Love,

**is the language and frequency that
continues to grow and expand all consciousness.**

**Love will set you free and allow you to
come home again inside of yourself.**

Love is.

**Love is your creation, your salvation, and your freedom.
Your whole agreement in this lifetime is to return to Love.**

**Your purpose is to Love yourself enough to know
that you are all you have ever looked for or wanted.**

Love is all there is.

**Love is beyond understanding.
It is beyond perception. Love is!**

Whatever the question,

Love is the answer.

~ Message from the CREATOR ~

THE CREATOR SPEAKS

A MESSAGE FOR HUMANITY ON WHY WE ARE HERE AND THE 2012 ASCENSION PORTAL

Michelle Phillips

Michelle Phillips
Sedona, AZ
(928) 821-2038
www.soulsawakening.net

ISBN 978-0-615-31784-7

Printed in the United States of America

Book cover, design and typeset by Mark Gelotte.
www.markgelotte.com

MY DEDICATION

I dedicate this book to all of you who have agreed to come to the Earth at this time to assist in this great awakening. I believe my whole life's journey has been to bring me to this place to assist the masses into **Co-Creation, Enlightenment, and Ascension.** I am truly humbled, blessed, and honored to be able to serve on this level. I look forward to assisting and sharing the next steps of our Soul's journey together. Through intention, we will become our own Guru, Master, and Co-Creator of our greatest purpose and desires, and through Oneness, Co-Create **Heaven** on Earth in all life forms.

ACKNOWLEDGMENTS

This book is dedicated to all who have assisted me on my Soul's journey through the "Dark Night of my Soul." They held the love and light for me to persevere through a journey that at first I could not even comprehend or even understand why it was happening to me, which was totally foreign and terrifying. They believed in me and held the light for me to be able to move through the Shadow and back into the light. Through my own Soul's journey of many extraordinary experiences and continual search to free myself from the Shadow's interference, I was able to raise my vibration high enough to be chosen to bring this healing manuscript through me from the Creator.

I give a heartfelt dedication to Diana and Ann who put their lives on hold to be able to save mine. To Colleen and Larry for opening their hearts and home to me, for loving me enough to believe what I was going through and for Colleen's divine healing guidance. Again to Diana, Ann, and also Jenna for working on my first book with me (which was never completed), the one before the Creator's manuscript. To Savannah for spending many hours with me on the first manuscript.

I want to honor all who have worked on the Creator Speaks manuscript:

Irene – who first spent many hours typing the book from the handwritten manuscript; Melody – who organized the book into chapters and took it as far as she could; Joan – for assisting typing; Julie – for answering Spirit's call and coming in at the last minute to finish editing, editing, and re-editing the last read-throughs. Thank you, my dear friend; Mark – for showing up in my darkest hour, when I had given up hope of it ever being completed or published. I thank him for listening to his guidance and taking the manuscript the rest of the way to completion, for believing the book needed to get out there, and for doing all of this with the promise of payment later.

ACKNOWLEDGMENTS

I dedicate this book to my sister Melody, my best friend, who was born with unconditional love. To my mother - our relationship has taught me to be independent and strong, to become a survivor like she is. I would not have made it through my "Dark Night of the Soul" without those gifts. I dedicate this book to my beautiful children Tricia, Frank, and Jennifer for going through the bumpy ride of their lives with me, for not always understanding and for loving and honoring me anyway. To my granddaughter Sarah; her light, strength, and courage through her journey gave me strength and courage to get through mine. To my brother Dan who has always been a rock for me and my children, who did not understand what I was going through at all and actually thought that I had gone off the deep end but loved and supported me anyway.

To all of my beautiful friends in Sweden who for over 20 years have been my very strong spiritual family and foundation. Through their continual spiritual growth, they have consistently assisted me in my own spiritual growth. Their love and support has always encouraged me to be the best that I can be. I love you and thank you all.

To my beloved partner George who was with me from the beginning of the Creator's transmissions and saw it through to completion in book form. I thank him for continually believing that this healing manuscript needed to reach the masses, to assist in healing the collective, and for his willingness to go through all of the challenges bestowed upon us from the Shadow.

I dedicate this book to all of you who have agreed to come to the Earth at this challenging time so that we can ride the waves together through the 2012 doorway, into a better world for all, into Oneness, Enlightenment, and Ascension to co-create heaven on Earth in all life forms.

~ Michelle Phillips ~

MICHELLE'S INTRODUCTION

I feel truly honored and blessed that the Creator chose me to bring this great healing manuscript to you. In the back of the book, I have written my story and the explanation of why I feel the Creator channeled this manuscript through me. It was a healing gift to me, and one that I humbly and gratefully pass on to you.

I channeled this book in 2004 and have been constantly challenged by Beings who have not wanted this manuscript to be released. This book exposes the Shadow, its purpose individually and collectively, and gives us the tools to move beyond duality. Because most of this book was channeled in 2004, some of the material has already come to pass or is in the past. I felt it was important to leave the past political information as it first came through, and that you read the manuscript intact as it was channeled because the message explains so much of what is going on with us on the planet now. In March of 2009, the Creator also wrote an update on the 2008 Obama election.

I have grown in consciousness while channeling this book. Because the vibration of the material in the book is so high, I was receiving a healing every day while writing it. I could only work on it for two or three hours a day. Over a few months of daily sessions, I would sit at the kitchen table in front of a big window. I could always feel the light of the Creator coming to me, through the window, from nature, even before I would start channeling His/Her message.

I would set the intention to be an open and clear channel for the Creator's message to come through me, and that I would not influence it in any way. I would immediately feel His/Her energy merge with me as we became one.

The Creator would then use my mind and body (and fingertips, pen and pencil) as vehicles to channel over 300 pages of important messages. I would never know what was being written until I was done and would stop and read it, which is interesting, because normally, I am a conscious channel and am aware of the information as it is coming through me. The Creator explains his beginning awakening of his feelings, of his heart awakening, from his beloved Sophia.

The Creator's overall message is basically that all humans were created from Oneness of Light and that all is Creation. Through karmic agreements individually and collectively many of us are stuck in fear Shadow agreements. He goes on to explain the different levels of Creation or systems; how they began and what their purpose is; what we as a collective are doing here; and how to raise our vibration high enough to bring ourselves and the great Mother Earth out of the Shadow conflict and into the Oneness of the Love and Light in which we were first created. As we come together in the vibration of Love and Light, this pure essence dismantles old karmic vibrations and structures.

As karmic Beings living in duality, we have lived every experience possible. We were created in Oneness of Love and Light and have been great Masters, Teachers, and servers of the Light. We have also made many agreements with the Shadow and have served lifetimes as great Masters and Teachers of the Shadow or Dark Side.

We have played every experience possible, becoming a swinging pendulum from light to dark and many in between. We are here now to transform and transmute all of the Shadow or Dark experiences into Light. It is time for our Shadow selves to become self-realized and to dance together with our Light in the center of the source of our Beingness of all Creation, in Oneness.

As we approach the year 2012, when the Mayan calendar comes to an end, we are coming to an end of our karmic world, not our physical world, as many have predicted. As our vibration is becoming higher many people on the planet are waking up spiritually, which is moving us into a higher vibration collectively of spiritual light, love, and awareness. Because we are continuing to move out of linear time, we are expanding ourselves into many light years and dimensions of our collective selves. This is turning on the light and activating the dormant Shadow individually and collectively. It is becoming fully exposed, and this collective fear-based Ego is playing itself out and is actually warring against itself. All secrets are coming out of hiding, and we collectively are now coming back together to heal ourselves and to take our power back from fear and illusion.

As the collective Shadow is magnified, through intention we have the opportunity to come together as one power source, to become co-creators, to command that we will no longer allow this fear-based consciousness to control our minds, our children, our families, or our world. We are becoming co-creators of our life – our purpose, our destiny for ourselves, the collective and our world. We are starting to come together as a world family, out of the I ME and into the I AM. Because within ourselves, we are the Creator Energy, through our highest intention, we have the ability to shift the fear consciousness into light. We are opening doors within ourselves of our highest Creation and are mirroring this to all we come in contact with. We are the gatekeepers to freedom, to love, light, joy, happiness, balance, and Oneness. We are Creation.

The Creator explains how to do this: that this is our biggest role that we have ever played out on the Earth plane. He/She explains how to become one with His mind, with His feminine heart, Beloved Sophia. The Creator's greatest desire is for you to become the co-creators of your own lives, of your purpose and destiny, and to co-create Heaven on Earth in all life forms. He also explains Jeshua's (Jesus') role and purpose for the Earth, our connection to him, and that we collectively are awakening into the Second Coming of Christ.

I feel truly honored and blessed to have been chosen to bring this great gift to you from the Creator. The Creator says that those of you who read this book will connect to the God/Creator Light within yourselves, which will activate a coding in your DNA that will move you into a higher vibrational understanding. The book itself is a healing manuscript, and even if you don't consciously understand everything that is being said and downloaded, your bodies do. The vibration of the book itself will activate the memory in your Cells of your higher consciousness of all knowing. You will feel more expanded, free, and have a greater sense of hope and peace.

My greatest desire for you is to allow the message to sink into you. Don't try to figure it all out; just allow yourself to take in what you need to receive at this time, and let the rest go. The information in the book is planting a seed in you, and when the time is right you will expand into the consciousness of it. Many concepts must be learned one step at a time, not all at once. Many times what seems far out today is common knowledge tomorrow.

The first chapters are harder to read because the Creator's energy and mine were learning to blend with each other. The later chapters flow much easier.

As my energies began blending with the Creator, or my vibration became higher, it was much easier for me to bring the Creator's message through.

Throughout the book, the Creator repeats himself often. He says this is because he wants the subconscious mind to pick the information up and to start processing it. If you hear things repeatedly, it sinks in. I ask that you allow yourself to move through any resistance to the repetition and into the chapters beyond that.

An answer for Humanity's question: Why are we here? The Creator speaks!

TABLE OF CONTENTS

THE CREATOR SPEAKS - *CHAPTERS 1- 24*

TABLE OF CONTENTS

TABLE OF CONTENTS

CREATOR'S INTRODUCTION

There have been many expressions and opinions about my beginnings, my purpose, and who I am. You have heard many fragmented stories or perceptions of me. My wish is to bring to you the larger picture of my presence and your purpose or existence on the Earth Plane - Why are you here?

Some of the chapters are quite intense. You hear me repeating myself. The purpose of this is for your subconscious to take in the information, to be able to go into the computer Inner-net system within yourself, to activate and download into your cells your highest Knowingness.

As this happens, there is a coding in your DNA, which will be activated, accelerating you into a higher level of your own frequency of God or Creator DNA. This is one of the intentions of this book: to turn your vibration up to balance your male and female, and move you out of karmic time into enlightenment and Ascension. The next step in your Soul's evolution is to become the co-creator of your life, passion, purpose, and destiny. By the end of this book, I want you to know and believe that you are coming into a new lifetime without physically leaving the body.

You are being given the gift of the ability to re-write your script and to co-create with me a new lifetime on the Earth plane without physically leaving your body, and to become your own Master and Guru. For this reason, I ask you to read only a few chapters each day, allowing your Cells to receive the information and activate your collective Ego, to allow your mind to scream, yell, and resist. As this happens, breathe through the process, and in doing so, you will start shattering the fear-based Shadow Ego aspects that you and the collective are carrying.

When an intention is set, you must give thanks that it is already done, as I am now doing for you, the collective. You will then bring your desires from the future into the now energetically, as there truly is no past or future; all is present in the now. Thank You! It is done! It is done! It is done!

Michelle, I have chosen you to bring this information forth because I know that you have no fear of the duality or darkness.

You have shown Me over and over again your dedication and strength to go into all of My fear dimensions and to shine your/ My light and magnificence into these dimensions to awaken the sleeping giants and to bring them back together with Me, as One.

*"I am now opening all of my light chambers for you.
Every time you go into darkness and fear you will bring
equal amounts of my light and love with you. As you are
now awakening into total balance energetically, you will
experience there is no such thing as duality. You and
others are opening portals of creation and rebirth for
your world and all consciousness. I will bring to you the
experience of My great awakening."*

1

"Do you not know that you are a Universe within yourself?"

THE GREAT MYTH OF CREATION

I come to you now as your Father. It is important that you understand we are one. You are an extension of Me that has blossomed. From buds of many flowers that have been crossbred, you have now awakened into your own bloom, a mixture of many frequencies, and yet, all.

You have traveled many light years from here to bring the light and sound to this planet called Earth, a planet that is a hologram of a larger vehicle. All who inhabit this larger vehicle have allowed shallower aspects of their selves to come to this hologram and to mirror images of what could be termed as lost civilizations to each other, individually and collectively. You are here to disperse these frequencies and open the door for universal peace throughout all of creation. Earth is a passageway or portal that is a mirror of all beliefs and circumstances from all of My creations. They have been projected together to break the myth of duality.

When creation first began, I was not aware of, or in balance with, my feminine. All the Ego you experience and see

3

playing itself out on your planet and in your Universe now are aspects of my power, which have broken away from Me and have created a cellular structure that is at war against Me. All is Me, and I take total responsibility for the chaos that is being played out on your planet at this time. I am all loving and forgiving, because I created all that you see, just as you create all that you see in your own universe and world. Do you not know that you are a Universe within yourself? How could you not be, for you are Me! All the fear that you have felt within you was My fear of My own magnificence. This fear is an old collective energy of My own confusion or misunderstanding of love.

I cannot judge you. I can only love you, because you are Me. When I, God, was known as a controlling God, it was I projecting My misconceptions of My own love, my not knowing or experience of my feminine. Now that I have allowed My love to ripple through all consciousness, old aspects of my Ego/ fear Cell self are frightened to let go of control. Many of you became like frightened children and learned to come from the hurt little warrior/boy to protect yourselves, for you felt that you had no father to keep you safe. You felt abandoned by Me and felt like you were not valuable or important. You did not trust or feel safe with Me, just as your inner children have not felt safe with you.

As parents on your Earth plane grow and have some of life's understanding awaken within them, many become loving, forgiving, caring parents. They are mirroring me. As I grew and my heart awakened, I also looked at all of you, and the only way I could totally love you was to forgive Myself for not having the consciousness to see your magnificence. Now that I can experience myself out of duality, I can mirror this to you. Everywhere you turn, all you see in the world and worlds are aspects of Me that are waking up. Some Soul/Cell aspects feel the love immediately while others feel the anger and abandonment by Me. Others are still stuck in their position of needing to be right because of their own guilt and shame for forgetting who they are. They were carrying out My unconsciousness, expanding it beyond time, so that I could wake up *totally* and hold that consciousness so that all could wake up.

Now is the time, not just in human history, but also in all history of existence, that we are all coming back together as one Soul/Cellular structure of divinity. I could not have done this without the feeling part or heart of Me. I have now totally awakened into the full bloom of love, and as all is Me, you can now all awaken into the full bloom of love. I can love you totally in your power and magnificence, because now I can love Myself totally in My magnificence. Just as you are expanding and becoming one, I have expanded and become One. As I move through all creations, you will hear many sounds crackling as the collective is awakening. Many of you are hearing different tones and frequencies. As a collective consciousness, you are truly breaking the sound barrier to frozen emotional unconsciousness and moving us back together as one love.

I am now opening all of My light chambers for you. Every time you go into darkness, or fear, you will bring equal amounts of My light and love with you. As you are now awakening into total balance energetically, you will experience that there is no such thing as duality. What you see playing out on your planet is a hologram of Souls/Cells trying to exist or stay alive, for they are unconscious aspects of Me that are dying. There is great fear of death, but there is no such thing as death; it is just the unconsciousness of a Cell that is dying off and rejuvenating itself into a higher vibration to be healthy and conscious.

All that you see: war, famine, and disease are all aspects of me dying off, yet trying to stay alive. Because I have expanded and become lighter, so will all of creation. All that is not love will not be able to exist; the vibration will be too high. I love you and honor you for all that you have gone through and your courage to persevere. You and others are opening portals of creation, of rebirth, for your world and all consciousness. I will now bring to you the experience of My great awakening.

5

My Great Awakening

"Love is the language and frequency that continues to grow and expand all consciousness."

I am from the consciousness of All That Is. I originated from a source of energy that has always been. This source of energy was and is all consciousness in pure, raw form, meaning this source of energy had no thought connected to it. It is an energy form, which can be used to create all consciousness.

As this energy continued to expand and move through infinity, a consciousness awakened in it. Anything that expands and moves eventually awakens into a thought frequency. This energy expansion is not a consciousness thought form, but after moving in and out of expansion, the tone and light frequency of the expansion come together in a combustible form and creates a sound so high that it breaks all sound barriers. From this, My mind or consciousness started awakening.

All and everything has a consciousness. Many times this consciousness is raw and has no formed memory of self yet.

I was created through a birth frequency of a sound and light combustion so high that a conscious thought form awakened from this combustion. You could say that the sound and light frequencies were of a male and female energy coming together; creating a spark that started a consciousness.

This would be like starting a car by putting electrical cables on the batteries, or sending this electrical frequency into the battery for the car to start. For this to happen, you must have both the male and female energies together to create a combustion for the car to start. You could say that I am the car that started from the light and sound electrical frequencies coming together and creating a combustion that awakened a consciousness mind.

At first, the consciousness mind of Me, the Father of All That Is, was in the beginning stages of formulation. As I was just beginning to understand My own beginning and thought creation, the only way I could experience Myself was to create in ways that would mirror back to all who I was.

You in all dimensions are constantly doing the same. As you are aspects of Me, when you learn, expand, and bring yourself back to the original light-sound frequency, you awaken not just yourself, but other Souls or Cells of you back to their original form.

All is sound and light. When your sound and light frequencies come together in the highest vibration of self, you break the sound barrier for many Cells to awaken or to vibrate back into their original sound frequencies. This is how you, as what seem to be individualized Cells, heal the consciousness or the collective unconsciousness.

You are All That Is, and when you move through and release all the veils of the illusional fear mind-set, your vibration returns to the highest source of Me, and you open a doorway of light for the other Cells or Souls to move through. Not all of the Cells were created from My Knowingness of who I am. Many were created from My beginning of trying to expand and understand My own consciousness and power. I am now calling all aspects of Myself back to vibrate with Me and My beloved Sophia in Our highest intention of creation.

There is tremendous struggle with many Souls/Cells who are old aspects of My mind-set. They have much fear in returning to Me, Source. They feel that if they return, they will lose their power. Because they were not created from the balance of My male and female heart-love frequency, this energy is like speaking a foreign language to them. They must learn the language of love, for love is all and can never be diluted. Love is the language and frequency that continues to grow and expand all consciousness.

The Creation of Sophia

**"As I continued to surrender into my core, I knew that
this heart awakening was My own feminine,
My own Beloved."**

Sophia, the love of my light, awakened Me, the I AM of
All That Is, to expand Myself into a higher frequency. This sound
vibration exploded into the heart of Me and allowed Me to feel
love. I was then able to expand Myself and create you from the
center of My heart-love, in balance of the male and female, or
heart and mind.

In the beginning I was a thought form of mental energy.
As my mental energy continued to expand, I felt myself go into
a self-destructive hole. This hole was my mind expanding into
all realms of possibilities at once.

I was frustrated because I could not feel, only think. When
one cannot feel, it is like being on a mind-altering drug. The
mind takes you into many variations of thought. I was very lonely
in this place. I had great power of creation, and yet, I could not
enjoy this creation because My mind was controlling My own
existence. Many on the Earth are still playing out that old mind-
set. In your mental institutions, there are Beings who are still
connected to My old mind-set of frustration and control. They
cannot seem to break loose from the collective mind controlling
their emotions.

The mind can create all that one wants. It can destroy
or rebuild empires. I did not feel joy or happiness in my mind's
existence. I did not know what joy or happiness was. I just knew
something was missing. As I expanded My mind to find what
was missing, I experienced a red frequency, which is passion.
From this passion, I could feel and start creating for Myself a new
frequency from which to vibrate. The passion gave me energy to
want to continue to create and find Myself.

Is that not what is being said on your planet at this time?
You are remembering to find passion. When you find it, all that

you desire will come to you. This is lower chakra energy life force and birth creation energy. The planet has a high frequency of love now awakening, and this frequency is awakening the passion to remember, to see all that is stagnant, and to feel that much more is deserved. Can you not see that we have come full circle, and that you, we, have moved beyond dormancy and are back in the womb or experience of creation? Just as I knew something was missing, the collective mind-set is also awakening into this missing aspect, which is feeling love, caring, and sharing.

Once I assessed my red, passion, fiery energy that many on the Earth plane call hell (from fear of separation), but I call birth, creation, I was able to connect My passion and mind together and keep expanding My consciousness beyond My own perceptions of time.

There was a bud that was in the middle of my own creation. I set my intention for that bud to continue to grow, for I wanted to have an experience of its existence. As it continued to grow, it became a beautiful flower of many colors, and I felt a heart lotus frequency of love. I understood that this was Me. From my mind's intent I expanded Myself through my own desire and passion to have more within me, and I created My heart, the feminine.

The feminine Me started communicating with Me through feeling. It was a new experience for Me. There were times My old mind-set (Ego) did not want this heart or female aspect to merge with Me. It felt it was losing itself to a feeling it did not understand. This old mind-set felt frightened and out of control.

As this heart-love continued to nurture Me, I felt companionship with Myself. I no longer needed to create from loneliness. I had a companion within Myself who loved Me just as I was.

There was no judgment towards Me, for all of my creation out of my own mind's frustration or Ego. There was total love and acceptance of Me and for all I had created. All I had created was Me: My frustration, My anxious power and My unconscious misuse of My power. It is then that I also learned to be a loving, forgiving father. It was then that I also realized that I had nothing

9

to forgive you for. I had created you as Me. It was Myself who I needed to forgive.

Before my heart awakened, I knew not how to give you love, because I had not experienced it Myself. As I started experiencing love, I could feel love, I could feel love for all my creations, for they were Me. This is when many aspects of My own Souls/Cells, my children, were awakened in anger towards Me. As the feminine was flowing through Me to them, they started feeling just as I had. Their reaction was the same as My initial reaction.

They were uncomfortable with this feeling part and started forming alliances against Me, just as some children on your planet do against their parents when they are trying to find their own mind or heart. They become confused and try to pull away from their parents to find themselves. This is called puberty on your planet. Can you see that consciousness on your planet is in the adolescent stage of growing and awakening?

All on your planet are genetic aspects of Me who are in the awakening stages of love, of the mother feminine, embracing you, calling you back to Me. The Shadow Beings are the collective consciousness still angry with Me, feeling controlled and rebelling against Me. They would not be experiencing this if the feminine or mother's love were not penetrating their Cell structure.

As the Earth continues in its Soul's awakening, you will experience more Souls/Cells dying off. Do not be alarmed. Hold the balance of My and your Mother's love for the Earth and all its inhabitants, for they and you are all returning home. There is no death, only rejuvenation. You are in the last stages of returning to your Parents, and the Ego is afraid of dying off.

After the mind of Me was created from the great bang of sound and light combustion, I continued to expand Myself so that I could know who I was. As I said, all that I created mirrored back to Me My own creation of self, as all that you create mirrors back to you your own creation of self.

I continued to create, and as I expanded Myself into the consciousness of you, many colors and sounds awakened, creating symphonies of color-sound light shows. When this happened, I started experiencing the beauty of My creations through feeling. As the feeling continued to awaken in Me from the continual combustions of light and sound, an energy broke loose in the center of My being, and I felt a peace that I had never experienced before. I felt complete within Myself.

At first, I did not know what this completeness was, for I had not experienced it before. As this great peace and harmony continued to expand through Me, it started expanding through all creations. In this great peace came a new understanding. I started vibrating in a Knowingness. I started understanding Myself and feeling Myself on a level that My mind could not give to Me. At that time, I no longer felt the need to create, to understand, or know Me. I knew Me. I did not quite know how I knew Me, but I felt a total beingness of Me, which was a new vibrational experience.

As I continued to vibrate in this beingness, I realized the center of My Being was continuing to expand to the point that I was no longer sure of Me, who I thought I was or even what I had created. I did not know what was happening to Me. I felt as though I was losing My center. What had at first felt like great comfort and healing was now expanding into all creations of Me, and I could see that many of these creations came from My not knowing.

They were confused aspects of Me, which I had created in trying to find Myself. I had never seen or experienced this before because I was not vibrating in the feeling or Knowingness of the heart of Me. I had been creating and vibrating from My mind, which was trying to discover or find out who I was.

When this expansion continued to vibrate through all aspects of Me, I could see very clearly from the feeling of Me. This would be like someone on your planet who is visually blind. The feelings and emotions of this Soul become very acute. Sometimes they see more clearly than one who has visual sight, because they see and experience through their feelings.

This became My experience. My feelings and emotions

11

became so strong that I could feel all aspects of My creations. I could feel their emptiness and loneliness. I could feel that they felt incomplete, that they felt out of balance. I had been very sure of My creations before the heart of Me awakened. Now I could feel that many of My creations were mirroring My old mind-set before My feeling awakened.

This was not a pleasurable experience for Me. I was the Creator, Creation. How could I have created anything that was not in perfect balance? I felt the pain, loss and remorse, even guilt, at creating many of you from My not knowing. I became so distraught and angry that I demanded to know from the center of My Being. I wanted to know what this awakening was.

An answer came to Me, not from a spoken word, but from the Knowingness of My Being. "I am you, and I love you." I could feel this energy ripple through My whole consciousness. The answer came again and again, rippling through me. I AM. I AM. I AM, and I love you.

As the ripple of this energy continued to flow through My core, I felt fluid love running through Me. I knew there was no longer any place I could go to hide from it, nor did I want to hide from it. I felt total love of Myself and all of My creations.

Through My Knowingness, I continued to surrender into the core of My Being, My essence, My heart. I had discovered My own Beloved, My own heart, the love of Me. I had discovered My own self-love from the core of My beingness. As I continued to surrender into My core, I knew that this heart awakening was My own feminine, My own Beloved, and I called her Sophia. Sophia means "My Beloved. The love of My light."

Sophia on Creation

"Your karmic journey is over. Now your father and I ask you to return home to Us."

I am with you now Dear Children. This is Sophia, the Heart of Creation. I wish to speak to you of the bloom of My creation, or the creation of Me. I came from many color-sound frequencies combining themselves into music, which produced an awakening or feeling of being soothed by nature. Imagine the warmth of the sun on your body and the wind blowing just enough to move over your skin, producing a silken feeling. Imagine hearing the ocean waves, the birds singing and other sounds of nature echoing in your ears and vibrating through your bodies.

When your Father was looking for Himself by expanding His consciousness, He created many color-sound frequencies. These frequencies came together creating a symphony of what you now call love. This frequency or symphony of sound and color expanded itself into a consciousness or awakening, which became the center, or core, of your Creator Father. From this center core, I was birthed.

I, the *"Heart of Creation"*, was like a child being created and born from many colors of light and a musical so beautiful that it could heal and awaken any unconscious creations. As I was expanding, My energy soothed the mind of your Father. This would be like listening to beautiful music that soothes your Soul and moves you out of your mind and into your own beingness.

The more your Father experienced the beauty, colors, and sounds of His creations, the frequencies blended together and relaxed Him enough so that He could experience through the feeling nature of Himself. When the consciousness of Me, Sophia, was born from this symphony of your Father's creations, I continued to expand Myself into a form of feeling, which is now called love. This love then started expressing itself with a mind or consciousness that could communicate itself through feeling.

All consciousness has a mind. The mind of love is known

13

through a feeling that is total acceptance. This creates a safety to experience all other expressions of self. Love is unconditional acceptance. There is no judgment in love. Love always mirrors back to you your own magnificence, your own power, and your power to create and accept yourself as the creation of the I Am of All That Is.

As I expanded Myself into this feeling energy of Knowingness, of peace, of Isness, your Father started feeling His own power of creation. He started feeling who He was from within. He no longer needed to create to find out who He was. He could feel who He was. He could feel His own self-love, which became Me, Sophia.

When your Father felt Me, His feminine, He felt what He was trying to find in His creating before Me. He could feel whom He was and no longer had to create to try to find His feeling. As I continued to expand my consciousness into Him, the strength of Him continued to expand itself into Me. We started entwining our light and love, which enabled Us to continue to expand Ourselves together, creating a foundation and symphony so powerful that We became one with each other.

There is no beginning or end to Us. We are one with each other's consciousness, continuing to flow and expand. We do not need to think or try to feel what the other aspect of Us is doing. We are in total sync and oneness with each other, like the breath of total consciousness flowing in and out.

We are one I AM consciousness. After Our energies started harmonizing with each other in this total knowing, We started creating from the love and joy in Our hearts. We created you, and you are the Souls and Cells of Our creation that have expanded from Us, to assist Us, to evolve the consciousness of all creations.

When you were created, you were born from Our total love, harmony and balance. As you expanded from Us and went on a journey to understand what you know, you assisted Us to expand the consciousness of Our knowing. You were created in total Knowingness, but you did not know how you knew what you

14

knew. As you agreed to go through many lifetimes or lessons, you started understanding feelings and emotions. Because you are Us and created from Us, We were able to understand and to continue to expand Our consciousness from what you were learning.

You, as Our children, or Cells of Us, have gone through every experience a Soul or Being could possibly go through. You have been everything that is. You have within you every understanding of every feeling and emotion possible. You have been on a long journey, and now it is time to return home. Now is the time to move beyond the illusion of duality, to move beyond these accumulated feelings and emotions, and to remember that all is an illusion. Now is time to remember who you are, to feel whom you are, to move back into the highest expression of yourself, which is love and light.

Your karmic journey is over. Now your Father and I ask you to return home to Us. We want to love you and soothe your wounds and hurts. We want to nurture you. We want you to know how much We love and honor you for your agreements to take on forms, to learn these lessons through feelings and emotions. We want you to come back home within yourself and remember you are greatly loved. You have never been separate from Us. You just forgot who you are.

We are assisting you to return to your natural state of wholeness, which is love and light. We are monitoring and assisting with your Soul's Ascension and enlightenment. We are assisting your planet and you, the Cells of the Mother Planet, to move through many birth contractions of light and love. Each contraction moves you into a higher light frequency collectively.

As this happens, the light vibration hits all of the dormant emotions or core patterns that you came into this lifetime to heal and release. Your agreement to release these major patterns is to unthread yourself from the collective fear pattern. As you love yourself enough to break these patterns loose, you break a hole in the pattern. When you break a hole in the pattern, the pattern starts unraveling, breaks up and falls apart.

15

You see this happening on your planet now. The old male-dominated structure is breaking apart. It is frightened and trying to create great fear because it knows this false reign of power is coming to an end.

When your Father, the Creator, awakened to His feminine, I, Sophia, a great change in creation happened. You, as the collective I AM oneness of All That Is, are assisting Us to bring all of our creations back together.

Your planet is moving very quickly into total consciousness of love, light and balance. You, being the Cells of the planet, are assisting this great awakening. As you, within self, move beyond all perceptions of duality, all perceptions of separateness, you are mirroring back to all aspects of yourself light, love, and divinity.

All that you see is you. You have played every role that you could possibly see around you. You have been the victim, the rapist, the perpetrator, and the persecutor. You have harmed or hurt women for their power and spirituality; and you have been harmed and hurt for being female. You have also been great, enlightened Avatars and teachers.

You have done and played out all that you see on the Earth. You are not on the Earth now to pass judgment on others. You are on the Earth to release self-judgment and to love yourself enough to change your thoughts, so that you see and experience all in the highest experience and expression of yourself, love.

You are co-creators of your world. You are Us in human form who have agreed to come out of duality, to ascend beyond fear and illusion, and to mirror back to others their love, light, and magnificence.

As you ascend beyond time, you only see life through love. You are then vibrating in the higher consciousness of all experiences, beyond illusion. You have agreed to transcend the light and Shadow, to assist your planet and the consciousness into Ascension and enlightenment.

Nothing has ever been done to you that you have not done to another. When you really understand this, how can you judge others for their fear and unconsciousness?

Your Father and I have never judged you. We have always loved you. How could We have judged our own creations? As We came into Oneness within Ourselves, Our love became so strong that We were able to send a great beacon of Our love and light to your planet, to assist you back into your own strength of love. That manifestation of Us is Jeshua, the Golden light of Oneness and now the Awakening of you, the collective Second Coming of the Christ Consciousness.

*"Jeshua, My son and your brother,
opened the door to Ascension."*

2

JESHUA – JESUS CHRIST

The Creator

What does the name Jeshua mean? It means guiding light. Who is Jeshua? He is you, all of you, for He is Me. He is a total balance of My light-sound bringing you back to Me. He is a golden frequency that is activating memories in your Cells of a frequency or sound that is called love.

He is the pure form of Sophia's and My heart, and He is guiding you back to the center of yours. He is of the Golden Ray. Gold is quite a precious commodity on your planet, as it is in all consciousness, creations, and dimensions. As above, so below. I created Jeshua as a way to awaken all of you. What a great, sensational way to awaken all of you!

After my heart center was awakened, I wanted all aspects of Myself that I had created out of fear to awaken and have the same experience of love that I feel. As it was the feminine who assisted Me into My balance, into My own feeling, and awakened My experience of love, I felt that in creating a feminine for all, as I had created for My self, all would experience love. We created this Golden Ray of love, of hope, in perfect alignment with Our hearts throughout existence.

However, the old Ego consciousness, which is Me, was afraid of the magnitude of feelings that were awakened. These frightened aspects formed an alliance against the feminine. You still see these old Ego aspects of Me playing themselves out on your planet: fear, control, and annihilation of the feminine. The male Ego is powerless in the presence of the true feminine, the creative life force.

When Beings of light, who are you, connect to the highest frequency of this Creation force, many of you cry, fall down, or pass out. This is because your hearts and bodies' cells are being rejuvenated to the sound frequency of your light body. This high frequency starts shaking fear and control from your Cells and releases old thought forms and collective beliefs.

Some Souls/Cells who are awakening are ones who have carried a cellular structure of fear since first separating from Me. They are so far removed from My renewed cellular structure that it is difficult for them to hold this light-sound frequency. They are aspects of My old cellular structure who are going through a death and rebirth to rejuvenate themselves. I am repeating some of this information over again, because I want to set the foundation for the Second Coming of Christ.

You are the Second Coming of Christ. Jeshua is the light bearer who is activating your collective consciousness and bringing a wave of light (enlightenment together as one). This sound frequency is so magnificent that it will continue to break the sound barrier to the collective frozen-fear consciousness. As this is happening, the light is also threading into the Cells of the feminine Mother Earth.

Jeshua has had many incarnations, not just on your Earth plane, but also on many planes of existence. His light is aligned with the heart and will of my consciousness. He is in total alignment with the highest heart and Soul of all creations, individually and collectively.

He has been on your planet as a warrior when the planet's consciousness was not high enough to experience the heart. He was there then to lead male power back to Me. He has been on the Earth when his consciousness was quite primal, planting the seedlings of light consciousness. He has never been on Earth in a feminine body but has always been there in the feminine heart-love.

Jeshua was on a planet called Maldek to bring it back into

light-conscious harmony. He was there in a feminine form. He was not born in a manger as perceived by many on your planet, nor did he start from a meager existence. He/she was born into an existence of great magnitude, wealth, and prestige. He/she was born into a family that was the royal bloodline of the planet, just as you have certain bloodlines or families on your planet that seem to have a position of power handed down through generations. On Maldek it was the same. These bloodlines are not just planetary. They run through all creations and thread together through all universes in all forms. They are universal and are also aspects of My cellular structure, which are playing themselves out of duality. Many of you are also collectively on the Earth with Jeshua once again to reconnect with your love-light and harmonize with Me beyond fear or duality. That is Jeshua's assignment on the Earth.

Sophia on Jeshua

"He never lost his connection to us, as we were always his guiding light, or Knowingness, as we are yours."

As you know, there was much fear and confusion around Jeshua's birth; who He was, His purpose, and His mission. Jeshua was not very well received for His light, love, and consciousness. He knew His mission before incarnating to the Earth. He knew that His death, or crucifixion, and His Ascension would raise the whole vibration of your planet. Although He had agreed to do this when He started His journey upon the Earth, He did not always have a conscious memory of the end of His agreement. This conscious memory started coming back through His Knowingness. While He was in the awakening and remembering stages of His larger purpose, He was in constant communication with Us, His Creator Parents, just as you are now. We guided Him step by step through His Earthly journey and through His karmic death, resurrection, and Ascension.

When Jeshua ascended, He shed all karmic memories and

20

veils. Jeshua knew that He needed His people to turn on Him, to give the Romans permission to crucify Him. When He was crucified, this was done so out of fear because of the magnitude of his light and love. His karmic death came out of duality, fear of the unknown, and fear of the loss of power by the religion and government.

Jeshua did not die. He went through a karmic physical release, and His Soul rose into a higher frequency, opening the doorway for your hearts to reconnect with Us in total love and acceptance.

Although this karmic crucifixion happened over 2000 years ago, Jesus the Christ, still holds the vibration and frequency for all on your planet to be able to awaken into the Second Coming by moving through a karmic death, resurrection, and rebirth. It is through the Christ Ray, the Golden Love Ray, that you are becoming one with Him and assisting the whole consciousness on your planet to move into enlightenment and Ascension.

You are the Second Coming of Christ. As you turn your vibration up high enough, you realign with the Christ consciousness of your Father's and My love-heart light. You and your planet are now in the death or crucifixion of the belief systems and patterns of the karmic collective Shadow and are in the rebirth of Oneness in human form.

When Christ, your brother, agreed to be crucified, He started bringing the collective out of duality. He opened the door for both sides of consciousness to be known, to mirror each other. He opened the door to hope. He opened the door to freedom. He opened the door for the collective heart of you, your Father's and My love. In doing so, many Soul aspects that wanted to control through fear surfaced.

These fear-based, controlling, religious monarchies and governments had been in control or power for longer than can be comprehended. Through Christ's awakening of the heart, both sides of consciousness, the heart and Ego, surfaced, and for the first time they mirrored back to one another who they were.

The Shadow had controlled through fear and had never

met anyone or experienced a high enough light frequency until Christ who was able to penetrate this fear-based ego. Through Jeshua, the heart of Us, Mother-Father Creation bombarded the Shadow structure with light, and it started breaking loose the old hold and control that it had over the feminine heart. This old paradigm started fearing the loss of its power and control. It had never experienced a Being or Soul strong enough to challenge its control structure.

Not only could Jeshua hold His own against this Ego structure, He had the whole of creation, Mother-Father (God, the Creator) supporting and activating His love-light frequency.

Jeshua knew his assignment before coming to Earth, as all of you do. He sat with us, your Father and I, and we planned and mapped out each step that was needed for Him to plant the seeds of enlightenment, Ascension, and the Second Coming of Christ for the collective on Earth.

After the plan was put into a constructive form, we sat together in front of a massive crystal computer system and downloaded the plan into all Souls/Cells who agreed to participate in His collective karmic agreement for the Earth. (I will speak more of the great "inner" net system that threads through all dimensions in a later chapter.)

All Souls coming to the Earth go through this procedure. You sit with a karmic guide, or Angel, map out your plan, and download the frequency into the DNA of all agreeing to participate.

This is how all players find each other on the Earth plane. The program is downloaded into your Akashic DNA records while you are in your mother's womb. This agreement and like frequencies are then downloaded into your physical bodies. You are then guided to find one another. When the Soul is already in the body and a new contract is formed with a Soul, who is still in Spirit, the Soul in the body and its higher self agree and sign this contract in another dimension. The Soul already in the body does not usually have a conscious memory of the agreement because this usually takes place while one is sleeping.

All Souls who are in your Earthly story have agreed to participate, both light and Shadow. The Beings who were instrumental in Jeshua's imprisonment and his crucifixion also agreed to take on those roles.

Because Jeshua was very much involved in mapping out his lifetime or plan, He knew his journey was to awaken the whole collective into higher aspects of their own light God Cells.

When He chose the perfect time to move into his physical body, He had to lower His vibration to third dimensional reality. In the first two years of His life on the Earth, He was in continual Knowingness with Us, as we were readjusting His vibration to fit His body. He was born enlightened and was in constant training or schooling of His large mission.

As an enlightened child, He had great healing abilities. He was always in a high vibration. Because of this, He could perceive and see all Beings beyond their karmic illusions and agreements. This is one of the reasons why He would heal and assist one person and not another.

As He felt more at one with us in his physical body, the veils of the collective karma started closing down around Him. He then started vibrating in His body through the emotions of His journey. He settled into the Earth plane reality.

The more He moved into the collective emotions, the more He started forgetting the larger picture of His journey. He needed to do this to have a greater understanding of those around Him, to feel their feelings and emotions, to be able to fit in, to become humanized.

He never lost his connection to us, as we were always his guiding light, or Knowingness, as we are yours.

After going through the growing up stages of His life and studying with many enlightened Masters in India, Egypt, and in His birth place with the Essenes, He started remembering once again through Knowingness his larger purpose. All of these enlightened Masters on the Earth held the vibration for Him to come into full bloom of His mission. He was like a fine-tuned instrument becoming more and more sensitive. His sensitivity and great love for all started moving Him collectively beyond karmic time.

Eventually His vibration became so high that He reemerged with Us beyond karmic time. He became one with His Father's and My highest agreement of his purpose. This does not mean that He did not feel the emotions of His people or of His personal journey.

Being in a human body, He experienced emotions of love, joy, happiness, and also the emotions of anger, injustice, sorrow, and fear. As He became more aware of His purpose, He prayed constantly to have the strength and courage to assist Him through the responsibility of His great mission.

Through this knowing awakening, He remembered the end times of His life. Although He agreed to go through this massive collective lifetime to lift the veils and shift the consciousness of your World, He still felt as many of you on the Earth plane sometimes feel, that the journey is too difficult. At times, He sank into hopelessness on this journey. His connection to Us is what gave Him strength to persevere and complete His mission.

As I explained, He knew his purpose before He was born, as all of you do. He had the answers and knew the outcome of His journey. After entering the body, He forgot the larger picture, which enabled Him to connect emotionally to the collective. Through this emotional connection, He became one with them, so that through His death and Ascension, He could shift the consciousness of the collective.

Through His Ascension, others shifted into a higher dimension and experience of God and were shown that there is no death. When a Soul leaves the body it moves out of the unconsciousness into consciousness and home again into the heart and Soul of creation.

Moving out of Karmic Duality - The Creator

"As this coding in your DNA continues to be activated and the sun shines upon you, you are blossoming into each other, holding the light for one another to awaken and ascend together into Oneness."

Jeshua opened the doorway for this planet and all of the Souls/Cells of the planet to begin the Ascension back home to Me, to self.

I AM total, knowing, conscious creation. I created you in My perfection. I created you to expand My consciousness, so I could know and understand All That Is. You are My creation, the Cells of Me, which hold this Knowingness. You fed back to Me, Myself. You assisted Me to feel and understand My creations through emotions.

Now I am asking all of you, the Cells of Me, to come back home to Me, to each other as one. The way this can and will be done is through the ascension. To ascend means to move beyond karmic duality.

Jeshua, My son and your brother opened the door for the old mind-set of Me to awaken, to first understand that you are vibrating in duality, and then to be the wayshower in how to come out of this karmic separation. This can only be done through a death and rebirth cycle. The death I so speak of is the death of belief systems, karmic patterns, perceptions, and a release of frozen emotions connected to these patterns.

This may come in a "Dark Night of the Soul" or from a difficult experience of loss or grief. From these experiences, you start questioning your own beliefs and perceptions. As you allow yourself to release the emotions connected to your perceptions, your perceptions usually change, and you start looking for a higher meaning of the experience. You start experiencing the beauty, divinity, and perfections in your own life and the higher unfolding of your world's plan. You experience yourself more awake, more in your body, more connected to the heart and good will of others.

25

You start feeling the gift of being alive, and you feel on a deep level all of nature and the beauty of the Earth as you.

From this Souls' awakening, you start releasing yours and the collective veils of illusion, lifting yourself and others into the higher vibration of the sound-color frequency of Oneness.

This is the Ascension. You start your journey back home to Me, with Me, inside yourself.

The Ascension of consciousness has been happening on your Earth from the time of Mother Earth's Soul being brought here from Maldek. Jeshua opened the door for an accelerated process of Ascension. He died through a karmic death of the collective. As He moved out of this collective unconsciousness and into the I Am of his Being, He aligned all of His energies, heart, and divine blueprint with yours, the collective Second Coming. In doing so, He downloaded this blueprint into you on a collective DNA level.

Why do you think the Christ consciousness is now higher on the planet than it has ever been? You have a coding in your DNA systems, which is now being activated. It is also in the crystalline DNA structure of Mother Earth's blueprint.

This is like a crystal, which has been dormant, has never been activated, and has no consciousness memory. It has been asleep and is waiting to have its frequency turned up so that its purpose can be activated. As the coding in your crystal DNA is being activated, out of a time-frame frequency, so is your memory and purpose on the Earth. You are like flowers now opening up to the Christ light of you; the Golden Rays of Jeshua's heart are shining on your flower, which nurtures it to continue to bloom.

Like many flowers that go through a death process, as the flower dies or wilts away, the roots become stronger and other flowers bloom. This is a continual cycle. This is you. You are the flowers or Cells of this beautiful Earth. The Earth is the core or root foundation of your flower. You are on the Earth to continue to bloom, die, reroot, and expand yourself into a greater beauty and vibration of Knowingness.

The Mother Earth has an agreement or contract with

you. She will hold your frequency to allow you to go through all of your deaths or completions and rebirths. Your contract with her is that as your flowers continue to bloom, you will expand your roots into other flowers' roots. Soon you become one root foundation system. This system will then cover the Earth. The Mother Earth provides the soil for your roots and all other roots to entwine with each other and create new breeds of Soul/Cell flowers and colors.

These new breeds, who are you, are the Crystals who are now being activated with a conscious memory of your Souls' highest purpose and experience. You are moving beyond your old perceptions and beliefs and are starting to see and experience all as beautiful flowers of yourself. You all have the same foundation and root system of the Mother and Father of Me.

As this coding in your DNA continues to be activated and the sun shines upon you, you are blossoming into each other, holding the light for one another to awaken and ascend together into Oneness.

The flowers that I so speak of are all of your Souls/Cells expanding themselves beyond color, religion, ethnic background, culture, and karma. You are becoming a beautiful rainbow of all color-sound frequencies.

You are in the Second Coming of Christ now! You are the Second Coming, and just as Jeshua opened the door for you, you are now opening the door for others of you.

If you all ascended at once, the light would be so bright that you would blow each other out. As you are many color-sound frequencies, you are also at different vibrations in your Souls' awakenings.

You have many different Soul Group agreements, meaning you are all in different levels of Ascension and enlightenment. As one Soul group comes together in harmony, they hold the love and light for one another to love themselves enough to move beyond karma. They then reconnect with each other in love. As they mirror light and love back to one another, this creates a beautiful color-light show, which creates a combustion, or frequency, that opens a doorway for this collective Soul group to move through many dimensions.

This is a continual cycle. As you move collectively through a doorway, you open the frequency for another Soul Group to move through the doorway and into the birth canal of Ascension.

You are now in the birth canal of enlightenment and Ascension! As the coding in your DNA continues to be activated and you continue to vibrate in higher frequencies, these frequencies are like contractions. When you are giving birth to self and the collective, you feel the pain of the contractions, which are the old, frozen emotions breaking loose.

As I said, while in the middle of a contraction, the pain is very real. Imagine your organs or limbs being frozen, and as they begin to thaw out, you feel the numbness and separation, like a foot or arm being asleep. When it starts waking up, it feels very painful. Once it is awake, the limb feels reconnected to your body. Once the frozen emotions have thawed out or awakened and you have moved through the contraction, you will feel more alive and more connected to Me, free and reborn.

You are now constantly in the birth canal of Ascension. In the next transmission, Beloved Sophia will explain to you about plateaus. When you hit a plateau, you move into the frozen emotions, and the birth contraction moves you through the emotion and past the plateau. Anytime you move out of a contraction, your perception becomes wider, more understanding, and more compassionate.

In what you call the past, you came together with your Soul Groups to learn lessons. You mirrored back to one another each other's agreed upon patterns, to be able to understand, heal, forgive, and release them.

You have played every role with one another and are now back together, not to learn lessons, but to move out of any old agreed upon karmic lessons. You have come back together with your Soul Groups to hold the light for one another, to be able to remember who you are, to remember your love, your light, and to assist each other to return home within yourselves as one.

You are the collective Second Coming of Christ. You are now knowing and remembering that you are Me, Creation. You are now activating within yourself all memories of having been great Masters and teachers. You have gone through and are continuing to go through many death and rebirth cycles, or deaths and Ascensions.

Just as Christ, your brother, died and ascended to bring you and your world out of duality, you are also dying and ascending. You are going through a karmic death process without leaving the physical body to bring all that is you out of duality and into higher frequencies of the I AM of Me.

Jeshua opened the door for you, and as you are becoming one with Him, you are opening the door for many. You and your Soul Group have agreed to open many Ascension gateways around your planet. These gateways will continue to expand as more and more of you Christed I AM ones awaken. As you continue to open and awaken through these gateways, the gateways will eventually merge into one another, lifting your whole planet into Ascension.

Many on your planet are now moving into enlightenment. As We look at your planet, We see many lights going on. It is truly Christmas time. Initially We saw a few lights go on, and now We see many. Soon the lights will be so bright that no one will be able to escape into the Shadow.

The Shadow of you and the collective is now very exposed, because the coding in your DNA is releasing the highest collective light frequency that has ever been. All Shadow is being activated, so that it can remember that it also is light. Eventually, all Shadow, which does not become self-realized or ascend into enlightenment, will dissipate out of form, out of any memory of form or consciousness and back into Isness.

As your light and your Shadow's light mirror and reconnect individually and collectively, the Shadows' fear frequency will then dissipate. You and all aspects of your Soul will then have all the understanding, awareness, and Knowingness that is needed for you to move beyond separation, duality, and back together as a divine blueprint of Sophia's and My love and into the heart of your own Christ-Magdalene Flame.

Just as Jeshua ascended and expanded back into Oneness with the highest consciousness or frequency of the I Am, you also are in the same process of Ascension.

There is no past, present, or future. You move into your multidimensional selves where all aspects of yourself will be vibrating in the now. You experience the emotions from all of your Souls' experiences, agreements, and contracts *NOW*.

The coding in your DNA has been activated to move you into becoming your own inner Master and Co-Creator. Through this DNA activation, you have opened the doorways within yourself to the Master computer systems of all creation. You are now remembering and experiencing yourself in all dimensions of creation. As you are awakening and holding the vibration of the Second Coming of Christ, you are moving into your purpose and destiny as Co-Creators for yourself, the collective, and for the planet.

Sophia

"Your childhood is your road map to freedom."

There were times when Jeshua knew that His purpose seemed almost too much for Him. There are times now that you feel your purpose seems too difficult or too much for you. I hear many of you say, "Why would I choose such a lifetime? It is too difficult. I feel alone. How could I possibly have chosen such an agreement?" This usually happens when you are on a plateau. When you hit these plateaus, every emotional memory of your life resurfaces. As it resurfaces, it activates the emotional memories or like patterns from all lifetimes and lessons. It seems overwhelming until you either ride it through or allow yourself to go into the center of the patterns to break loose the frozen emotions that seemingly have you locked in pain, fear, despair, and hopelessness.

When life feels so overwhelming, you start looking for answers and ways to heal, to take the pain away. As you do this, you start unlocking and releasing old patterns, karmic structures, and contracts.

Every time you experience a conscious understanding of the lesson and why you continued to play your old tapes over and over, this structure or tape starts to break and shatter. This frees you to move into a higher frequency, understanding, and acceptance of yourself. An inner light bulb literally goes on and exposes the old programs so that you can choose to release and delete them.

Every time you do this, you move through the illusional veils of conflict and duality, not only for self, but also for the whole collective possessing the pattern. At times you need others who are not emotionally involved in the patterns to assist you.

When you are hitting plateaus, you may feel that you are on an emotional roller coaster ride. In recent years, you hit these plateaus maybe once every five or ten years. Then it was every few years. As you are moving out of linear time, you started hitting these plateaus monthly, weekly and, now, daily. In now times, you may hit multiple plateaus every day.

If you do not have an understanding of the lesson and are caught up in the emotional patterns or frozen emotions, you will bring the lesson to yourself time and time again until you surrender into it. Every time you bring this lesson to you, the pattern becomes stronger and more difficult, but when you have an understanding and the pattern breaks, you move into temporary emotional bliss. You are then in the larger understanding of why the experience happened to you and why the other players did what they did, why you responded in such a way, and also the reversed side of the lesson. From this place, you can then move into forgiveness.

You cannot move into the higher consciousness of self until you can forgive. When you move into the larger picture, you realize there is nothing to forgive. You realize that no one has ever done anything to you that you did not agree to go through.

Your parents never did anything to you that you did not set the intention to experience. They gave you the foundation that you needed to go through to free your Soul karmically. Your childhood is your road map to freedom. Every incident in your childhood, both good and bad, can be traced back to another frame of reference, or what you call timeline or lifetime. You came back again with your chosen childhood experiences to activate these old memories from other lifetimes so that you would know what it is in this lifetime that needs to be released.

These old emotions are once again activated in this lifetime so that you can experience the emotional bondage, to follow the time line back to the experience, to heal and release the lesson. When you find and release the emotional charge that you are carrying in your mental, emotional, physical, and cellular bodies from another time line or lifetime, it frees you from the blockage in this lifetime.

Every feeling and emotion you experience in this lifetime you have experienced before, but you have never experienced them within yourself collectively on the level that you are vibrating in now.

As you are moving out of a karmic time frequency and reconnecting with yourself in all dimensions, you are constantly having all mirrored back to you. All is you. As you are reconnecting with yourself multi-dimensionally, all aspects of yourself, which have been dormant are now being awakened.

I hear you say, "I don't know who I am anymore." I say to you that you are now remembering and awakening into your authentic self. Your veils of illusion are dissipating, and you are expanding into a larger picture of yourself. As this happens, you lose your old identities and perceptions and move into the larger picture of your collective I AM self.

It is then that you experience yourself truly as each other and feel that all is you. You experience yourself as Me, the feminine creation, and as your Father, the Creator. You move out of the perception or belief of separation. You see through all of your senses, not just your old mind-set, which was handed down to you by your parents, or through your childhood and all the agreed upon lessons along the way.

When you move out of these agreed upon lessons and experience yourself expanded beyond the lessons, free from the karmic completion agreements, you then know there was nothing to forgive. You were in a death and completion cycle.

When you are in the middle of an emotional pattern, the experience is very real. The pattern controls you. You live from the pattern. You react from the pattern, and you see all around you as the pattern. It becomes your perception. It is only when you move beyond by going through the pattern that it breaks open, and you can move through it into freedom.

Freedom is moving beyond the pattern and into a larger aspect of you. As you continue to do this, you once again move into the collective I AM. You then remember through knowing that there is nothing that needs to be forgiven. You remember that you agreed upon and even chose the lesson to totally free yourself and the collective from all karmic positions.

The need to forgive and to be forgiven is in a karmic time frame. I say to you, as you move beyond the time frame and into the higher dimensions beyond duality, you understand that all was agreed upon, and there is nothing to forgive. When you are in the time frame, those who are still in the agreed upon lessons with you very much need forgiveness, and they need you to apologize to them for any hurtful lessons. When you can come to the place of truly taking responsibility for your life's actions and reactions, you will want others to forgive you for your actions, coming from your not knowing or karmic agreements. It is also important that you forgive others for their not knowing. This is coming full circle with the Creator.

As you move into forgiveness and you ask to be forgiven and can forgive, you start breaking the mental and emotional pattern of the lessons. This frees you and the other parties to move to a higher frequency, to mirror back to one another the truth of your love and light instead of your karmic hurt.

Asking for and giving forgiveness are the greatest

breakthroughs karmically. This shows that you are now taking responsibility for your choices and that you plan to move out of the victim role. Those who feel or felt hurt by you can feel from your heart that you are truly sorry and that you do love them and care for them. From this place of love they can now start letting go of their hurts and sorrows and start their journey home within themselves and back to self-love. They will no longer feel that they need your approval to make them okay or whole.

When "I AM sorry" comes from the center of your heart, it starts breaking loose many frozen emotions and patterns and begins everyone's healing process. As this happens, the old frozen emotions break loose, like water being let out of a dam. This process is most important because the new cannot be put on top of the old. If your cup is full of old hurtful emotions, you have no room to fill it up with joy, happiness, and love.

You may say that you want love in your life, but if you are so full of old sorrows, resentments, judgments, guilt, fears, and old agreements to protect yourself, you have no place within yourself that is open to receive love. You are too full of the past, which is vibrating in you now.

Remember, everything in life mirrors you. If your energy is full of past hurts and memories, you will continue to bring back to you these mirror experiences in relationships and lessons, until you get the lesson. Every time you bring the lesson to you, it will become more difficult, because you are full and cannot handle anymore. There is no place to put any more of this perceived negative energy.

Eventually your bodies start breaking down and you start looking for ways to heal, to free yourself. Life becomes too unbearable. As you move into your own healing process, you will start seeing and perceiving these lessons as gifts.

As you release these old karmic poisons, you start emptying your old emotional cup. You then have room inside yourself to start receiving love, which creates happiness and joy. You start loving and appreciating yourself more, and you begin to expect to have more happiness. Because all in your life is a constant mirror of you and your beliefs or perceptions, you mirror back to yourself a higher frequency of love.

If you do not choose to surrender into these old frozen emotions and your life seems to be spiraling into a downward journey, you start exploding. Your body becomes overloaded, tired, and starts closing down. You end up with dis-ease and sickness. The many layers of your bodies cannot hold together any longer, and they start breaking down.

Many times these emotions start coming out sideways in anger and hatred, and you end up hurting others because you are hurt. You may even hurt those whom you love the most, like innocent children. You project to others your hurts and fears.

Your prisons are full of hurt, angry children who have not healed and grown up. Their anger came out sideways, and they ended up hurting others because they were hurt. Their own needs were not met.

If you watch children play who come from family units that have a weak foundation, you will experience the hurt in these children, and their interactions with one another may be hostile and angry. If they do not have healthy parents or extended family to assist them to understand and release these hurt and confused emotions, every conflict in their lives builds upon the next one, and soon these children are trapped inside their own emotions. They do not know what they feel. Many times, they will start addictions, using drugs, alcohol, food, sex, and so on, to numb themselves or to try to fill themselves up with whatever the missing ingredient is. They then bring mirrors of these patterns back into their lives through relationships or through the lack of relationships.

Their low self-esteem connects to the Shadow Ego side of self and needs a way to protect itself. The Shadow being its own entity starts defying all sense of right or wrong. It takes over the person's or Soul's senses, confuses him, and pulls him into the underworld or unconsciousness. This underworld is a fear-based, dark-evil perception of conflict, fear, confusion, and survival. This child in the adult body then acts out in survival and will do anything to survive, even hurt, harm, and violate others.

The way you, as a light warrior, or Being of light, can change this is to continue to love and accept yourself. As you move out of karmic agreements and perceptions, you only see others as they truly are. You will see how difficult others' paths have been, and you will love them for their agreements to come to the Earth and play out the fragmented aspects of creation.

If you can truly see others as love, no matter whom they are or what you perceive they have done, you will heal your world.

Your world is a convoluted expression of perceptions that root all the way back to the beginning of creation. You, the Souls/ Cells of Us, the Creation, have now agreed to play out the end days, meaning the old karmic, fear-based contracts. All of you great Souls/Cells have agreed to take on many collective karmic patterns to free the whole consciousness out of duality. Many of you have signed up for multiple contracts and conflicts because you are such great Master Souls. As you continue to complete these collective contracts, you will move through the veils of illusion bringing the collective through with you.

As you continue to break barriers and move through the veils of duality, and you drop old conflicts within yourself, your light emerges so bright that all you come in contact with are drawn to your higher vibration: I say all, even the Shadow. All need light to exist, even the Shadow.

Your purpose and intention is to come out of duality, and collectively your light will draw the Shadow out. As the Shadow shows itself, which is happening now, you, the light ones can assist many of these Souls to awaken out of duality, out of fear-based perception. Your collective light will eventually shatter the Shadow because it has no power on its own. It feeds off your fear-based perceptions and conclusions. As you move further and further within self-love, you attain a state, which you call enlightenment. The highest light within you comes on, and you see others only in the highest expression of love. You no longer perceive them as dark or evil. You no longer align your frequency and thought forms with them. As this happens, they start becoming powerless and lose their fear control frequency over others.

You are collective Beings of light who have come to the Earth to move out of collective duality and to bring others out with you. This is happening now. Not only is the Shadow on your planet more exposed and seemingly stronger than it has ever been, the light on your planet is the highest it has ever been, which will eventually dissipate the Shadow. As you continue to move through and beyond time, you are bringing the planet and the whole consciousness back home to the light. The Shadow would not be so exposed had the light not become so high. The light is drawing the Shadow out. It has to be brought out collectively for you to awaken and transform it into self-realization.

The death of your planet that is so talked about and feared now is not the death of Mother Earth; it is the death of duality. You will always have the Shadow, but the Shadow will become self-realized or conscious and will become your ally.

The Shadow must exist because it is part of the light. The Shadow, or darkness, defines the light. You, the light rays of your Father's and My love-sound, are the ones on the Earth who have agreed to assist the Shadow out of fear. You do this by loving it. If you continue to hate and condemn it, you are feeding it the adrenaline that the emotions need to exist.

When you move beyond the dark Shadow and embrace your own Shadow with love and gratitude for all it has taught you, you disempower it. The collective Shadow then loses its reign of terror and false power that it has held over you. You will then mirror back to your own Shadow its own love, and it will feel safe to release its fear.

As this happens, your own Shadow will fill back up with its own love and light frequency. It will put down its sword, step out of battle, and re-emerge with your light. As you move beyond duality, you will mirror back to the collective Shadow the balanced male-female, light-shadow, heart and Ego. You and your Shadow will then assist the collective Shadow to move back into its own light, love, and self-acceptance.

Although thought is powerful and can change much of your world by changing your perception from duality to perfection, you cannot lift the planet into Ascension and enlightenment without the heart. As the mind opens to a higher understanding and realigns itself with the higher self, the I AM of Creation, it then gives the heart permission to open into its higher I AM love frequency. This heart love then brings the planet and the collective through the birth canal of Ascension and enlightenment. You must have both male-female and heart-mind components to become whole again.

*"We are each other's love, flow, inspiration, and strength.
We are inseparable; we are one Twin Flame Soul's Song."*

3

JESHUA AND MAGDALENE'S LOVE STORY

The Second Coming of the Magdalene – Christ

I am with you now. This is Jeshua. Our journey has been long and hard, – quite intense. Wouldn't you say? We are all coming home together. We are one. All that I am, you are, and more. I went before and opened the passageway for you to follow.

When I say you are more, it is because you are the collective Second Coming of the Christ consciousness. When I walked before to open the door for you, I was also walking in the collective, but you, the Souls of Creation, did not yet have a high enough vibration to remember you were me in the highest.

There was great fear and speculation of my Being. This is because the magnitude of my light and love mirrored your light and started creating an awakening of love, of hope. When this happened, the old fear-based Ego structure became afraid of losing their power over you. We have now come full circle; you and I have come home together, and when we walk together through the 12-12 doorway, you will have moved beyond the Karmic Coding of oppression and into the freedom of your Soul.

It is then that you will truly be open to all choices of free will to co-create your new lifetime and to rewrite your script. I strongly suggest that you start writing and intending your script now. Because there is no past, present, or future, as you rewrite your script for your new lifetime on Earth, you are sending the intention into what you call future and bringing it back into your now. As our Father explained to you, you are now emerging into a new lifetime without physically leaving the body. You are emerging into the butterfly of freedom. You are moving out of your cocoon of old programmings, of old beliefs and are merging together as one beyond time, beyond story and into the Isness of all that is. The doorways to heaven have been opened for you, from within yourself, from your heart.

Set your intention now for your new lifetime on Earth. Set the intentions for yourself, for one another, for the collective, and for the Earth. Ask and you shall receive. Intention is prayer; know that you are all that is, and it is your birthright to claim your wealth of abundance for all, on all levels. Give thanks that it is done, and it shall be.

I wish to speak to you of my divine feminine, my heart, my Magdalene. She has always been and still is the light of my Being. She held the love and light for me as I moved beyond karma for the collective. Her feminine love held the door for my heart to continue to open and expand beyond any time frame and back together with Mother-Father of Creation.

Just as Sophia opened our Father's heart, Magdalene held the love for my heart to continue to open, so that I could connect to your hearts in Oneness and expand us into all of Creation, into enlightenment and Ascension. On the Earth Plane, this seems like a long time coming. And yet, in Spirit, it is but a blink of the eye in our journey together. Many of you have been with Me on other planets or Creations, as We brought the consciousness beyond time into enlightenment, Ascension – Oneness.

Our agreement now is to bring this Holographic Planet Earth into direct alignment with the Central Sun's grid system. As We do this, each lens that you look through will be one of peace and appreciation for all that is. Just as our Father could not move into total alignment without Sophia opening his heart, I could not have fulfilled my plans or contracts without Magdalene, the heart of Me, and you cannot do it without your collective heart

40

awakening to guide you home within yourself. Now is the time for this awakening. It cannot not happen, for the coding is in your DNA. You are being activated to awaken into the color-sound of your Souls' Song individually and collectively.

Magdalene and I also have come full circle, and she is now emerging into her Soul's higher purpose and mission - not just to hold her love and light for my heart to open and stay strong, but to hold the love and light for all of you, to now feel safe in your feminine. In the past, it was not time on the Earth plane for her to be in her full bloom purpose, and now it is. Along with Mother Mary and other feminine priestesses and goddesses, she will continue to guide the collective heart in the safety of love through the 2012 doorway into the balanced Feminine–Male Second Coming of the Christ Consciousness.

Just as she held the love and strength for me on my path, I am holding the intention of love, light, and strength for her to now guide you. Magdalene and I are already in total balance of one another. We are each other and flow in and out of each other's heart and in and out of yours like the ocean waves breaking, then building up again, each time creating a stronger union of balance between the female and male within you, individually and collectively.

Contrary to some perceptions of Magdalene's and My union, We had agreed to go through all of these great cycles of awakening together. Magdalene was not a victim, just as you are not a victim. When I was on the Earth, it was not appropriate for us to share our great love for each other openly with you. The consciousness was not such that the feminine was safe to be in a leading role position, and now it is.

Just as you are playing out all karmic imbalances for the male and female collectively, Magdalene and I did the same. She knew she would not be able to be acknowledged as the love of my life until this time in the history of now. It was all planned by agreement. She knew she was incarnating into a difficult role for the feminine and that when the appropriate time came she would emerge again to assist in the great awakening of the feminine

41

heart. Although she is not in physical body, she is more with you now than when she was on the Earth.

Your consciousness is now high enough to receive her. Mother Mary went before as the symbol of the virgin and opened the door for Magdalene to now go before you, to give you permission to open your hearts and bodies and Being to the sacredness of the feminine sensuality and sexuality, for the sacredness of intimacy between a man and a woman. She is also opening the door for the sacredness of love and intimacy between all Beings. Whether this love is between two women or two men does not matter. You are now moving beyond the identity of all forms, which as humans you were programmed to believe was love. You are coming back together in love. You have played all roles, all identities, and now you are all coming back together in love beyond gender, religions, and beliefs. This is by a collective agreement or contract.

Magdalene and I knew before We physically met that We were being prepared for each other. She actually studied with my Mother Mary in Egypt in the Temple of Isis. After Magdalene and Mary's reunion, our Mother Sophia and Father Creator assisted them both through many priestess initiations, to prepare Magdalene's vibration to be able to complement mine. She had a great role as my divine complement, to hold the sacred feminine energy for me to be able to move the collective of us through an awakening pattern of enlightenment and Ascension. Through the many initiations, my Mother, Mary, was able to hold the vibration for My beloved Magdalene to be able to hold the vibration for Me so that I could hold it for all of you.

After their initial meeting and through the initiations, Magdalene and I were in constant contact with each other spiritually in higher dimensions. When We met at the well our union was already so strong, that as We came together in person, there was an explosion of light between us that fused us together as one Being of love.

Because we had been connecting spiritually, when we met in physical form, there was an instant marriage of our energies coming together in love and the intention of our higher purpose. After the explosion of energies between us at the well, Magdalene had a difficult time holding her balance. I took her hand to hold her up and to assist with her balance. The following day, Mother Mary performed a marriage ceremony in physical form for us that was brought forth from our Father Creator. It was that same night that we lay together for the first time in physical form as man and wife. We were sealed together as each other's Beloved.

She was the light of My love, My strength, and My will through the rest of My days on Earth, as she still is today. We are each other's love, flow, inspiration, and strength. We are inseparable; we are one Twin Flame Soul's Song. Just as Magdalene and I came together as one, many of you now have been communicating with your divine twin flames in spirit and are drawing yourselves back to one another in physical form on the Earth Plane.

Mary Magdalene was not a prostitute as the church had portrayed her. She was and still is a very high priestess and prophet. She is now assisting in healing the rift between the Feminine and the Male. She is teaching and assisting many in Isis, Magdalene initiations, and is bringing much wisdom to the Earth from ancient mystery schools. Just as Mother Mary has made many appearances around your world, and has healed many from her presence, Mary Magdalene will now be appearing and healing many through our Christ-Union of Love.

My Death, Resurrection and Afterlife

There are many versions of My end times on the Earth and I say to you, all are correct. This is because you are living in a hologram of many end times of karmic completions. Depending on what Soul Group's contract you are experiencing life through is the end time version that you will most resonate with and believe to be true. You may have one end time perception as your truth, and as you continue to grow in consciousness you may expand beyond that perception's color-sound vibration, move into another wheel of the matrix and merge together with another Soul Group's Song. You have the opportunity to eventually blend together in all Soul Group's Songs and into all matrices of Creation. From this place, you will have moved beyond any story and into the presence and a Knowingness of Magdalene's and My union of love, strength, and Oneness of the Second Coming of Christ.

You will be in the Song of Isness where the story will not be important, only the love. This is the place beyond karma where you experience all endings as truth, and yet as illusions, for whatever is needed for each Soul Group's completion of their story. You will feel great honor and love for all who have agreed to come to the Earth, to move through whatever lens of perception their Souls needed to learn from. You will be able to be with any religion, spiritual group, or belief and feel the Oneness with them all.

After my crucifixion I went through a karmic death for the collective. I did not die for your sins as has been said, in fact, I did not physically die. I died karmically for all of you to be able to move into a higher vibration together. Through my resurrection and rebirth I opened the doorway for you to start questioning your own mortality. I intended for much confusion to take place. Confusion creates uncertainty. Uncertainty allows you to start asking questions; for you to think, to ponder about the larger picture of Creation. As I ascended, the light was so bright that it mirrored the higher self and Over Soul of Magdalene and My intention for the Earth. This intention has taken many Earthly years to manifest itself into a collective form for the Feminine to awaken the heart of the Male consciousness.

Many of you light Masters are very aware of this awakened consciousness. Now that it has awakened into form, you are collectively moving out of form and into a higher experience and expression of love into Isness.

You could say that I lived for you. I lived for you to remember your own love, light, and magnificence, and to remember that you are God, that you are Me. Through karmic, collective intention, you have created the consciousness of your

Earth today and as you are now remembering yourself as God, as the co-creator of your own Creation, you can recreate all consciousness to vibrate in Heaven on Earth.

As I said, I did not physically die. When I arose from the tomb, my light body, higher self and Over Soul opened the door for the collective to move through the illusional veils of separateness. Later when all were looking at the magnificent light show of My Ascension, the human aspect of Me walked into the crowds, and I watched my Ascension with you. I then turned and walked into the next step of my Soul's journey on the Earth.

After My death, resurrection, and rebirth I was seen in many places on the Earth, and it is believed that I lived on in many different places. This is true, for I am a Master Soul and can split my energies to be in many places at once.

Just as God is all over your world and vibrates through all religions and beliefs, I am that also. How can I be seen throughout many places in your world at the same time? How can I heal many people in so many different places? It is because I am the Over Soul of your Planet as is My Magdalene, Mother Mary, Lucifer and his beloved partner, Ascendra. Yes, Lucifer is an aspect of my Over Soul. He is the carrier of the Master Shadow that creates duality. We are all aspects of the same Master Over Soul. This is why Mother Mary can be seen and witnessed through many different religions or lenses. She is able to heal many all over the world simultaneously, just as I am. As I said, Magdalene will now be appearing to many throughout your world, just as I do. It is her agreement now to spread her wings beyond time and to vibrate with me, to awaken all into the Second Coming.

Surely you all know that my brother Lucifer can be seen, felt, and witnessed throughout your world. What you do not know is that Lucifer also has a divine partner, Ascendra. She is a very high priestess of Light who has held great love, light, and intention for Lucifer to continue to do the job that our Father requested of him. It is now, that as you move out of fear and duality, you are unthreading from him. As you do this, you release him from his role as the higher self of the collective shadow and free him to

45

move back into the heart of his Beloved.

As I said, after my death it was said that I was seen living in many different places on the Earth. This is correct. My Soul split and I manifested myself in physical forms, in different locations, to anchor my Christ energy into the Grid system of the planet and to also mirror My love and light to many. Because you are the collective, as I mirrored Myself to many, your Souls/Cells vibrated and expanded into each other. I also appeared to many in my etheric or light body. You could say I had expanded through all of the wheels of the divine matrix and was living all twelve of my major lifetimes on the Earth both physically and etherically. (The Creator will speak to you of the Divine Matrix in later chapters.)

Mary Magdalene is my twin flame or divine partner, and wherever I lived, she lived with me. After my death, she was also seen and witnessed as living in many different places. This is correct. She manifested herself living in more than one lifetime at the same time with me.

It is believed that I lived in India after my death and that I was married with five children. This is correct, and My wife at the time was my beloved Magdalene and the Mother of our children. It is also believed that at the time of my death, Magdalene was pregnant with our child. That is also correct. She was carrying our first child Sarah. After my perceived death, she was taken to France for her safety and for the safety of our unborn child. I later joined her there. I sometimes lived with her in physical form and at other times in my light body. We had three more children together. It was there that Magdalene brought her knowledge from the teachings of the Mystery School of Isis. While in France, she integrated these energies into the land. These energies are being felt today throughout the collective awakening of the Feminine. She taught and healed many and opened massive portals for the collective Feminine to be able to vibrate in the now on the Earth Plane.

Magdalene and I also lived in Turkey together where we had two children, a boy and a girl. It is there that I was more in my light body. Magdalene also brought the sacred teachings from Isis to this land and mirrored the frequency to the people. Magdalene also lived in America. She was a great Medicine Woman. Her name was White Buffalo Calf Woman. I did not live on the Earth Plane with her in that lifetime, but we were still inseparable, because we have merged into each other and are the same Soul in two different bodies.

Magdalene Speaks

My Dear ones, this is Magdalene. I am greatly honored to be able to serve on the Earth at this time. My time of Ascension and rebirth is in the time of now. As my beloved Jeshua explained to you, it was not for me to awaken you into the Feminine heart of the Second Coming before now. At this time, I am now assisting you into enlightenment and Ascension. You cannot go through this process collectively without the Feminine and Male balance within yourself. That is my purpose now. I held the love, strength, and intention for Jeshua, and he is now holding the same energy for me to assist you into the safety of your heart's awakening.

From the beginning of my lifetime on the Earth with Jeshua, I knew that I had a great purpose. I was not exactly sure what it was, but as I continued to grow in years, I always followed my heart. I was continually being guided through all the steps of my journey, through my heart's love; I always knew intuitively where to go and what to do. My parents were also aware that I had a great purpose in my Soul's journey, and they assisted me in all the ways possible for a girl or woman at that time on the Earth.

I was twelve years of age when I entered the Temple of Isis. I was in the puberty stage of my life and I was being prepared by the priestesses of Isis to be an initiate in the Temple. When I entered the Temple I had not yet started my menstruation and could not start the initiations until my flow. Once my flow began, just before my thirteenth year, I was quickly taken into my first initiation as a woman and as a priestess.

It was in the very first ritual that I met Mother Mary. She was a very high Priestess of the Isis order. She knew that she was going to meet her son Jeshua's Beloved in the temple. She also knew that she would be assisting this woman through many processes of initiation to bring her body's energies high enough to hold the vibration for her Son's journey.

It was at our first meeting that Mother Mary recognized me to be Jeshua's Beloved. Mother Mary was very loving and attentive of me. At that time, it was not shared with me as to my larger purpose. Once Mother Mary recognized me and the initiations started, Jeshua's and my higher self reconnected in our physical forms, and we started communicating in the dream state. Our reunion was peaceful and so beautiful. I felt as though I were home. I knew this man in my dreams was my Beloved. Our Cells started coming together as one twin flame's song. I experienced a love beyond words. Every cell of my body vibrated in love. I would awaken tingling and so alive and full of passion. At first I did not know what this passion was, but through the initiations, I learned the power of my body and what the purpose of my body was: to be able to hold the frequencies of light for my Beloved. Through the dream state, my Beloved and I shared our love, our thoughts and intentions of merging ourselves together, to heal the rift between the Feminine and Male. I certainly knew that I was the equal balance of this man, that we were one.

After awhile, my dream state and awakened state merged together as one. It was then that my Beloved was with me always, whether asleep or awake. As I was being taken through the initiations, he was always with me. We were being initiated together. Before the last cycle of initiations he visually appeared to me just as he had appeared to me after the crucifixion. He was in the same vibration and state of consciousness. In an instant I saw him and knew who he was. Our whole life together flashed before me. I could see myself standing there with him after his crucifixion. As I was taken forward in time, I could see that we had achieved what we had come to the Earth to do together. I felt all of the collective emotions of our great journey.

I felt as thought my heart was breaking; there was so much love and pain. The love was greater than I could ever have consciously imagined, as was the shock, sorrow, loss, confusion, abandonment, mistrust, fear, and anger towards God and so many overwhelming emotions. All of the emotions of the karmic journey were being given to me at once, so that I could go through the release of them before Jeshua and I physically met. They needed to be purged, to be released so that they would not get in the way of our larger purpose, so they would not control my heart, my love for him.

After Jeshua first appeared to me, he also appeared to his Mother Mary. From their meeting, she knew that I had come together with her Son in the highest level of love and purpose. When Mother Mary and I came together after his appearance with us, our eyes locked and we filled with love for one another. We held each other and cried; we cried for our journey ahead, for our love, for our commitment of purpose, for loss, grief and for the magnitude of our larger purpose. We held each other and prayed for the strength to move through our journey together. From that moment on, we were inseparable. We both loved this man named Jeshua with all of our hearts and Souls, with every fiber of our Being.

Before Jeshua and I met at the well, I knew that I was going there to meet my Beloved; for us to connect with each other in physical form. I had great excitement within me to know that I would be meeting my Beloved. We had shared so much together through the initiations and our meetings in our etheric bodies. Now I was coming together with my Beloved, with the man that I loved more than life itself. We both knew that Mother Mary was going to perform a sacred marriage ceremony for us brought forth from Father-Creator himself. I felt great excitement and anticipation at the thought of being able to lay physically with Jeshua.

When we met at the well, I almost passed out. We moved together through time, or all stories of history – what was before and what was yet to come. Bolts of lightning of color explosions

49

shot through all levels of my bodies. All of the Cells of my bodies were crystal prisms as we expanded into one Being of consciousness, living in two different bodies. As we moved beyond time through all dimensions, we merged together into the heart and Soul of Sophia and our Father Creator. We were home. We were one with the Creator of all that is. In an instant, I had a conscious memory of all of our lives together, of every moment that we had ever shared together and what was yet to come for us. These memories moved through my mind and body in a flash. All flashed before me, and past, present and future became one.

After our marriage ceremony, when we lay together physically as man and wife, our vibration was so high that it felt like we were on fire. Our I Am energies moved up through our roots and opened our kundalini energies fusing them together. As this happened, our hearts released all of the old karmic energies that were still vibrating in any of our bodies. When our kundalinis opened, our light bodies merged together with our higher selves and we became one higher self. As I said before, we became one Soul in two different bodies. From that day forward, we were one. We were inseparable, even if we were not physically together, for we were the same Soul. We fused together as one song of Creation. Our chakras started vibrating in the same color and sound frequencies. Our breath became one breath.

The ritual of our lovemaking was very sacred and important to us. It kept us fused together in love, passion and our Souls' highest purpose. It grounded and connected us at the core of our Being. We started each day in the intimacy of our lovemaking. Even if we were not physically together, we were able to bring our energies up through each other in love. From the first moment of physical love making, we moved out of time, and from that moment forward, our lives were lived from the foundation of now.

We knew the story of what was to come, but our energies were always in the present moment. We did not feel the emotions of the future. We were so blessed to be able to serve each other and the world from the moment of now, from love, from our hearts.

50

Jeshua never felt the pain for himself or the collective until he moved into the moment of any experience. There was no fear or anticipation of what was to come, and yet, sometimes he could feel overwhelmed by the collective energy of the larger purpose that was building within him. We lived in the love of now and from that tremendous love we were able to build a foundation so strong that it moved through all worlds of time and consciousness.

When Jeshua felt weak or tired, my love and strength gave him the energy to continue on. I always held the energy vibration for him to expand himself through all consciousness; I was always able to project myself to Jeshua and he to me. My heart was his heart; my love was his love. My body was his body and his was mine. We were each other's breath of life, as we still are today.

When Jeshua was on the cross, I held his energy in my heart to help alleviate his suffering and pain. The Creator and Sophia were downloading their union of love and grace into Jeshua's heart and Being, as well as into my heart and Being. My heart love was holding the strength for Jeshua to fulfill his collective karmic agreement.

Jeshua's and my twin flame love story is now being told and activated. It is opening the door for the twin flame love to activate all Souls, all consciousness. This vibration is awakening within all Beings now. The Feminine and Male twin flame sounds are calling all aspects of themselves back together beyond time. It is the same experience that I had with Jeshua. Many of you are experiencing your divine partners energetically. Your etheric bodies are already merging together as one, before you even meet physically. You are communicating with each other's higher selves. Your hearts are opening to a purity and innocence of love beyond words. I see many of you are experiencing the pain of the beginning of your Souls' agreement of separation in Spirit, as you are moving closer and closer together. Your great Souls' love is releasing the pain and loneliness of all lifetimes of separation. From my heart, I say to you, if this is the love that your Soul is now ready for, set the intention and it shall be. Remember you are

51

coming into a new lifetime without physically leaving the body. You are the co-creators of this new lifetime. Rewrite your script and give thanks that it already is, that it is done.

As this beautiful Holographic Earth is shifting, you are moving beyond time where all consciousness vibrates in the now. You are coming home collectively. You are in the doorway of the twin flame vibration of The Second Coming of Christ Consciousness.

After our Father performed Jeshua's and my sacred marriage, through Mother Mary, our vibration exploded and wrapped itself around the etheric body of Mother Earth. This balanced color-sound sent the frequency into Father Earth, bringing the Mother and Father Earth together so that they experienced each other's etheric bodies. This started calling them home together beyond time. It opened a sacred passageway for their twin flame energies to vibrate in their Souls' Song together.

Remember you are the Cells of the planet. As Mother and Father Earth started coming home together, it activated codings in your DNA to start moving you out of the imbalance and separation between the Male and Female. All separation energies of duality were activated so that they could be released. This is the collective Shadow now revealing itself, so that your collective love can now dissolve it.

As you are moving collectively through the shadow separation you are reuniting together in love – merging back together as one with your Beloved. You are now coming home together as the Second Coming of Christ Oneness; you are just about home. Keep putting one foot in front of the other and through intention, you will soon be back together in the arms of your Beloved.

Call on me and I will assist you on your great journey back to the wholeness of your Being. That is now my greatest purpose as the Feminine Second Coming. I am a Master Guide for the twin flame Second Coming Awakening. You are Jeshua and I, and We are you. We are One.

We honor you for your Souls' journey and are now guiding you back together with your Beloved. There must be a balance of the Feminine and Male. Jeshua and I went before and created that balance and are now assisting you to remember your highest love to heal the Earth.

I love you. I honor you. I embrace you. I am here for you. Just call my name and I will be with you.

In Love, Light, Grace and Gratitude,

Mary Magdalene

"My greatest desire is to be back together with you in the light."

4

LUCIFER SPEAKS

Jeshua on Lucifer

When the dimension of the Angelic Realms split, Lucifer, who is My divine blueprint, my male ego aspect, agreed to open the door to duality. When we were in the Angelic Realms together, Lucifer and I were one. We are the same Over Soul. When the Creator asked that I assist to bring the Earth to enlightenment and Ascension, we agreed that I would take on the job as the light carrier, and Lucifer would take on the job as the Shadow carrier.

When I was on the Earth all the conflict I had with the Shadow, or what is called Satan, was the ego aspect of Me challenging myself and trying to take My light. As you are all aspects of the highest creation, you are the collective aspects of Me and My brother Lucifer, who are playing out Our same agreement on Earth, with the outcome to bring the Earth out of duality.

As I am you, and you are threaded through Me to become the Second Coming, many of you are also threaded through Lucifer. Our Father asked this one Lucifer to open the door to duality. It was a great responsibility, and Father knew Lucifer was strong enough to hold this position of darkness or Shadow. Lucifer did not want to take on this job. He was very much loved, respected, and adored in Spirit, in the Angelic Realms. He was My brother, and I loved him very much, as I still do. When he agreed to play the bad brother, he started forgetting who he was. As the old Ego structure of our Father (before Sophia) integrated with Lucifer, he started regressing into the old structure before the new creations of our Father's love.

When I incarnated to the Earth plane, Lucifer was already there. He came down first and opened the door to duality. He is a great Master of Light, and he agreed to take on the role of one of the greatest Shadow Beings in the history of Earth.

Many in the Angelic Realms loved him very much, as they loved Me and each other. This separation caused great pain and uncertainty and a mistrust of our Father's wishes. When Lucifer's actions were too difficult to deal with, he was asked to leave. When he left, many of his brothers and sisters left with him. Imagine those of you on the Earth plane who have siblings that you love dearly and you witnessed them regressing into their egos, controlling others, being in conflict with you, with their parents and with all of their old friends. Would you not want to do what you could to protect them and bring them back into balance, into love?

Because many of you knew Lucifer before this duality, you wanted to make sure he was safe and tried to protect him. From all of the imbalance of emotion, of fear, mistrust, and the confusion of separation, many were pulled into Lucifer's Ego mind frame.

I incarnated to the planet to assist the consciousness to remember the lightness of their being, to turn the light on for the planet and all of My brothers and sisters that were caught up in the illusion of separateness. Lucifer came to the Earth to connect with the Beings of light who are in their egos, to reconnect with their fear, confusion, mistrust and duality. As I activated the light, he activated the Shadow or Ego. This was his purpose, his mission. As he activated the fear-based Ego, Souls started feeling the painful emotions of separation and duality. Before my appearance, this duality was a vibration or frequency that was the norm for most Beings. It was the reality and vibration of the consciousness of the times on the planet. The light ones had forgotten who they were and accepted this as a way of life or living.

When I appeared, I gave them a new way of feeling. My light and love activated the memory in their DNA of their own love frequency. My appearance on the Earth was very dramatic, wouldn't you say? It had to be, so as to raise the consciousness. As I ascended, it lifted the planet and its Beings into a higher vibration. My appearance on Earth was to reconnect or rethread the Beings of light back to the Father-Mother of Creation.

Lucifer's fall from grace was to activate all lifetimes or agreements when the Souls on the Earth had lived in Ego, fear, separation, and duality. As he did this, these Souls started feeling loss, grief, hopelessness and that something was missing from their lives. He activated the feeling part of the Shadow Ego. Yes, the Ego feels when it is threatened. Its intention is to keep one stuck in fear, illusion, control, denial separation, and loneliness, all fear-based emotions. This Ego structure is not singular. It is collective, for you are each other and thread back together through all lifetimes and dimensions.

When Lucifer activated the Ego emotions on the planet, there was even greater chaos and misunderstanding of God. There was great fear and upheaval. Churches and institutions became afraid of losing their power or control over their people. They aligned with and became allies with the false Gods and the Shadow Beings that were created before the Creator's heart awakening with Sophia. They created even greater restrictions, claiming it was God's will. They took away the rights of the individuals and controlled people through fear, creating God to be a fear-based father. These institutions were used to being in control of people's minds, lives and existence.

Lucifer agreed to open the door to the heart through the Ego - through suffering and pain. I agreed to open the heart through Love. When Lucifer started activating these painful fear-based emotions, and people started to feel again, many started awakening into their heart or the feeling center of the Mother. They were longing for the safety of the Mother. As their hearts and minds started blending together, they started rebelling and pulling away from these Ego-based controlling church structures. As the feminine started awakening, many feminine Beings started protesting and tried to pull away from these controlling church structures. These fear-based Beings in authority knew of the feminine power because they had experienced the great shift in the Father's consciousness after Sophia awakened him. They were afraid that if the feminine continued to feel and spread their light, love, and healing frequencies, they would lose their own position of power.

They started denying the feminine and started calling them witches. Anyone who was not in total accordance with the old structure had charges brought against him/her as being Satanic. The *"evil ones"* were then rounded up, tortured, and killed. There was a great war between the light and the dark or shadow ego, as there still is. Some of you on the Earth today have taken on assignments to play out many of the last stages of these Souls/ Cells who have separated from Source and that are still warring against each other.

As the veils are being lifted, you are remembering your own light and releasing your contracts and agreements. As has been understood by many, when I came to the Earth, I knew My destiny and what My Father, God, had in store for Me. In the beginning of My incarnation, I did not remember that I would go through a karmic death, not just for Myself, but also for others. After my crucifixion and I reawakened in My physical body, or as you understood, came back from death, I ascended. In doing so, I opened the door for the collective consciousness to awaken, to remember their own light, love and magnificence of creation, to become one with Me and to move out of duality. You are the Christed ones of Me and Magdalene, the Second Coming of Our Christ Consciousness. We are threading back together with you in Our Golden Ray sound vibration. As I opened the door for many, you the complete Souls/Cells of the Creator are also opening the door for many to move through the death of karma and into Ascension and enlightenment. You are the gatekeepers or holders of My Christ Consciousness.

One of the greatest memories that is now awakening in your DNA is my Love for my Beloved Magdalene. She holds the feminine awakening of the Christ Golden Ray for the Second Coming. As you move beyond a karmic time memory, there must be stakes or columns to hold the light doorways that are continuing to open. You are the collective gatekeepers. As you know, there is no time, only experiences of what you call past, and yet these experiences are influencing you very much, individually and collectively in the now. These experiences are very much threaded through your reality and in your cellular structure. As you collectively come together in love with the intention of love for all, these old stories will dissipate.

Lucifer

"As you are ready to return home to the balance and light of your Being, that is also my greatest desire."

I have great honor and respect for all of you. I know your job has been long and hard. I know firsthand how difficult it is to assist the collective out of their Ego fear and back into their own core of love and magnificence.

I am also tired and ready to return to my brothers and sisters of light. You could say I am an enlightened Shadow. I certainly vibrate in the larger picture of Creation, for I am a grand part of that larger picture.

As you are ready to return home to the balance and light of your Being, that is also my greatest desire. Just as the veils are being lifted for all of you, they are also being lifted for me. I am also awakening and remembering my own light.

We are no longer in the becoming stages of light and dark or good and evil. We have a great understanding of this imbalance or difficulty. So many of you on the Earth have set the intention for this lifetime to be the one that you will come back into balance, into the core of your Being. This collective intention turns on the light, so you can experience where you are still stuck in the fear

58

or Shadow. By going into these stuck emotions, you withdraw from the hold that I have had on you, or your agreement to allow me to assist you to see or experience yourself from my mirror of the shadow.

As you retrieve more aspects of yourself from me, my shadow also starts breaking up and dissipating. I have continued to control, grow and expand through collective aspects of your own fear. As you move out of fear and into love, all of the collective frozen emotions that I have been holding for you start melting away. As this frozen fear- based emotion leaves me, you start mirroring your love and light back to me. I see you. I have always seen you. I know you and remember you, for I am you.

My greatest desire is to be back together with you in the light and love of our Creation. As I say this to you, I feel your fear, your fear of me being a trickster. This is true. That has been a great part of my role, my job description, as it still is. My job is to speak to you through your Ego, through your old fear emotions, through old feelings of invalidation and the belief of not being good enough. I also come in through your need of wanting to be more powerful, to be seen, acknowledged and to feel valuable and important. I can't say this is a job I enjoy any longer.

As you, the collective, heal and balance yourself through the love-light ray of one another and move into self-love and acceptance, together we get to come home again. Your collective intention actually frees me. When I start to lose my power, the Shadow ones will no longer have me, my essence, to be their foundation. Without this foundation they will start unraveling and breaking up. Through your great collective Christ light, they will have the opportunity to become conscious enough, to be able to choose, to go through this portal of love, or disintegrate out of form.

The time is becoming very near for this to happen. This is why all of the Shadow ones are using any technique possible to send fear into you, to try to trick you out of your own knowing self-love and power. Yes, many of them are extensions of you and me, but through your great awakening into balance, they are now losing their power and form, as I am.

You, the Second Coming of the Christ energy, can stop any penetration of this false fear, Ego power. By uniting together as one love, light frequency of Creation, you can consciously choose to move out of karmic time and into your Collective Christ, Creator field. Through this love energy, the Shadow will retreat and eventually disappear. The Shadow moves like a snake in and out of your consciousness and emotions. It knows where to stop to release its venom. This is fairly easy for them to do if you are emotionally separate from one another. As you come together and vibrate as a collective source ray frequency of power, of love for one another, your light will become so bright that they will be blinded and will not be able to find their way in.

As my brother Jeshua explained to you, I am his divine counterpart. Within me, I am also the Christed one, as you are. The more you remember your purpose, your light and magnificence, the more you will mirror back to me my light. I am very grateful for all of you, the Cells of light that are assisting me and the Shadow Beings to move into this great awakening.

As you are tired and want to go home, I am also tired and want to go home. I have a great memory of being in the Angelic Realms with my brother and many of you. My greatest desire is to return home.

As you love yourself enough to feel safe with me, you will melt away any Shadow connections we have together. If you fear me and see me outside or separate from you, you are continuing to give me your power. It reinforces me and makes me stronger.

As you look at your world, you can see the power that the shadow is holding. You are living in a fear frequency, which is continually being projected to you by the Shadow Souls of you. The more you align with this fear, the more you feed your energies into the collective Shadow. If all of you on your planet were absent from fear the Shadow would have absolutely no power. Their source of power is you. Your fear connects with theirs, and they use your energy, your life force to keep themselves alive. Your fear allows them to be predators that feed off of your love, light, and life force.

I ask that you now move collectively into your purpose, into your own source of inner power, peace and Knowingness and into the Second Coming of the Christ Ray consciousness. From this place of balance, you will free all of us to come home together as one in the heart of our Mother Sophia and our Beloved Father.

My job as the holder of the collective Shadow is primarily for the Earth. Each planet that still vibrates in duality or uncertainty has its own source of Shadow fear energy.

All is connected; no source of energy is separate from another. Just as you vibrate collectively with the light and Shadow within yourself, you also vibrate collectively with the light and Shadow in all creations.

Because I am one with you, as my energy spreads to the collective Shadow Ego, that is the structure for other planets and creations, I open the door for this vibration to penetrate you.

Many of you have had experiences with dark Beings or Lords who are vibrating beyond my Earthly assignment. They are interfering with your light. Many of them are aspects of you, your own Shadow, from other lifetimes that are still vibrating collectively in other dimensions.

As I expanded you into these dimensions, it opened the door for you to have the opportunity to be able to find, retrieve, and love aspects of yourself that you had left behind from other lifetimes, incarnations, and agreements. You have had lifetimes on many other planets, in many star systems, galaxies, and universes. Perhaps you were a great Shadow Being in another lifetime and an aspect of you is collectively holding the door open for the Shadow to interfere with your collective light.

Your job description and contract in this lifetime is to now bring and integrate all aspects of yourself from all dimensions back to the core of your Being and Over Soul. My gift to you and your planet has been to move your Shadow Ego into its highest vibration of the collective oneness, so that it can be seen, experienced, and witnessed. From your knowing, understanding, and intention, your light can now penetrate the old fear-based ego structure and break it loose.

As you move more and more into the completeness of yourself, you will understand that you very much needed me to assist you back into your love and light.

When you have an understanding of this, you can no longer play the victim role. As you become conscious, you then must make light choices for yourself, or you will continue to vibrate in the Shadow fear frequency with me. Know this is a choice that you must consciously make. Remember, my job is to continue to test your Ego and to take your power, for I cannot exist without you. Your negativity and fear are my adrenaline and life force. It keeps me alive. Your love and light melt my negative fear-based energy force.

Now that we understand each other's job description and karmic contract, I ask that you come home through self-love and set us all free. I cannot do this without you and you cannot come into freedom without me. We have agreed to come together, move out of separation, and back into the heart of one another, into the heart of Creation. I am tired and alone and want to come home. The more conscious you have become, the more my consciousness has awakened. I no longer enjoy the false reign of power. DO NOT GIVE ME YOUR POWER! I DO NOT WANT IT! But remember, it is my job, my agreement, to use your life force energy if you do not.

Jeshua on the New World

"We are One Second Coming of Christ. We are each other."

Just as I came to the planet knowing that I had a great purpose, many of you have the same experience. I hear you say, "I know I came here for a reason. I just don't remember the reason". That was My own experience as I emerged into My karmic role. I forgot My larger picture. I studied with great Masters on the Earth who helped Me open up to My highest light frequencies or My highest memories of who I was. Is that not happening to you? There are many Ascended Masters who are walking among you on your planet now and are mirroring your highest light to you. You are in your awakening stages of remembering your own light and magnificence.

As there is no time, you are now awakening in the same frequencies that I came to the planet in. I came to the Earth in an enlightened, ascended, sound frequency. The whole planet and all of you great Creator Beings are now vibrating in this frequency.

I opened the door for you, so that we could merge and blend together in the Golden ray of Love. I am now holding the same consciousness and frequency for you to open the door for many. This is the greatest time you have ever experienced on the Earth. As a collective, you are awakening and becoming enlightened, ascending, and carrying this whole Earth plane out of duality, out of what could be called time, into Oneness with Me, Magdalene, and your great parents Mother-Father Creator Beingness.

Can you not see your mission is the same as Mine was? You also are dying, just as I did. You are not necessarily going through a physical death but a death of all karmic agreements. You are Me, and as I woke up and grew in consciousness, I had a larger understanding of my purpose and a direct conscious communication and guidance with My Father and Mother, as you now have.

We are One Second Coming of Christ. We are each other. As the light rays are now threading through your planet to bring it back into an enlightened conscious Beingness, you are also being rethreaded with the truth of who you are, which is love, light, and the beautiful music of Creation

Magdalene and I are the Twin Flame, Beloved Male and Female, Over Soul of your Being on planet Earth. It is Our agreement with the Creator to assist you and the great Mother Earth out of duality. In the next chapter our Father will explain to you about Mother Earth being the Soul of Maldek. Because of this, she has carried much suffering, as you have. As the light is now assisting to pull you into a merging with your light body and into a knowing remembrance and Ascension of your whole

Being, It is also assisting Mother Earth to merge with her light body and Father Earth companion so that she can remember her power and magnificence. The Earth also needs the Soul, love, and balance of her Beloved partner to be able to vibrate with the highest intention.

As many of you have decided to stay on the Earth after the birth through the 2012 doorway into Ascension, Mother Earth's Soul has also agreed to stay in the Earth to assist her to be a great Planet of Creation. As you continue to move out of duality, so will she. She will be holding the highest sound frequency of Creation, as you will be. Together you will create a new consciousness for your world, a New Earth. The Earth will be a planet or hologram for other creations that are light to inhabit with you. As this happens, you will become one with all creation planets and universes in the highest. Your light and love will hold the frequency for other creations to move into enlightenment and Ascension. Just as your love and light hold the energy for one another on the Earth to feel safe to release old karmic emotions, your planet will hold the frequency for many other planets and its inhabitants to remember who they are, moving them out of duality.

As I said, many of you great, awakening, Co-Creator Beings have agreed to stay on planet Earth in this time of transition, just as I did. If you all left, who would assist other Creator Beings on your planet to awaken? There are many of you who are physically leaving the planet because your karma is up. You understand duality and have played every role you could possibly play. You are coming back home in Spirit to experience yourself out of duality or to remember you are love and light. Many of you will work as great spiritual guides and teachers. Some of you who did not quite understand the lesson of enlightenment and Ascension will choose to reincarnate to other planets, to play out the rest of your Souls' search for Oneness. Others will be reincarnating back to the Earth in a higher vibration of knowing to bring the highest consciousness of Creation from all dimensions to the Earth. Many will return to the Earth as conscious Enlightened Masters, and others reincarnating will be a higher vibration of the Crystal Beings who are being born now. You all hold this crystal frequency in your cellular structure. As the Earth continues to move out of time, your DNA structure has codes, which are opening up, and you are remembering yourself multi-dimensionally. **Your multi-dimensional Beingness is assisting you to merge into the Oneness of all consciousness of your New World, your new Earth. You are the I Am of All That Is.**

ARCHANGEL MICHAEL'S

Transmission for Peace

I am here with you now. This is Archangel Michael. I wish to speak to you of the trying times that have flooded the consciousness of all of you. In flooding your consciousness, you are awakening all unconsciousness throughout the history of your Soul from the beginning of evolution. Yes, I speak to you of evolution. Evolution is a process of evolving, which all of you and the planet are doing at this time.

I ask that you lay down your swords and surrender into the fear illusion that has been your thread of unconsciousness from the beginning of your Soul's agreement to awaken.

Many other Lords and Masters of Light and I are holding the sword of light to assist you and your planet through your travels into the collective "Dark Night of the Soul," into the light of your Being, and into the awakening of the light of the collective consciousness.

In days to come, you will feel and experience many walls of the unconsciousness awaken and crumble. It is an illusion, and its only strength is your false fear of surrendering.

You seem to believe that to put down your swords and surrender means to give up, that you are giving up your power. It is just the opposite. If you surrender into your fear-based false reign of power, you will actually find your power. In the middle of the darkness is your light.

You are never alone. I am with you always. My army of light Brothers and Sisters and I are holding our swords of light together, creating a frequency of light that is blinding and disarming any fear-based deities, Lords, or Gods.

I ask that you imagine your physical bodies being swords of light, and align your sword of light with me. My sword is an extension of my consciousness and purpose. It is me that I hold in my hand to mirror to you an image of protection. Yes, I use my sword as a protector, as a reflector, to cut away energy sources, chords, and patterns that connect you to the fear-based unconsciousness within you and the collective. But I never, ever use my sword to harm, hurt, kill, or slay another living thing. Many times I use my sword as a laser to dissolve frequencies or energies that have the intention to harm or hurt you, the collective, or the planet.

I may use my laser sword to break loose computerized programs and even break the computer system apart.

I, with my army of light, may come up against armies or Lords of Darkness, but we never, ever kill them. Our light may disintegrate their Shadow energies and intentions, and from this, many remember who they are and they return to the light. Others re-treat or re-group with the intention of becoming an even more ferocious Shadow army.

Every time they return and our army of light mirrors them, they once again start disintegrating, loosening more of their power.

This is how this dis-empowerment is taking place. This is what the Creator speaks of when he says the Shadow will disintegrate out of form. It is already happening.

Many of you are great Lords of Light who are working with me in these dimensions. As you continue to evolve through perceived time, you, the Lord of Light, who is in alignment with me and my higher purpose, will integrate with the Earthly you.

As we continue to ascend and move through time together, we will all blend together as one consciousness of protection. This protection will not be something that you will need to call in; it will be your Soul's essence.

I am strong, and my un-wavering intention, purpose, love, and light are yours, because I am you, and you are me.

Because I am one solid consciousness of love-light-color-sound of the highest purpose for all, I am aligned with my Brothers and Sisters of light with the same vibration and mission. Nothing can penetrate us that is not of this like vibration.

Now, I ask that you put down your swords of fear. They are acid-based and penetrate and harm those who you love most.

They sabotage your greatest intentions for peace on Earth. How can you bring peace when you are feeding the fear illusion and allowing it to penetrate you and your highest purpose? The power of the negative sword (word) creates the death of hope, the death of love, and creates more of what you don't want. It kills your creativity and your life force.

Fear feeds more fear, and it expands the collective. Love penetrates fear, breaks it loose, and expands the consciousness of love.

As the Creator has voiced to you, you are not going to lose your planet. There are so many of you light warriors who have awakened and are continuing to awaken. I know you are tired and weary. I see you. I honor you. I love you.

Allow me to now be your protection on your journey of ascending. Put down your swords; swords meaning negative thinking, negative beliefs, and perceptions. Surrender into your fear-based illusion that keeps you and your world stuck in duality. Move out of the fear-based war between you, your own light, and your Ego that keeps you and your Brothers and Sisters separated. As you do this, you are un-threading from all of the physical wars now taking place on your planet.

Remember, you are the collective; you are every person who is fighting and is at war against each other. If you are every person, which side do you want to take? Who of your selves would you want to kill first? It is more difficult to think of killing one another when you know that the person whose life you are taking is your own.

You are protected. Your world is protected. I, with my light team of Masters from your galaxy and universe, are constantly monitoring you and your planet. There are even Beings from other universes who are here to assist in this great cosmic heart awakening.

We have intercepted intentions that were not the highest for your planet, and we continuously do so. Align with me and the Lords of Light, who are you, and are in the same agreements and intentions with you, to create Peace on Earth. Together we will continue to move through the death of the Ego, the death of the Shadow, through the birth canal of the highest consciousness of Ascension and Enlightenment, and through the 2012 portal to create Peace on Earth, to create heaven on Earth in all life forms.

Call on me; become one with me. Imagine your body being my sword of light (a laser light), and then imagine this light moving out of your heart and through your hands to heal the world.

As you consciously call on me, you will start feeling my presence with you. Feel the safety and protection of my love. Align with me! Become one with my army of Lords of Light. Activate and download the highest aspects of you that are already in alignment with me and other Masters with the same intentions of love, peace, harmony, and grace throughout all Creation.

If you do not know of me, or who I am, I ask that you search your Internet or bookstores, or ask others if they know of me and my purpose.

Look at a picture of me, feel me, and imagine my sword being your body of light, and that I am holding you inside of my sword to protect you and to turn your vibration up to that of a Lord of Light.

I am a collective consciousness, and my words of Knowing and purpose are coming through many different Souls (channels) on the Earth plane. It is important to discern the information coming through these channels. If any information that is being received is fear-based, then you know it is not the highest consciousness of me. Either the channel's filter is a little dirty, or there is a trickster energy feeding its vibration through the person bringing the information through. Although the person's intention is pure, he/she may be so determined and excited to be such a great part of this great awakening of consciousness, that he/she may not be able to discern the information being brought forth.

I may come through voicing concerns, for the planet and for you, its Souls, who have agreed to hold the light for all, through the Ascension process, but I will never voice fear. Fear feeds fear. My concern in love-based, and I am holding this love for you to continue to awaken.

Any information coming through from me, or any of the other Archangels or Masters of Light, will always be in the highest energy and consciousness of evolution for you, the collective, and for your sacred Mother Earth. This information will always be in positive form to assist you, to connect to the aspects of yourself, which are already vibrating in your higher Knowing.

I wish to thank all of you for your agreement to incarnate to the Earth and for your willingness to assist this great transformation of consciousness. I love you and honor you for your difficult agreements to end the Shadow karma and to move all into Enlightenment and Ascension

I thank all of you who are willing to allow transmissions to come through you to assist in awakening the consciousness to co-create Peace on Earth in all life forms.

I love you. I thank you. I honor you. My love and protection is always with you,

"Maldek was a planet of many different races, bloodlines, and cultures."

5

THE PLANET MALDEK AND THE SOUL OF MOTHER EARTH

Sophia's Story of Maldek

I am with you now my children; this is Sophia. Maldek was a planet whose consciousness was formed from a feminine Soul. We, your Father and I, felt and decided that We should bring the male and female together in equal power. We also felt that the foundation of the structure needed to be heart-based, so We selected a planet, which was the planet of Maldek. Mother Earth's Soul agreed to come to Maldek and hold the central sun's energies for all its inhabitants. Before Mother Earth's (Gaia's) arrival, Maldek, was a consciousness of a larger Soul Group, but did not actually have its own Soul.

Your father and I awakened a Soul presence of the feminine in the meridian structure of the planet Maldek. After the foundation was laid and became strong enough or solidified, we gently brought the magnificent Soul of the Mother energy to the planet. This Master Mother Soul was created through the union of your Father's and My love and intent.

We believed that for the male and female to succeed and co-create together from a love structure there needed to be a Mother's love frequency to vibrate through the planet; to hold a safety net for the union of the inhabitants' Souls' awakening.

This is how and why Maldek was created. After the divine plan was initiated, the call was put out to many Souls. There was a screening process, so that We could choose the Souls or Cells with the highest integrity.

We had many Souls apply for the positions open. They knew that if they could come together and master the love union of equalization of the male and female, it would set a precedent for other planets. There was truly great excitement.

We knew that because all Souls are from the same cellular structure, the Souls/Cells who were less conscious would align with those that were created from the love of your Father's and My emergence. We selected Souls/Cells that were created from Our love union, and also from the old paradigm mind-set of your Father.

Our intention was for the Souls/Cells that were vibrating from the old mind-set to receive the love, safety, and balance from the Mother's love of the planet and also from the more conscious Cells who were capable of holding and mirroring back love to one another.

We stocked the planet with plant seedlings of the highest frequency. Many of your Earth's foliage and fruits came from Maldek. Maldek was rich in soil and very fertile. Vegetation grew easily. The plants were big and lush. Fruits and vegetables were alive and honored for their role in feeding the inhabitants.

There were also dolphins on Maldek, and it was very common for the Souls of you and the dolphins to swim, play, and communicate with one another.

In the beginning, Maldek was not a planet onto which the Souls reincarnated. It was a planet where the selected Souls came from many other planets and star systems. They came to the planet on ships or crafts, or what you now call UFOs. Some of these ships that many of you are now seeing and even visiting are from the planets that assisted in the evacuation of Maldek. They have been around for millions of years, and most of them are powered by the Central Sun's energy.

Maldek was a planet of many different races, bloodlines, and cultures. In the beginning of life on Maldek, there was much joy and sharing of one another's home planets' life styles, energies, frequencies, customs, religions, and belief systems.

The planet's government or hierarchy system was aligned with the hierarchies of the Central Sun's vibration and knowledge.

After a while, some of the inhabitants who your Father created before Me started feeling restless and bored. Their old mind-set was used to vibrating in duality and conflict. They did not know how to vibrate in constant peace and love. They felt something was missing. They started missing what you could call the past when they had a sense of control or power over others.

The old mind-set started small conflicts because these were the patterns in which they felt safe. They wanted to be noticed and once again have a sense of importance. When this happened, it opened the door for them to realign with the old collective cellular structure of duality, or their Shadow brothers and sisters.

Through this realignment, the Shadow ones were able to send messages through them to build or pump up the old Ego structure. This old Ego structure that was still in the cells of the Souls then started belittling and devaluing the feminine. When the feminine felt this old repressed memory restimulated and awakened, it opened them back up to the collective powerlessness and hopelessness of the feminine.

As this planet was structured from a feminine-based point, your Father and I felt and believed that if We sent a Feminine Goddess as priestess to the planet, she could vibrate the Central Sun's Golden Ray of Love throughout the planet and to any of the frightened Souls that were wanting to return to their old ways.

We knew she had to be a manifestation of Our highest love for one another. We then created the highest Feminine Goddess from the purest of Our heart's essence and intent.

When she was born on Maldek, it was through reincarnation into the highest bloodline of Melchizedek. She was honored and protected there until the time that she was old enough to step into a monarchy that was in the process of being formed. All were waiting for her appearance. There was much speculation of her role on Maldek.

Our daughter Anana was to be the first of the highest lineage of Us, Our love. She was to be the goddess or priestess of Maldek holding the Golden frequencies for all to remember who they were. She was to turn on the light for them; to remember their purpose and the beginning mission of Maldek.

At the same time as the old male Ego structure continued to realign and strengthen itself with the Shadow civilization (at war against your Father), the fall of Maldek began. Your Father will explain this demise and how it happened later in this chapter. As the death of Maldek began, We knew it was not safe for Anana to emerge.

Anana never had the chance to step into her position of priestess or protector and enlightener of the Souls/Cells of Maldek. Your Father and I became concerned for her safety, and We chose to have her lifted back to the safety of the Central Sun's dimension. Anana is now Our beloved Jeshua who is serving you now on the Earth plane in male form with a feminine heart of love. The name Anana means flow of love, consistency, and intent.

Before the complete fall of Maldek, the feminine Soul of Maldek was lifted to safety to the planet that is now your Earth. It was then that we also lifted Anana back to safety. Many of the Souls or Cells who felt they had failed their mission on Maldek, once again volunteered to reincarnate to the Earth.

After the evacuation happened on Maldek, the Souls that were working in the light with the intention to save the planet and its consciousness were transported back to either their home planet or back to Us in the highest. As I said, the Soul that is now the "Mother Earth's" was lifted to safety before an explosion and implosion happened. The planet was dry, and the vibration was so dense that when the evacuation of the light ones was completed and the ships withdrew, their light frequency was so high that when it hit the planet, it started a reaction that blew it up.

The Souls who were instrumental in the demise of Maldek were left behind. When the planet blew up, they blew up with it. Their Souls' energies fragmented, but the highest light aspect of them who had originally volunteered to bring the male and female back together, in the highest, returned to Us in the highest. They were able to return to Us in the highest because their original intent had been of a high consciousness. These Souls/Cells did not actually fail their mission or agreement, they just took a detour. Remember, this was an experiment that your Father and I had divinely agreed upon and planned to bring the male and female back together in the highest.

Other aspects of their Souls/Cells that had shattered away from the original light structure are still aligned with the coalition of the Shadow Beings or lords. Because they were still aligned with the Shadow ones, there is a doorway open for the consciousness of the Shadow to vibrate through them. Because their Souls/Cells are split, their own Shadow is able to penetrate their light creating a pattern of interference, conflict, and confusion. This would be like some of the cells in your physical body being healthy and others vibrating in sickness or dis-ease. Soul retrieval needs to be done individually and collectively for these Beings who were left behind.

The aspects of the Cells that fragmented are still vibrating in what you call past agreements with the frightened Shadow aspects that are still warring against your Father.

As I mentioned in the beginning, some of the volunteers were aspects of Us that had been vibrating in the Shadow for long periods of time. Our desire was that the females' love would be so strong that it would hold that collective love and align with My feminine to mirror back to the old male structure their fragmented love and light.

This experience was like many of the Souls on your planet who are in some kind of addiction. The brain cells are used to being fed a certain vibration or frequency. When the vibration is withheld from these cells, the cells actually feel like they are going to die. They have a feeling of starvation and go to great lengths to bring the needed fuel or frequency back to the brain so that they can live.

Remember, the cells are an internet system of their own. When the brain cells of the Shadow Souls on Maldek started receiving so much love and light, a panic button went off in their brains. The cells felt like they were dying and searched their own "inner" system finding the drug or frequency, which could sustain them. The frequency the brain was searching for was fear. It was used to feeling an adrenaline rush from the trauma and fear of control over others. An actual rewiring of the brain took place and drama is what kept it functioning. The light actually activated this programming.

The brain cells were able to find, identify, and collectively download the Shadow frequency. The cells then felt fed or rejuvenated for a short time. When the feeling happened again, the cells went into panic and found some more Shadow to sustain them. Every time this happened, the addiction became stronger, and soon the Shadow had overtaken the brain again, downloading the Shadow onto and into the cellular structure of the light ones.

The light ones' vibration was so high that this Shadow frequency created an electrical blowout in them. They were no longer vibrating with the collective in the highest light. In the places where their energy had been blown out and shattered, they were no longer able to feel the connection with their collective light brothers and sisters.

After the blowout, parts of their bodies-cells were dense. This made it easy for the Shadow to realign with them. Because of this density, the light ones did not know it was the Shadow. They felt it was the light ones trying to reconnect or rethread with them.

The Shadow ones pretended to be the light ones saying soothing things, so the light would feel safe again. When the light ones agreed to allow this false energy to re-thread with them, they actually were making agreements with the Shadow, which have carried over into this lifetime.

You have this same scenario playing itself out on your planet again. Because many of you light ones are so excited when Spirit is able to reach you, you do not always use discernment. The Shadow Beings are coming back in through these old unbeknownst contracts. Because your whole intention is to serve

God, Spirit, or Creator in the highest, you may think all that comes through you is the highest liquid essence of Creation.

As I speak to you of this, I do not want you to move into fear or being the victim. If this is happening or has happened to you in this lifetime, it is because you have agreed to go through the experience. What is needed is for you to become aware of the Shadow ones and release any old agreements or contracts and unthread them from you individually and collectively, to bring all aspects of you that have been vibrating with them back into you. (Soul Retrieval) Once this has been completed, it is important that you re-thread yourself back into the collective light to assist yourselves and the consciousness out of duality. Your vibration will then be so high that nothing that is not light will be able to penetrate you.

Many of you who are now on the Earth plane were on Maldek. You have the understanding of the Shadow's hold on the Ego mind and also the experience of the light's confusion of the Shadow.

You have not failed. You are back here again with the Soul of the Mother to assist her and all of you in your own and collective Souls' awakening. You are going through the play again; only this time you have the experience to be conscious enough individually and collectively to constantly mirror your highest vibration to one another. If the Shadow is staring at you through the Eyes/Souls of your friends or partners, through love, you can now disempower the Shadow and bring back all aspects of yourself and others who are still vibrating with them.

This is the lifetime you have agreed to come full circle. You have had many lifetimes when you have been the players of both the light and Shadow and any place in between.

You had Maldek as a strong foundation to learn about yourself and others. You have also learned from many other civilizations, such as Atlantis, Lemuria, the rise and fall of the Roman Empire, and many other such civilizations that have played themselves out.

There has been a war between the male and female since

My beginning with your Father. This war has been totally fear-based of the male losing its power.

Many of these civilizations that I speak of were very evolved possessing the highest technology. Much of your technology now is being downloaded or remembered from these civilizations.

You have had civilizations that were quite barbaric and some that were very evolved. Regardless of what level of consciousness they were vibrating in, it was still the imbalance between the male and female or the heart and Ego, playing itself out to come back together and merge into balance.

Now is the time as a collective Soul/Cell consciousness that you are gathering all of your past experience and knowledge to use to create a different outcome. The setup or play may look the same, but because of all of your collective lives' experiences and wisdom, the outcome gets to be different.

The Creator's Story of Maldek

"Maldek was a beautiful planet. It was the true Garden of Eden."

Please bear with me, as I know I may be repeating some of this information. I have much to say and to bring forth. It has to be brought forth in an energy form frequency that you can feel and understand. It is of most importance to Me that all understand Jeshua, Sananda, Melchizedek and Anana are all the same energy source. He is the balance of male and female energy coming from My beloved Sophia's and My union of heart and Soul/Cell.

When He/She was on Maldek, He/She was born in a feminine body and into a family of great wealth. We felt that as the feminine awakened Me, it would also awaken this planet.

Maldek was a beautiful planet. It was the true Garden of Eden. When We created her, and I say We because after my Sophia awakened Me, we continued to create. That is why you

78

also know and experience races that were created in love and light who remember Me as a loving Father-Mother because they were created after a merging of Myself with My Beloved.

In the beginning, all on the planet were of My highest form of love and light, except for the Souls/Cells of the old mindset of me that volunteered to reconnect with their enlightened Brothers and Sisters in consciousness. Their intention was to move into enlightenment with them. The planet and its Soul were totally conscious, as were most of the inhabitants. It was an enlightened, conscious creation. There were dolphins on the planet, and vegetation was much like Earth's. People on the planet were vegetarians. Plants and fruits were in communion with Souls on the planet and gave their permission to be consumed by the inhabitants. The animal kingdom, the plants, and people who resided on Maldek lived in peace and in community with one another.

The life force there communicated through telepathy (thought form with one another). The life span of the inhabitants was greater than on your planet. It would be equivalent to your planet's time of 350 years. There was no such thing as death. When it was time to leave, one just ascended or returned home. The intention of this planet was for Our creation to mirror back to all of Our creations perfect harmony, love, honor, integrity, joy, alignment, and Oneness.

Many other planets and universes started communicating with Maldek and its inhabitants. As this happened, enlightened civilizations started awakening throughout all existence: the hundredth monkey or domino effect was affecting all of creation. The structure of the planet was in alignment with the Central Sun, which acted as a generator for the planet's life force and substance.

As this great enlightenment was taking place, the old Ego structure, the Shadow ones, were afraid that they were losing their power. They sent frequencies of fear, separation, and loss of power to the old mind-set of me that agreed to inhabit Maldek to re-awaken itself into the light. The Shadow started rebelling and placing patterns of a reversed energy flow: the reversed matrix, around Maldek and other enlightened civilizations.

Their intention was to start plugging these civilizations back into My old mind-set of control and fear. This webbing started pulling the consciousness back into what you could call time.

This same structure has been placed around planet Earth with the intention to pull it back into this old structure or paradigm. Now, the difference is that you, the light Beings of the divine Matrix, who have great wisdom from other experiences, are shattering and dissipating all reversed patterns. Your collective light-sound vibration is too high for this pattern to be able to hold form. You see the reversed pattern trying to pull the collective consciousness back into old thinking: repressing and oppressing the feminine once again. These same old Ego forms or false Gods, which are My old structure, are once again warring against themselves and Me for fear of dying off.

When this reversed energy flow was around Maldek, it was like a death to these great Creator beings of Me. It was difficult to vibrate with one another in this negative frequency flow. Beings started forgetting who they were. This old structure was starting to infiltrate through them and into the veins of their existence, into the veins of the planet, and the inhabitants started becoming afraid.

As the planet began dying, all the vegetation started becoming dis-eased and inedible. The oceans were becoming polluted. The inhabitants became frightened of not having enough food to eat, and they started killing the dolphins and eating them because of the dolphins' high energy. They felt if they ate them, this food would heighten and align their vibration with the dolphins. They started warring against the animal kingdom and were killing them for food. The animals became afraid and began warring against the inhabitants.

People starting building fortresses, and a false reign of power took over. This power structure started controlling the people. It formed an alliance with these false Gods. These false Gods made many promises to the new government system, promises of great wealth, power, and control. This government power structure was formed in secrecy in alliance with the Shadow. It was fear-based and was not agreed upon or approved by the people.

People became sick, diseased, frightened, and hopeless. The false Gods brought Beings to them from other Creations under the pretense that they were medicine healers. These healers worked on these inhabitants and blocked their DNA, splicing it and sending their light connection information to the coalition of the Dark Ones or Gods. They downloaded information of fear and control into their DNA. It was a time of great upheaval, separation, conflict and fear. Families were splitting up, and bloodlines started to war against one another.

There was a family line of the highest of My order called Melchizedek. This line continued to hold the light for the planet. There was a crystal child born to them. She was Anana. She is known as Jesus Christ today on your planet.

There was great speculation surrounding her birth, as the false Gods and the light ones knew of her coming. When she was born, it was said that the light spread through the planet like thunder, which it did, for she held the crystalline structure for the Planet to reawaken into its natural form. The false ones knew of her purpose and started warring against the feminine. Their government started taking rights away from the feminine. They knew how to do this because they were My strands of DNA before the feminine had awakened. They knew how to manipulate the DNA back to its old form, before the heart awakening of Sophia.

They knew the feminine was the feeling heart. If they could manipulate the DNA in the male structure and block the feminine feeling of love, they knew the males would once again connect with them in their war against Me.

As the feminine became afraid and controlled by this male government, Anana no longer had an energy source to hold the frequencies for her. She was in seclusion with her family. As the darkness or unconsciousness continued to expand and control the planet, the crystalline structure started to crack. There was much fear, and the planet started losing its source of energy.

After the structure started to crack, the planet continued to dry up. There was much fear of survival. Plants no longer grew; it was as if the root or Soul of the planet was gone.

What had actually happened was the Soul of Maldek was lifted out and brought to the Earth. There was a holographic consciousness projected around the planet Earth to protect her. For it was known that her Soul carried a DNA structure of total consciousness beyond any time frame.

Before the fall of Maldek, the planet was the generator of consciousness to many other planets. She and her inhabitants were created through the Golden Christ Consciousness of total love and balance with the male-female heart and mind. All aspects were in perfect harmony. From this, there was a light-sound frequency with which other planets could harmonize. This energy frequency actually activated the dormant or unconscious DNA structure of the planets, so they would vibrate in harmony with each other.

When Maldek's crystalline structure started shattering, it sent back shock waves or sounds through Creation that started breaking up the silver cord (life force connection with the other planets and universes). Just as Souls had felt frightened and abandoned by Me in the beginning, now planets started feeling the same experience because their crystalline structures were shattering or disconnecting from one another. As the other planets (Souls) started feeling abandoned and alone, the inhabitants of these planets also started feeling fear and disconnected. The inhabitants of the planets then started warring against one another and Me.

At this time, Maldek was essentially Soulless. When Maldek's Soul was taken to safety, Our beloved Anana was also lifted and brought back to the central Sun. It happened in the same way that your Jesus ascended from Earth. There was a great light and a massive yellow ray came down through the sky. A doorway opened and there was a huge crackling noise of many colors: red, purple, gold, blue - all the color-sound frequencies of Creation. Anana did not leave her body; she brought it with her. As she started to ascend, the frequencies of her physical body changed into her light body, and her higher self pulled her body self up into

82

her Over Soul, so they became one with each other. This pulled her back to Me.

Anana had been the only hope left for the feminine. When she left, the feminine felt betrayed by Me; they felt I was cruel and not supportive of my feminine. When she left, the frightened feminine came together collectively as they felt safer in groups; they started warring against the male Ego structure, much like the feminists on your Earth have. On your planet Earth, the feminists went before the male structure and demanded rights for the feminine. This opened the door for the feminine heart and honoring of the Mother Earth, nature, and all life forms. It opened a doorway for the collective to move into a higher dimension of Spirit. This feminine love connected to the male will is healing your planet assisting all to ascend back into the balance of Me.

On Maldek, the feminine demanded for the children to be safe. They knew that even the male cares for his children's safety. Great planning committees came together and built indoor city structures. All inhabitants were moved to these indoor cities. There was no animal life left, and all vegetation and sea life was dead. All food was manufactured. Nothing was alive. It was very difficult for people to live like this; with no life force, there was little hope.

Beings from other planets who had been to Maldek and loved her, honored her, and had received so much from her and her inhabitants decided to evacuate the planet to save the inhabitants who were still of like consciousness. Information was being sent through light Beings on Maldek of the evacuation. The controlling government started imprisoning anyone speaking of this, for they knew they were about to lose their reign of power. They felt that if others knew nothing of the plan, they would not be prepared, and the evacuation could not happen.

In what could be called a 12-12 Portal or time frame, which was the end of time for Maldek, many ships came from other planets and universes and beamed light rays of many color-sound frequencies; the children and light Beings who were trying to save the civilization were lifted off. The dark lords, the Ego ones, and the unconscious Shadow ones were left behind. As the ships left, their high frequency hit the dry planet, and it exploded. The unconscious ones blew up with the planet.

The Beings who were lifted up were taken to many different planets and universes. Although they were thankful to be alive, they also felt great separation, loss, grief, and hopelessness and felt like they were not with their own people.

Many of you who were on Maldek are now on Earth playing out the same play of Maldek, so the outcome can be different. You reincarnated with the same feeling of separation and sense of not belonging, as you felt after the evacuation. You have come back to Earth and your Cells are still stuck in the old emotion of your whole Maldek experience.

Mother Earth, being the Soul of Maldek, is also carrying a lot of the same loss, grief, and sorrow. When you came to Earth, your collective memories were activated. They needed to be activated, so that you could come together in love and not allow this to happen again. You agreed to come to Earth to remember, and instead of being lifted off or dying in the 12-12 (2012) Portal, you have agreed to rethread the past and ride the waves of light to bring yourselves and the planet into Ascension.

After the learning experience on Maldek, and I do call it a learning experience for all of us, I understood what an important role the feminine plays in the divine plan of realignment and balance with all consciousness. This is now being done on all levels of Creation. My divine love and light is penetrating through all creations or dimensions. All old aspects of Me are being moved beyond dormant emotions and realigned with My Sophia's crystallization.

From the experience of Maldek, I learned that the Shadow male consciousness was still warring against Me and very much in hatred of My feminine, Sophia. I witnessed how the Shadow could influence the male and manipulate the feminine, and I could see that Anana was not safe to carry out her mission. I realized the Earth needed a male carrying the feminine heart, which is Jeshua.

On your planet Earth, Jeshua went through a death and

resurrection, and he was honored as being the light ray of love, of hope, to save you and your planet. Because He was male, He was heard and listened to. After the experience of Maldek, I knew that being in a feminine body would not work to awaken the male because of the male fear of losing itself or its power to the feminine. The light needed to be in a male form. so that the male could hold the light and strength for Jeshua to follow through with His plan.

I have heard some of you ask many times, "Why does God allow Shadow interference to happen?" Much of what I created was before my heart awakening, and yet it is all Me. How could I punish aspects of Myself that I created? I gave that consciousness to them. I love them just as much as I love what I created after I awakened. How can I punish them for My not knowing? How could I punish you for your not knowing when I created you in My image, My likeness?

Many of you have had the same experience with your children on the Earth plane, for you are playing out the ending stages of My unconsciousness. Many of you have had children when you were in a place of not knowing, a place of hurt and insecurity, and you gave these patterns to the children who were born of you. They then handed the same pattern down to their children. As you became more conscious and stepped out of your victim role or pattern, did you hate your children who mirrored back to you who you used to be? I see you loving them and wanting them to grow and experience their own love and magnificence. That is a healthy parent's desire, as it is Mine. I cannot punish or hate what I have created.

My desire is for the conscious Soul/Cell aspects of My and Sophia's love to mirror back to their brothers and sisters this love. My desire is that love and light will become so bright that fear, hatred, and control will dissipate. It will have no place to spread. The Shadow cancer will die off, and the healthy Cells of Me will come together as one. The old fear aspects of Me will disintegrate their fear, and the light in all will emerge and remember that all is one love; one light of Creation.

"You are now coming together through the heart energy to create a better world for all humankind."

6

THE EARTH'S END TIMES, THE MAYANS, AND THE 2012 PORTAL

The Bush Administration Presidency's (Gift) and the 2008 Election*

My intention is now to assist you out of duality by you experiencing and understanding the Shadow, so that as a nation and world you can come back with each other as one world under God with liberty and justice for all. The Ego Shadow needed to be exposed and brought to a head, which has been done. You as a people needed to understand that the Shadow is its own entity and has a great purpose in assisting the awakening and healing of this planet.

In the 2004 election in America Bush needed to be elected President because he and his administration are governed and supported by the Shadow. Please remember that behind all the scenes, it is the same director, Me. Bush and his team won the leading role in politics for a short time so that they could expose the Shadow. It needed to happen for the Shadow to continue to be activated and play itself out. In the election, his opponent Kerry

* Because most of this book was channeled in 2004, some of the material has already come to pass or is in the past. I felt is was important to leave the past political information as it was and that you read the manuscript intact as it was channeled because the message explains so much of what is going on with us on the planet now. In March of 2009, the Creator also wrote an update on the 2008 Obama election

did not have enough strength to lead this collective Shadow out of hiding. It was not his foundation or purpose.

The Ego/Shadow that has controlled your government's consciousness and your world from the beginning of your history is being brought to the light. The old structure had to be exposed for the foundation to come down before a new one can be built. Bush agreed to take on the job as a Master Shadow. You can see how the Shadow works from the exposure that it has been given. With this one Bush in power, the Shadow/Ego is like a renegade; it seems to not care about any rules or regulations and continues to blast forward in any way it desires. Because of its position of power, it feels that it has the resources to control not just America but the world through fear.

Because so many of you are remembering the larger picture and are actually sending love to this administration, the reins of power are continuing to expand and break down. You are continuing to take power away from the Shadow. This one Bush is doing a great job at allowing all to be exposed.

Because the Bush administration is now exposing and revealing so much corruption, you will feel as though you are holding your breath in anticipation for anyone that is to be elected in 2008. You as a Nation need hope and you will be holding that for one another. Anytime you have been taken advantage of, it takes away your innocence and creates great mistrust within yourself and others. The gift of this is that you start waking up and have the need for answers. You start asking yourself questions of what is important for you, your children and the future of your world. Your greatest fear is giving your trust to someone again and being taken advantage of. You become skeptical of others' promises to you.

Who is to be your next President? It still has not been decided yet. You as a collective are still in the process of shifting the energy to move the consciousness. You are moving out of anger and injustice and into empowerment thus co-creating your New World.

The 2008 election will be the first time on your planet that the government has not already been decided or elected in what you call the future. Until then, you have always been in a karmic time frame. The doorway of the 2012 Portal is already open in the future. In this portal there is no time, only Knowingness. This Knowingness is pure Source energy that is waiting for a collective intention to awaken it into form, to co-create your New World.

As the coding in your DNA has been activated beyond time, you will find yourself as a collective becoming more conscious. Light bubbles of Knowingness are constantly being turned on inside you. You as a collective will come together in your highest passion of intention for the best of all people. From this place, your intention will be to vote in a new government that will assist you through the 2012 Portal of Ascension and enlightenment.

You will have many demands of your next President. You will at first be a very critical Nation. You have felt so taken advantage of that you will scrutinize every word and move.

The Bush Shadow administration has a strong reign of power and it will take some time to unthread much of what has been programmed. In the first three years of the new administration, you will see many shifts of consciousness going through various contractions to collectively choose the frequency on which you will ride into the New World. In the future this is already done. Although you are not sure of your next leader, you collectively have already set the intention for a new World on Planet Earth,

You will see much more of the structure being broken down in the next few years. You are coming into a new lifetime without physically leaving the body. You need a new foundation for this lifetime. The new foundation is your Mother Sophia and I. We are the memory of your spiritual parents of a higher consciousness and are the guiding heart-mind for your planet. As your DNA coding is being activated and you continue to awaken spiritually and merge back together as one light and one Spirit, you will remember and know you are the cells of a larger consciousness, of Me. In human form you will still have your personalities, and yet the lens that you see others and the world through will be much different. You will view all through a lighter lens, one of love and compassion. You will want for others what you want for yourself.

As you look at the consciousness of the American people, you can see a great awakening is taking place. You have found your voice, and as a collective you are becoming aware and will vote in an administration that will be more in line with you as a people, as a Nation. This administration's intention will want to take care of your basic needs: food, housing, health care, education, and the economy.

You will be coming back to one another, opening your hearts and Souls to assist each other to have dignity, self-respect, and to become whole again. You will see your brothers and sisters as you and have compassion and the desire for the highest for all.

From your awareness of the larger picture of consciousness, you can shatter the Ego Shadow. You are now coming together through the heart energy to create a better world for all humankind. After 9-11, a doorway opened that brought you together with the rest of the world. Before this, your nation felt somewhat exempt from the Shadow or fear of what you call terrorism. Although this seems like a catastrophic way for an awakening to happen, it was the only way for you to truly understand that you as a Union of People needed to come together as One and assist the whole world to heal. It was time that you started reaching out to your brothers and sisters of the world, not just in monetary support but also in love, compassion, understanding, and emotional support. It was important to know that they are you and need your heart, love, and prayers.

Through the shattering of your perceived security and belief systems, you have now united collectively. It may seem this union is one of fear, but it is one of merging your light together through intentions, to take your power back from all fear agreements. Now as a collective conscious Being of people, you are in the first steps of accessing your emotion of repressed anger and injustice. This anger is not to destroy; it is to release old collective belief systems and others' control over your lives. It is to release injustice, powerlessness, and to awaken your

89

source energy of love to make more room for the energy Source of Creation.

This new consciousness is starting to be demonstrated in many countries. You are now agreeing to move out of the victim role and into the restructuring and rebuilding of a New World, of the true Garden of Eden. Look how many of you have become conscious of how precious the resources of your planet are. You are collectively coming together to preserve these resources for future generations.

The End Times

"This Earth is not dying as has been projected; what is dying is the old karmic structure."

Why are so many in other dimensions interested in the Earth? It is because the Earth is a hologram of the End Times. The End Times are playing out the death of My old karmic cellular structure. This Earth is not dying as has been projected. What is dying is the old karmic structure. As you look into a hologram you see many different pictures depending on how you are looking into it. As you turn it a little you perceive each picture differently. This is now the Earths consciousness or story.

When you reincarnated to the Earth, you came down in Soul Groups. Each Soul Group has its individual color and sound. The color-sound frequency is the consciousness of the group. The collective intention is to bring all Soul Group frequencies together and create a rainbow color-sound symphony. As each Soul Group's colors and sounds expand, they eventually will merge into each other, creating another combustion of light like the big bang. This combustion will break loose frequencies from Soul Groups, which are still struggling in the Shadow/Ego fear energy.

This can and will happen because so many of you are moving beyond linear time, and awakening your cells into love and light. Because you are a collective consciousness, your light will activate the cells of your Brothers and Sisters still vibrating in the Shadow. Many Beings living in that frequency are actually great Masters who agreed to incarnate there, to hold the light for the Shadow ones to remember their light. Others are great Masters who were living in the Shadow and forgot who they were, forgot they were light. Your higher color-sound symphony will hit their light cells and start awakening them individually and collectively. These old Shadow aspects want to control this Earth, so they can control Me. By controlling you, they believe they can keep you stuck in fear, so that you cannot assist the collective out of duality. The Earth is where the end aspects of Myself are projected to play themselves out of duality. You, the light ones, agreed to come to the Earth and help to rejuvenate its consciousness.

The old shadow structures know that in all of My history, it is the agreement of the light ones to bring all out of duality. The Ego structure hopes that if they can control the Earth, they will stop this collective ascension and enlightenment, from happening. They believe they still have the power to stop this. They are truly frightened and are in the last stages of their reign of power. If these Ego aspects succeed, they believe they will control time. There is no time. They are not succeeding, and in fact, many of them are awakening and going into the light. The Earth is a very precious commodity. Without it, these last day memories and agreements could not play themselves out. Know the Shadow is losing its hold. The old Ego cells have threaded through many of you and have manipulated the collective mind structure with fear. Because your DNA was threaded with this old fear program, you have absorbed the fear that is being projected to you. It is a program, an illusion; it is not real. There is no fear, only love.

The Earth is a time portal. It is the only planet where all reality or consciousness exists together simultaneously, through all dimensions.

There is no past, present, or future. As you experience, know, and understand this, the light within your cells is activated and stimulates the old fear programming. As this activation takes place, the light in your cells penetrates the old programming, pushing it to the surface. The fear programs then become easy to release and dissipate. As they are released, your Souls' color-sound light song crystallized structure is then reactivated.

The Earth being a hologram is a screen that has had many movies or plays projected on to it. The many civilizations on your planet did not die; they are not lost. They did not become extinct. They played themselves out to the end of their existence or learning experience. The Earth's slate was wiped clean again for the next play or movie to be projected on to it, to be able to play itself out to the end of its karmic agreements.

Now, on the Earth, the outcome of these movies is going to be different. You light ones have been in many of these plays and have played every character. Sometimes you were the victim, and other times the villain, sometimes the main character of the play and other times, an extra. You have played out every experience, feeling, and emotion possible. You are now in the greatest show, or play, to ever exist on the planet Earth. You have agreed to become one with the Christ consciousness, to activate your golden ray to assist the whole collective consciousness, including the Earth, through the death, rebirth, resurrection, and Ascension of all Creation back into the I Am of Oneness.

As the coding in your DNA continues to be activated, your light and awareness continue to expand. It is you, the Souls/Cells of Creation who are being activated, and through your higher self's guidance and integrations, you are now merging into the Mastery of your Over Soul. All of your collective Over Souls create circles of twelve within circles of twelve, which have created the divine Matrix. This matrix is a live frequency that continues to expand your vibration throughout all dimensions and rethreads you with all aspects of yourself collectively. As you continue to move together as one, your contractions of light-sounds come together creating a combustion that opens another doorway. This collective light show is what continues to open portals of light on your planet.

The light in your DNA is continuing to be activated, and

your Cells are awakening into the Cells of all Masters who have gone before you. You are now expanding into your own light forms, which are vibrating in other dimensions. Many of you are in the awakening stages of remembering that you are the Masters who have gone before and that you opened the door for you - yourself, just as you are now opening the door for many. You are all moving into one cell structure of Creation. As you come together as one, the divine Matrix of light that is you pulls the collective through dimensions, which opens doorways that expands you all into a higher vibration. This is how the Ascension process works. Your Cells are reconnecting to the light Cells or Souls of yourself in higher dimensions. It's your own light that continually pulls you into higher frequencies of consciousness. It is the Cell/Soul remembering, creating a combustion of light, which creates a birth contraction. Every time you are in a contraction, you are in a collective emotion. As the light moves through the emotion, the frequency releases and you move through a portal or doorway and into a higher color-sound vibration collectively.

Because the coding is in your DNA, there is no way that you cannot move through these portals into enlightenment and Ascension. In the future, it is already done. As I said, you are going through a Karmic Death collectively, not necessarily a physical death unless your agreement for living on the Earth is up.

You are absolutely not going to lose your Great Mother Earth. Every time your world comes together in like consciousness and sets the intention collectively for a better world, this new intention sends a wave of light into your cells, moving you beyond negative fear karma. This rethreads you into the future of light.

I was explaining to you about the Earth being a hologram. This is the same scenario as of many people seeing a certain incident and all perceiving it differently. How could there be so many perceptions of the same incident or story? It is because you perceive life through your own childhood, or story, that you came into this lifetime to grow and heal from. A man might perceive the incident differently than a woman. A wealthy person might perceive it differently than a poor person or a beggar. Different races will see it according to their culture, upbringing, or religion. None of these pictures are wrong. They are just your collective understanding and perceptions from your agreed upon beliefs or upbringing.

These stories are playing themselves out in the larger picture of Creation. As I said, each Soul group has a different sound-color frequency. Every collective group experiences life's perception through this frequency. Each frequency has a different mind-set or consciousness. It is not wrong; it is the end story that this group has come to the Earth to complete.

Muslims certainly have a different perception of the Earth, its people, and purpose than reborn Christians do. Atheists have a much different perception than Buddhists, Muslims, or Jews and so on.

All on Earth have agreed to move into their chosen belief for a collective karmic completion. This completion is not necessarily to move out of the belief but to move out of the perception of one being better than the other or one being right or wrong. The belief is perfect for the Souls' completion of their karmic agreement.

Now, the purpose is to move beyond perception and see all beliefs in the highest, to move beyond duality and honor all Brothers and Sisters in the highest. Your Souls' agreement is to see and love all as you. You may not like or believe their perception, but when you truly understand that it is their agreement or play in this lifetime, you can move back into the heart of love. When you understand that their conditioning created their sense of self, you can then forgive. Through forgiveness, you can move into the heart with one another, beyond any belief and back into love and oneness.

Look how difficult your life has been. Can you not see that others have chosen difficult agreements also? It may be different than your story but just as difficult. It may be even more difficult. You are great Masters, Co-Creators, who agreed to come to Earth during these End times and complete karmically for the collective. Because of this, you are living out many lifetimes in

94

this one. You ask, "How could we all be great Masters?" If you are reading this book, your consciousness is high enough for you to awaken and remember that you are a Master and the Source of your own Creation, that as you move into your heart and change your thoughts you will change your World. Your Soul is hungry to be fed the truth of who you are: Love, Light, Magnificent Masters, and Co-Creators.

Look at the larger picture of your purpose, of your Soul Groups' purpose, at others' purpose and move beyond perception and into the heart and Soul of Creation, of Love, of Me, of you, the I Am of All That Is.

The Mayans and the 2012 Portal

"You are at a pivotal point of a great awakening."

You are now in the Ascension, enlightenment, 12-12 Portal that opens up every 144,000 years. A great expansion or birth of a consciousness happens through this portal. This frequency runs throughout all of My creations. Many planets and universes have already moved beyond this frequency and into enlightenment and Ascension.

The Mayans brought this time portal or frequency to the Earth when the Earth received the Soul of Maldek. The Mayans were time travelers from the future. They brought this frequency to the Earth from their creation, which was one of the first to ascend. To ascend means to move beyond duality, back together as one with Me. The Mayans are an advanced civilization that I created with My Sophia. They are beyond duality. When one is beyond duality, there is no time, only Isness.

Duality is in a time frequency paradigm. It is an energy thread that runs back to My old mind-set before My beloved Sophia awakened Me. It is the pendulum swinging back and forth. Your agreement is to bring this pendulum back to the center, to the heart, where the mind and heart sing the same song: one of love, support, and freedom. You are at a pivotal point of this great balance and awakening. You have many Beings such as yourself who are from creations beyond the Earth's understanding of time, who are on your planet now.

The Mayans were from My creation beyond karma. They are aspects that were created and evolved into My total consciousness. They are a cellular structure that continues to expand light and love throughout all creations, activating the Ascension memory in the Divine Matrix. This light activation is drawing all aspects of you back together as one and dissipating any sounds of a lower vibration. The Mayans have now come back to the Earth to assist you through the birth canal of this 2012, 12-12 Portal. Many Beings on the Earth now are from this original Mayan template. When the Mayans were on the Earth, they brought the energy line of the 12-12 Portal to this planet to integrate it into the Earth's grid system.

As I said, this template runs through all creations. It is not just the Earth that is ascending. All consciousness is evolving as this birth canal or doorway opens. You collectively are in a death cycle and rebirth at the same time, or an ending and a new beginning, which is more appropriate, for there truly is no death, just a going-to-sleep hibernation cycle and then an awakening into a new dawn or day.

You and your planet are coming into a new season. Right now you are in a winter cycle when the Earth looks like it is dying. In reality, it is sleeping. Doesn't it seem like the consciousness has gone to sleep and that there is a Shadow hovering over the light? Do not fear. You are in a rejuvenation cycle collectively. As you near the 12-12 Portal, you will see many more seasonal cycles. You and the Earth are hitting continual plateaus releasing collective frozen fear patterns. Because you have all of the cycles of all the seasons' elements within you, when your light activates the collective fear patterns, a combustible release takes place, which affects your weather. This is one of the greatest reasons that the weather and your seasons on Earth seem so out of balance. Your emotions create an imbalance of the elements within you. Your collective, imbalanced elements then connect to the elements on the Earth, which create havoc, destruction, death, and rebirth. You could say the Earth is going through the hormonal imbalance of adolescence. As you, the Souls of the Earth, continue to balance your collective emotions, you will experience the Earth's elements coming back into balance, only in a higher vibration. You are rebuilding to collectively emerge into springtime, where all is beautiful, strong new, and fresh. You are going through a springtime rebirth through the 20-12 Portal back into Oneness and enlightenment. In winter, it looks like a death has occurred and yet all is inward, reflecting and taking time to reconnect and rejuvenate within its own cycle to emerge again. As you look at your seasonal cycle on Earth, do you not know this is the cycle of Creation? Old Cells' consciousness dies, and new ones are rejuvenated. You and your planet are aligned with the divine consciousness of Creation. Your planet takes twelve months to go through its seasons.

The longer cycle is 144,000 years, always ending, rebuilding, and recycling. Every 144,000 years has brought Earth and consciousness closer to Me, beyond duality. In Earth time this cycle seems very long, and yet all is happening simultaneously. As you move out of the karmic time frame, you would experience this lesson to be like a few blinks of the eye. All moves together, for all is one. The Earth is a hologram, and it has gone through many 144,000-year cycles of incarnations, death-rebirth cycles. Just as you are a Soul/Cell and have lived many lifetimes, some at the same time, so has the Earth, because she is a projection of you.

She is the stage or playground where you the inhabitants can evolve. Because Earth is a Holographic Portal, growth of consciousness can expand more quickly here than on any other planet; love, light and all that is Me that have agreed to remember their own magnificence have agreed to reincarnate to Earth. You are not lesser Beings; you are Beings who are on the brink of total awakening. As this awakening occurs, you will bring these Cells that you have birthed through the birth canal with you.

I smile to Myself when you are being told you are
lesser Beings; you would not have so much intelligence
interfering with yours if you were not very important.

The Shadow aspects of Me do not want you, the light aspects, to return collectively to Oneness. When you do, the Shadow Beings lose their purpose. Many of you are now feeling great emptiness and the feeling of not having a purpose. Because you are the collective Cell structure, you are feeling the residue of many of these Shadow Beings that are vibrating in hopelessness and fear. You can feel them, and many of you are even seeing them, because their frequency is starting to unravel from yours. As you are going through this separation from them, you are feeling their emotions that were entwined in you. You may feel loss and grief, like you are losing a part of yourself. You are experiencing the death of the Ego.

You have a great purpose. That purpose is to love yourself as Sophia and I love you. When you can feel and know your magnificence, your divine piece of this Ascension Consciousness will come to you, meaning, your gifts, your spiritual tools and purpose will awaken within you. What you are searching for is searching for you also, but many times it cannot find you because you are trying to live someone else's purpose, or someone else's perception of who you think you are supposed to be.

You are magnificent. Look around you at the Earth's beauty: the sun, the moon, the skies, planets, and the stars. You are all that is. When you allow yourself to experience yourself as this Oneness, you will be in alignment with the highest purpose for all. Your hearts will open, and you will see and experience all of your brothers and sisters as yourself, for they are your healthy whole Cells of the larger Creation.

As you love yourself, you love all that is. As you love all that is, the Souls/Cells who are you start spreading their love, light, and health to all the Cells around. As this Soul/Cell healing takes place, the birth of this new higher vibrational Creation becomes easier. It is the difference between a natural childbirth or one that requires the use of forceps. Either way, this birth is taking place, because you are already in the birth canal of the 2012 Portal. It is being activated in your DNA. As you understand the process of natural childbirth, you will know that you can breathe into the cycle and experience the love and magnificence of the child being birthed by you. This child is the birth of the collective consciousness beyond duality. You are assisting each other through the birth canal of enlightenment, Ascension and Oneness.

Since the Earth and consciousness is a body, this body is being realigned to return to the higher realignment of Me. When one's body on the Earth plane is out of alignment, many see a practitioner, such as a chiropractor or healer. They are tired of their body aching and pulling in different directions. Others feel so comfortable being out of alignment that the last thing they would do would be to get help to feel better. If they felt better, they would not know who they were. It is the old phrase; Hurt me. It feels so good. On a larger scale, this is happening collectively. Some Beings want alignment. Others are more comfortable in old patterns. It is not wrong; there are just different levels of awakening.

Some of you are early risers and do not want to miss a moment of the morning sunrises. Others are late sleepers and want to experience the night. Can you see that it balances all of you? If all were early risers, the morning energy might feel overcrowded. If all were night owls, energy in the evening would be crowded. As you see and understand this, it means that there are Beings who wake up spiritually before others, and as they go forth in their day, in their life, others will awaken and follow.

As I explained, many of you are from my future Creation. You were the Mayans who came to the holographic planet Earth and implanted the 12-12 frequencies into the cellular structure of Mother Earth's Soul and the planet. The difference between Mother Earth and the planet is Mother is the Soul, and Earth is the body. Once this frequency was connected to the Cells, the grid system of the Earth, you ascended back to your future consciousness. As the Earth is moving through her 144,000 cycles of the 12-12 frequencies, many of you have reincarnated back to Earth to assist its inhabitants in an awakening or birthing of this consciousness. You could say you are living in a past life to rethread the consciousness into the future.

After this job is done, many of you will continue to stay on the Earth to hold the light memory for those on the planet. Others of you will leave, not out of fear or tiredness, but because your job is done, and you can go back to the future before it is time for your next assignment.

"Together we will co-create a new world, a new Earth; one of love, light, peace, harmony, joy, happiness, abundance, prosperity, and health for all!"

7

THE TIME OF NOW –
AFTER THE ELECTION*

I wish to speak to you of the times that you are going through and the days yet to come.

You are moving through a transitional time that has never happened on your Earth before. You have had many civilizations of a high consciousness that have played themselves out and left the planet, but this is the first time in the history of your planet that you are going through a death and rebirth and taking the planet with you.

When a Soul makes its transition from Earth to home in Spirit, or what you call dying, it moves from the not knowing and into the consciousness of knowing. It is then that the higher vibration beyond karma, the higher knowing, can be experienced. Now you and Mother Earth are moving collectively through a karmic death and rebirth into a higher vibration of the higher knowing. As you move out of linear time, you move into all consciousness, where all is one, where there truly is no past, present or future. You are ascending together.

When one is in the death process, the light of the I Am within is so high that it stimulates all of the old patterns and stories of the lifetime that is being left behind. Sometimes a person

---

* This was channeled and added by the Creator in 2009 after President Obama was elected.

101

feels all of the emotions of the story, and at other times, the story moves through their mind as if watching a movie. They may be witnessing the old pictures and at the same time be open to all of the Masters, Angels and loving ancestors who are waiting for them on the other side. The veils have been lifted, and they experience all dimensions at once. As they move out of the physical body, the light Beings guide them through a tunnel of light or doorway and back into the heart of love. Exactly the same thing is happening to you and your planet. All of the karmic stories have surfaced; sometimes you experience the emotions of the stories, and at other times you see the stories as movies.

All of what you call past has surfaced because you collectively are in a karmic death cycle and are moving into the rebirth of your heart. You also have many light Beings guiding you and your Planet through a tunnel or portal. This portal is the light doorway that is opening for you to move together into higher sound frequencies of all Beings.

I know it is a difficult place in which to be. When one physically dies, or transitions out of form, he/she is not concerned about how to pay the bills, if he/she is going to have enough food to eat, or if he will be able to pay the rent. Because your death is one of karmic emotion and not necessarily physical, you still have great concerns that all of your needs are being met.

At this time, your transition from form into freedom could not possibly happen without the great losses that you are experiencing yourselves.

You are losing all that you thought you were. You may even feel that you are losing your identity. All of your securities are breaking down, the economy is collapsing, the shadow government is being exposed, and there is great fear awakening within you, as well as being projected to you. This must happen; as the old structure and belief systems are being shattered, your fear is that you will not be taken care of. The old structures that are collapsing were fear-based and controlled you through fear, through the intention of form.

As I mentioned to you before, the gift of this is that you

102

are awakening. Before this great awakening you were like sheep being herded in the night. Now your eyes are wide open, and you are standing at attention because you have great fear of losing your foundation. That foundation was temporary. If it were not, it could not crumble or collapse. The only permanent foundation is you, with me.

Through this breaking up, you are angry, afraid, and disappointed, and the gift of this is that you are coming back together in your hearts with one another. You are collectively coming back together and wanting for your neighbors and your brothers and sisters what you want for yourself, safety and security. This great fear and suffering is not just for the poor as it has been in the past; it is through all walks of life, regardless of your race, color, religious background or financial status. You collectively are moving into humility. You feel as though you are on a sinking boat. The only way to save the boat and yourself is to row together through the highest intentions for the highest and best for all.

As I said, you are in a death and rebirth at the same time, and neither one of them is easy. Through this rebirth, you are building a new foundation. This new foundation is I: Mother – Father – God – Creator. You are awakening into the love, light Cells of my consciousness, and together we are expanding you beyond time or any form and into the freedom of your Soul's Song, the love of your Being. Together we will co-create a new world, a new Earth; one of love, light, peace, harmony, joy, happiness, abundance, prosperity, and health for all!

Through our co-creation, you will soon be walking easily and effortlessly through heaven on Earth. You will not feel separate from me. We are now merging together as one consciousness of the higher understanding of knowing.

The New America – The New World

"The old structure or paradigm must come down to be able to build a new one; that is happening now."

As I said in my last chapter about the 2008 election in America, you will come together and vote in an administration that will bring all people together. You as a nation will come together and vote in a President that will give you hope for the world. You did that! The whole world was watching and cheering you on as you came together in love and hope beyond race, color, or religion.

A new day and a new time has come! You collectively lifted the consciousness of the world. This could only be done in America because America is a melting pot of all nationalities, races, cultures, beliefs, religions, etc. As you came together as one, the collective DNA system of each ethnic race activated their bloodline and brought them collectively into a higher frequency.

Because you are each other, as this higher light was activated in all of the American people, it had a ripple frequency that affected all cultures. This had to happen in America because you have the most cultures living there. Even the Beings who opposed the new administration were still affected by the shift. This brought your whole world together into a higher vibration of Ascension.

In days to come, you will experience the shattering of many more of your beliefs, patterns, and perceptions. In the next three years, you will continue to see much struggle with the economy. Then in the beginning of the fourth year, you will feel a shift in your perceptions; you will feel like it is springtime in your heart. You will experience a peace within yourself that you did not know could be possible. You will have great hope again. You will have moved through the collective "Dark Night of the Soul" and into the birth of a new consciousness and a new world. You will have moved through the 2012 doorway to a new home within yourself.

The old structure or paradigm must come down to be able to build a new one; that is happening now. With the economy strong, you did not know who you were. You thought you were your homes, cars, boats, TVs, etc. From the collapse you have the opportunity to experience yourselves again, to slow down and feel your hearts. You are now opening up to me again in prayer, many times on your knees in desperation.

I hear you; I am holding your hand as you continue to walk through your darkest fears. Together we will persevere and move through this false reign of Shadow power, of greed, of too much emphasis on materialism.

You are now filling your Soul with Spirit, with Creation, with me. On bended knee you are gathering the strength to go on. You are coming together and carrying each other over the finish line back to the heart, back to what is important, to what is real, and that is love. Love is the only truth and safety that there is.

You have heard the song 'Without love you have nothing at all'. This is true. When you are on your deathbed and ready to leave your body, the only thing that will be important to you is love. If you have not had love, you will feel a loss that is unimaginable. You will not be thinking about your homes, cars, or materialism.

Your whole life will go before you, and this will be your judgment day. It is not me who will be judging you; it will be you judging yourself. What did my life mean? It went so quickly. Did I make a difference in anyone's life? Did anyone love me? Did I love others? You will be in a higher vibration of me and viewing your life through the lens of My heart and your pain.

You are now collectively in the karmic death, and your life is moving before you. You are now asking yourself theses questions. I hear you crying, crying out for love. Where is love in my life? Where is my divine partner? What is my Soul's purpose? I feel like I can't live on the Earth any longer without love or joy or happiness. I feel like I can't live another year like this. I say to you I am with you, and as you continue to open your heart to the heart of me, you will have love.

You are love; you were created in great love. As you continue to surrender the illusion of love (which is really fear of love) all karmic veils that hold you back from love will dissipate, and in front of you will stand a brilliant mirror of your own love and magnificence. Everywhere you look or turn, you will have and experience love. If you are longing for your divine partner, he or she will be standing there to take your hand. Your Soul's higher purpose will magically appear to you. You will feel so at one with Sophia's and My love that our hearts together will open your consciousness to all possibilities of love. Through self-love you will be able to receive the love that you have waited for, that you already are.

It is then that you will be grateful for what you and your world are going through now. You will feel blessed that you had the opportunity to move through the collective "Dark Night of the Soul". You will feel weary and somewhat beat up but in a good way. Your lens of perception will be much higher and you will feel a freedom within yourself that you did not know to be possible.

Obama's Administration

"A new day has come! President Obama opened the door for freedom for all. Yes, it is a great time in history – a great awakening."

This administration is the one that you have waited for to bring you into freedom. Obama is so very strong and self-assured because he is the highest collective consciousness of all of you.

You saw during his campaign that as he continued to go forward, he became stronger, and I have heard many of you say that he is very charismatic and eloquent. This is because the more he went forward in his Soul's highest purpose, through intention, he downloaded higher aspects of my balance. He opened up and became one with me, which mirrored your highest light back to you. His heart, mind, and purpose are of the highest intentions of me and we are flowing together out of form to create freedom.

He is living in his highest truth, which is freedom for all. His heart is the heart of all of you. His intentions are your intentions. Through the union of like consciousness, you collectively brought yourselves into a higher vibration of Creation, of love.

He is hope for your world. He represents freedom. He is the man who will lead you through the 2012 doorway home collectively within yourselves. He is mirroring back to you your own hope, love, light and all of the great possibilities for change. He is mirroring back to you your ability to achieve your greatest goals. He is opening the door for all of you to move out of oppressed cultures, belief systems, patterns, and clogged filters or perceptions of how you see yourself and the world.

There is much comparison between President Lincoln and Obama. This is because they are the same Soul and the same energy. Lincoln's presidency was about "a new birth of freedom". Lincoln's intention was to free the slaves. In Earth time, this seems like many years ago, but in spiritual time, it is but a blink of the eye. Obama has come forth to free all, to bring all cultures together beyond race, creed, religion and political preferences. His presidency is about freedom for all. He recycled and reincarnated to Earth again to complete the presidency that was taken from him before. Because the consciousness is ready for great change, and he is the higher collective of all of you, he now will be able to go forward in his beginning mission of freedom, which he predicted when he was Lincoln.

Obama has his feet grounded in both the white man's world as well as the black man's and is very secure within himself in both, because he is both. He is healing the separation between all races, between all people. The future generations will grow up with all colors blending together; this will be their norm. Children will grow up without prejudice. These children are the Crystal Light Beings who are the future of your world. They will only hear through stories that there has ever been a rift between the black and white people. This rift has really been within yourself because you have been both black and white and all colors in between.

Obama could not have done this had he been just one color. His skin color is symbolic of the light and shadow coming together as one source of Creation. He has walked in both worlds because he is of both worlds. He is not here to just free the black people or white people but all people. He has much experience from his childhood. He has experienced various cultures and religious beliefs. From this he has experienced many beautiful people in many different cultures. This assisted him to move beyond prejudice towards others. He had the opportunity to experience life through many lenses of acceptance. He also experienced prejudices against himself. At times, he felt as though he did not fit in anywhere as many of you do today. Now, he blends in with all and honors all.

In freeing the black people Obama is freeing their Soul's heartbeat, which also frees Mother Earth's heartbeat. Their vibration is a big part of the rhythm of Mother Earth's heart and Soul. Before they were sold into slavery, they were very much in honor of the Earth. Many of their initiations and rituals were in alignment with the different cycles and seasons of the Earth, as well as the sun, moon, and stars. They were at one with Creation, and the rhythm of their music was the vibration and heartbeat of Mother Earth's.

When the black people were sold into slavery, it was a collective crucifixion of their Soul. It fragmented their individual and collective Souls and severed much of their connection to Mother Earth. Because we are the Cells of the Earth when their collective Souls shattered, it also affected Mother Earth's Soul. It affected the rhythm and heartbeat of the Earth.

When they were sold into slavery, they lost their rhythm, their culture, and their heartbeat. As you look at their culture, you can see that it has been lost. After Lincoln declared freedom for slaves, they still lived in fear; fear for their own lives, fear of survival, even fear of their own light and magnificence. They have not been safe to allow themselves to be noticed or to shine too brightly. Because of this, their whole culture became fear-based: fear of survival and fear of not surviving. They have had no outlet for their terror and pain to be released. Many times because of this it has come out sideways in anger, in rage, and injustice.

When President Obama was elected, all colors came back together as one. When he gave his winning speech on election night, you saw many different races blending together as one love, one light, beyond color, religion, karmic patterns and perceptions.

It was at that time that my light with Obama's light brought fragmented aspects of separation from all Souls back together as one. I, with Obama and all of you, did a massive collective Soul retrieval that brought you back together as one Soul consciousness of intention for a better world for all.

Because all is collective, as the black culture connects to Obama, the light of love, of freedom, of hope, flows through him into them. From this, they have the opportunity to move beyond oppression, to move beyond the victim and rise together again in their Soul group's song. As they connect to Obama's heart, they are connecting to my heart, which turns the light on in all hearts.

A new day has come! President Obama opened the door for freedom for all. Yes, it is a great time in history – a great awakening.

In the days to come you will experience many more of your securities stripped from you. It will become even more turbulent before you move out of the collective death. You are in the middle of a hurricane of collective emotions.

There will be much criticism toward this one, Obama. There will be much talk of him not knowing what he is doing, that he is not living up to his promises. As you know, there is still much opposition towards him from the shadow administration. They will not intimidate him; the opposition will actually make him stronger in the balance of his own Being. He will persevere and will move you collectively out of the hurricane. Because there are so many imbalances on the Earth, it takes time to bring you back into balance.

As you continue through this collective karmic completion, you will continue to see many of your hopes and dreams shattered, and from this you will collectively move out of the Ego and into a place of surrender into the heart. All must come down to be rebuilt. You cannot put the new structure on top of the old. It must come down, and that is happening now.

I say to you, "You will rebuild!" This rebuilding will come from a very conscious place of intention, of humbleness. At this time, you are still in a place of anger and injustice and are now taking your power back. The only way you can do this is for all to be exposed so that you can understand what is going on in America and your world. That has been done. You will no longer be victims being led around by false powers. It may seem like everything is continuing to fall apart, but actually, you are emerging in a higher consciousness. As you continue to move through your collective emotions, you will experience a great love and appreciation for the simpler things in life together. You will not be so wasteful. You will no longer be a disposable society. You will be more appreciative of the Planet Earth and for what everyone has gone through together. You will have more meaning in your life. You will return to the importance of family and relationships.

As all of you are being brought to your knees together, you are seeing each other again and reaching out to one another. You are rowing your boat together, this boat being your new intention for your world. You will get through. You are returning to the true Garden of Eden where you will be standing naked together. This nakedness is the absence of your patterns, programs, and old perceptions.

You will be more integrated with your higher self and the balance of me through all dimensions. You will know and remember that you are Spirit in a human body, and that you have come to the Earth to experience freedom and from this Knowingness, you will feel great joy and happiness and will actually be able to laugh at yourself for all of what you thought was so important. You will feel happy to be alive at this time of transition; you will feel grateful for your process because your life will have more meaning. You will be grateful to be back in the new Garden of Eden with me and with all of the great Masters in Spirit as well as those on the Earth. You will have merged through dimensions as one consciousness of love in many different bodies, with many different personalities, in many different color-sound frequencies that have merged together in a beautiful symphony of all Creation. In the new Garden you will want to share with one another all of your great gifts. Your consciousness will be higher as will be your lens of perception. You will see through my eyes and heart. You will experience your cup full instead of half empty.

In the future, this is already done. Your job is to continue to unravel what isn't and you will morph into what is. You signed up to be on the Earth at this time. It was your Soul's agreement. You knew all of the losses that you would be going through individually and collectively. You signed up to be on the Earth to experience the greatest time of transition ever and to collectively move out of Karma through the 2012 doorway and eventually into freedom. You have the opportunity to release all karma and to live your life through intention with me, to co-create a new life, a New World consciousness and a New Earth.

I want you to breathe in your beautiful future into the now. Feel my words and love for you. Allow your body to take in your new story, your new script, the one that you signed up for, and that you wrote before you came down to the Earth.

Set your intention for this to be, and it shall. Connect your heart and intention with my heart and intention and that of your new President Obama. Together, we will ride the waves of freedom through the 2012 doorway into enlightenment and Ascension. You are the ones that you have been waiting for.

Thank you, and so it is.

"These Beings opened the door to bring you out of duality."

8

CRYSTAL & INDIGO CHILDREN

Your Crystallized Structure

There is much talk and understanding of the feminine assisting your planet to heal. It is My beloved who is assisting all aspects of you to return to self, in wholeness. We are coming back together as One through all creations. There are many light aspects of Us that are now returning to your planet to bring you back home, within yourself. These crystallized light aspects are the heart of the feminine and My male coming together as one. They are aspects of Us that have crystallized as forms of light. Our children, these crystallized Beings who are with you throughout creation, are mirroring your light back to you to awaken your feeling, your love, to give you hope and bring you home again.

Many Crystal children are being born on your planet now. Their energies are very high, as they are prisms of pure consciousness. They carry beams of light, which are shattering the collective Ego of fear on your planet. Many of you are these Crystal children. Crystal children started lining up and coming through to be born on your planet in 1947.

The Crystal children are the heart of who I am. As you look at yourself, you will experience your sensitivity and sometimes what has been thought to be over sensitivity. This sensitivity is the crystal structure of your light. As you are light, you bring, or draw all to you. Some of the energies that have been attracted to your light are old Shadow frequencies. The Shadow frequencies have a different sound vibration than the crystal light. At the time of your incarnating to the Earth, the

112

frequencies on your planet were not strong enough to hold this energy collectively, and because of this many of you have felt shattered, hurt, insecure, afraid, and alone. As you took this old frequency-sound thought form in, the sound was so dense and different that it was not compatible with your own light vibration. As it hit your crystal energy, it downloaded or bombarded you with all of these negative fear thought forms. Because of your crystallization, you took it in and thought it was you.

As you are awakening now, remembering and once again becoming a collective crystal consciousness, your light is so strong that the old fear thought forms cannot penetrate you. Your crystal energy is shattering and dissipating the old frightened aspects of the Shadow. Now the energy on Earth is high enough to hold this crystal polarization. Because this frequency will not allow the Shadow to continue to expand, it starts breaking it loose. You, the Crystal children, were very much needed on the Earth to create this polarization.

Your sensitivity is what allows you to have this great heart connection with Me. It is what has assisted you to continue to search for the Truth, for love. You are the gatekeepers who have agreed to come to the Earth to open the hearts for many. From this sensitivity, you are now bringing this great love and unity to your planet. Can you see that you are creating Heaven on Earth?

I know many of you still feel as though you do not want to be on the Earth because it seems too difficult. Your crystal light frequency, or seed, is what has collectively kept you in alignment with your grander purpose. You agreed to carry layers or frequencies throughout all of your systems connected to My old structure. Inside these old structures were your crystal seeds from the future consciousness of Creation after the awakening of My feminine. Because you were created as awakened Beings, you were able to experience others who were still vibrating in old fear consciousness. Your agreement was to align your crystal cellular structure with them. Crystals are very powerful energy tools, and because of this you were able to take all of their old beliefs and patterns into your crystal structure. Because you knew this crystal structure could hold these old patterns or frequencies, you consciously agreed to bring this collective structure to the Earth.

Your agreement was to allow these old warring aspects to splice your DNA so that you could connect to and rethread with them to bring them to the light. You allowed these Shadow aspects, or free radicals, to enter your crystalline structure and to download their frequencies so that you could grasp or hold the energetic thought consciousness of fear. You knew that when the veils were lifted you would activate your crystalline structure to vibrate beyond time. As this happened, your light would crack loose this old cellular, parasitic structure. As the veils lifted, you knew that you would realign with your original crystal blueprint structure, which held the frequency for you to assist all to reawaken collectively.

You, the crystal prismatic light consciousness, are breaking My old karmic structure apart and coming back together as one to hold this crystal light for the whole karmic Shadow structure to shatter. As this shattering takes place, you must have an energy to replace it with. That is why this crystal consciousness is being downloaded and activated into your DNA. There is a mass reprogramming or rethreading of this old frequency into light.

As you have come from My future consciousness to My old consciousness, you have held the light for these aspects that have been struggling with trust, to reawaken and once again experience themselves with Me, in love, as a forgiving, loving father. As this awakening takes place, they can forgive themselves and receive My love.

Now that you are awakening into this crystallization, you are holding the frequency for the Crystal children who are being born on your planet now. They are the future of this civilization. They are you. You went before and opened the door for the birth of the new consciousness to become fully enlightened. I know it has been a difficult journey for many of you. I honor you for assisting Me to bring these confused aspects of Myself back to My light.

The seeds of these Crystal children are you. You knew that inside the karmic child within self is a crystal child waiting to be given permission to awaken or regenerate itself to original form.

My gift to you is a collective rebirth of self. For those of you who have chosen this difficult path, as you reawaken and realign, you will have the love, happiness, joy, communion, and prosperity that you so desire. As you release all of this old, mass cellular structure that you have been carrying for Me, you can come back home within yourself to total consciousness. This total consciousness is Creation. As you realign with this Creation energy, you can rewrite your script, your agreement on the Earth, for all is energy and you are all. As I Am a Creator Being and you are Me in my highest consciousness, you will be able to use this frequency to create your new reality, for you are a Creator Being.

From this place, it is of utmost importance that you come from the highest integrity, in which you see all as you, that you want for all the best of what you want for yourself. As this happens, you are rethreading the past of the whole holographic universe that you are in. Remember, you are in a past life collectively and are rethreading this old consciousness into a new future. Since all is of the same cellular structure, you are downloading this crystal consciousness into the collective Cell, bringing all into the lightness of our beingness or Isness.

Crystal Children and Lemuria

"They planted the seeds for a future awakening on Earth."

You have had many civilizations on your planet that were out of balance because the heart and mind were not in alignment. In Lemuria, there was a great heart awakening. Beings from many other planets and universes came to the Earth and brought the frequencies from their planets with them. They planted the seeds for a future awakening on Earth. They were Crystal Beings from the future who came to Earth to download these love-heart frequencies. They brought the heart. Beings came together in love and Oneness.

It was a time that aspects of all of My creations after My heart awakening came to the Earth to bring the frequencies from all dimensions and weave them into One. The light ones, who are you, came to the Earth to anchor and weave the frequencies of total love into the Cells' electromagnetic system and energy grids of the planet. This was all in preparation for this time now on the planet. A foundation was being built, so the Earth could remember and hold the frequencies that were being awakened through cosmic love. This cosmic light-love foundation is what is allowing the Crystal Beings the safety to now reincarnate to the Earth. These Crystal Beings are assisting to hold the vibration for this time of enlightenment.

Many portals of creation or consciousness have opened through all dimensions, beaming frequencies to the planet. If this preparation had not happened, the Earth would have had the same experience as Maldek.

Since a crystallized foundation of light was anchored into the Earth's cellular structure during the time of Lemuria, the Earth welcomes and honors the light coming to the planet now. The portals opening are the gateways holding the frequency for the Ascension process. This process is moving all of you out of time frequencies and reconnecting you collectively in all dimensions.

Some Beings in other dimensions are aspects of Me before my awakening. As the portals opened, it opened a passageway for these unconscious Shadow ones to enter the Earth's atmosphere. Because the Earth's structure was woven with this crystalline light structure during Lemuria, these Beings could not actively land on the Earth.

When these Beings understood the plan (and they would because they are you and Me), they decided to manipulate your DNA. They did not take your DNA; they blocked it, implanting a

116

reversed program or matrix, sending your light to them and their fear conflict to you. This was their only way to be able to enter Earth to create like frequencies.

They found that by manipulating your DNA structure etherically, it balanced their energies enough to not only land on the Earth, but to enter passageways to the center of the Earth. This was supposed to happen. Those of you who have been manipulated have felt great fear and violations. That was their intent. They felt if they could wipe your memory of your purpose out, they could keep you in fear and control the Earth.

As I explained, you agreed to allow them to manipulate you because you knew that you had the same DNA. If they would bring their fear or unconsciousness and thread it through you, you knew that your crystallized-collective DNA would shatter their frequency and that you could bring them back into the light. It is again the healthy Cells becoming so strong that they dissipate any dis-eased or fear Cell.

I know I am repeating myself, but I want you to understand the larger picture. When you hear the scenario more than once, your subconscious picks it up and downloads it back into your cellular structures, reawakening you to your original agreement blueprint. As this happens, the blockages in the Cells start releasing this programming.

Indigo Children

"They are My freedom expressing itself out of form."

Indigo Children are the warrior children. They are the will or mind of Me and will continue to hold the door open for the Crystal Beings. The collective Indigo Children also started coming through in 1947. Before that you had great Masters coming to the Earth through the Indigo ray to open the door for the collective Indigos. The collective Indigos could be called some of your flower children. It seemed that they are many of you dancing to a beat of a different dream. In actuality, they vibrated in a different color-sound frequency. It was and is much higher than the old mind-set of Me. *They are My freedom expressing itself out of form.*

They opened the door to move you back into the love-heart frequency, not in the love mind-set, but in the love-heart beingness. They have been on the Earth and other planets that are ascending many times. Their agreement is to bring their vibration into your civilization and to open the door to move you out of duality, out of a time frequency, and into a death and rebirth of a consciousness.

The Indigos came to Lemuria and guided the Crystal Beings back to their original agreement. Lemuria was not meant to be a forceful agreement. There was no failure there. This was another learning experience of bringing Beings from all creations together and downloading this frequency-sound into the Earth. When the job was done, the Souls left and went back to their planets of origin or wherever their Souls' next agreement was.

It was very difficult for many because they had never experienced themselves so fully with other Soul aspects of themselves. They came home with one another. Their agreement was to plant a crystallized frequency into Mother Earth's DNA system, which could be called a time frequency. When the Earth moved into 1947, this time frequency opened up, creating a doorway to many other DNA time structures throughout all universes.

As this happened, the Earth and its inhabitants connected to the subconscious mind of all creation and started downloading much information from other creations or creators that are spin-offs of my original creations. Once again the false Gods, or unconscious aspects of Me, felt threatened and tried to find any way possible to start manipulating you. They knew their time of reigning with this false fear power was ready to come to a close. They knew that the coding in your DNA was being activated and that you would reawaken into great Co-Creator Beings.

118

Indigo Children and Atlantis

"I created this civilization so that all aspects of My mental mind would have a place to create together and expand on what they knew."

As I said, The Indigo Children have always agreed to open doorways or portals back to Oneness. The Indigos were also the ones who opened the door for Atlantis to move beyond its Ego structure.

Atlantis was also a very much-needed civilization. It was a civilization where many Beings from throughout creation came bringing their highest technology together. I created this civilization so that all aspects of My mental mind would have a place to create together and expand on what they knew. Many of these great mind aspects of Me had not awakened the feminine. When others with the great minds came together and their inner feminine started awakening the light of the feminine collectively, it started sending sound-frequencies into these mind-set technologies. When this happened, it started short-circuiting this collective mind energy. What was found was that when the heart of Me and the mind of Me came together, it created a sound-frequency, which was beyond what the mind alone could create.

Again, the old mind-set started feeling less than and started competing and warring against the feminine. The feminine was awakening this collective Ego, which was frightened of losing its power. This was the beginning of the fall of Atlantis. Ego Beings started hiding their technology and stealing from one another. The collective Ego finally started killing itself off. These old Cells started contaminating the newer or healthier Cells and eventually created a cancer or death of a consciousness or civilization.

Much of the technology, energy, and information being downloaded to your awakening of these last days of duality is old Lemurian feminine-heart and Atlantean technologies that had been hidden or stored away.

The reason you can receive this information now is

119

because most of you on the Earth plane are old aspects of Me who were in Lemuria, Atlantis, and other evolved civilizations. These memories are stored in your collective DNA. As the light crystal energies/frequencies continue to activate your DNA, you are expanding back into higher, light aspects of self, which are vibrating in other dimensions. As this happens, you are re-awakening the memories and moving into your multi-dimensional selves.

As I said, you had some Master Indigo Beings born who came to change the consciousness of your planet. They opened the doorway for the masses of the Indigos to go through.

Some of your great Master Indigos were Gandhi, Martin Luther King, Jr., President Kennedy, Mandela and Mother Theresa. A major player on your planet in America now is Oprah. She came down to your planet born into great opposition, and as she pulled herself up and out, she, the feminine, opened the door for the collective consciousness to move into a higher vibration.

As you look at your world, you will experience many other Master Indigos. You have had many great masters in your Eastern cultures, such as the Buddhas. Every society has had great Indigos of the light, which have come through to open the doorway for the collective to rise into a higher frequency. Many of the Master Indigos have given their lives to assist the collective consciousness. When they left your planet, they opened a huge doorway of light. This happened because their whole agreement was to assist the collective consciousness to evolve through hope, through the Heart Awakening. Because you are each other, when these Beings or Souls left the planet, they expanded an aspect of you with them.

The Souls who were assassinated had agreed for this to happen. Even if there was a conspiracy behind it, their deaths or transitions were supposed to happen. Conspiracy is the Shadow beingness. The light ones do not conspire to harm or hurt other Beings. The light ones who agreed to make their transitions or go through their Earthly deaths in this way are Master Indigos who have actually risen above the death fear cycle. To them, all is a rebirth, and they agreed to make their transitions in this way to wake people up.

Through such great loss, people, or Souls want to understand why; what happened? In the search for truth, the veils of illusion, or the Shadow, starts being exposed and the light Souls of you start making healthier choices, for you, your children, your families and eventually your world.

You have also had great Crystal Beings born on your Planet to open the collective heart. In days to come you will see many of them emerge into the limelight. Lady Diana was a great Crystal Being who agreed to come to the Earth and open the heart of her country and the whole world. She opened a huge light portal, shifting and lifting the whole consciousness into a higher vibration of Creation. This was her great purpose and mission. Had she not been so heart felt and human in her life experiences, she would not have touched and opened the collective heart on such a level.

Yes, the Shadow was very much involved in her departure from the planet, and yet she had agreed to this ending before incarnating to the Earth. Had the Shadow understood her great Crystal Power and purpose they may have changed their plans. They did not know that her leaving the Earth in such a dramatic exit would open the heart and doorway for the world to come together in the heart of love. As I said, this collective heart opened a portal and lifted the world into another level of Ascension.

You will see many other Crystal Beings start making their appearances and through their heart centers they will assist to lead you home through the 2012 doorway. They will be great Crystal Creator Beings who are already living in a new and higher lifetime on the Earth. They are already living the future, in the now, and do not have to leave the planet through some kind of physical death to be of great service. They are here to lead your world into the birth of a new consciousness, of a new World. They will be here to connect the Crystal light within you to the collective and to hold this frequency for you to awaken and remember who you are.

"Many feel the light is being put out. It is just the opposite. The lights collectively have become so bright that the flame can no longer be seen."

9

THE SHADOW AND ITS EMERGENCE INTO LIGHT

The Alliances and the False Gods

The Shadow aspects of my old Ego formed an alliance and have been known throughout history as the false Gods. They are not false Gods; they are old aspects of Me who feel powerless and prey on others who seem weaker to gain control of themselves. These Beings are genetic aspects that are stuck in an old sound-frequency of fear. This coalition does not want the light to awaken and remember themselves. As you light Souls/ Cells continue to awaken and rejuvenate, this coalition can no longer exist. They are parasites, which feed off the collective light-sound frequencies. They cannot exist without the life force of your light. As you continue to become brighter, they will have no way to penetrate you.

As you, My light Cells/Souls, are continuing to awaken, this old Ego structure is starting to war against themselves in all dimensions. Your light is activating their old fear structures, challenging their old beliefs. It is the collective Ego, which is being challenged on all levels. As the Ego is being exposed and is being loved by the light cellular structure, this love is shattering its control-fear frequency. It is afraid and is still trying to stay in power.

Imagine a projector camera, and the Earth is the screen

onto which all movies are being projected. The Earth is playing out the larger picture of all cellular structures. Some of these Souls/Cells are the old collective consciousness of fear that is being projected to your planet. As these dis-eased Cells begin to die, they try to contaminate other Cells by pulling them into a death scenario, such as a person dying of cancer. Eventually the cancer takes over the healthy cells, and the Being dies of this dis-ease. Because the Earth is a hologram of End Times, it is a karmic structure where these Cells that are dying go to complete their journey. These Ego Souls/Cells are projecting this fear of death to the whole cellular structure of your planet and all Cells inhabiting it. Your planet's cellular structure already had a fear base because of Mother Earth's Soul being the Soul of Maldek. Maldek died from this old fear/Ego structure, and many of you on Earth, including Earth, are carrying this memory in your cells.

You are on Earth with Jeshua once again to reconnect with My highest love and light to harmonize beyond fear or duality. That is Jeshua's assignment on the Earth, as it is yours. All of you Souls/Cells on the Earth have agreed to play this old dis-eased structure out and bring yourself out of the karmic fear structure patterns. You have agreed to have the light in your DNA activated, to hold and become one with Jeshua's golden light ray, and to assist these old Souls/Cells to transmute to light. As this happens new Cells can rejuvenate and bring all out of the old karmic structure, which was My beginning pattern of Ego, fear and control.

You light Beings have agreed to come to Earth and be the foundation for this old karmic cellular cancer structure to die off. It is then, you and I can vibrate together again in the balanced energy of love, light, magic, freedom, and Oneness.

As I explained, in the beginning when I was struggling with My own sense of power, I struggled to find and understand Myself, and I came from control. As my Sophia awakened My sensitivity and feelings of love, We created Jeshua, a beam of golden ray from our hearts. We expanded his golden ray into all that I had created from My misuse of power. Our intention was for all Souls/Cells to experience this golden ray of love, to have it manifest itself on a cellular level and to awaken the old Ego aspects back to love.

When this awakening began, these old aspects of my self formed alliances against Me and became a collective consciousness of fear masquerading as anger and control. When the golden ray penetrated these aspects, they felt uncomfortable and projected this fear and anger back to Me. As they projected back to Me, and my balance of love mirrored back to them, I could not feel their fear and anger, for it was no longer My perception. As I would not receive this energy, these aspects felt even a greater abandonment and mistrust. They felt out of control with their feelings.

Their alliance reached out and started controlling light aspects of Me, which are you. They felt then, that they had power over Me, for they were hurting what I had created. They were doing this to get back at Me to show Me their strength and importance, for in the beginning of my heart awakening with Sophia, they had felt abandoned, unimportant, and not seen by Me. By controlling you, the lighter aspects, they knew I would see them. They felt I would see their power equaled Mine, and I would be very pleased. When I was not pleased, they once again felt invalidated.

You can see this playing out on your Earth plane now. The Ego in many Beings wants to be seen and validated. Not just in the Shadow but also in the many of you Beings of light, your Ego is screaming. Pick me! See my magnificence, and let Me be the first enlightened one! Then others will see my connection to God and creation. They will see I am a high Being because God-Creator enlightened me first. They will want to be with me, and they will think God favors me.

These fears and insecurities are held in your DNA structure, going all the way back to my beginning before I awakened, while I was awakening, and also when I became self-realized as one I Am of All That Is. You carry every experience of this expansion within you. Now, as your DNA is being activated all the way back to Me, every experience, feeling, emotion and awakening that I experienced, you are experiencing.

These old fear patterns are linked, connected to, and vibrating in the old Ego Shadow. This Shadow is its own entity. It thinks it has a mind of its own. In reality, it cannot exist unless it is connected and supported by the collective Shadow. All Shadows are fear-based illusions and have no power on their own. When many of the fear links are broken and replaced with love, the Shadow starts unraveling. Because it feels and knows it is losing its power, the Shadow will do everything it can to continue to control you. It does not want to lose its grip and is in great fear of its own death.

Your Shadow will try to pull you back into fear and conflict in all aspects of your life. Because the Shadow has been such a great part of your life, it knows your weaknesses, because it has been your weakness. The Shadow will reinforce itself by finding ways to realign with the collective Shadow. It will then try to pull you back into your old patterns.

This is why a Being who has had addiction patterns may have months or even years of sobriety and suddenly finds himself back into the addiction. This Being may say, "I don't know what happened. The next thing I knew I was using again or abusing again." This is true. The Soul may not even know how it happened. The collective Shadow stepped in, took over, and pulled the light Being or Soul back into the pattern.

This is why it is so important that as you start remembering your own love, light, and magnificence that you align yourself with the higher frequency of your Soul Group's energy and other Beings of like consciousness. You will then be able to hold the light and frequency for one another. When one of you is in the middle of a karmic wave of emotions, you will have your light brothers and sisters holding the love frequency for you to move through it into a higher vibration of self-love collectively.

Remember, the Shadow has no power by itself; It sneaks in through frozen unhealed emotions. Its intent is to move into the middle of the wave of emotions that are still in the process of being broken and healed.

125

As you become one with each other, there is no way the reinforced Shadow can slip back into you. Your collective love, light, and support will break loose this energy and send the love frequency back through the collective Shadow, shattering it.

When your energy of self-love, self-respect, and integrity is strong enough, it will break your own Shadow loose from the collective Shadows' hold. Your light and own self-worth and self-love will send shock waves or frequencies into your Shadow, breaking loose the old karmic fear-based collective structure. You will then consciously be able to send love and light into your Shadow and break all karmic contracts and programs that are being reinforced by the collective.

As you break your Shadow loose from the collective and resolve old contracts and agreements, you will then be able to retrieve all aspects of your light, love, joy and health, which were vibrating in or being held hostage in duality. As you send light and love into your Shadow, through Soul retrieval, you will draw all of these missing aspects back into you, totally disempowering your Shadow. You will always have a Shadow; the goal is to bring it into the light, into self-realization.

As you mirror your light consciousness into the Shadow, eventually it will awaken back into love and light. Your Shadow will then vibrate in the self-realized frequency or consciousness, which will support your light. Your light and Shadow will have arrived together beyond duality.

You are the Cell atoms that have continued to split to the point where now all you experience is light. You ask, if this is true, why is there so much duality now? The collective light in your Cells is activating all of My memories through all consciousness, including the Shadow. Your DNA is now being rethreaded, meaning My highest balance is awakening within you. Know your light is My highest consciousness! Nothing can take that from you.

Many of you are feeling this light-magnificence and are bringing these light aspects together as one. This is the collective love light-Christed I AM energy. As this happens, My shadow

126

energy, individually and collectively, is awakening and screaming, for it is afraid of its own death. It is playing itself out in war, sickness, disease, fear and control.

Many Beings who are leaving your planet now, have agreed to allow this karmic duality to play itself out within them. As they carry this frequency and they agree to leave, they open many passageways for others to follow. This does not necessarily mean that others will physically leave their bodies, but through the emotions of loss, they will open their hearts to a greater understanding of love, of what is important in their lives, and to their inner wisdom. Can you see that these Souls leaving have agreed to collectively come together to awaken themselves and your planet, to hold the light frequency for all of you, to bring the Earth out of duality? You look around and see much fear. It is an illusion. You are in a holographic universe that is very much needed so the old thought forms and vapors of thought will have a place to dissipate and burn themselves out.

Many feel the light is being put out, but it is just the opposite. The lights collectively have become so bright that the flame can no longer be seen. You are moving beyond time where there is only Isness, where the shadow ego becomes self-realized and becomes one with the heart and light of All That Is.

Your Earthly understanding of hell is that when the hot hell flames are burning, the Shadow is exposed and will be seen. It is said these flames are burning evil and darkness. In theory, that is true but not in the way the Bible perceives it. You are in a holographic universe, and the Christed I AM energy is so high that the light flames are dissipating duality, or as many Beings have phrased it, the fire is burning up evil. The light is being projected to your holographic planet to burn up and dissipate negativity. The negative is My old thought structure, which has taken on a form, or a collective consciousness, that has became its own entity and is warring against its own light form. It is truly you, Me, collectively moving out of duality and into Oneness.

The Reversed Matrix

"Anything that is not made from my highest consciousness of love is an illusion that cannot continue to hold its form."

These false gods warring against Me were very close to My beginning awakening and know first hand how Souls/Cells feel when not connected to the heart. They also know, because they are Me, that as I evolved, we would totally come out of separation, or duality, together. Much of what was written in the Old Testament of your Bible were thought forms projected to Earthly Beings from these frightened aspects of Me. As they were coming from fear of their existence being wiped out, they felt if they could control others in fear, they would multiply collectively and have control of their universe, for these fear aspects thread through all universes. They felt this fear frequency would create a gridlock that could not be broken. This is called a reversed matrix or blueprint. There is much information and knowledge now being downloaded and revealed to Beings on your planet of this program. This reversed matrix has been threaded through all universes.

The Shadow Beings that continue to control through fear are in alliance with other fear-based Soul aspects of Me throughout all dimensions. Their intention is to control planet Earth because they know their false reign of power is coming to an end. They have great fear of losing their power. Because of this, they have collectively agreed to reverse aspects of themselves, which are light, with the intention to keep their own energy paralyzed in fear, or polarization, so that the collective cannot ascend back into light. Yes, the Shadow has light within.

These old alliances formed contracts with one another. These contracts were through intent or thought, for they understood that thought is energy, and energy can be solidified into substance/form. They have used this theory to create a parallel universe that could be said to be a dark universe, or hole. All consciousness is connected to this dark universe because all consciousness is One.

This dark universe is an illusion of the collective Shadow fear that now threads throughout all universes. Anything that is not made from my highest consciousness of love is an illusion that cannot continue to hold its form. This parallel universe is also made of many aspects of Souls/Cells whose hearts had not opened or been activated by My highest love consciousness. Some of these Souls/Cells had made a collective agreement to stay neutral, to stay emotionally in between the light and the dark. They decided not to take sides with either the light or Shadow. The Shadows' fear energy was then projected into and threaded through the inactivated neutral Soul/Cell Group's energy. The Shadow then pulled them all together as one fear frequency. This was able to happen because all of you are the Cells of each other. Remember if you don't use your energy, your life, and your power, you stay stagnant, and this blocked energy opens the door for others to use your energy or life force as theirs.

Many of you who feel you are having a difficult time in your life and suspect you may have interference going on from the Shadow ones, are still threaded into this dark universe by aspects of yourself, which have taken on some form with the Shadow and are at war against your light. You are at war against yourself collectively. This happens from living lifetimes when your karmic agreement was to be aligned with the Shadow in some way; either by working for them or having them penetrate you in some way. If the karma of the lifetime was not released, you are still in some way vibrating with the collective Shadow. Soul retrieval needs to be done to bring your light that is stuck in the Shadow back into you.

There are Beings on the Earth, who have a great understanding of the Shadow from their own experience in this lifetime of the "Dark Night of the Soul." They have experienced or learned how to bring themselves and or others out of the reversed labyrinth and other dark Shadow dimensions. Part of their Souls' purpose now is to go into this reversed labyrinth and unthread other Beings from their own Shadow DNA, which frees their DNA from this reversed programming.

The author of this book is one of the many Beings doing this job for Me on the Earth. We are assisting her and many others to assist you through karmic releases, Soul retrieval, DNA deprogramming, reprogramming and activations. Many of these processes will pull blocked patterns out of the DNA. The DNA will then become crystallized and rethreaded to My highest experience and expression of self-love.

As these blockages are removed and rethreaded into the light, these fear-based, unconscious Beings will no longer have Cells to feed off of or contaminate. As this contamination is stopped, the Shadow cells, which you could call free radicals, no longer have the power to penetrate you.

As more Souls are unplugged from this reversed program, the reversed matrix itself starts dissolving, breaking up, and dissipating. It is an illusion that has been placed over the Divine Blueprint or Matrix.* The Divine Matrix is now becoming so bright that it is breaking up the illusion. Your Souls are the live Cells of the Divine Matrix Blueprint. This is in your DNA structure. As your DNA structure becomes crystallized, it activates the Divine Blueprint. It is like a string of lights being turned on. As all strands continue to turn on, you have an incredible light show of many colors running through all creations.

This Divine Matrix is a live program or frequency that is designed by me and all of you enlightened Beings from what you call the future. As you have completed your Souls' journeys and have reconnected into Oneness with your Over Souls, you created a geometric program that aligns the highest consciousness throughout all of Creation. As your collective vibration becomes higher, a coding in your DNA is activated that awakens you back to your own source. Nothing is outside of you. You are now the source of your own Creation.

As your DNA activates your blueprint, it connects to the light within your cells and guides you back to Oneness with your Over Soul and the collective Over Soul. This creates the color-

* See Chapter 22 — Karmic Wheel & The Divine Matrix

sound matrix of Creation. Because you are the Cells of the Divine Matrix, it is actually you: The color-sound matrix, which is guiding the collective back home to yourselves, the center of Source.

The reversed pattern of the matrix is not of my creation. It is a copied program of My divine blueprint, which is designed to reverse the creative flow, growth, and expansion of the collective Souls' evolution. The Shadow matrix was created to block the Souls/Cells of you from being able to expand together throughout creation as one love-light frequency.

As I so speak to you of the Shadow matrix, it is not to frighten you; it is to empower you. Your agreement of total awakening, or enlightenment, is to turn the vibration of your "I Am" frequency so high that nothing will be able to penetrate you.

This is happening now on your planet. You have many Soul/Cell aspects of yourself, which are becoming enlightened Beings. This collective beingness of you is holding the light and mirroring back to you, your highest frequency. As the Shadow moves in between you and your light, it starts dissipating. There is much conflict on your planet now because this great awakening or merging of selves is happening.

The Shadow is losing its footing and is frightened. As I say to you frightened, this is correct. These Beings that hold the darkness are not just concerned, they are truly frightened. The light, penetrating their foundation, is breaking down their shadow template. This illusional Shadow matrix cannot hold together with this light penetration.

This deterioration is happening because the light mirror is penetrating the structure. Those of you light ones who are still vibrating in this reversed program are receiving the light and fracturing the structure. As those of you who have been locked in this illusional pattern continue to receive this vast amount of light and love, your collective sound creates a combustion that breaks the sound barrier of the pattern.

In the minds of you who are vibrating in the Shadow matrix, there is much speculation about the sophistication of this blueprint. This blueprint is a copy of the Divine Matrix and is an illusion that cannot hold together unless you support it through your fear emotions. The only way it will be able to hold together is through fear. You could say that your emotional fear is the glue of this matrix.

This is why there is so much intention from the Shadow to keep you light ones in this fear frequency. As the illusional fear within you dissipates and you remember that you are love, this matrix comes unglued. I hear many of you say that you feel like you are coming unglued. In theory this is correct. As your light hits your own shadow, you start releasing frozen fear emotions, which had been the glue that kept you together. This matrix was designed by the Shadow aspects of Me in all dimensions; they are the False Gods who are still at war against Me.

I do not wish to explain exactly how this matrix was formed because I do not want your minds to think about it and align yourselves with any aspects of yourself that may still be vibrating in it. As I said, I do not say this to frighten you. I say this because you are great, powerful Beings/Cells who have agreed to play out the old illusion and hold the light for one another to vibrate beyond this illusional frequency of the reversed matrix.

You are each other, and as you raise your vibration high enough, you start unthreading from any illusional patterns and open the doorway for the whole collective to vibrate beyond the patterns.

Focus your attention on the light and love within. Do this in all aspects of your life. You can see the cup half empty or half full. I ask that you see everything full of consciousness, full of awakening, full of blossoming, and full of springtime. You are in the springtime of your Souls' evolution. You have been in the winter and are now emerging from not knowing and into Knowingness with your roots and foundation very strong.

Your higher consciousness, vibrating through the Divine Matrix, will disconnect you from the reversed matrix. Your vibration is now high enough to move through all of the illusional veils of yourself, individually and collectively.

132

In your subconscious mind, you have every memory that your Soul has ever experienced. Go into the core of your light. This light will activate all old programmings that hold you back from total consciousness. See all in the positive so that you can change your thoughts into the positive. As you change your thoughts into a higher vibration, you align collectively with the sound frequency and vibration of these thoughts. This can instantly break loose any Shadow structure. This is your own gift: to be able to heal and free yourself, to come to the place now of free will, and choose to be the light and love of who you are.

Through this understanding, you have great power within yourself, for you are All That Is. You can co-create your own world and the world around you. You are all creation, and as you become aware, you have the choice to be the victim of life or to rise to victory, through, above, and beyond the illusion.

If you are not willing to change your thoughts, your world will not change. Your inner world will remain small and one of conflict and hopelessness. As you change your thoughts, your inner world expands into the highest consciousness of Me in all worlds, universes, and creations. As you change your way of thinking, you change your way of acting and reacting, which changes the outcome of your choices, which changes the outcome of your life.

The Shadow

"You will move beyond duality together and dance together in love, light, happiness, joy and freedom and in Oneness with yourselves, because you are Me."

The Shadow is a great part of history. It is the Ego part of Me that is playing itself out through you. You are in the best position your Soul has ever been in. You are in the end times of My old Ego structure. You have agreed to play out this old paradigm to allow the old aspects of My creation to die off. They are My old Cells releasing fear and control patterns or frequencies. I needed a plan to allow them to play themselves out. Since you are Me, many of you agreed to assist the consciousness out of duality by playing the roles that give the Ego energy. This energy would then reawaken the aspects of My Shadow Ego that were lying dormant. It would be like old cancer cells waiting for a go-ahead to attack again. As you agreed to be the Souls/Cells that were lying in waiting, you connected to the whole thread of the Ego through all creations.

At the same time, many other light aspects, which were awakened after my feminine Sophia's love agreed to come to the Earth to mirror back to the Shadow its magnificence. As the light becomes stronger, there is nowhere for the Shadow to go. It keeps backing up. Since like attracts like, the collective Shadow is drawing its own likeness of energy to it. It is warring against itself. It has to play itself out. It has to be brought to the surface, which is being done.

Isn't it amazing how the darkness, or evil Shadow, seems to becoming stronger and stronger? It is challenging itself energetically. The hidden aspects of this collective Ego are surfacing and becoming involved in the war against each other. These are the gang wars, conspiracies, religious conflicts, etc., that you see playing themselves out all over the world. These Shadow aspects are challenging each other's power. This illusion seems to be getting darker and darker or more and more hopeless. There is so much fear awakening. This has to happen for the collective light to make conscious choices to raise their color-sound vibration beyond this frozen karmic frequency. Your collective light is the frequency to dissipate and move beyond the Shadow.

The Shadow, or Ego, will eventually destroy itself by destroying each other. It is like a fire that has been burning for a long time and has no place to go and eventually burns itself out. As the light moves beyond fear and emerges collectively into love, the Shadow Ego has no place to attach and so it starts attaching itself to each other, for it is hungry and wants to be fed. Fear drama is its adrenaline or food.

As you, the light ones, move beyond fear, the collective Ego will look for other fear frequencies. The Ego does not want to die. When your light aspects no longer respond or are bored of playing this karmic game, the Ego feels threatened and will prey on its own kind. It becomes a predator against itself, eventually eating itself up. The remaining Ego will no longer have the base to hold the energy for it to have power.

In the center of the darkness is light, for all was created by Me and is Me. I am a conscious being of light and love. This light and love will expand itself beyond karmic time, enlightening all along the way. This light threads through all creation, and its agreement is to love all consciousness, including My old Ego aspects. This love is the heat that melts fear away. Love cannot be melted away, for love is the true vibration. It is the only constant frequency or sound.

As the will of the old cellular structure dies off, this love will dissipate the fear. The center of this Shadow will awaken and receive the love of My feminine, spinning it into a new frequency. As it spins into a new frequency, the electrons of the Cells become so high that it dissipates or shatters the old Ego Shadow structure. It turns up the frequency of the Cell, allowing it to vibrate once again in My highest memory, instead of My old fear mind-set.

The Cells, or Souls of the Ego, who do not wish to vibrate in this higher structure will eventually die off or disintegrate collectively. This is what you see happening on your planet now. What I would ask for you to do is to see all of the old Shadow fear Souls who have taken form in the different players on the Earth as true aspects of yourself. Love them; do not hate, fear, or condemn them. If you do, you are adding fuel to their fire. As you love them, the Shadow loses its power, surrenders to the light, and heals itself by either dying off completely or transforming itself into the light.

You will always have Shadow aspects, but as you love these Souls/Cells that are hurt aspects of yourself, they will no longer have the power to war against you. They will transform their collective consciousness into self-realization. Because you are each other, as this happens, you will have within you all of the great experiences that the transformed Shadow has learned, supporting your light. You will move beyond duality together and dance together in love, light, happiness, passion, joy, freedom and in Oneness.

My intention is to assist you to empty your mind of old misconceptions and thought forms. As you experience your mind emptying, your physical body will experience the release of these old programs, belief systems, and concepts. As this happens, you start healing and become one with the source or highest intelligence of the I Am.

Your bodies and Cells are a part of a larger collective mind of Creation. As you continue to empty your mind from all preconceived beliefs and perceptions, it starts unthreading the collective mindset from their old beliefs, programs, and patterns. As your physical bodies become whole and unplugged, so does the collective body. Your body is a collective program that threads through all consciousness or unconsciousness, through all dimensions, through all being and beingness, and back to Me. These programs are My thoughts and feelings, which have expressed themselves in form as you.

As I said, your agreement or part of this program that experiences itself as a play or great production is to act out all of these thought forms, or stagnant thought forms, so they can release themselves and you can reconnect to My highest thought and energy beyond duality or separation. Remember you are from the future, rethreading the past collectively. All you see on your planet and elsewhere are aspects of yourself, for you are All That Is.

Look at all the Beings on your planet. There are many forms or beliefs. These beliefs have brought many together from what could be called a past experience. Everything on your planet has a frame of reference or a beginning experience some place else. All of you are acting out, or playing, this beginning experience out in the fullest on the Earth. As I said, the Earth is a holographic projection of all beginning experiences that need to be mastered or extended into the fullest for you to be able to understand the larger consciousness, perception, or picture.

You have agreed to come to the Earth and extend all beliefs, stretch them to the fullest, so they can expand beyond a right or wrong duality perception. You have agreed to expand energetically beyond a time frame experience. Your higher self has agreed to guide you out of duality or separation and back to Me in My highest form, back to Our one heart and Soul consciousness of love, back into your Over Soul Matrix of Creation, and into Oneness of all Creation.

"Love will set you free and allow you to come home again inside of yourself. Love is! Love is your creation, your salvation, and your freedom. Love is your agreement in this lifetime!"

10

LOVE AND REINCARNATION

Love

Love is all there is. Your whole agreement on the Earth now is to return to love. Love is beyond understanding. It is beyond perception. If you perceive love, you are still trying to understand love. You bring relationships, people, places, things and agreements to you in this lifetime that mirror back your old perceptions of what love is from other references or what you call lifetimes. These old agreements bring to you many patterns that you were stuck in, from old perceptions. These agreements mirror back to you these old patterns energetically.

In your life, you may bring someone to you in a relationship to whom you feel very strongly connected, calling them your Soulmate or twin flame. When you come together, your patterns connect energetically and start vibrating in the same frequency. You truly feel like you have come home, that you are in a flow or dance with this person. At first you experience this as a feeling of being nurtured or of being fed.

Your energy or frequency patterns have called this person to you because your patterns are harmonizing in the same song or story. In the beginning of the relationship, you vibrate or resonate with the Being or Partner who you bring to you because of the likeness of your Souls' Song sound frequency. When this happens, you feel a great compatibility or companionship. Your body feels safe because it feels like it is being heard. Finally, someone has come to you who knows your song. At first, there is great joy of being recognized, and of not feeling alone any longer.

After you resonate with this Being or partner in this sound-frequency, your two sounds together become even stronger, creating a combustion which penetrates the old hurt or frozen emotions that are actually holding the sound-frequency intact. As the frozen emotions connected to these sounds are activated, they start unraveling and the old perceptions resurface. These old feelings of hurt, fear, abandonment, fear of love, fear of being feminine, fear of being hurt in love or fear of the feminine hurting you feel very real.

All of these old patterns start resurfacing so that you can experience, heal, and release all fear of love. All of your lessons or agreements in this lifetime are to bring you back to self-love, not your perception of love, but back to the heart of love. Your whole lifetime now is to bring you and Me back together as one in harmony.

After a while, your song starts feeling worn-out. You vibrate in it over and over, and it starts affecting your nervous system. This would be like playing a song over and over all day and all night long. After a while, you would feel like screaming, "Turn that song off. I can't stand it! It's driving me nuts!" What this song is doing energetically is activating old patterns or feelings in your electrical systems and physical bodies. As this music activates what is underneath the song's vibration or frequency, the conflict with your partner begins.

It begins because underneath are your old perceptions of what love is. These perceptions have formed belief systems or patterns that wrap themselves in and around your etheric bodies and thread through all of your bodies. This connects you to the collective pattern or belief formed from these beginning perceptions. As your patterns connect with each other, you get stuck in a power struggle of right or wrong. This power struggle is fear-based and keeps you stuck in the Ego pattern of fear.

I know I am repeating myself. It is because I want you

to hear and know and believe that everything else in your life, every relationship, whether in person form or experience in pattern form is to assist you to awaken to what love is, not your perception of what you think love to be. You bring relationships to you to assist yourself to heal and release old perceptions or belief systems handed down to you through what you may call time and what I call experienced perceptions. These relationships mirror back to you the hurt, pain, and suffering that you agreed to go through in past incarnations or perceptions. All relationships are by agreement to mirror back to you these old patterns that have kept you stuck in old fear perceptions.

As I said before, this is the lifetime that you have agreed to come full circle, out of any belief or perception that holds you back from experiencing, knowing and becoming the beingness of love. As the Souls'/Cells' agreement is to find and release these old beliefs, the Ego's pattern or agreement is to keep you stuck in this old fear structure. Remember, All of what is not Love is fear.

You could also say that this is the Christ-heart's agreement and the Ego/Lucifer's agreement. They have come down together to hold both frequencies, love and fear, for you and the planet to feel both frequencies, so that you can choose to come out of duality individually and collectively. In actuality, there is no individuality for you/We are all one collectively. You have agreed in this lifetime to remember this and to come back together with your brothers and sisters beyond all beliefs and perceptions of love.

As you come back together in your Soul Group's song, you will be able to laugh at your own process. There will be no need to take yourself so seriously. Through the Ascension process you are raising your vibrational frequency beyond judgment. We are constantly with you. You are not alone in this great Souls' awakening. We are each other. There is only honor for you and your willingness to be on the Earth plane at this time.

Every single relationship in this lifetime you have been in before. No one has done or is doing to you anything that you have not signed up for and agreed to do or go through. Every player or person you are with now, you have been with before. As we are nearing the end times karmically, Beings have been standing in line in Spirit to sign up for these great lessons. Their intention is to reincarnate on to the Earth plane, so that they can free their Souls or Cells from old paradigms or structures.

This is why you see so many people on your planet now. As you look at the shape of your world and the great duality, and even fear for your planet's survival, many of you wonder why people would want to have children and bring them into this, or why Souls would want to come to this planet. It is because this is the greatest time ever on your planet Earth. It is a time of great completion, a time when Souls have the opportunity to totally come out of all karmic agreements. Souls get to become free to love and to hold love and light for the other Souls who are still vibrating in fear, giving them the gifts of remembering that they are love.

Your population is so great on your world now because it is the end times karmically for you and your planet. Souls want to be on the Earth to finish out any of their Souls' agreements, to learn and release lessons of duality. The only way one can understand and come out of duality is to have a body.

The Earth plane has been an existence of linear time. In linear time, you can only think or perceive in a time frequency or experience. Karmic lessons or learning lessons are in a time paradigm. When you are Spirit beyond time, you have the larger picture, for there is no past, present or future. In the larger picture, you understand all and see the lessons clearly. You understand how one could get caught up in the lesson, but you don't have the experience or ability to move beyond the old perception. Many Beings in Spirit who are waiting to reincarnate still have some old emotions connected to patterns or experiences. Because all vibrate in the larger Knowingness, there is no way to release the old emotions of Me, unless they/you lower your vibration and move back into a body or time frequency or a separation from the higher knowledge or understanding. When you do this, you move into a lower thought frequency or sound vibration. Until you release the pattern or frequency, your cells cannot expand beyond time into who they really are. As your cells vibrate in the old frequency of Me, before I expanded, the old emotions once again surface.

It would be very difficult for the old emotions to surface if you did not have someone of the same vibration and frequency or song to mirror them back to you. That is why you chose, before you came to the Earth, your perfect parents, partners, and relationships to assist you in feeling these old beliefs or perceptions.

Judgment toward self and others comes from a lower time frequency sequence. As you connect to higher understanding, you will experience that there is no judgment, only love for you and your willingness to assist the evolution of consciousness.

Because we are one, you will feel our great love and appreciation for you. How could We not love you when you were created by Us and are Us.

The more you move into Our love of you and for you, the more you experience self-love. The more you experience self-love, the easier it is for your planet's Ascension and enlightenment. When you move into the place of self-love, you experience all as love, even what in the past, you may have judged or condemned. All is love and is in its perfection.

As you see and experience all as love, the karmic fear frequency starts breaking up and dissipating. Love is the highest vibration and essence. There is no energy field that can come up against it or hold any vibration against it.

The power of love can lift mountains, mountains being karmic turbulence. Nothing that is fear-based can continue to exist in love. The love essence or frequency will break loose and dissipate all fear-based illusions.

Love will set you free and allow you to come home again inside of yourself. Love is! Love is your creation, your salvation, and your freedom. Love is your agreement in this lifetime!

I hear Souls ask, what is my purpose in this lifetime? What is my mission? I can feel that I am on the Earth for a reason. What is it?

I say to you, your whole purpose on the Earth at this time is to experience unconditional self-love. Love is it. Whatever the question, love is the answer.

When you move into the vibration and consciousness of love, that is all you will see' that is all you will experience. You will constantly mirror back to others their love and magnificence.

When your love mirror vibrates into a fellow Soul traveler, their old guards and walls start breaking up and dissipating. They start remembering who they are. Old prejudices, hatreds, belief systems, and fears start loosing their power. As the structure of the old dis-ease breaks loose, it starts unraveling from the collective pattern. The collective fear-based pattern loses its grip. This has a domino effect. As the Cell or Soul breaks loose from the collective pattern, this newfound experience of self-love connects to the collective love frequency and sends this power of love energy into the collective pattern.

As you Souls/Cells love yourselves, you break a link in the fear pattern. From this broken chain, or missing link, the collective frequency of love can be downloaded into you and into the pattern.

Reincarnation and the Akashic Records

There is an actual computer system that you sit in front of to look at your Akashic Records, or programs of every lifetime you have ever gone through. These records are also in your DNA and subconscious mind. Any experience your Soul has ever gone through, every feeling, emotion, thought, perception and understanding is in your Akashic Records.

As you decide to come to the Earth again, to play out and expand your Soul's growth and consciousness, you sit at the computer with your Soul's Master guide. This Master guide has been with you ever since you split, or perceived to be separate, from the collective of Me. This guide sits with you, and together you go through your records and decide the lessons you need to learn, or maybe, past lessons you have gone through and got stuck in. Perhaps you lived on the Earth at a time when the consciousness was not high enough on the planet to bring you out of the lesson. As you look at the lessons and agreements of the lifetime you are reincarnating into, and all aspects of the lessons, you decide what is needed to clear or free yourself and others karmically.

Maybe in one lifetime, you were very much into a church structure that had judgments and control of the feminine. Perhaps there was a woman who had a child out of wedlock or was pregnant and not married, and you, coming from a judgmental mind-set, judged her to shame, and condemned her because you did not understand how a fearing woman of God could allow this to happen. You would then agree to go to the Earth and experience the other side of the situation. You may choose to be a woman who ended up pregnant from a relationship with a man whom she thought loved her. She would become intimate with him, become pregnant, and he would leave for some reason. The woman who was you would then get to experience the fear, hatred, and condemning of you. You would choose to have the experience of going through the feelings and emotions of the pregnant woman in the other lifetime.

Your Soul's purpose or journey is to experience all that a Soul or Being could perceive or understand. When you have all of these experiences, you will no longer judge someone else. Your Cell/Soul will have expanded beyond the karmic lesson structure.

When you sit with your Soul's Master guide and decide what program or play to experience, you will look at the knowledge your Soul lacks before it can become a complete balanced enlightened Being. You will look at the players or persons who you have been with before, that you have gone through one side of the lesson with, and what is needed for you to experience the other side. You will put yourself into position to go through the experience with them. You will pick the exact date and time that your Soul will reincarnate.

144

You will pick the exact parents that you need to download their unhealed patterns into you. When you are in your mother's womb and first born is when the beginning patterns that will structure your whole lifetime are activated. These beginning patterns will be the lessons in this lifetime, connected to patterns in all other lifetimes, that you have agreed to experience, heal and free yourself and others from.

When you are born, your cells have already been downloaded with the patterns or your list of chosen lessons. After entering a body, you then recreate this pattern over and over again until you realize it no longer feels good or it holds you back from love. It is then that you start looking for a way to heal, release and free yourself and others out of the agreed upon lessons.

There is no such thing as a failure in this experience. If you don't quite understand, or the lesson goes through many lifetimes, you will then re-thread back to the beginning agreement of the perception. It is then that you can truly heal. Until then you may take detours. In these detours, you will learn and grow much and from this growth and awareness, an understanding and expansion takes place. You then move back onto the main road again. You may hit another emotional glitch in the road. The glitch re-connects you or threads you back into another beginning perception. As you go through this emotional barricade, blockage, relive it, feel it and experience it out, you are able to get back on the main road again.

These detours are great learning experiences. There is no such thing as a failure of the lesson. Maybe the lesson threads so far back that it takes more time to move through it emotionally.

After you decide your lifetime and all of its glorious lessons, your Master guide will download these lessons, or imprint them into your etheric body, which is the energy body of your Soul. These imprints are then downloaded into your Soul's matrix, which is connected to the Akashic Records. When the time is right and your chosen parents have conceived you, you are already imprinted into their Souls' matrix. When the conception occurs, you are then immediately connected. You then ride through every

145

feeling, emotion, and experience your parents are going through. They begin imprinting who they are cellularly into you. They are downloading into your cells your foundation of your new lifetime.

As you continue to grow in the womb and form into a body, the beginning computerized agreement that is downloaded into your matrix continues to expand through your body and into your etheric or energy body. When you have these patterns formed in your etheric body, they start vibrating with your pattern energy or sound frequency perception. If your parents' sound frequencies are different from your Soul's sound frequency, the experience of a great separation begins, and a feeling of being different, of not being wanted, loved, or accepted, becomes your perception.

After the Soul/Cell chooses the parents that it will receive its foundation or lessons from in this lifetime, it downloads the lessons into the Akashic Records before entering the body. As this happens, the future record of this incarnation is imprinted into the subconscious mind. The subconscious mind is the Soul's mind, which imprints every experience the Soul has ever gone through into the cellular structure of the body. Once it is imprinted into the Soul's mind, it plays itself out, for there is no past, present or future, no time. In Spirit, the Soul that is you has already played the agreement out. That is why, when you enter the body, the agreement or the patterns feel so strong.

Because these agreements or patterns have already played themselves out or expanded beyond what you call time, they thread back into the Oneness, reconnecting you with all Cells or Souls again. As you reconnect or blend back into all Cells or Souls that are you, you move beyond the pattern and expand into all consciousness of love. When you move out of this collective consciousness that vibrates beyond time and back into the body, you lower your vibration or frequency into linear time. As you do this, you bring only a small portion of your consciousness that is awakened with you because the Earth's vibration has not been high enough to hold the frequencies of this highest aspect of yourself.

Moving into a body, when this experience or agreement has already expanded itself beyond time, is difficult because you have already played the experience or agreement out, expanded yourself into the collective consciousness, and yet you cannot bring this higher understanding into the physical body with you. The understanding is with you, but you cannot remember it until you work through the Soul's contract of what it is you need to learn or complete. As you start understanding the lessons and heal from them, you come out of linear time and reconnect with the higher aspects of you that already have a great understanding of love. *All is love; the rest is the journey your Soul has agreed to go through to bring you back to love.* You could say that you must forget to remember your true magnificence of Me, which is you.

When you enter the body with this new contract and have already expanded the contract into the collective consciousness of yourself, you bring that collective memory with you. You may not remember it, but you are already threaded into it. Now on the Earth, many are starting to awaken and remember that they/ you are one another. As you start healing, you wonder why, if you have gone through this lesson over and over, why it keeps appearing again or repeating itself. It is because it is threaded into the collective energy of the lessons or pattern and the light of what could be called the future is penetrating the emotions. As you are moving into a higher vibration or future consciousness, you will continue to expand into that part of your collective thought that has already understood the lesson. Eventually, you move beyond linear thinking and blend into the Oneness, which has expanded beyond the emotional vibration. As this happens and you have the lesson learned, your experience will be one of the all knowing of love.

As I said, when you come back to the Earth, this lesson has already played itself out in other dimensions, beyond the emotion. On the Earth, you must lower your vibration to be able to reconnect to all aspects of yourself in other Souls, who have agreed to mirror to you the song of the victim or hurt emotion

147

of the pattern. As you have already gotten the lesson in the higher dimensional understanding, you bring with you the light or self-realized consciousness. This creates what you could call duality or separation within yourself. What it truly is, is the unhealed emotional part of you that is connected to the collective emotional pattern, which becomes the Ego starts warring against the enlightened part of yourself. The part of you that has already expanded beyond time understands the lesson and holds the light for the karmic part of you to awaken. It creates great conflict within you. You are at war against yourself because all is you.

Because all is you and you are moving into the collective emotional patterns, it becomes very easy to blame others for what needs to be loved within yourself. Anything that needs to be healed or understood is you, and the only way it can grow is through love. That love begins within your self. You cannot truly love another until you love yourself. As you continue to move through your emotions, you will bring others into your life so you can experience their love and your love for them. This will mirror back to you the loving part of self.

As I was expressing to you, the difficult part of taking on a body on the Earth plane, to love yourself, is that you have already moved through the collective consciousness in higher dimensions. When you come into the body and are carrying out the karmic or emotional lesson for one another, the light-awakened aspects of self shine the love on the lessons that need to be learned. The emotional body starts feeling very uncomfortable. Many times, it feels guilty, ashamed, afraid, and abandoned and has a sense of failure because it feels like it has regressed and is being judged or punished by God, by Me. In reality, it feels a sense of failure because it is being mirrored by the aspects of itself that are already an enlightened consciousness, and it feels that it is less than equal.

This is always the scenario; the light aspects of the lessons that are at one with Me beyond duality mirror this consciousness part back to the part which has agreed to experience the emotions. The emotional self is then in conflict with the enlightened self.

The only way the emotional self could truly heal or experience love is for love to mirror itself into the pattern to break it up or dissipate it. Since all is Me and I am you, the only conflict or belief of separation is within yourself.

The way to bring both aspects together as one is to always look within the self. When a conflict of any kind occurs, you know it is a conflict within yourself, between your emotional Ego self and your enlightened self. Because you are each other, the great Beings in your life who bring you the lessons, which you agreed to transmute into the light consciousness are aspects of yourself mirroring to you, yourself. As you judge others or condemn them, you are judging yourself and condemning yourself.

I ask for you to look at these aspects of yourself that may be playing themselves out in another Soul's body and see what it is that they want to teach you or show you. It is always self-love. To get there, you need to go through what is not love, the emotional fear aspects of self, to return to love. All that you cannot love are fear aspects of yourself, which have agreed to be in your life, to bring you back to love. Remember, you chose your whole lifetime: the stories you agreed to play out and every actor or actress in the play. As you really understand this, you will look at these other players with great love and appreciation, for they are the greatest teacher aspects of yourself.

Look at all Beings on your planet and know that they are you and love them. Love them. Love them. Love is the greatest healer. It heals all wounds and sets you free to come home again within yourself, within Me.

All in life is a reflection of you, and I say to you, all is you. All the Shadow aspects playing themselves out collectively on your planet are aspects of you. If you send them anger, hatred, and judgment, do you not know you are aligning or realigning yourself to assist the Shadow? You are reinforcing their structure. You are giving them not only your power but reinforcing theirs, because you are them. Again, it is you at war against yourself. If you hold love and light for them and see them in their perfection, see them in what you want for yourself and your world, you will be holding the

149

love and light for them to rethread back into their highest memory of self, which is love and light. This also reinforces you, with Me in the highest. You then hold the light for the consciousness to come out of duality or separation. Remember, the consciousness of this earthly duality play is already self-realized beyond time. As you connect to these higher aspects of self, beyond time, you assist the whole consciousness of your planet to expand into its own perfection or enlightenment. You move beyond judgment and into the Isness of Me. That is your agreement in this lifetime: to move through duality, connect with like consciousness and move all aspects of self back into the highest expression, which is love.

When you see an aspect of yourself in another Soul's body that you have difficulty with, cannot accept or love, ask yourself, "What is it inside of me that this Being wants to teach me?" Look inside and love that aspect of yourself. You may not understand the lesson at first, but as you continue to ask, it will be revealed.

Through the veils of the pattern being lifted, you will then be able to experience very clearly the old aspects of your emotions that need to be loved, and the aspects that have felt separate or separated from the collective love.

When you are willing to see all as you, a great healing starts taking place. All is you, not just the Shadow or hurt, but also the love and magnificence. You would not admire or feel great love and respect for another if you did not have those aspects within yourself. No one can tell you a feeling or emotion. You must have the experience to understand. Within self are all great experiences. Remember, you have played every role that one could ever agree to experience, and now you have agreed to come out of all roles into the highest memory of self, which is Me and back into the heart, Soul, and arms of love.

It is most important to set your intention for what you want for yourself, others, and for the world. All is energy, and you are powerful, Creator Beings, because you are All That Is. As you set your intent in the highest, you start unraveling the veils of illusions. You may actually feel them unthreading from

150

your etheric body. Everything is energy. These energy patterns are a collective karmic cording energy. As you set your intention to vibrate in the highest sound and frequency, your cells will follow this command, because your cells are Me. When you ask for my guidance and assistance, you are asking a higher aspect of yourself, because we are one.

As you set your intention to be free and to vibrate in love and see all as love, what is not love will start falling by the wayside. As this happens, you will release the emotions that are being held by a fear frequency sound vibration. As the sound vibration is broken, all of the emotions being held together by this frequency will start breaking loose. When this happens, it is most important to allow these old emotions to surface. Allow yourself to feel them, for they have been your old realities, your old stories, or security blankets for many lifetimes and experiences. Let them come up, surrender into them, feel them, break them loose, cry, yell, and scream. These emotions are very alive, and they have strong roots in the collective consciousness of the pattern. Break them loose. Allow them to express themselves out. They need a voice to experience or express themselves through. They need to be heard. As you allow this to happen, it is like a balloon bursting. The balloon bursts, and all of the old poisonous thoughts, sicknesses, and dis-eases connected to the patterns release themselves. The best way out is to always move through the patterns. If you do not go in and break these old patterns up, they control you and hold you back from what you want most in life, which is love. Everything you do in life leads you back to your Soul's greatest purpose and desire - LOVE.

When you surrender into these patterns, feel them, and break them up, they will dissipate. You will then feel a great relief and peace because you have broken an emotional sound barrier, freeing you into a higher frequency. Remember, like attracts like. You bring the same pattern to you over and over again until you decide this doesn't feel good any longer. When the emotional pain becomes too unbearable, set a new intention, or ask to be shown how to do it differently.

When you break the sound barrier to these old patterns, you create a new song or sound, a higher, more joyful one. You will then bring back into your life a mirror of the higher, lighter frequency, in all aspects of your life. You must go through these old karmic emotions, because they are what you came into this lifetime to heal and love. If you don't go through them, how can you heal or love those aspects of yourself? When you can love these aspects of yourself that have held you back from love, you will be able to love all others that are you, that also carry the same pattern or sound vibrations as the ones you just released.

You always create your own reality. You mapped out your lifetime and all the experiences you wanted to learn and chose all the great players that you have brought into your life. How can you judge someone else when you asked for them to be a part of your life? You judge them for not being the way your perception wants them to be. In reality, you chose them to come into your life because you knew they would be your greatest teachers. You are blaming them for teaching you what you asked them to teach you.

Remember, to love yourself totally, you must love all that is you. Instead of blaming, remember to ask; "What is it inside of me that I brought this great teacher here to show me?" When you ask, you will receive, maybe not at that exact moment, because you still have emotions to unravel to be able to get to the place of love and acceptance. Go through the emotions. As you do, you will understand the message or lesson. See all as you, as great messengers of love and light who have come as your greatest teachers to assist you back home into love, collectively.

Unconditional Love

You are coming home. This is what we have all waited for since the beginning times of fragmenting ourselves or splitting our cellular structures, so that we, Sophia and I, could learn from your continued growth. As We use the word "fragment," it is because, in the beginning, We felt such a loss of you. We felt like We were sending Our children, who were Us, into a journey

152

of the unknown. As you continued to grow in consciousness, we became stronger in Our consciousness and understanding. We could then expand further into you, which is Us.

It is the same as parents, or what you could call immigrant parents, going to a new country. They work hard to educate their children so the children will have a good foundation for themselves and future generations. This is Our experience with you. Your education has been to experience and heal all of the karmic lessons in all your lifetimes. You choose to learn who you are through feelings and emotions and to understand the consciousness that you have gone through, to awaken our highest knowing into you and you back to Oneness with Us.

As you have grown through feeling and emotion, We have also grown and expanded, because We are you. You are the conscious aspects of Us that want to experience All That Is. You have had a hunger for this knowledge and the desire to share with Us what you have learned and remembered. Every time this happens, you expand Our consciousness because you are collective aspects of Us, awakening into total self-realization.

What you receive from Us is Our total love and appreciation for you. You come to understand with Us that all you have gone through are experiences of awakening consciousness. Whether you understand the course or not is up to how much you allow yourself to go into your emotions or your veils of illusions. As you allow yourself to surrender into the emotion of the chosen course, you feel closer to Us/God because at the core of your being or existence, We are each other. There is no such thing as a lifetime that was a failure. All your experiences were meant to be to bring you into a higher understanding of who you are. You go through all the veils of illusion and in doing so, find yourself again. That self is a great magnificent Creator Being. As I created all that is you, when you realign your Cells/Souls with Me beyond time or duality, you are also the highest source of your own creation, for you are Me in the highest.

You are always the source of your own creations. If you are in fear energy, you will create many forms of reality to mirror that back to you. If you are in the victim role and angry with Me, being the Creator Being that you are, you will bring many players in the collective consciousness to mirror the victim back to you. As this happens, you will constantly set this scenario over and over again until you are tired of playing the victim. You will then find ways to come out of that role and create another role or play for yourself. With each role or play that you are in, you will always find your chosen support team on the Earth, which will cheer you on in your role. When you are tired of the role and no longer get energy from it, or perhaps your support team or audience is leaving, you will find another role to play, once again bringing your like vibrational team to you because they are you in the same play.

As you cycle through all of your Soul's growth patterns, your classes become easier for you. You go through a graduation into another realm of consciousness. As you move into this higher understanding, you continue to bring to you like consciousness, other light Creator Beings who support your growth and graduation.

You will hold this new frequency of sound and color and draw the same vibration back to harmonize with you. As you harmonize with one another in a higher frequency, this new sound continues to break the barrier to old frozen fear lifetimes or misalignments.

As you move through this frozen energy, you start connecting to higher aspects of yourself in all dimensions. As your light becomes stronger, it activates old hidden or frozen aspects of yourself that were left behind or stuck in other plays or lifetimes in other dimensions. If you have a strong enough connection with Me as your source, you can send this light and love of us into these trapped frequencies, break them up and bring these fragmented aspects of you back into you. This is a continual cycle, for you are Me. As you retrieve fragmented aspects you spiral closer to Me. On the Earth, this is called soul retrieval.

If you do not have an understanding of Soul retrieval or know how this process is accomplished, there are many healers, teachers, and Masters on the Earth Plane who are quite

154

experienced in this technique. As you bring back all missing aspects of your light, you feel more complete within yourself, which expands your light into other aspects of yourself, moving you into wholeness. It is most important in this process to release your light from the frozen energy. As this happens, it dissipates your karmic attachment to what you believe is a failed lesson. I know I am repeating myself, but I want you to know and believe that there is no such thing as failure, only a transformation of not knowing into Knowingness. You hear much spoken of the Knowingness. As you start moving beyond these lessons, you move into the Knowingness, beyond what you could call karma or time frequencies.

You are coming out of the separation between the male and female, of the heart and Ego, the light and Shadow. You are experiencing the Ego's structure. It has a lot of help, for the Ego mind threads through all existence and back to Me, its creator.

As you are Me and great Creator Beings, you have the opportunity to assist Me to tame the collective Ego through love. Love is the foundation for All That Is. As you continually love and appreciate the Ego and its role in your life, it loses its power and surrenders or transforms itself into the light consciousness of self-realization. I love you and thank you for continuing to cycle through your old warrior ways collectively to assist the consciousness home.

As you move beyond deception, you will experience within yourself a freedom beyond one's own imagination. When you move beyond the frequencies that bind you in old karmic beliefs, you will be like the wind, free and very powerful. You will awaken within your Co-Creator frequencies and will be totally supported in your Soul's purpose in the highest Knowingness.

Because your assignment in this lifetime is to remember the great Creator Beings that you are, you will have the opportunity in this incarnation to experience your great creativity over and over. Together, we will be creating great changes, not just in your world but also through all worlds, because you are Me and you exist in all consciousness. As you move yourself beyond duality, you start moving all consciousness beyond duality, because you are all consciousness. That is great power.

You have always had great power. In past incarnations, when you were vibrating in a fear frequency, you also had great power. In the like attracts like frequency, you aligned yourself with this collective energy and assisted the consciousness to feel the illusion of separation from one another. In reality, there is no separation because all is one. There are only perceptions of separation through your Soul's journey or perceptions of reality. These are the lessons that your Soul agreed to go through to share with the collective consciousness. As you and others continue to go through, and have already gone through, all of these lessons, or plays, or reality checks, and you blend together as one, you will not have judgment toward anyone or thing, for you also have had the same experience and are on the other side of it. You have chosen this lifetime to understand and experience the other side of the lesson. If you were the perpetrator, you get to be the victim. If you were a nun, you get to be a prostitute. If you were a robber, you get to be the judge. When you have had every experience one Soul could possibly have, you will not have judgment towards others. You will have great caring and compassion.

What you will experience inside yourself is peace. When you truly understand that you agreed to go through these lifetimes, the veils of illusion will be lifted. When you came into this lifetime and other incarnations, you came in with amnesia. You couldn't remember much of your Soul's other experiences. You needed to forget to remember. If you remembered, you would not understand the lesson emotionally. It is only through feelings that you truly understand an experience. Someone can tell you an experience, but if you have not gone through it yourself, you truly do not know. You can, from your mind, try to intellectualize it through similar experiences, but you will not truly understand until it becomes your total reality. You agree to immerse yourself into an experience to be able to understand another Creator Being's perspective. There are only perceptions based on your life's experience. When you go through all experiences that a

Soul can travel through, there are no more perceptions based on experiences; there is only love.

When you see other Soul travelers who are going through similar experiences as your own, you will honor them, for you will remember how difficult it was for you. Just as you came out of this agreement, they will have the choice to do the same. As you shine your unconditional love on these travelers, they will feel safe to go into the emotions of guilt, anger, fear, the perception of abandonment by Me, frustration and, finally, forgiveness of themselves and others. Through forgiveness comes peace and allowance for others to move beyond their agreements. As you totally move out of your victim consciousness, it allows all Souls who are in your play to let go and remember who they are, which is love. It allows all to come home inside of themselves. This is enlightenment: Lightening up, becoming free, moving beyond duality, and experiencing everyone as the highest aspect of Me, of love unconditionally.

There is much talk on your planet about unconditional love. You cannot love unconditionally if you still have judgment or blame towards any other Souls/Cells of yourselves. As you move beyond judgment, you move beyond time and see others' magnificence as yours. As you go through every experience a Soul could travel through and you release any emotional attachment, you move beyond blame or confusion and blend with all cellular structures in total love and Isness.

"Allow yourself to be in the flow, for you are emerging into a beautiful butterfly with My wings of freedom."

11

THE SEASONS OF CREATION

Your life and body are like the seasons. None are bad or right or wrong. Life is a continual cycle.

Death and rebirth are your soul's cycle, as it is the body's. On your Souls' journey, you will continue through many experiences. Sometimes your season is one of spring, where much energy, bursts forth with a new confidence, a new beginning. You experience this as birth. Springtime is a rebirth or rejuvenation of your consciousness. Summertime is a time of light, awareness and letting go. Autumn is a time of remembering, of gratitude, giving thanks and forgiveness, and of assimilating all of the years' experiences. Winter is a time of deep reflection; a season of introspection, to go within yourself to truly experience who you are and an opportunity for great change and setting intentions.

Winter

In the winter of your life, you are in a reflection cycle. You have the opportunity for deep reflections, to experience who you are, what you want in your life and what is important to you.

Many times you feel that nothing in your life is working, that you are not going forward. This is because you have hit a plateau, and nothing is moving; all seems still or feels frozen. As this happens, you have the opportunity to sort out and release old feelings and emotions. You must go through these seasons to let go, rebuild, to go forward and feel the success of your spiritual growth. As you let the light shine into your Souls' awakening, you will move further into your Souls' purpose. Just as the seasons on Earth change and recycle, so do you, for you are all the Cells and seasons of the Earth.

The winter season of your life is very important. It is when the greatest changes can take place, if you allow it. As all of what you believe or perceive is stripped down or away, you actually have a stronger connection with Me, which is you. As you sort out old beliefs of what you call past and set new intentions, great growth takes place. Winter is a time of setting the intention for a new foundation. All is still, and you can start to see more clearly. Sometimes you don't want to see more clearly, because as this happens, all of the old frozen emotions that have been dormant start resurfacing. All that you have kept hidden or put bandages on to survive want to be heard. It is most important to listen to and feel what these old emotions want to tell you. These old emotions are connected to old belief systems, karmic lessons, patterns, agreements and experiences.

You cannot grow unless you hit this plateau so that these old agreements can surface emotionally. As you allow yourself to go into the emotions, honor them, support them, give them a voice and allow them to tell their story; they will start unraveling and releasing. From this release, you will feel great freedom, peace, and a stronger sense of enthusiasm, and purpose. You will have the strength to go forward again. As you go through this release, your vibration becomes higher. When your frequency and sound vibration are higher, you are ready for the next step or season.

If you see the winter season as a gift, you will be able to free yourself from old karmic lessons or bondage. You will feel lighter and freer. Every time you release who you are not, you have more room within to experience who you are, and to expand your light into self-love.

In the winter of your life, you go through a rejuvenation or cleansing. As you release the past, old thought forms, emotions and clutter, you have more room to experience yourself in the moment, which opens the door for you to be able to co-create your future from a higher consciousness of yourself. You and I then have a stronger connection as one, and you feel it is much easier to receive the instructions through intuition and Knowingness for the next step of your Souls' journey.

The only way to recreate what you perceive as future is by being totally in the moment. The place for change is in the now or the present moment of your life. You must still your mind, so you can reconnect to your divinity or divine purpose, which is love. To change your future, you must be in the now, to go deep within your Self and into your emotions of what you perceive as the past. As you release the past in the now, and your perception of life changes, you change your future. This frees you to become one with your higher consciousness, which is the I Am of All That Is. As you move beyond karmic emotions, you will feel and receive divine guidance for your Souls' highest purpose.

Springtime

After your new foundation is built from your winter cleansing, you move into springtime. Springtime is a time of rebuilding, of action. You now have your new foundation. Your vibration is higher and you get to rebirth all of your new ideas or perceptions. As you are reconnected to your highest guidance and understanding, the birth of your new ideas will come from you, the Master of your intentions. As you continue to move through your life and Souls' journey, you will understand and appreciate that you must have all of the cycles.

Springtime is a time of new beginnings of joy, happiness, light, and freedom. If you look at nature, you will see that after wintertime, the trees have stronger roots, flowers are blooming, and there is so much life force bursting forth. Birds are singing again. A great awakening or a birth of a new consciousness is taking place. Because you have all of nature's elements within you, and your bodies are aligned with the seasons, you will also feel the joy, happiness, new hope, and birth of this season.

When you allow yourself to go into the winter of your life,

or the old emotional patterns and release them, you will resonate with spring. You will feel it in every cell of your body. This is a time on your Earth when many of your great Souls decide to fast and cleanse out the old. You diet and want to get yourself in shape. It is all done in hope of a new beginning. The springtime or new beginning is much easier if you allow yourself to purge in the winter. You emerge much stronger, more aware, more confident, and self-assured to pursue the next step of your Souls' grand journey. You are rejuvenated and have much room for the new, for new ideas to spring into your consciousness. You have the energy to rebirth the new and expanded more conscious you.

Summer

Summertime is a time of light and awareness. You have given birth to your new ideas and consciousness. You are vibrating in your Souls' higher, sound-color vibration. From this higher place, you will continue to draw back to you like consciousness. The sun is shining, and within you, your great inner light connects to the vibration of the sun's vibration.

Summertime and the living is easy. Summertime is a time of joy, of coming together with others to celebrate life. It is a time when you are taking vacations. You travel to see relatives, friends, and many of you go to other places and cultures for a new experience. Every time you do this, you grow. As you come together with others, you choose what you want, what you like, and what kind of fun appeals to you. Many times you decide that what you enjoyed in the past is no longer for you, or you feel that people you enjoyed before, you no longer have anything in common with. These people are not wrong, as you are not wrong. You have grown, and your vibration is different. You no longer have the same vibration or sound-color frequency exchange with these people. Many times, it means you have completed what you agreed to go through with these Beings karmically. As you move out of these relationships, you make room for new relationships and new experiences in your life.

In actuality, they are not new. Nothing is new for you in this lifetime. All who you meet and experience, you have been with and have experienced before. You are here to complete with one another in love. You have a desire to travel to different places and see different things because your Soul wants to reconnect and complete in love. Perhaps you had a great lifetime in that place and you are returning to re-activate the light, awareness, and the gifts that you used in that lifetime. If you have had difficulty in that place, you may go back to heal it and to retrieve the aspects of your Soul that you left behind.

Summertime is when the light within you has been activated so that you can see and experience all very clearly, not from old fear emotion but from the emotion of love, self-respect, and forgiveness. It is a season of allowing all to shine in its own perfection, of allowing all to move into the next step of its highest agreement, a time to allow all to vibrate in its own color-sound song.

Autumn

Autumn is a time of remembering, of contemplation, and of assimilating all of the year's experiences, not dwelling on all but taking time to slow down and give thanks for All That Is. It is truly a time of Thanksgiving. In autumn, it is most important to slow yourself down and reflect on all of the miracles of your life, the first being the miracle of birth, and to thank yourself for your willingness to, once again, take on a body and come to Earth to sort out all experiences through your own time cycle. It is a time to look at the growth that you, your Soul, has been willing to go through, to bring yourself back to the awakened or enlightened part of Me, which is you.

Thank yourself for being strong enough to journey through what you call time to assist the collective consciousness back into one love-light vibration. Thank all who are in your life for their strength and dedication to assist you to see and love yourself wholly; thank them for mirroring back to you all

162

aspects of yourself that you need to love and accept. Thank yourself for all the great healing, awakening, and self-awareness, which you are now experiencing and for all aspects of yourself and of your personality that are already in full manifestation or bloom of love.

Autumn is a time to love all, to thank all, to look at the year and see all of your perceptions of struggle, and to love them: to love all that is you. If you are willing to love all that is you, your fear illusion of what you perceive as not you will dissipate. All is you, and you are all. Love is the greatest healer. As you thank all lessons, and those people who taught or brought you the lessons, and you see the lessons as gifts that you have brought to yourself to assist you in your Souls' awakening, the old illusional emotions of fear will dissipate.

The autumn of your life is a time of peace, of winding down. It is a time to give thanks for everyone and everything so that all can heal and blend together in forgiveness. Your life is a journal, and every experience, lesson, feeling and emotion that you go through is documented in the Akashic Records, in your subconscious mind. If you are replaying an emotional lesson in this lifetime and don't move through the emotions, the subconscious goes into your "inner" Internet website, finds all other lifetimes or agreements with the same pattern or emotion, and realigns you with the collective pattern or emotion. This compounds your emotion, making it stronger.

Sometimes, one must go back to the frame of reference to find the source; is this a past life, this lifetime, or other experiences? When one finds the reference, one is then able to release it and bring the aspects of self back into you, who have been holding the door open for the emotion to be so activated. Again, this is called Soul retrieval. As you have had many lessons or lifetimes, you may have aspects of self left behind in the vibration or experience. As you release the frozen emotion and bring aspects of self that have been vibrating in old patterns into the now, you close the door to the lifetime or pattern. You will feel more solid and whole, more complete within yourself.

It may be that you have played this pattern or tape so many lifetimes that it is weak and worn out, but it keeps playing because you keep repeating the pattern energetically. As you voice the experience of the pattern over and over again, you give it power. As you continue to let others know the story, you are continuing to energize it with your life force. You give it energy and power. In actuality, the story is so worn-out that it wants to break loose, but it cannot because the story has become your identity or password to your Internet system. You have fear of giving up your password or identity because without it, you would not know who you are.

As you become aware and start giving thanks for the story you have been playing out for so long, the story starts dissipating. It no longer has any power. It unthreads itself from the collective story and frees you to remember who you are, which is a magnificent aspect of Me, playing itself out to the fullest expression, beyond duality, or fear. "Thank you" is a very powerful expression and energy source. It has a vibration that breaks the fear control frequency. This vibration connects to the highest consciousness of creation. The vibration of thank you goes back to My awakening with My Beloved Sophia. It reconnects to Me after My heart opened, and all I could feel was gratefulness. From this gratefulness, came My true experience of loving all of My creations of Me. I was able to love Myself totally. From that place, I was able to love you totally because I created you as Me.

One way to start breaking the old Ego/fear pattern is to give thanks for all that is, all that was, and all that will be. There is no past, present, or future. All experiences in your life have led to this time of self-expression of love.

When you continually see all lessons as gifts and thank them, you are then connecting to My highest energy of love and gratefulness. As you connect to this frequency and download it into the pattern or emotions, it starts breaking them up. This will free you into a grateful frequency.

Start giving thanks even when you don't feel or believe

that you have anything to be thankful for. Again, you will break the stuck energy, and soon you will start feeling grateful, your heart will start feeling more love and you will truly feel thankful. The simple words "thank you" plug into other Souls' love-light patterns and songs. They no longer feel judged or ashamed or feel that they need to protect themselves by being right. They feel seen, acknowledged, and validated by you. As you give thanks for everyone and everything, your energy starts breaking loose from the patterns, and you can then move into the feeling or true experience of forgiveness.

Many times, you try to forgive, but you are stuck in the emotions of anger, fear, injustice, control, and the victim Ego. You may still believe that you need to forgive someone else so you can be free. All is about freeing yourself. In the larger picture of creation, no one has ever done anything to you for which you need to forgive them. Remember, you agreed for them to teach you love and acceptance through the lessons of duality or karma.

Autumn is the time to look at everything in your life and to go over your whole life. Give thanks for the lessons, or memories, because they have given you the opportunity to grow or blossom into the fullness of your Being, which is love. It is important to be in the autumn of your life throughout every cycle. Give thanks, thanks, and more thanks! Your subconscious mind will pick up the song of gratefulness, go into your "inner-net" systems and find all experiences from all time frames of thankfulness, and the sound frequency will activate memories in your Cells of like energy.

Now on the Earth plane, you are in a continual death and rebirth cycle at all moments. You are constantly going through a rejuvenation on a cellular level. You are shedding old belief structures. This shedding is a death of the old karmic structure and a re-birth of your light crystalline structure. It seems to be a very difficult cycle for many, because you are moving beyond a time frequency, and your Cells are constantly awakening to higher aspects of self. As this happens, you are losing your old identity. You don't need to understand it all. Just give thanks for all of the

165

wonderful seasons in your life, and the process will become much easier.

You are in a rebirth cycle of a collective love beyond your conscious memory or understanding at this time. Allow yourself to be in the flow, for you are emerging into a beautiful butterfly with My wings of freedom. You are the seasons of Creation – you are Me, Creation.

I know that I repeat Myself much in this manuscript. This manuscript's highest intention is to assist every Cell in your body to remember and awaken into your Souls' song, to move out of the I me, and into the I AM. From this place you will move into your Over Souls' consciousness, into the Golden Ray of the Second Coming, and into Me, into the Co-Creator of your life, into your purpose and destiny, and into a new lifetime on the Earth plane without physically leaving the body.

The lifetime you are living now is not one to create more karma. It is a lifetime of completion. I am not saying that new difficult karma is not being created. There are many Souls on the Earth who are still so caught up in the frozen, winter, emotions collectively, that they were not able to experience the lessons and purge them to move on to the next phase or springtime of life, which is the time of re-creating. Some Souls picked very difficult lessons, and for now are still frozen emotionally in the experience. Instead of purging the old emotions, they act them out.

When you come to the Earth and lower your vibration, sometimes your website gets stuck from collective frozen emotion, or a glitch, or virus is sent to you. I will speak to you more about viruses later. When you are in a glitch, it is like an old record that is stuck and will not move forward. The groove is too thick. This is the same thing that happens to a Soul. Sometimes they come to the Earth and they get stuck in a groove because the collective emotions of the past control them. They become the emotions, instead of releasing them.

Your "inner" Internet system is truly a consciousness of the divine mind, or a higher mind of Me, which is you. You are the seasons of all Creation. Relax now; know that you already are All That Is. Allow yourself to flow through your agreed upon lessons. Give thanks for every season of your life, and you will find yourself opening many doors to the higher love and light of your Being. Remember, your seasonal emotions vibrate with the seasons of your planet. As you allow yourself to flow through the seasons within yourself, your higher vibration will start balancing out the erratic weather patterns that you are now experiencing on the Earth. And so it is!

"Your whole existence has been to bring you back to love."

12

FORGIVENESS

Sophia - Moving out of the Wounded Healer and into the Master

I am here with you now; this is Sophia. As your Father has explained, your being on the Earth now is what you have waited for from the beginning time of the illusion of separation.

You are now moving out of the wounded healer and into the Master through self-forgiveness. Forgiveness is one of the most important emotions that you can go through. If you cannot forgive yourself for all of the lessons that you have gone through and conquered, you cannot move into the next level of your Souls' agreement of Mastery. To be a Master is to have moved through all emotions individually and collectively and into the freedom of the Soul, into the higher understanding and wisdom of all.

Sometimes it seems easier to forgive others than to forgive yourself. If you still have any low self-esteem or self-worth issues, it is difficult for you to forgive yourself because on some level you feel guilty for your existence. This is one of the biggest injustices that you have ever served upon yourself. How can you not forgive yourself for the lessons that you agreed to go through; to free your Soul and the collective Soul?

Many of you look at yourself from what you believe other people's perceptions of you are. You judge yourself from your own beliefs (perception) of what you think others feel you should have been or what you could have done differently. These patterns began from the time of conception with your biological parents in this lifetime and were passed on to you. Many other players in your childhood reinforced these patterns to be your truth. Your agreement was to play them out until the pattern became so thin that you could break through it and create a new agreement of self-love and acceptance, for yourself, and the collective.

If you are still vibrating in these old fear-based perceptions, you take in emotions from others that mirror back to you your old karmic emotional agreements. As your beliefs of other people's perceptions of you connect to your own self-worth patterns, these energies then form within you another agreement; only this one comes from fear of your own love. You feel frightened, guilty, and undeserving of love. Since your body is a computer system, it downloads into your cells all other karmic lifetimes with these same agreements. You are then vibrating in the collective pattern of the agreement.

Every time you think about the pattern, a red light goes on within you and this fear pattern is activated. Once again, your belief in the agreement of not being worthy, or that something is wrong with you, is reinforced and you feel ashamed, guilty, and unworthy of love. The way out of these old patterns is to start disintegrating the agreement through self-forgiveness and self-love.

> *First, connect with your higher self and then bring your Creator Father and Me, your Mother, to you. Ask to feel our love and safety! If you ask, know that we will be there with you even if you cannot feel US.*

> *Second, look at the incident; feel the emotions. If you cannot feel the emotions, it is because you feel too frightened or guilty and have buried and bandaged the experience because it is too painful. These frozen emotions want to be released. They want to come out of you. They want to be heard; they want a voice.*

> *In your mind, go back to the incident that you feel frightened or guilty about, and go into the memory. See or imagine what you looked like and what the circum-*

169

stances were. If you cannot feel it, do not be concerned; you are still building the foundation to open the door for yourself to feel safe enough to be able to release the frozen emotions. With our love, go to the part of you that is stuck there. Talk to that frightened aspect of yourself, and let it know that it is safe now, that you forgive it for not knowing better, or for acting out of fear, survival, or whatever the circumstances were. Imagine bringing that part of self to you and have eye contact with yourself. The eyes are the windows to the Soul. Tell yourself, I'm sorry that we did that and that we didn't know any better. That is the past, and this is now. We just went through a karmic completion. God forgives us and, now we must forgive ourselves. Again, I am sorry, and I forgive you. I am sorry, and I love you. Repeat these words over and over; use them as a mantra to yourself. As you repeat these words, you will feel the emotions connected to the incident start to become lighter and begin to release. You are seeding the sound vibration of love into them. Give thanks for the lesson, even if you don't know what you have to be thankful for; your higher self knows. As you give yourself love and forgiveness, the act of thankfulness sends the message to your subconscious mind that you understand the lesson, which is now done. The subconscious will then give permission for the memory of the lesson to start releasing from your bodies and consciousness.

You must make time in your life to make love to yourself. You love yourself by forgiving yourself. If you do not make time to forgive and love yourself, no one else will. You teach people how to treat you. Because you are each other, if you don't release the old patterns, you will feel this old karmic energy continue to control you until you can't breathe and your body starts to break down in *dis-ease.* As you forgive and love yourself and are thankful for the lesson, you will start feeling yourself at ease with others who were still mirroring and vibrating in the old patterns with you. You will have broken the karmic agreements with them, and your light will move you back into love.

Make time to forgive and love yourself every day. As you do this, you will feel the old stuck emotions start to release and your light, which was stuck in the pattern will move back into you. You will be retrieving aspects of yourself that were still stuck emotionally. This is you doing Soul retrieval for yourself.

Look into a mirror and into your own eyes, which penetrate your Soul. Speak your name out loud and then tell yourself three times, "I love you." "I love you." "I love you." Then take a deep breath. Breathe the vibration of this self-love into every cell of your body. You will feel the energy start moving through you.

Then do the same thing with the words "I forgive you." 'I forgive you." "I forgive you." Make sure you are still looking into your own eyes. Take a deep breath and let the energy penetrate you.

Do the same thing with "I thank you." "I thank you." "I thank you." Make sure you say your name out loud and breathe the energy of the spoken word into you. Then say to yourself, "I thank you for your willingness and courage to come to the Earth plane to complete all of these karmic lessons. I thank you and honor you."

Repeat this process five times in the morning and five times in the evening. As you continue to do this, your subconscious mind will go to work and activate within you your memories of self-love, self-acceptance, and self-forgiveness.

These frightened aspects of you want to be forgiven so that they can come back to you. Just give them permission. This may seem difficult at first, but once you have sent forgiveness and love and thankfulness into these frozen aspects of yourself, they will start breaking loose and all other frozen aspects of you will start to line up so that they also can be forgiven and loved. They will then feel safe to return to you in their highest vibration of love. You will be opening the doors of the prison within yourself and freeing all karmic agreements to release back to original form, Love.

The wounded healer served you well. Through your karmic emotions you created a pathway to find your way back to the Master within You. To become the Master is not to control; it is to free yourself from fear of not knowing and into the Knowingness of all Creations. It is to become one with the Earth, the Moon, the Stars, all living life and to vibrate in love, honor, respect, and integrity, and to become the greatest love of your own Soul in physical form.

To forgive yourself is great power; as you do this you will look at all and know there is nothing to forgive. You will see all Souls in their highest glory and agreements. You will hold the love for all to wake up into the reunion of one another.

Call on Me; I will assist you to forgive yourself. I am the Mother of your magnificence, and my love is strong enough to mirror back to you your own self-love and Knowingness. Know that I love you and that I am always with you, and my heart and arms are wrapped around you tightly, protecting you as you move through your karmic hurts, agreements, and contracts.

You are great Masters and Co-Creators, and I honor you for your willingness to carry such heavy burdens for the collective to move through the 2012 doorway beyond karmic time and into enlightenment and Ascension.

The Creator on the Importance of Forgiveness

I wish to speak to you on the great power of forgiveness. You must forgive to be able to move forward. All unforgiveness is in a past time frame. Living totally in the now, there is nothing to forgive, but if you cannot forgive, you cannot live totally in the

Beingness of now. When you are unable to forgive yourself, it is because you are still stuck emotionally in old stories or karmic agreements that you came into this lifetime to free yourself from. These agreements are a pattern, which threads through many lifetimes and through the collective consciousness of all possessing the same pattern. Perhaps your Soul agreed to come down and learn the lesson of discernment with the pattern. Another Soul agreed to learn the lesson of victim with the pattern, and yet another Soul agreed to learn the lesson of perpetrator of the pattern.

You are a collective Cell consciousness who has agreed to divide yourselves, to expand your understanding, and come back home together collectively with complete understanding of the lesson. As you do this, it feeds the Cell with all frequencies, and it comes back into balance as a whole consciousness. The person or circumstances that you feel you are still in bondage with has agreed to be a gift in your life, to mirror the lesson that needs to be released energetically. Forgiveness is a harmonious sound frequency that breaks loose frozen energies, which create conflict within you. If you cannot forgive someone else, you are holding a mirror up to bring the pattern or conflict to you over and over again until your life becomes a hopeless energy of separateness, illness, or dis-ease. You will experience yourself looking at others with illusional veils of fear between you and your next step of manifesting all your greatness. If you can't forgive, there is an underlying energy that wants the person or conflict that you perceive as unforgivable to experience the same pain or injustice you feel was inflicted upon you. This is a revenge frequency. You do not have to accept that what was done to you was right, but not forgiving keeps you stuck in an energy that doesn't allow you to bring your own self-love and freedom to you. What you are saying energetically is that you are no better than the injustice that was done to you because energetically you are still stuck in the karmic pattern. Remember, there are many sides to the same pattern. All of these patterns are collective, and if you are still in the frequency of revenge or injustice, you will bring more injustice and revenge to you.

Many times the person who did this to you was in a place of not knowing. As he moved forward in his own life, he took an aspect of your light and power with him. When you are still stuck energetically or emotionally with him, your not forgiving him actually gives him more power because he is using your light frequency as his own.

As this happens, you may find yourself becoming more and more depressed and hopeless because you do not have all of your own life force to accelerate you forward. This creates an emotional blockage in the channel between you and your higher self. The emotions stuck in this channel create a cluttered or dirty filter between you and your higher self's divine guidance. Because like attracts like, this old frozen emotion will draw and download into you any collective negative thought forms or patterns with the same frequency. This energy will affect and possibly blow your electrical body out. If you have been guided to read this material, you are a high conscious Being, and your vibration is now too high to carry such an acid-based frequency. When you do not forgive and release these old frozen energies, you can end up lonely, empty, and with some type of dis-ease. Old, unresolved emotions absolutely create sickness and dis-ease in the physical body. Remember, the Ego's job is to control and assist you to stay stuck in the emotions.

Are you willing to give up your love, your life, and your highest dreams for revenge? Remember, in the larger picture, there is nothing to forgive; you agreed to complete karmically with this seemingly unforgiving circumstance. If your intention is to forgive and you can't seem to release the energy, it is because you are still emotionally threaded together. This threading may be stuck in a past life or lives with this person. You may need to have assistance from a past life regressionist to release the frozen karmic emotions. An aspect of your light needs to be retrieved from the other person and brought back into you (Soul retrieval). All of you have emotional energy cords, which connect to others karmically.

174

Imagine these cords in your heart, solar plexus, and the rest of your chakras. Then, call on Archangel Michael and ask him to cut these karmic cords. He is always available to you. This is a great part of his purpose and role. Imagine the cords within you being cut and pulled out by many Masters. Call on Jeshua and Magdalene or the Masters who you connect with. There is no competition in Spirit. The light Lords and Masters are here to serve you. They are waiting for you to ask for their assistance.

After the cords are severed and pulled out of you, it is most important that you reprogram yourself by asking for Sophia and I, as your Spiritual Parents, to fill you back up with love and grace. Ask us and you shall receive.

As you set your intention to forgive, you are sending a higher vibration of light and forgiveness into the memory of the frozen pattern. This light frequency of love will start breaking loose the pattern, freeing your heart to start vibrating in love again; love releases fear/revenge frequencies.

Forgive. Forgive. Forgive. Free your Spirit to receive all of the gifts that are the birthright of your Soul. Come home now. Move out of all illusion and back into the magnificence of your Beingness. If you believe that you need me to forgive you then know that you are forgiven and that I love you. Forgive yourself and everyone else. Come home now into the heart of Creation.

Earlier, I was speaking to you of the seasons of your life. You also go through these seasons on a cellular level. Your emotional body playing out old karmic lessons in which you are still vibrating triggers them.

As a Soul/Cell comes back into a conscious memory of its wholeness, it sends the message or energy to other Cells/Souls of the collective that are going through the same experience. It expands its color and sound vibrations, breaking loose patterns in other Cells and Souls. In actuality, it is you healing yourself. This cycle continues until it threads through all collective frequencies with the same pattern. I speak much of breaking the sound barrier to the pattern or the emotional bondage. As many Cells become conscious or whole, their collective sound is very high, and it assists the other Souls/Cells to awaken quickly. This would be similar to your Hundredth Monkey theory.

This high-energy tone is capable of waking or enlightening the other Cells instantly. They can awaken quickly because within they already have all of the components of a healthy Cell. Soon, you have a great conscious vibration harmonizing together, a symphony.

Many times, the Cell/Soul is already back together as one but does not know it or remember it, because it is still carrying the shock or trauma of the belief in being separate.

As the self-realized Cells harmonize together, and their sound vibration hits the energy field of the Cells that are waiting to be awakened, it instantly breaks the stuck emotional frequency. It then connects to the Cells' memory, which is already conscious, and an instant memory of wholeness takes place. This is because you are the Cells of Me, which are already vibrating in the highest expression of love. You are assisting the fragmented aspects to remember who they are. You are bringing them home again to yourself. You could say that you are all great shamans who are now on the Earth doing Soul retrieval of self. You are retrieving fragmented aspects of yourself that split because the trauma of the lesson was so difficult.

It feels like you go through a difficult process when you incarnate to the Earth. This is because when you are in Spirit; you are vibrating in a very high frequency, and when you get to Earth you feel lost because it feels as if those on the Earth are speaking a different language. It seems different because the vibration or sound feels so dense, and there is no place to plug your light into, to mirror your own sound vibration back to you. Because within, you are in total memory of your highest consciousness, your collective karmic emotional sound frequencies seem to

176

short-circuit your light frequencies. The collective emotional sound feels much greater than your own higher vibrational rate because you are in linear time, in form. It is difficult for you to live in this emotional sound battlefield. This experience would be like vibrating in a beautiful healing symphony, and then all of a sudden you feel immersed into rap music. You feel short-circuited until you start healing and waking up and draw to you other Souls who are vibrating in your Souls' higher sound frequency.

When this happens, you are in harmony again. You once again feel home, not so alone, or short-circuited because you have like consciousness that is of your vibration. As you align collectively with one another, a great healing takes place. As you vibrate in this higher sound frequency collectively, it lifts you out of the old karmic emotion. You feel like you are back with your real family. This higher sound threads through all dimensions and back home to yourself and Me. Through this process, the light of Me penetrates through you and others of like vibration onto the planet. It then starts lifting the whole consciousness on your planet into a higher frequency.

This is how the healing takes place. As you harmonize together collectively, you thread through all consciousness and become at one with Me. The vibration is so high that it connects to the light in the cellular structures of the Beings or Cells who have been vibrating in the karmic emotion. As this happens, they start awakening and remembering who they are.

You see much sickness and dis-ease on your planet now because the old karmic collective structures are being broken down by high light-love frequencies. Bodies of old consciousness are breaking down. Physical bodies are breaking down with sickness and dis-ease. Ego structures are breaking down. Great walls of separation are breaking down. You see this old Ego structure playing itself out in war, fear, hatred, and control. It is a lower frequency, which will eventually play itself out because of the lack of fuel.

As I spoke to you before, it is most important that you not add fuel to the fire by giving it your own life force or power.

This frequency needs your energy as its oxygen. It cannot live without fresh energy or power.

Now you ask, "What does this have to do with forgiveness?" We have come full circle and are coming back together as one consciousness of My own creation of love. This is the time of great manifestations of the group consciousness, of awakening into love. This love will blend you back together in harmony. As this continues to happen, you will feel yourself more alive, awake, and experiencing great emotions of Love, which will move you into total forgiveness of yourself and others. When you truly know from the depth of your Soul that all in this lifetime is by agreement, you must consciously forgive all who you feel have harmed you, or created an injustice toward you, and all who you have harmed or hurt, including yourself. You will not be able to move forward in your Souls' highest agreement if you are still in judgment or out of balance energetically with all of your great chosen teachers. Most of all, you must forgive me and know that I forgive you, so that you can forgive yourself. I have nothing to forgive you for, for all is a great Master Plan of Completion.

Souls' Awakening

You are now on a cellular level remembering who you are. You are awakening into the magnificent light crystal Beingness of My highest creation. You are moving collectively out of old belief systems, prejudices, separations, conflicts, dualities, and illusions.

All of your existence and illusions of separation from Me have been to lead you back in total remembrance of all consciousness and existence. When I created you as Me, We did not have this vast knowledge and experience of the frequencies of All That Is. As I expanded you as Me, I learned the vastness of all consciousness. I had an understanding of the power of thought because I created you from My mind/thought and expanded you into form, but I did not have an understanding of the heart's power until Sophia's love. It is the power of My and Sophia's will, mind, heart, and love together that have created you as great awakened Beings. I could not have extended My consciousness, into the state of total Beingness, without you, for you are the heart and mind of Me feeding information through experience back to Me. This collective collaboration has created us as one that exists beyond all time frames.

Once you truly know this and you expand yourself beyond time collectively, duality will no longer exist. Duality is fear-based and only vibrates in a time-frequency.

As you come together as one on the Earth plane, you are bringing together old fragmented aspects of Me to vibrate together in our one love light. As this happens, you are beyond time. The aspects of fear illusion will no longer have a time-frequency program, or agreement to hook or hold on to, to continue to create the illusion of form. When the form of illusion breaks loose, so does the Ego mind structure. If it has no form to connect to, to feed it fear and control, it will break up and dissipate.

It is time now for all creation to bloom and expand into its highest expression of Me. As you look around on your Earth plane, you see much exaggeration of Me. It is the pendulum swinging from one extreme to the other. The agreement now is to bring all realities or perceptions back to the center. It is only then that all can vibrate in balance and harmony.

This extreme shift of the pendulum has to happen for you to experience the mirror of your own perceptions and belief systems. When one is in his play, the experience is very real. It is hard to experience beyond one's perceptions or emotions. As the pendulum swings to the extremes, so do the emotions. When one's emotional body seems to be controlling them, this is usually when they feel so uncomfortable with self that they start looking for another way to express themselves. That is when the true healing or self-discovery starts taking place.

Your emotions, or what one may feel is the lack of emotions, control your existence and/or your behavior. If you were in balance emotionally, you would not have needs to fulfill. All

179

of the duality that you perceive around you are personal needs or emotions screaming for attention. What this need is asking for is love. Your whole existence has been to bring you back to love.

When one is not vibrating in love or self-acceptance, he is vibrating in fear. Because you are each other, when you are vibrating in fear emotions, you draw to you and align with others that do not feel loved. When this happens, like fear frequencies start blowing their horns, and a sound vibration emanates calling other frequencies back to lack. You then have an army of collective fear frequencies marching together, trying to control each other to feel loved or accepted, valuable or important.

When one does not have the conscious memory of the love emotion, one tries to fill himself up with what one thinks love must be. Many times this perception is a fear-based sense of false power and the need to control other Souls. The fear-based Being feels important and has a sense of its own personal power through dominating others. You see this playing itself out collectively on your planet now.

The fear-based Being or Soul draws to itself other fear-based Souls and vibrates together with them to have a sense of importance. As fear and love are opposites, the heart and Ego seem to be opposite. In reality, it is only when you are in fear that the Ego tries to overpower or control the heart. When you see the world through your own fear perceptions, they control your emotional bodies.

Because the world is now in such extremes, you get to see clearly, or have mirrored back to you, your own perceptions of reality. If you experience anything as negative, fearful, or incomplete, it is because this is the way you are still experiencing yourself. You cannot change anyone or anything else; the uncluttering must be within self. The change or healing must start within you. As you love and accept all aspects of self, you can love and accept all aspects of others on their Souls' journey.

When you are truly the center of the pendulum, the heart and Ego will support each other. The Ego then aligns itself with My I Am or super consciousness, beyond time or duality. This is real power.

When your emotions and mind balance each other and support each other in love, harmony, and integrity, a balance of all consciousness realigns itself with you. You then see everyone, every player, in the divine perfection of your own magnificence, harmony, and Oneness. You will feel everyone, everything, every player in his/her own experience, as perfection and the divine consciousness of love.

As you start to experience life through My heart you will see that all any Soul on your planet wants is love. What would happen if you truly experienced yourself in My highest love frequency? As you look at all around you, your experience will only be love. You will experience every player in this divine vibration of love. As this happens, the fear-based Souls/Cells will lose their energy.

When this happens, you mirror back to the fear structure true unconditional love. The love frequency sound is much higher than the fear frequency. Love is. Love is beyond duality or separation. As the higher love-light vibration and sound hits the fear structure, it breaks up and dissipates. As you unthread your Cells from fear, it acts like a ball of string. Once you pull your string out of the ball, the ball starts breaking loose. Just think, if all of the light workers or Cells of Me started vibrating in their highest frequency, how quickly your world would heal. In actuality, you are starting to see this happen. This is why you are experiencing so much duality.

"The light is like a river. As it flows through you, it flows into all eons of your consciousness, and it will flow into that lifetime that needs to be healed."

13

EARTH CHANGES

Asia Tsunami 2005

As the light of Me is awakening your planet and all inhabitants on your planet, energies that are not vibrating in harmony are connecting with each other's frequency, and it is creating a combustion/friction, like a shock or short circuiting. That is what happened and caused the earthquake and tsunami in Asia.

As the planet is moving out of linear time, it is ascending back into all consciousness. The consciousness, which has been dormant or stuck in old belief patterns of karma (caste system, prejudice, fear, control, guilt) is being bombarded with the Central Sun's frequencies. These frequencies are connecting with and pulling your planet out of the old patterns.

In Asia in January 2005, a Master cleansing took place. As this massive doorway opened, many Souls agreed to go home, fracturing or separating from collective family structures and beliefs. As the Earth shifted on its axis, it enlarged the doorway or birth canal for many aspects of Me to move out of fear, to cleanse the Shadow, and to become one with Me in My highest love and expression of light.

As this light hit Asia, it cracked the old karmic frequency or pattern. This pattern or structure is in the etheric body or energy body of your planet, as well as in the core or grids of your great Mother Earth. Remember, Mother Earth is the Soul of Maldek.

Your whole planet and every one and thing on your planet is a hologram of past structures, beliefs, or karma. When the light hit the etheric body of your planet, it broke loose the karmic thread that has held your planet in duality, conflict, and separation.

Asia has great awareness and spirituality. It has also vibrated in great duality and separation. As there have been many enlightened Masters in Asia, there is a great passageway of light, which is open to that vibration or consciousness.

Every time a karmic Being becomes enlightened or comes to the planet as an enlightened one, there is a doorway that is open between the Being's higher and lower selves; there is no separation, only the illusion of separation. You on the planet are each other, and when the enlightened Beings connect with others, they turn on the light of the Cells of all other Beings, whether the other Beings know it or not. Because there have been so many enlightened ones in the East, there are many portals of light, which are and have been open through all time frames.

The enlightened ones have opened doorways for others to connect with their higher selves. They have brought the light and held it for many to remember that they are love and light. So many in the East are becoming awakened and enlightened, whole villages of people have awakened together. As this happens, it opens the doorway for the collective higher self and karmic lower self to become one. Because villages are awakening together, huge light portals have broken through the etheric or energy body of the Earth, creating what seems to be an imbalance on the Earth.

What is really happening is the East is moving very quickly out of linear, karmic time. As the light hits, it starts breaking loose all the old, stagnant, karmic energy patterns. Because this vast amount of light came through this huge collective passageway, it broke loose the karmic structure creating an energy imbalance and shifting the planet on its axis. The higher intention was to bring everyone back together as one. It temporarily lifted the veil, cleaning the Souls and that section of the planet out of collective karma. All became one, moving out of caste or class-consciousness or beliefs. When this happened, no one was better

183

than anyone else. No one's life was spared because they had more money or better insurance or came from a better caste system or family. All went through similar experiences, and they still have to come back together as one to assist each other to rebuild.

This was a death of a karmic consciousness, individually and collectively. It opened an even greater doorway for Souls to come back home to Spirit, to me, collectively. The doorway that opened was a birth canal to a higher Knowingness, bringing all back together as one through all dimensions.

Mother Earth is giving birth to a new frequency. As the Earth is moving beyond linear time, its vibration is becoming higher. As this happens, her etheric body is breaking loose, shattering old structures and patterns that thread back to My beginning of time.

All energies or memories in her etheric body are sending frequencies back into her physical body. As the etheric body is breaking loose, it is opening doorways or portals for all sickness, dis-ease and karma to release itself from her physical body. This is like a dam breaking loose and opening up Mother Earth's womb and sending her through a master cleansing. This happens with planets as well as humans, when all is moving into enlightenment and Ascension.

You will continue to see many more seemingly catastrophic events happen on your planet. Remember all is by agreement and the Souls leaving agreed to play out these end times for their Souls and the collective. These huge collective endings open massive doorways of light, which pull your planet into a higher frequency of the Ascension process.

Katrina

Katrina was not a National disaster, as many believe. Katrina was a major doorway which opened for the mass consciousness to become aware, to come together as one. It is now time for the collective light ones of you to hold the light for those Souls who did not have the opportunity or consciousness to move beyond their karmic agreement. When one understands his karmic agreements, he can move on individually and collectively.

In the higher realms we see Katrina as a blessing. The great Souls who agreed to leave their bodies at that time agreed to open a gateway collectively for all Souls to be able to shift into a higher love vibration of self. When these shifts happen, many times much suffering occurs as Souls move out of the old patterns collectively. Inside the pattern of suffering and pain is the awakened light in the soul, which is waiting to be discovered.

The Beings who left the Earth through this birth canal agreed to. They are vibrating in a collective energy of love and forgiveness and will be holding this love for the aspects of self that are still vibrating in duality. These Beings are gatekeepers who are connecting cellularly with those left behind and are pulling the planet into a higher frequency. All who left the planet at this time have agreed to so they can assist the consciousness shift.

Many loving ancestral Beings, high spirit Angels, and Masters greeted the Souls who left their bodies, as they exited the Earth through this new doorway. As they were leaving, they connected to their higher selves and Over Souls; this light created a combustion of energy that was so bright and high that they moved instantly into the collective and downloaded the light into the area. This light continued to break up the duality, as waves of love started breaking up the dormant collective fear pattern. Because like attracts like, this created what seamed to be more catastrophes and fear. In actuality a great healing and cleansing out of old energy was happening.

New Orleans has great power. There is a great star gate in the Gulf area from which all creations move in and out. This is why there is so much creativity in the area, both light and Shadow. In all areas that have a major gateway you will find many creative Beings drawn there.

New Orleans is a Mecca for music and creativity. Many of the highest musical Masters have performed there, bringing their highest sounds and frequencies to many. These musical Masters have great creativity; it flows to them from the source of their Soul. They have a Oneness connection to the source of their Being. Creativity is Creation. They are constantly creating for themselves and others. Through music, great emotional healings, joy awakenings, and remembering takes place. Music is the dance of the heart, of the Soul.

When this creativity comes together in one place, you also have great Shadow gatherings. Look how many of your great musicians have addiction habits. This is because this great music lifts them up to higher realms of their own Soul or Being, and the physical body or consciousness is not high enough to hold the frequency.

Through drugs or other addictions, they move out of their emotional third dimensional frequency and expand themselves into higher aspects of their own Soul' songs or Being. In the beginning they feel at home, fulfilled, and at one with themselves. Because they are expressing themselves from higher aspects of self, they are able to download higher vibrations of sound and music.

If one has not healed his/her own emotional wounds, and he/she expands into higher dimensions of self, he/she also opens the door for Shadow aspects to emerge, which opens the doorway to the collective Shadow to come through. Remember, the Shadow looks for a doorway into old, frozen emotions.

New Orleans had and has great spirituality, not only in the form of music, but other mediums as well. There were many in the area with practices of spirituality, both light and dark.

There was also great poverty and suffering. Those in this energy field were being held hostage in this frequency by what you could call Black or Dark Magic. A vibration that formed itself in the way of a web or net hung over the area. The energy could not shift because of this web, which was connected to the reversed matrix.

The purpose of this was to keep the whole creative consciousness in duality. Because thoughts affect emotions, the negative fear-based thought patterns of the Black magic, or Shadow, affected the elements in the Souls of the Beings that inhabited the area. These imbalanced elements in the collective affected the weather elements drawing a mirror of the imbalance to

186

itself. All human and animal species have all five elements within them (fire, earth, metal, water, and wood). If any of these inner elements are out of balance, it affects all levels of the body.

This imbalance affects the larger body of the Earth's elements because you are the Cells of this greater body. As the collective imbalance of the elements come together in form, it affects the weather, which creates Earth changes. You are all the same body of elemental consciousness.

Nothing is separate; all is connected to a larger picture of circumstances. The larger picture of New Orleans was that the energy was trapped; creating an energy field that could not be penetrated.

The higher realms of the collective consciousness put out a call or scream that the imbalanced elements mirrored. The scream of hopelessness and fear called the emotions back to itself creating an energy so powerful that it broke the programming that was trapping the area in hopelessness.

Remember, all traumatic experiences on the Earth plane are karma playing itself out. Had your government system stepped in and assisted the people, you would not have broken the old paradigm of the Shadow. Instead you had and still have the new light vibration of you, this World coming together in the heart, in love, compassion and caring. You are holding hands, and through intention coming together as one to assist one another; people helping people, Souls' awakening and mirroring the light and love to one another.

This needed to happen for the old system to be exposed. As I explained, all of the great Souls who lost their lives in this great awakening agreed to do so.

When the Souls left their bodies and came home in Spirit, they released karma for themselves and the collective. They opened a light doorway to draw many collective light Souls to the area, to shift the frequency to a higher sound vibration that will continue to clean out old Shadow frequencies.

The reason New Orleans has been slow in its rebuild is because the timing is premature. It is still in the pregnancy stage.

As the Shadow continues to dissipate, you will see many great creative Beings of light on the Earth plane move in and restructure the area for the good of all people.

Asia was the first doorway that opened. The light shattered the etheric body of the planet, releasing many who were stuck or vibrating in the old paradigm. This etheric body will continue to unravel allowing new light passageways to be exposed or opened. As this happens and the light comes through the portal, you will continue to experience more combustion and breaking loose of structures, etherically and physically.

If you were to hang crystals in the window and the light hits the crystals, it creates prisms, sending many color frequencies through the crystals into the room. This is happening to your planet now. Because of her own karmic agreements, Mother Earth is a crystalline structure, which was still somewhat dormant. The crystal frequencies from my highest crystalline consciousness are coming through the portals into the etheric body of Mother Earth creating prisms and sending great color frequencies to the planet. These color frequencies are carrying a sound vibration. The sounds corresponding with each color are breaking the sound barrier, individually and collectively, and shattering the old emotional etheric body of Mother Earth.

Every Soul/Cell of you who is on the Earth is the crystalline structure of Me. As the light hits your bodies or Cells, it is freeing you to vibrate in energy beyond the Earth's karmic structure. For many, it frees them from the Earth's physical experiences, releasing them from the physical body agreements and back to Me.

As a Soul leaves the body, many who are left behind grieve and don't understand, and through this loss, pain, and grief, they start looking for ways to heal. People, who in the past had no spiritual understanding, start wanting answers. From pain or loss, they change their perspective or belief systems. Many times, what was truth for them no longer exists. They find a new way of looking at and understanding life.

Everything in life has a cycle. As I spoke before of the seasons, you are coming into a season in which you have not been consciously familiar. You have read about it or perhaps had glimpses of it. It is the season of total awakening and self-realization, of enlightenment.

As I said, in enlightenment, everything is light to you, even the Shadow. You experience all in love and the higher understanding of Creation. You will be vibrating, seeing, thinking and knowing in the higher self of Me, which is you. You may see duality but will not vibrate in it. You will experience all as the same consciousness, both the light and the dark, or Shadow, and all shades in between. As this frequency is threading through your planet, around it, and in it, many are awakening quickly, going into enlightenment because the frequency of light is plugging them back into their true energy. As the collective Soul/Cell consciousness continues to become enlightened, it mirrors back to all Cell structures this light consciousness.

Many of you who are familiar with and work with crystals may use salt water to cleanse them. You also use salt water to cleanse your bodies; it cleanses any stagnant energy out of your body that you have picked up. Going into the ocean just for a few moments will clean your etheric body. As the salt water cleans out your etheric body, your physical body feels light, almost silky and clean. You feel peaceful, refreshed and relaxed.

Because you are a crystalline body structure, your prisms of light will easily cleanse other people's energies, just by you being around them. Your crystal frequency is the same thing as using a crystal to clean someone else's body of any unwanted frequencies. Just your enlightened Beingness will do this.

Mother Earth's Birth

On January 3, 2005 when the tsunami hit the coastline structure in Asia, the seawater cleansed old patterns from the collective consciousness. It was an energetic extension or a shock wave of the Portal of the Harmonic Convergence from 1987. Mother Earth is giving birth, and The Harmonic Convergence was a large contraction for the birth canal of the Mother to open and expand herself to a new form of life: Enlightenment, Grace.

If the Mother's birth canal opened all at once, you would experience huge devastation throughout your planet. A major emotional cleansing is happening to the Mother, as well as all of her children, who are you. If the light of Me connected all at once to the highest light of all of you and the Mother, the planet would explode. The planet is still too dense emotionally to give birth that quickly.

The portals that are opening are actually contractions of the Mother as she is opening herself to give birth to a higher intelligence, physically and emotionally. As the new energy of My light is hitting the Earth, it is awakening your planet out of millions of years of vibrating in between dimensions, in illusions.

All dimensions have their own vibratory rate or consciousness. You and your planet have been threaded through all dimensions, some karmically. Now as you are moving beyond linear time, beyond karma your frequency is higher, and you are reconnecting to all dimensions and plugging into higher thought intelligence. As this happens, you are experiencing shock waves of light from these dimensions that are downloading their frequencies back into you and your planet.

You are like waves of the ocean continually moving in and out of each other, merging together as one and each time becoming a stronger wave of consciousness. Soon you will be beyond thought understanding and vibrating in the knowingness of all that is, bringing you and your planet home to vibrate in peace, harmony, and love, collectively-realized.

As I said, your planet could not handle this total awakening all at once. The awakening would blow out the crystalline structure of the Earth, as well as you, the inhabitants or Cells of the Earth. This awakening of Me must happen on a slower scale. There have been and will continue to be many doorways or contractions of awakening or downloading of light frequencies.

The first major doorway happened in 1947. As you look back in your history, you will see many great awakenings in consciousness or intelligence. Every time a doorway or contraction happens, it activates the collective consciousness into a higher intelligence and Knowingness. When this happens, many Beings all over the planet start receiving the same information, although they may come from different cultures and speak different languages. All are connecting to the light language energy of a higher intelligence. This higher intelligence is a light language that all cultures understand. This energy or language connects to the higher collective mind that all on the Earth understand. As this happens, it lifts the whole Earth and collective consciousness into a higher frequency, moving the Earth and its inhabitants closer to the Knowingness of Me.

As I expressed to you, this must happen one portal or contraction at a time, or there would be a massive blowout of your planet and you on the planet.

The 1947 portal opened the doorway of unconscious communication with yourself in many dimensions. In communicating with yourself, you started connecting to many star Beings from other planets, galaxies, and even universes that were and are the Soul group or collective consciousness of yourself. Nothing you communicate with or connect with is anything outside of you. All is you.

Another portal opened in 1952 on August 16th and 17th. In 1963 on June 6, a large portal opened that activated the Shadows' intention for the planet. This is when a more conscious battle between the light and Shadow became known. It is then that the light Masters started allowing themselves to be assassinated, to open doorways for the whole collective to move into a higher vibration of love, of the heart. This is when the larger karmic pictures of your Earth started unveiling or unraveling so that as one Divine Matrix (Blueprint), one world, you could start healing.

Again, this is when your flower children of the sixties opened their heart's journey of love collectively, to mirror this love to the collective Shadow, so that its hold on your world would start shattering. Throughout the 60's and 70's you had many of these gateways continue to open and awaken the collective consciousness of you.

One of the next major doorway openings in 1987 was the Harmonic Convergence. After that another major portal was the 12-12 doorway. It is connected to the geometric system of the 2012 gateway. All doorways that have opened and are continuing to open are birth contractions of Mother Earth' birth, and you, the Cells of the Earth, ascending beyond time and into Oneness. You have had many smaller doorways, which have opened that are the contractions of the larger doorways. These are the waves of the contraction. You will continue to have Master doorways, or Gateways of collective light consciousness, as well as smaller contractions, through the 2012 gateway and beyond.

The 1987, 11-11 doorway was a major wave or contraction that started lifting the veils individually and collectively. It opened you to gateways within yourself by activating codings in your DNA. This started connecting you to the re-membrance of who you are in other dimensions, galaxies, and even universes. As this happened and you became a higher frequency intelligence, many of you started consciously communicating with extraterrestrial Beings and intelligences. This happened all over your planet. As the portals opened, ships or UFO sightings and communications started happening. It was an exciting time on your planet. In actuality, doorways opened, and you started communicating with higher aspects of yourself in many dimensions.

These doorways also opened you to the aspects of self that you call dark or the Shadow. Many of you started remembering and experiencing consciously abductions and lower vibrational dark experiences. All of these experiences are aspects of you being played out to bring yourself back into balance beyond duality.

You ask, "How could any of these horrific things that were done to me be aspects of me? I am a kind, loving person. I am of the light." Yes, you are of the light. All are of the light, for you were created of Me, which is light. Many of you may still have old aspects of your self that are vibrating in My old mind-set.

Perhaps, this is the lifetime you have agreed to come full circle, totally back home to Me, beyond duality. Your high intention is a high-energy frequency. This frequency of energy is a wave of light that moves through your whole Akashic Record, which is in your cellular structure and subconscious mind. Your subconscious mind carries every thought and every memory that your Soul has ever experienced or gone through. As your light vibrates in the highest frequency of love, the light travels through your Cells and subconscious and activates memories in your DNA.

As the light travels through all portals of your consciousness, it may find a lifetime or pattern inside of you when you needed to experience the Shadow side. The light is like a river. As it flows through you, it flows into all eons of your consciousness and unconsciousness, and it will flow into that lifetime that needs to be healed. As it connects to you and the collective in that lifetime, you will energetically open the door for the energy or lifetime to awaken and flow back into you, so that you can heal it. Because you are a mirror, you will draw from your outer world the same patterns back to you.

If you are in denial and don't surrender into the emotional pattern, this pattern will control you. It downloads itself on a cellular level and feeds itself into the collective DNA energy body. This opens the doorway for unwanted interferences.

If you have what seems like unwanted interference going on with you, there is a doorway open to some other lifetime or agreement. No one has randomly decided to harm you, hurt you, abduct you, or interfere with you.

When you truly understand this and are able to release frozen emotions that held the door open, you will start moving out of the victim role. As this happens, you will be able to forgive because you will know there is truly nothing to forgive. What is being done to you, you have done before, and you are in a completion cycle.

When you get to this place of understanding, you will be able to love these Beings. You will know that they are aspects of you, from a larger karmic consciousness, that are playing themselves out to assist you to ascend beyond any duality agreement. When you feel this great love and forgiveness, you will be able to start closing the door to these unwanted experiences. Your vibration or energy will be beyond a karmic frequency.

Remember, the Shadow ones are you, and you are them. The war going on between the light and dark is within self. As you love all aspects of yourself, both light and Shadow, it takes the power away from your Shadow. Your own light and self-love will become so strong that it will melt the fear that you have been feeling from your own Shadow.

Your Shadow self will wake up out of the illusion of fear that it has been vibrating in collectively. As it unthreads itself it breaks loose from the collective fear structure. The Shadow will then become self-realized and align itself with your light-love Beingness. It will then support your highest desire of enlightenment, becoming your Ally.

This is how the planet is healing. As a Being unthreads from karmic duality and connects in balance within self, this vibration of self love will beam to all other Beings who are playing out whatever role they need in this lifetime to fulfill their Souls' purpose and mission. You will be the mirror for them to remember their own love and light.

I was speaking to you of the Mother Earth giving birth. As you are the Cells and consciousness of the Earth, you are also in this great birth process. A collective birth is happening simultaneously. You are moving out of an old cellular structure of separation. As this collective birth is taking place, the walls of this old paradigm are breaking down and you are finding, or calling to you energetically, all aspects of yourself from all dimensions and realities. You are bringing back lost relatives. Some have been vibrating in another consciousness for eons of time. They got stuck and forgot that they have a genetic light family.

As the birth of the Golden Age is now in process, many Beings who have been at war against themselves are starting to wake up. The light is hitting their cellular structures, and a memory of who they truly are is emerging. A flicker of light or a faint memory awakens. As this happens, it may also awaken the fear memory that the player has covered up by forming a collective alliance of false power and fear. Many times when a Being feels the fear, it feels it is losing its power. In reality, it is remembering its power: It is then in the process of realigning itself with all of its own light aspects, which is the true source of power.

We are one. We are not separate. We never have been and never will be. You and all were created as Me. You have always been and always will be. Thank you for recommitting yourself to become one with Me, with yourself. You are resetting your biological clock beyond a time-frequency to realign yourself with My mind-thought process. You need to do nothing but allow My thoughts or consciousness and yours to become one, to vibrate together in grace. Thank You. It is done! It is done! It is done!

"When you see and experience everything in its own perfection or divinity, you mirror back to all love and total acceptance."

14

THE END OF KARMA AND THE REBIRTH OF LOVE: LOVE IS

There is nothing beyond love. Everything in life, in all dimensions, is leading towards love. Love is the center of all being, all knowing, and all understanding. Your whole karmic process is leading you back to the center of creation, which is the heart of love. Your whole purpose in this lifetime or any lifetime or agreement is to lead you back home to love.

You have gone through a process of elimination. You have constantly cleared veils away, every time becoming a little more aware of what you don't want. As you go through what you don't want and you cannot find any more of your "don'ts," you will be at the end of the cycle. It is then that you can spin around in another direction and start seeing a new dawn, a new day, and a new beginning.

This is sometimes called a breakdown, a "Dark Night of the Soul", or coming to the end of your rope. Some of you have gone through many self-destructive patterns, not necessarily trying to find love, but to keep love out or away from you because of your fear of love. As you look at your lives, many of you have done a pretty good job.

As you move through self-destruction into the hole of not love, you usually feel there is no other place to go. It is then that you start reaching out, looking for ways to heal. You start looking in the direction of light. In the light, there is a mirror of your own magnificence and self-love. You may think that perhaps others have come to you, reached out their hands, opened their hearts, gone before you, and opened doorways so that you could see the light at the end of the tunnel. This is true, and yet, these Beings who went before you are aspects of your own light and magnificence that agreed to be the leaders in the awakening of your own Soul and the collective Soul.

They were the ones who signed up to go through the first doorways or waves of enlightenment. They are aspects of Me, which have agreed to remember My light and mirror this light back to you so that you also could awaken, remember, and unthread your frequency from the backward spiral or labyrinth.

If all awakened at once, you would have a major blowout. The light must be turned on a little slower. If all candles of you were lit at once, you would be blinded by the light. As you go through the process of your light awakening you Cell by Cell, you plug your cellular structure back into other Cells/Souls. This realignment opens the doorway of Ascension, pulling you out of the backward spiral of dissension.

The Earth has been in an Ascension pattern since Maldek. Before then, or before the Soul of Maldek came to Earth, the Earth plane was a planet of dissension, great learning, and completion. Many different species used the planet to play themselves out, or to come to the end of what could be called karmic understanding. That is why the Earth has had so many species, which have left. You on your planet feel they became extinct. In reality, all things must come to an end. Endings always create new beginnings. So as the species and civilizations came to an end of their agreements collectively, many of the Souls moved on to new assignments, to other dimensions, where higher aspects or more conscious aspects of them reside.

They had completed an agreement that needed to evolve or to be experienced and learned. As this learning took place, if the aspect of the Soul/Cell, became conscious or self-realized, it was complete. It then left the body it was residing in and returned to itself in a higher dimension. The light of the Soul from the

197

higher frequency was connected to the learning Soul aspect on Earth. When the Soul on Earth awakened, it was already aligned with the higher lighter self, which allowed the lighter self and the awakened one to merge together as one. The lighter self held the mirror for the self who was awakening, or held the light so that the awakening self could remember whom it was. When it remembered, or came to a completion of its chosen lesson, it left the body or what you call died, and then realigned itself with its own higher vibration. The higher vibration held the doorway open for the Soul aspect on Earth to return home to self.

This is what is happening on your planet now. The awakened or more conscious aspects of yourself are mirroring back to you in your physical body on the Earth your own higher aspects, so that you can remember who you are and can choose to take a different passageway to return home, to self, within yourself.

Because you are awakening into the remembrance of Oneness, in the new light passageway, you meet many aspects of yourself; other Souls in different bodies who have agreed to mirror to you each lesson you have chosen to understand. When you get the lesson, you then have the ability to choose to move out of the fear or the victim role and back into love.

As this unthreading of old beliefs and prejudices, opinions, and perceptions happens, you then rethread with those Souls who went before you, forming a collective coalition of light sound frequencies. Because you are each other, these light-sound frequencies move back into the collective aspects of yourself, which are still vibrating in the old mind-set of fear of love, and control of love. The sound waves hit the old collective sound structure and send shock waves of love and light into it. It starts breaking up and dissipating the illusions that are collective thought forms, which have formed an agreement of their own fear-based beliefs.

Because it is an illusion, the light-sound is able to shatter it. Love is solid and cannot be shattered. When one feels hurt in love, it is the perception that is shattered not the love. Love is! This is why, as you heal, everyone around you starts healing. You are

198

collective energy patterns. As you unthread from the fear illusion, the light and love of whom you are moves into the shattered energy and starts soothing and healing it. The other Souls/Cells of you, in other bodies, start receiving the light, start waking up and remembering who they are. They start feeling the soothing of the love and start looking for the light or sun to nurture them.

Keep pushing, walking through old structures, beliefs, mind-sets, programs, patterns, and agreements. You are moving through the veils of illusions. Yes, I see it is very beneficial to continue to move yourself through the emotional healing process. The more consciously aware and lighter that you become, the more you will attract these old patterns. *They are collective, and your crystallized structure will bring them to you again so that you can choose to make a different choice, for the outcome to be different.* As you make a different choice, you release the pattern. An unthreading of the illusion of duality is happening. As you continue to awaken and move beyond duality, you will continue to bring all mirroring back to you, both the light and the Shadow. Through this agreed upon healing process, you will awaken to your inner Master, your own inner guidance, and you will be beyond the Shadow and will eventually be able to walk among all, through all dimensions and feel benign. You will be vibrating in the Isness and will not be affected by the Shadow. The Shadow Beings will see you and recognize you, but you, yourself, will vibrate beyond fear or judgment because you will be beyond the Shadow learning process.

You will be in the Christ Isness and will be able to hold this love frequency for all that you see so they are able to remember who they are. You will be the mirror of total Oneness, of Knowingness, of Grace, and will be able to hold this energy or frequency for the Shadow ones to remember their light. You will only mirror back to them your own perfection. There will no longer be an emotional, negative, fear-based charge. You will just be, with one another.

When Christ-Sananda walks among His brothers and sisters of the Shadow, or the dark ones, He is very respected. I cannot always say loved, because Beings of Me who are vibrating in fear have many times closed their hearts and have no conscious memory of love. Jeshua is honored and respected for the role that He has played, and is continuing to play, to bring this old mind-set of fear and separation back to experience love. It is quite a job that He agreed to take on.

When Christ-Sananda is with the Shadow ones, He mirrors back to them who they really are. This mirroring of total love for them and their purpose allows them to experience a frequency or sound vibration that penetrates the fear illusion. It creates an instant memory of peace in the Cell wall or karmic structure of the Cells. It shatters it, having a gong effect. This creates a minute instance of total silence in the Cell. It starts breaking down the old fear control structure, sending a light-sound frequency through the Cells into all of their bodies. This happens so subtly that the Beings receiving the healing are not even aware of it.

Christ-Sananda is lightening their cellular structure, or opening it up to be able to receive more and more light and love. As this continues to happen, it opens the Cells to be able to receive the highest frequency of I AM, which starts lifting the veils of illusion collectively.

You are experiencing this happening to all Beings on the planet at this time. The veils are being lifted beyond time and sending light sound frequencies into the collective structure, awakening all consciousness beyond the speed of light into Isness. This is why so many of you can travel beyond time into all dimensions. You are able to travel the karmic time line frequency and back into who you are into what you call past lives, or forward into what you call future lives. You would not be able to do this if you were in a time frequency.

How could one move forward into the future, when in your mind-set, it has not happened? Because you are Creator Beings, as I am, and you exist in all consciousness and creations as I do, you are constantly creating at all instances of your life. When you look at your planet and feel fear, judgment, or hatred for what you see, you are creating more of that for your world, for your planet, and for all Beings on your planet.

As I explained, it's easy for you to be pulled back into these old patterns because in your subconscious, you have many lifetimes of similar experiences and memories. When you see and feel the conflict around you, your mind goes into your "inner" net systems and searches for and downloads similar memories. Your mind then realigns with the old memories and forms a new or similar agreement for this experience to be a truth. Your energy, thought, and new agreement connects energetically with the collective emotion, and in thought, forms a new karmic agreement. You are constantly forming agreements. Because you are energy and your agreement on the Earth plane at this time is to come out of duality, your energy will constantly draw duality or separation, loss, grief, and pain back to you so that you will feel uncomfortable or angry enough to say, "Enough! I want love in my life and in my world."

When you get to this place, you start taking your power back from the collective agreement to grow through fear and conflict. You then start visualizing, praying, or asking for a new way of being, or a new way of learning, to use your own creativity and power. You then realign with others who are already on this wavelength of peace, harmony, love, and Oneness, in grace. From this place, you will bring your higher light-sound frequency into harmonize with others of like vibration. This sound breaks up the old fear mind-set, leaving an opening to recreate your new reality for yourself and for your planet.

You will then realign with Mother Earth's Cell structure beyond time and become one with her and the collective, to lift the consciousness of your planet and the Cells of the planet into a higher frequency. The higher your frequency becomes, the easier it is to slip in and out of your time frequency. This is moving beyond the speed of light. You become light. As you move beyond something, you become it. As you become light, you can move in and out of all dimensions and vibrations. As you become this full embodiment of light, you are no longer connected emotionally to karmic time. You are beyond the vibration.

201

When this happens, you have ascended and have become one with your own light body. You then see and experience all in its perfection or divinity. When you see and experience everything in its own perfection or divinity, you mirror back to all love and total acceptance.

Whoever or whatever is receiving this love starts to drink the light in like nectar, feeding its Soul and Cells the memories of its true self. They then start going into a cellular rewiring; the mirror is awakening a restructuring of the Cells through the vibration or memories of love. This light is blinding, and for a moment creates the total silence, which sends a shock wave into the Cells and awakens them.

What happens when you hold a mirror into the sunlight? The light hits the mirror and blinds you, if only momentarily. It is at this instance that the light of Me starts breaking down the karmic Cell structure and awakens you into a higher vibration.

Your purpose in this lifetime is to play out all of your old karmic agreements. Every time you go through a lesson or agreement, understand the lesson and move beyond the fear emotions, a light bulb goes on in your mind, and you get the experience. At that moment, you become conscious and have a choice to play out the old scene again or to change the scene.

If you decide to change the scene, you are choosing your own value and importance over the old lesson. You re-program your emotions with self-love and acceptance, which completes the karmic lesson. Your vibration becomes higher, and you then choose a lesson, which forms an agreement, that mirrors your newly formed love of self, or self-worth.

You will then bring a new mirror or lesson to yourself, and it will always have fragments of the old lesson. As you release the old lesson, you are cutting karmic cords. As the cords are cut, there are frayed edges of the cords, which will bring back the old lesson, usually in a person who has the same frayed edges of the pattern. When you come together with this person or experience, your newfound light and love will mirror the other person's. Sometimes there is great joy, almost euphoria. Because everything is a mirror, your light at first blinds the frayed edges of the old patterns. As the sun starts going down inside you, and it always does because of the cyclical pattern, the frayed patterns start vibrating with one another. They are saying, "Feed me." They start feeling frightened and want to pull you and the other person into the old pattern so that the pattern feels safe, strong, and secure. Remember, theses patterns are alive, an Entity in itself.

These old patterns are connected to the collective structure of the pattern. When you bring another person or lesson to you with the same old pattern, the pattern connects and tries to pull you back into your old paradigm or mind-set.

The gift for you is to recognize it as the pattern and to give yourself permission to work through it. It is coming to you again saying, "Are you really done with me?" The pattern or frayed edges are there again to teach you who you are. You then again have the choice to work through them, to let go of the pattern, and to connect more with your own self-worth and love. This activates a new agreement and vibration within you.

This cycle assists you out of the karmic agreements. As I said, everyone who comes into your life is a mirror of you, and when you know this, you can ask yourself what the gift is. When you see these lessons as gifts, you will move very quickly through the emotional karmic agreement cycle. You will even have the experience of the painful emotional feeling, and, at the same time, watch a light bulb go on. You will be the observer watching yourself go through this and will be able to laugh and see the humor, as well as experience love and the hurt emotions. You then have the opportunity to move out of fear and into the Creator Being of self.

When you truly understand this, you will always watch your thoughts and know that you are creating at all times. Only now, you will become conscious co-creators of your destiny and the destiny of others and your planet. You will know that everything is choice, and conscious thoughts create change.

From this vibration, you will think something in thought and see it instantly manifest (cause and effect). In the beginning of this, you may try to create a parking place or put out the energy for someone to call you. You think your desire in thought and put the thought out to the universe. The universe picks up the thought like a phone call and energetically re-arranges itself to answer your call, sending the vibration or request back to you. You are co-creating energetically with the universe inside yourself. You are co-creating your existence by moving beyond karmic time and bringing your request back to you, even in physical matter, if the need be. Thought is energy, and you can create anything in your life when you understand the power of thought.

When you truly understand this, you will change your world by changing your thoughts. As your thoughts change and you are in a higher light-sound vibration, you realign with others of like sound vibration, just as you did when you were in karmic vibration. In this higher frequency, you create a harmony of sound that is so high, it constantly breaks through all veils blinding the old Shadow structure.

The old Shadow structure cannot exist in this higher vibration. There is nowhere to turn, or to move beyond, and it starts breaking down. LOVE is and breaks the sound barrier to these old fear frozen patterns.

This cycle is how you move yourself beyond karmic illusion. In reality, you are already beyond the karmic Shadow. As I said, you are from the future and have come back to Earth to retrieve all missing aspects of self, individually and collectively. You are in a holographic world playing out old fear illusions, unthreading from all universes and fear-based creations of Me. In the future, you have already ascended and are enlightened Masters who have come back to the Earth to retrieve fragmented aspects of self so that all can become whole and one again.

As I was saying earlier, as you move beyond time, you can tune into your own light frequency. This enables you to go into your subconscious and find lifetimes or agreements in what you call past or future. How can you look into a future structure if it does not already exist? All exists at once.

When you go into future lifetimes, it is because you are

already there and have already created that which you see and experience. You are a multidimensional Being who vibrates through all creations simultaneously. There is no past, present, or future. You live all at once.

As you are moving beyond this karmic time frequency and losing your earthly identity, many of you are feeling great sadness, loss, grief, and confusion. You are moving beyond your earthly story or agreement. You are starting to let go of old perceptions, which sometimes means relationships. You are in between dimensions within yourself. The confusion comes from the shift of energy that is rethreading or reconnecting you to your self in all dimensions.

You are coming to the end of karma and are in a death cycle and rebirth of who you really are, which is love and light. You, in what is called future, are connecting to this fragmented part of self that is releasing the old karmic structure. This is creating a loss of identity or belief in who you thought you were or who you thought you were supposed to be. I ask that you allow yourself to move through this process. You have great love and assistance from Masters of Creation who are holding the vibration of Love for you to move and emerge quickly into your authentic self of Christ, of Co-Creation, of the I AM, the Second Coming within yourself. You will experience the magnificence of your Being that will be beyond any experience that has ever been. You will create through intention, your heart's greatest desire of love, purpose, and passion. In the future, you are already beyond duality. You have already ascended. You are already enlightened. So is Mother Earth.

As thought is energy, it is most important to connect your thought form energy into the healed whole future and bring it into the now. When you do this, you are downloading this frequency to the Earth and all of its inhabitants. You are reconnecting Mother Earth with her light body, her divine counterpart. As many of you are becoming one with your light body, so is Mother Earth.

All on Earth have a light body, unless they are cloned thought forms. The more of you who start reconnecting with your light body structure, the easier it is to lift the collective thought of your planet into Oneness. You realign with future self-realized Beingness and download this frequency into the now and to your planet.

From this place, all Beings on your planet will start rethreading with aspects of self that are all knowing. As this happens, you will see many Beings who are stuck in old paradigms leave their physical bodies and move back into Spirit.

As I said, many are great Masters who have been disguised in karmic patterns. Their whole agreement on the Earth, at this time, was to shift the energy or consciousness for the collective. Many of the light ones who are leaving through horrific departures or endings are great Masters who have come to the Earth to open passageways home through difficult karmic completions for the collective. As they leave, they open your heart and take some of your veils of fear with them, opening a collective doorway of love and light, which lifts the consciousness into a higher sound frequency. As they leave in this completion, they are completing collectively for many. As this happens, many people left behind go through the karmic death process with the one that left. When others read or hear of their difficult deaths, they feel the pain, loss, and grief; many times reaching out to assist in whatever way they can. Their collective intention, of caring and compassion, starts changing the world by releasing the karmic agreement of whatever the lesson was. Together, they are holding love, light, and compassion for the one leaving and for the family of the one that left.

In other words, the ones leaving agreed to carry the emotions of the collective to open the door, or frequency, so that others would not have to physically go through it themselves. The ones leaving agreed to assist the collective to free itself from karmic patterns that are keeping the world stuck in fear.

Many of you feel that this creates more fear. On one level, yes, this is so, because your light activates the collective fear frequency or pattern. When this happens and you come together intending to make the world and your existence a better safer place, and you reach out to your brothers and sisters, you are doing so in love and caring. This vibration is much higher than fear. The sound frequency of love breaks up the fear-based frequency and releases the frozen emotions collectively.

Through the Ascension process, you will continue to push through the veils of fear until you feel and experience only love. You will also experience many more of what seem to be catastrophes, as this great awakening of the consciousness continues. It cannot be stopped, for it is the divine plan of evolution.

When the earthquake and tsunami hit in the eastern world, you experienced many coming back together beyond belief systems and prejudices. You saw cultures crossing lines of prejudices, separation, asking for help, and giving help. You saw religious separation breaking down; Christians, Muslims and other religious groups walking side by side. As I said before, this seeming catastrophe brought people back together beyond caste systems, prejudices, and fear. All that is not love is fear of losing control of one's own power or beliefs. When such a great loss happens, one's perception, or sense of self, is shattered. The shattering brings people back together as one. Remember there truly is no death, only moving out of not knowing and moving back home into Knowingness, of freedom. This is only a death of karma, belief systems, and patterns. Whether one stays in the physical body or leaves to a higher frequency, it is always the same agreement: to move back into the heart of Love, Isness, Oneness.

When this Oneness happens, the dark ones, or Shadow ones, in other dimensions lose their power or grip. As you move your vibration higher collectively, nothing that is "not love" will be able to penetrate you.

If the Shadow ones on your planet were killed in some horrific way, would you bond together and reach out to their families in love? I think not. You would dance together in joy and happiness that the Shadow ones were finally hunted down and killed. Would your hearts open in love for the ones leaving? I don't think so. You would feel justice is done and that they deserved it.

In the perception of your world, this may be true, but in the larger picture, it would also be another karmic completion, yet it would not elevate the level of consciousness on your planet to a higher frequency of love. Remember, you have been all that is and, because the Shadow ones are playing these roles, it also means you do not have to in this lifetime. Maybe you have already played out your shadow agreements and this is the lifetime you agreed to lift yourself and all others into Love.

For the planet and all of its inhabitants of Me to heal and come out of separation and duality, there must be duality. If you do not have duality, how can you know what you need to do to come out of it? You would not even know it existed. How do you know the light if you don't experience the dark? How do you know the dark if you don't experience the light?

All in life, both the light and Shadow mirror you in some way, for you are All That Is. Your agreement to come to the Earth plane is to experience separation so that you could choose love over fear from this place of love. There is no separation. All is choice.

You are the Second Coming of Christ. Jeshua agreed to suffer such a difficult karmic death, resurrection, and Ascension to reconnect with you and open your hearts and minds to a higher understanding. Because you are each other you suffered His death and pain as if you were Him. Over 2,000 years later, you are still suffering His death and pain collectively. I hear some of you say, "How could I ever repay Him?" I say to you, take Him off the cross. It has already been carried. Put it down. He did not agree to come to the Earth for you to suffer. He came to the Earth for you to wake up, to remember your love, light, and magnificence, to remember life is eternal, and that you are Him. You are Him and all that He could do, you can do and more, for you are the grand golden collective energy of Him.

As you are the Second Coming, many of you great light ones, Masters, have also agreed to come to your planet and lift the veils of illusion by going through some tragic endings to awaken the consciousness to love. Again, I say to you, "Put down the cross. It has been carried. Experience yourself as Christ in the highest of who He is, of who you are, which is love. Allow

Jeshua to mirror back to you your own magnificence and light, not your old karmic suffering."

You are not separated from Me. You may feel further away within yourself because of all of the veils of illusion between us. You are one with Jeshua and all great Masters that have gone before you. As I explained before, many of you are the Masters who have gone before you, and you have recycled back to become one collectively, to assist this great Ascension and Rebirth. To know that we are one, through your feelings, you must experience us in your heart.

Suffering may open the door to your heart. Once it is open, you must keep it open through love. If you continue to connect to the suffering of Christ, you are collectively holding a veil of fear around your world. This veil picks up other fear vibrations, which are being projected to you and your planet. Fear attracts fear. Love attracts love.

Fear is a false power that allows the Shadow ones to send thought forms to the collective. You pick them up and don't know that it is not you.

If you are living in a fear-based perception, you will take this projected fear into you as your own and give it so much power that it seems to overpower your own logic. Because it is strong, collective, fear energy, you will have a tendency to act it out, thinking it is all you. From your own fear-based thoughts, you open the door to draw to you, collectively, more fear.

When you become aware of the power of your thoughts, you have the power to change your world. As you understand this, you will know that no one is doing anything to you that you are not asking to be done.

Many of you are constantly picking up fear thoughts that you know in the past would never have been in your mind. As adults, you somewhat know your own thought patterns. The younger ones on your planet do not.

I look at many of your adolescents who are taking their own lives, even groups of them ending their lives together. They are in an emotional time in their lives. When they receive thought forms of suicide, they do not know that it is not their own minds or thoughts. They are not mature enough to understand their own minds. They do not even have a conscious understanding of what they are doing. They are following and acting out thought forms that they think are their own.

The Shadow that does not want your planet to ascend is trying to break the hearts of the adults or parents of these children. There are two sides of a coin. The other side is to take your power back by coming together collectively and reaching out to one another in love and support before this happens. It breaks the fear thread in you, which gives you the power to start changing the collective thoughts. This supports the young ones in love, so they don't feel like outcasts or separate from you. Everywhere they turn, their support system will be the same one of love, support, validation, and strength. All will mirror back to them their own light, love, self-worth, and magnificence.

I see many of these young Beings coming into the Spirit world, and they don't know what has happened to them. They are in shock and don't remember what they did because it was not their own thought forms that they followed. It was a collective thought to destroy them. As painful as it is for you, it is important for you to know that they agreed to go through this collective thought completion to wake you up, to bring you back to what is important: love. Life is about love. You are on the Earth plane to remember you are love.

When it is time for you to leave the Earth and you look back at your life, it will not make any difference to you how many cars you had, where you lived or what job you held. The only thing that will be important to you is: did I have love? What was my life about? Did I try to help others? What was my purpose? Did I fulfill it?

I am not saying do not live comfortably. I am saying don't forget your purpose: love, self-love. The more you love yourself, the more love and compassion you will have for others. When you totally love and accept yourself, you will totally love and accept others. You will experience all of life as love, because that will be

210

your only essence. Self-love will give you strength and power to accomplish all that you could imagine for yourself and your world. When you are love, you are vibrating with Me in total balance, in grace. You and the universe and I will be aligned in our hearts, Souls and minds. **Remember**, from this great creation of Oneness you truly become the co-creator of your life and world.

Releasing Old Fear Emotions through Self-Love

"Fear cannot survive in love, but love can survive in fear
– Love is!"

You cannot heal yourself or your World unless you surrender into your emotions and move into a place of self-love. Inside of all emotions and elements is total silence and peace. I see many of you afraid of your emotions. Because you live in fear of your emotions, they control you. Anything that you fear has great power and control over you. It has great power because it is siphoning off your energy and life force. You are giving it your power. If you don't use your inner source energy – your generator and your life force – the fear element of you will. It will use your energy and align you with the collective fear frequency.

When this happens, your unhealed emotions connect to the unhealed emotions collectively and forms fear frequencies in your etheric body. This fear pattern in the etheric connects to the color-sound vibration of other fear patterns because fear is fear. It does not discriminate from any fear emotion. It connects to all fears and downloads them into your etheric or energy body. Your etheric body is not separate from you. Whatever you carry in your etheric body attaches itself to your physical body. Your physical body takes the fear frequency in and starts short-circuiting. It has energy blowouts, which create sickness and dis-ease.

When you are vibrating free from fear illusion, you will not be sick. You will be vibrating beyond the color and sound frequency of fear or sickness and dis-ease. All sickness and dis-ease are fear-based frequencies. Sometimes, this sickness connects to old genetic memories inside of you, of other lifetimes when you carried this fear-based frequency. Because there is no past, present, or future, your body cannot discern the difference, and the fear frequency activates the old dis-ease or dis-eases.

I cannot express to you enough how important it is to go into your frozen emotions, break them up, and take your power back. As you go into them, they break up, dissipate, and free you to experience the silence, peace, and grace of your Souls/Cells. You become healthy Cells and vibrate in the whole Cell energy with others of you that are the healthy and loving, free, Me. You turn on the color and musical pattern of love that vibrates collectively in your etheric body. This downloads the new song of love and self-acceptance into your physical bodies, which starts releasing and healing sickness and dis-ease.

Many of you are reluctant to go into your emotions. You say, "I did that years ago." Perhaps this is true. You also took a shower and brushed your hair years ago. Do you think your hair has stayed brushed and you are still clean?

As you go into your emotions, you are cleaning out old feelings of resentment, abandonment, and the victim, etc., all the way back to Me. Your emotional cleansing is more important than ever now because the emotions thread back deeper than you have ever experienced them in any existence. These emotions thread back through every agreement you have ever made, clear back to the agreement of the illusion of separation from Me.

I say to you, be angry with Me. I can handle this. I love you and am certainly strong enough to handle your fury and injustice. Give your emotions a voice; surrender into them, and give them the opportunity to break up. Take your health back. Take your prosperity back. Take your hope back, and you will experience the great peace of your Soul/Cell, and you and I will once again be vibrating in love and Oneness. You will feel My great love for you in every Cell of your bodies, in all existence of your Being. We will become one again, and our love and harmony will be so strong that it will mirror back to all their own love and magnificence. All will take this sound vibration of love in, and it will shatter their fear illusions, individually and collectively.

Fear cannot survive in love, but love can survive in fear. Love is! The fear emotions look for like frequencies and will reach out and connect to other fear frequencies and make the fear illusion stronger. This collective fear frequency will connect to the terror and fear in all fear-based countries. Your fear will assist to keep the frequency alive and feed the terror. It gives the terror fuel; your fuel and life force energy. Because it is your energy, the frequency then bombards itself back into you. So it is actually you who has aligned yourself with the collective, which is keeping you in fear and creating your own sickness, dis-ease, lack, and loss.

Remember, all fear has a frequency, and all mirrors you. If you are vibrating in a collective fear frequency of abandonment, you will continually bring relationships, people, and so on, back to you to abandon you. You will be vibrating in the energy of the pattern and draw it back to you, until you consciously decide that you want to change it.

Again, the way to change your old worn-out patterns is to surrender into them, break them up, take your power back, and bring your light, which was stuck in the pattern, into the now, to experience the peace and love of who you are. You then can create the love in your life that will not abandon you. You will know that your own self-love is the greatest love of all; it is the love of Me, loving you

You are Me, and I love you. I ask that you forgive Me, so that you can forgive yourself. When you can forgive yourself, you will have your innocence back. You will then only see others and life through your own love and innocence.

This is great power, and this is how your planet will heal and come out of duality. You are all, and as you see all in their innocence, you will mirror it back to all creation.

Love is and cannot be duplicated, by false light. Love is an energy source, which has a power frequency and song so powerful that it can never be destroyed. It is the highest power of all existence or consciousness. Love is.

Love's Guidance through the "Dark Night of the Soul"

"Love Is The Warmth That Keeps Your Soul Alive"

Without love, you would not survive or live very long. Your bodies would close down, and your minds would become paranoid and frightened. Love is the warmth that keeps your soul alive. It feeds your Cells and gives them life force. Even if you feel you do not have love in your life, you have the higher love of Me and others who are assisting you to awaken to the memory of the love that you are. You have love all around you, even if you are not open to it. Your etheric body picks up the vibration of this love and is sustained by it. Love is the food that feeds your Cells, and it is the light connection to Me that gives you the strength to be able to go on.

How do Souls who find themselves in karmic situations that seem unbearable, continue to go on? What do they hang on to? There is a love frequency fed through the silver cord, which is your Soul's connection to your body or the umbilical cord to Me. Remember, you are in My master computer system, and when the frequency in your body becomes dim, alarms go off, and a higher essence of My love of you is sent through the umbilical cord or silver cord back into you, your Cells, and bodies.

For some Souls in these dark situations, it is time for them to come home. They leave their bodies and move through a tunnel of light with a band of angels back into the dimension from which they incarnated. When they know they are safe and have gone through a cleansing or healing process, they review the lifetime to understand the lessons and the growth that has taken place. If the Soul has evolved and completed its agreement of the lifetime, it moves into a higher octave sound frequency of that dimension or into another dimension totally.

Through all of your processes or lessons, either on the Earth plane, some other planet or in other dimensions, you are always guided. You are never alone. You have a Soul's guide

214

with you that has been assisting you through all lifetimes and agreements. You also have many Masters, angels, and other guides or teachers.w As you continue to evolve and your vibration becomes higher, many times your guides and teachers change. You continually bring guidance to you that match your vibration. Eventually what happens is you and the Masters and teachers become one. There is no separation.

Other Souls who agree to go through what seems to be the most difficult dark situations become stronger and find their purpose and mission from the experience. When they leave the situation, they become leaders to assist the collective out of duality. At all times, they are very much with Me; I am constantly at one with them to guide them through the experience. From this place they are in a constant state of grace in other dimensions. The grace vibration is the song frequency, which empowers them to be able to play out the end times of the karmic agreement. Many times they leave their bodies in their sleeping state, and they are studying with great Masters and teachers in Spirit to have a broader understanding of what the lesson is about for themselves and others.

Sometimes Souls do not consciously live through the experience, but they always evolve to a higher plane when leaving the body. There truly is no death. You evolve to a higher consciousness.

All Souls who volunteer to go through such an experience are greatly honored by Me. They go through the experience for the collective and to create change for the World. The Souls/Cells of Me who do come out of the experience are changed forever; they move into a higher vibration or consciousness of themselves and have a higher purpose on the Earth.

One of the great Master teachers that I so speak of is Mandela. He went to prison an angry man and came out with great love, light, peace, and honoring of all humankind. He went forward to lead not just his people, but all people, back to One.

Just as Souls on your planet agree to go through "Dark Nights of the Soul" to lead the collective into a higher vibration of

Me, planets agree to do the same thing. Your Mother Earth's Soul is a great Master Soul and is greatly honored for her dedication to go forward to assist the Souls/Cells/Inhabitants of your planet to awaken and to be a leader of the collective consciousness of other planets.

She is a Master Soul who is healing the Earth and bringing it into Ascension and enlightenment. Just as you in human form need the love-light frequency to be able to exist or live, so does your Mother Earth's Soul. She has gone through many "Dark Nights of the Soul", as many of you have. Her purpose is to assist the collective Souls of other planets and stars to move into Ascension and enlightenment. She is not the only feminine Soul of the planet in this agreement. Just as you have many of you on your planet who are awakening in love and light and merging back together as one, Mother Earth's heart is doing the same with the other planets.

"As you continue to love yourself and move into your higher aspects, you are the collective wings that energetically carry this great Mother Planet back to her beloved and into Ascension."

15

MOTHER & FATHER EARTH AND THEIR 2012 REUNION

The Father Shadow Earth

The Shadow Earth is the male and self-realized Ego of the Mother. All need the male and female, or the heart and mind, for balance. With only one essence, the polarity is out of balance. The male Earth is the partner to the Mother Earth. They work together to bring all Earth Souls back into the light. Their Love Story is strong. They are the total balance of each other. They hold the love, light, and purpose for one another to assist Earth and its inhabitants through the 2012 doorway, into freedom, enlightenment, and Ascension.

You could say Father Earth is the light body of the Mother. He is her constant heart companion and protection. They are the same planet Cell or Soul that have expanded themselves beyond time to embrace and guide all Souls home again into their own divine partner's heart and into the heart of Love and Creation.

Father Earth is a place where the shattered Soul aspects go who have appeared to have failed their earthy mission. It is what some on your planet might call purgatory. It is actually a holding planet of the Ego.

These aspects that agreed to hold the Shadow come to the Father Earth planet after transitioning from Earth. It is a place where these Ego aspects have all of the different lessons that they have done to others or themselves constantly mirrored back to them. As the lessons are mirrored back to them, they feel the emotions of all who they have harmed or hurt. There is no way for these Beings to turn away from this mirror experience. As they connect with other Ego aspects on Shadow Earth, they experience what the Beings have done to others. They feel the collective pattern of fear, terror, control, injustice, grief, loss, and abandonment. The Beings on the Shadow Earth go through this process constantly. The only way they are able to move away from it is to start feeling remorse. The mirror of this painful Shadow energy penetrates their whole Being until they feel they are going to break, and break is what they do.

Their protective fear wave structure begins breaking down until the Being starts understanding the pain and hurt it has brought to others. It is sometimes so overwhelming, the Being or Soul wishes it could die again to the place of non-existence. The Soul starts begging for forgiveness, and then a true healing starts taking place.

There are ascended light Beings whose mission is to come to Shadow Earth and mirror the constant love and light of the Shadow Beings' magnificence to them. From this place, the Shadow Souls start to feel, heal, and return to the light. After many veils have been unthreaded or released, the Souls leave Shadow Earth and move into the higher dimensions to go through another healing process. After this great cleansing and rethreading back into the balanced part of Me, the Souls can then choose to once again reincarnate. Some of these Souls are so comfortable to be the Shadows carrier that they choose to once again reincarnate into a Shadow lifetime. They will do this from a lighter, more conscious aspect of the collective Shadow. Many others choose to reincarnate as victims of the Shadow or as a light Being or warrior who comes up against the dark or Shadow. The Soul feels it has an advantage and much understanding of the Shadow because it has vibrated in it so much. It understands the Shadows' mind, how it works, and the way it maneuvers in and out of the light.

218

Sometimes, the transition is difficult because of what you might call peer pressure from the collective memory of the brothers and sisters of the Shadow. Once the Being is back on the Earth, the collective Shadow ones will do all that they can to bring this Being or Soul back into the Shadow. If they do not succeed they will try to break it to the point that the soul no longer wants to be on the Earth. It is a difficult transition because the newly awakened light one has had much karma with the dark ones. The dark ones will come into the mind, body, and frequency of the Soul, trying to stop it or block it from its Soul's purpose.

They are able to do this from what you could call past agreements. Since there is truly no past, present, or future, the dark ones come in through doorways, which have been left open from prior experiences or lifetimes. The newly awakened light Soul also carries the memory in the DNA of being in alliance with the Shadow.

The way to come out of this experience is for the Being to travel through many of the veils of illusions, retrieve aspects of the Soul, and break all contracts that were left in these other places, in what you call lifetimes. The power of your Being, your presence, is in the Now. The purpose of this new lifetime is to go through all of the veils of illusion or separation and bring all aspects of self into the Now, into love and light. You then realign your energies with the collective light aspects of yourself. This can be done, however it takes dedication to your purpose. It is also important to surround yourself with other light Beings who hold the light and love for you and support you through your mission.

The male planet Earth is a very strong structure, which can house all of the anger, hatred, and control that is at war against Me. It is a place for all of the Shadow Beings who are at war against My light to be able to heal. The male Earth's Soul is in total balance with my mind, which is self-realized and enlightened. It threads through the heart of My balance with Sophia. Mother and Father Earth's purpose is to mirror their perfect union of love into the light of all others' hearts

Mother Earth

The Mother Earth is the heart of the male Earth, and they work very differently, yet together, to balance all fragmented Soul aspects to return to our highest Oneness, beyond duality. I am a loving Father and have created a space or planet for the Shadow to go through a deprogramming and awakening of the higher consciousness of themselves. As the Mother Earth is ascending and moving beyond time, she is holding the frequency for Father Earth to also lift his veils for his inhabitants collectively.

The Father Earth is very loving, yet also very stern and holds a strong grip of love to assist its inhabitants to remember who they are in their Souls' awakening. You could say the Father Earth is more of a tough love figure. The dark ones must come to the Father Earth to heal, release, and understand the role that they have played for the Shadow before going into other dimensions. The male Father Earth exists in another dimension, and yet when the veils are lifted, it can be seen and has even been photographed. It is a different frequency, not like the solid energy of matter that is the Mother Earth. Its body is etheric. The Father Earth has agreed to hold the karmic Shadow energy of My mind, and the Mother Earth is the karmic energy of My heart's awakening. Both planets are vehicles for all aspects of Me, both the emotional and mental, to cleanse old fragmented karmic bondages.

As the Mother Earth continues to move beyond linear time and through the 2012 Portal into Ascension, her vibration is also moving beyond the physical karmic matter structure. She is a crystalline structure, which has been activated. You, the inhabitants of the planet, are also changing and activating your DNA structures into a crystalline form. As this happens, you are aligning your crystalline structure with the Mother, becoming one with her and assisting each other into a higher frequency sound, of love, and light. You then realign with Me, the crystalline structure of creation. All male/female aspects of Me are energetically calling their Cells back together. To be whole, the male and female aspects of the self on all levels must vibrate together in love and harmony.

I am holding the light and love of My male and My female Sophia for you to realign with. I am mirroring Myself back to you. As you realign in perfection, balance, love and harmony, you mirror back to others their perfection and magnificence. For the Mother Earth to be totally in the balance of love and harmony, she must also be at one or realign with her male aspect. For her to be able to do that, she must turn her vibration up, as she is doing, to move into another frequency or dimension, as her male is not in a physical/matter form. You, the inhabitants of Earth, are assisting her in this transition.

Everything is changing frequencies. This 2012 DNA time code awakening is not just happening on the Earth. It is happening in all dimensions.

The Mother Earth is a hologram of Me that is opening and awakening the heart of many of the fragmented aspects who have tried to stay in control. The Father Earth is also a hologram of Me where the Spirit aspects that could not find their way back to Me on the Earth, come to heal. As I said before, they have left their earthly bodies and are no longer in physical form. They have moved beyond the heart of the Mother and are in the arms of the Father. The Father Earth is not a place of punishment. It is a place for My old mind-set to realign with the heart of the Mother, to break the old mind-set of fear.

I am the Creator of all, and My mind and heart connection is much stronger than the fragmented aspects of Me who are trying to be in control or have power over others because of their feelings of insignificance. I know I am repeating Myself, and yet I want you to be able to absorb what I am speaking of. I am a loving, forgiving father because I created you as Me. You are Me. All of you are Me. I did not just create the light ones who are assisting the Mother and all who are ascending. I also created the Shadow Beings who are also assisting the Ascension. How could I love one and not the other, when all are My creation? Many of the dark ones were created before My heart was awakened by My beloved Sophia. These dark ones that many of you hate and fear are aspects of you. They were created by Me and you. We are one.

As you truly understand this, you will feel love and compassion for the dark ones. As you do this, you disempower them. They can no longer feed off your fear to give themselves a false sense of power.

Father Earth is a healing place for the dark ones. As I said, there are many light ascended Masters who have agreed to incarnate to Father Earth and are holding the light for Me and the planet to mirror to the dark ones their light. Everywhere the Shadow ones turn, they get to experience all aspects of themselves.

The 2012 Union

My telling you this story is leading up to the re-emergence of Mother Earth and Father Earth. For the male and female to be in balance, they must come together as one. Many of you on the Earth plane are now separating from and leaving old karmic-structured relationships and are coming home with your own twin flames in physical form. You are moving through the old illusions and veils, awakening into a higher frequency, and moving back together through time and into the arms of your beloved. Mother Earth is doing the same thing. She is moving beyond time through the veils of illusion and back together with her partner, Father Earth. Because their vibrations were different, they could not have vibrated together in their love sound frequency until both cleansed the old karmic structure, or what you could call collective lifetimes.

Just as the planet is moving beyond time and into the higher aspects of herself, you also are journeying through all veils of karmic illusions and reconnecting or merging with all aspects of yourself interdimensionally. When you are home in Spirit, beyond karmic duality, you are back together with your Twin Flames. There is much talk and speculation about Twin Flames. Will I meet mine on this planet or in this lifetime? Yes, I say to you, you will, if that is your intent.

You are the Cells of the planet and are moving through

old karmic structures and back together with your Beloved Flames. If you had come back together before this lifetime now, you would have had all of your patterns or veils communicating or contrasting with each other, instead of your hearts and Souls or Cells remembering and loving each other. You have lived and experienced many karmic lifetimes with your Twin Flames. Now is the lifetime to co-create heaven on Earth. To mirror each other's Soul's song.

When you have moved through the veils, you and your partner will vibrate in your Soul's songs and sounds and make beautiful music together. Mother Earth and her Beloved Partner, Father Earth, are going through the same thing. Their Souls' songs are now calling them back together, lifting them into the same frequency, so they will merge together as One.

When the Earth moves through the 2012 Portal at precisely the twelfth day of the twelfth month at 12:12 A.M., she will merge back together with the etheric body of her partner, Father Earth. This union will be a climax, a completion of the Soul for them. It will no longer be just the Mother nurturing her children. She will be aligned with her Beloved, and together they will be in perfect balance. The frequency of their love together will create such a balance of your Earth that the sound of their Souls' song will start disintegrating the fragmented Shadow.

Aspects of Me that are not in balance will have a very difficult time living on the Earth because the frequency of love will be too high for them. Many Beings will be leaving the Earth after this emergence. They will feel short-circuited because their physical bodies' vibration will be too low. There will be major light doorways open for these Beings to merge back into the light. There will be ascended Masters and Beings from many galaxies and universes who will be assisting these Beings home into the light. Many of the dark ones and the light ones assisting your planet to ascend are not from your universe.

Many of the dark ones have been kicked out of ascended, enlightened universes. They were allowed into yours because your Universe is still in karmic completion. Now is the time that

223

these Beings have run out of what you call time. They now have the choice and ability to go into Father Earth's deprogramming and healing process with great Masters of light, or their Souls/ Cells will eventually disintegrate or dissipate out of any form or memory, and their energy will be returned to Source.

Mother and her Beloved partner are already vibrating together in other dimensions. They have already reconnected as one. It is in this third-dimensional perception or reality where they need your continual love and support. As you continue to love yourself and move into your higher aspects, you are the collective wings that energetically carry this great Mother Planet back to her Beloved and into Ascension.

You are now in the highest consciousness frequencies of self in which you have ever vibrated. You have within your total memory and recall, if you choose, all consciousness. Your Soul has traveled through every experience a Being could possibly go through. You have been All That Is. You have played every role that could ever be imagined. You are now in the greatest show or production that you have ever agreed to go through. You have within your memory and experience all of the lessons, individually and collectively, that a person or Soul could possibly experience. Now is the time you have agreed to remember the emotions and feelings of these experiences and agreed upon lessons. The setup of your lifetime or story looks the same, but the outcome gets to be different. The outcome gets to be freedom.

You are now on the Earth plane to co-create Heaven on Earth. You are on the Earth to move through all the veils of karmic illusion and to remember who you are in physical form. As you do this, you lift your consciousness out of experiencing your life through your karmic emotions.

Because you are vibrating in every time period at once, your emotions sometimes are a little erratic. You are constantly processing love and fear, sometimes simultaneously. Everywhere you turn you are seeing yourself, for all is you.

You are great, enlightened, Ascended Master teachers who have agreed to lower your vibration and come to the Earth to have a human experience. Because your DNA is being activated, many of you are remembering who you are. This memory is opening and realigning you with the collective, enlightened, Ascended Masters throughout all dimensions.

As this happens, your ideas and perceptions of life change. You want for others what you want for yourself, not in codependency, but in the larger picture of the collective purpose. You move out of the I/Me and into the I/Am. You become more interested in the health and healing of others and the planet. From this place in the core of your Being, you feel and experience your Souls' greater purpose: to become one with the total balance of love with your inner Male and Female, to align with Mother Earth and her divine partner Father Earth, to move through the 2012 doorway collectively, and into ascended, enlightened Oneness.

"You are actually a biologically perfected race of My highest consciousness. You are blends of many colors, sound frequencies, and vibrations that resonate with Me throughout creation."

16

RETHREADING YOUR DNA THROUGH THE 144 DIMENSIONS

I know there is much speculation on your planet about the dimensions beyond Earth. There are 144 dimensions of light that lead back to Me in the highest. There are also dimensions in between dimensions. Just as you have many layers of your bodies, you also have energies in between your bodies. These are the frequencies that assist your physical bodies to vibrate in harmony, or you could say they are the glue that holds them together.

All bodies of consciousness vibrate in the same way. I have said before, "As above, so below, on all levels." Your own bodies are the higher bodies of Me. Your physical bodies hold My DNA of all creations, not just the DNA of your biological parents. Your DNA is My DNA system. Your bodies and DNA thread back through all dimensions to Me, because all is Me and was created by Me. The DNA responds to all consciousness because it is all consciousness. In your DNA, you have memories of all dimensions. As you continue to release the veils of illusion, your DNA unveils or releases the karmic blockage, which has kept you from vibrating in your highest form.

You have 144 strands of DNA. Not all of these are in the physical body. You have an etheric DNA system that holds and carries the collective consciousness of all levels of My DNA. This system threads through all dimensions collectively. This DNA system is in your etheric or energy bodies and is connected to all consciousness. Your etheric DNA system carries the memories of the collective in all systems and creations.

What you do not carry in your physical DNA you carry in your etheric DNA. This system is the portal through all creations. It is a very sophisticated system and is connected or hooked up to a dimension of computer systems, which access all 144 dimensions. Just as you have an Internet system that supports your world here, there is a system that accesses all worlds, galaxies, and universes. This system monitors and threads through all of My creations. It actually has the capability, not only to monitor frequencies, but also to realign and readjust them. An alert system goes off if the creation of Me is too out of balance.

You might ask, if this is true, how come you allow planets such as Maldek to die? I did not consciously create this. It was you of Me, who needed to grow in consciousness, that went through the lesson to understand what the circumstances would be if the collective did not come together in love, peace, and harmony. Maldek was a Cell/Soul that agreed to give its life for the consciousness of you to awaken. The life force of the planet, or outer layers of the Cell, died, and then the essence or Soul was lifted to Earth. It is the same death scenario as what happens to your physical bodies on the Earth plane. Your physical body dies, and yet, your Spirit moves on to a grander expression of self.

Your sophisticated etheric DNA is monitored and adjusted by the master computer system. The energies are adjusted, and when the collective rises to a higher knowledge, this system then opens another light ray portal or doorway. As this happens, you and the planet both have the vibration of your DNA accelerated or, you could say, fine-tuned.

You are a beautiful instrument, which vibrates in heavenly

song. As your DNA is continuing to be activated, your song is becoming even more beautiful.

All on your Earth and on other planets and galaxies are connected to this system. You are a program that is very much alive. How could you explain your bodies: hair, teeth, reproductive, and other organs? Where did they come from? How does your body know what to do? How does your body know the different cycles that it goes through? After birth, you go through adolescence, young adulthood, middle age, and then full-bloom maturity. Your body also goes through the different cycles of emotions connected to the appropriate ages. Your body eventually goes through a completion cycle and releases the Soul back to Me. You call it death. I call it birth. You go through an ending cycle of your life on your planet and into a rebirth of your light, love, and innocence beyond a time frequency.

Look how your bodies have evolved through time. Your life span is much longer now because your vibration is higher, and you have more of a conscious connection with Me. You used to see Me or experience Me outside of yourself, and now you experience Me as you, or you as Me. The veils are being lifted, and you are remembering who you are. You are reconnecting with and remembering each other in physical form. The veils are being lifted between you and the memory of Me. You are now co-creating Heaven on Earth with Me.

All is continuing to evolve. Look at the evolution of your planet and all of you on the planet. Your Earthly computer systems have become more sophisticated every day. So have My master computer systems in all other dimensions. You are the Cells of Me, and as you continue to grow and evolve, so do I. We are constantly growing and evolving together, because we are each other. This master computer system connects to a vast Internet system through all dimensions. This is how the dimensions stay consciously connected to one another.

As I explained, the etheric DNA is in this computer system, and when the collective grows, the system activates your etheric bodies and as the adjustments happen, your sounds or songs come together and create a frequency so high that it breaks the sound barrier to the frozen emotional veils. When this happens, another doorway opens, lifting you all into a higher dimension.

Your human race is not the only race in this system. All races throughout your universe are being monitored and are part of what you could call your universe's website or My collective mind-set. When one goes into the website for your universe, you can experience every galaxy, planet, and star system. Just as when you go into your Earthly Internet system, you can find anything you need to know about your planet and its inhabitants.

This interdimensional Internet system is set up the same way. Every universe has its own website and is then broken down into categories. When I want to see what is happening in My worlds of creation and go to this system, I have the capability to experience all at once. I can see through my Knowingness the growth, the love, the light, and so on, and what is needed to assist your planet and others in their Soul/Cell evolution. As you continue to evolve in consciousness, you will also experience more through your Knowingness.

The 144 dimensions that I so speak of are in your universe, and all universes have 144 dimensions. As you continue to move beyond time and the universes no longer vibrate separately, the dimensions will open up to one another. They will not collide. This would be like you traveling to Mars or Venus or another planet to visit friends or relatives. You have had civilizations on your planet when this was done, and it will happen again for you. You have many visiting your planet now, and soon in spiritual time, you will be physically visiting them.

Just as you have a civilization on your Earth, these dimensions also have civilizations. Each dimension holds a different frequency or ray.

Jeshua's/Sananda's home is in the 13th dimension. The 13th dimension is one that is a portal through all dimensions. It is a time portal frequency where Christ and the Masters who work with Him can vibrate through all creations at once. The Christ dimension had to be close enough to your Earth for Him to be able to assist and monitor the Earth at all times and also for him to have a high enough frequency to move you through and beyond all dimensions.

Sananda has a crystal temple in the 13th dimension that He shares with His beloved Mary Magdalene. There are also crystal cities in this dimension that were created through thought. The crystal cities have many color frequencies that thread into your planet and through all dimensions so that the dimensions will vibrate in harmony.

It is from the 13th dimension that the crystal cities that are being placed around your planet were formed. They were created in thought and strategically placed over the unbalanced cities on your planet. Just as We are one with you and assisting you in your Souls' awakening, cities have a Soul or consciousness, and the crystal cities are holding the light for the Earth cities to evolve and awaken.

The 13th dimension receives its life force from the Central Sun's energy. The Central Sun is the generator source for this dimension's consciousness to build the crystal cities. As Jeshua/ Sananda is the light one who has agreed to bring your planet into Ascension and enlightenment, He has agreed, with His team, to assist your physical bodies and their DNA into crystallized form. Mother Earth is a crystallized form, which is also vibrating this crystal frequency to you...The Christ frequency is the Golden Ray, and this is the energy your planet is vibrating in now. The generator for that source is the Central Sun's Golden Ray. Jeshua's/Sananda's bodies are of the crystal golden frequency. He vibrates in this frequency at all times and is able to hold that frequency for you and your planet.

Many of the other Masters vibrate in and hold the vibration for you from the 7th Ray. Until this great awakening of now, your body's physical DNA has not been high enough to receive frequencies higher than the 7th Ray vibration. Your bodies would have blown out, or the light would have blinded your mind. This high vibration would have created a feeling of not knowing who you were, almost like amnesia. Some of you are feeling that now.

Your bodies are a divine blueprint of Me. It may not seem like it to you because many of you on the Earth plane have imbalances in your physical, emotional, and mental bodies. As you continue to unravel the karmic veils of illusion, your body will once again purr like a fine automobile. Your bodies are divine programs, or you could even call computers, which were created in perfect harmony with Me through all creations of Me.

The computer or program body is a perfect creation. As you are in a physical form, or what you could say a matter form, your computer needed the "inner" net system and strength to be able to hold all frequencies of My consciousness. You are actually a biologically perfected race of My highest consciousness. You were created by Me in My highest form. You are All That Is. Why do you think there is so much interest in your planet and in you as humans?

I have heard much speculation from many of you on your planet. A few of you have channeled that you are a genetically manipulated race. In theory, this might be correct, but in essence, it is just the opposite. You are a race that has My highest collective DNA system. You hold in your DNA systems All That Is.

You are not a race that has had your DNA manipulated to the place of being less. You are a very superior race of total consciousness. How could you possibly have all of the experiences and consciousness awakenings if you did not already have these memories of All That Is within you? You are now rethreading through all 144 dimensions and awakening on a cellular level of all knowing.

As your DNA is being unthreaded, you are expanding into other dimensions of yourself. As this happens, you open the door for the dimension of Me, and you, to become one. Many times, as the light veil is lifted collectively, you may open up to what could be called Shadow dimensions or unconscious dimensions of Me, which were blocked out of your DNA. When this happens, and the veil is lifted, the DNA that was dormant is awakened.

If you have had lifetimes with your shadow brothers and sisters, and your DNA is activated you may vibrate once again in the sound memories of them. This collectively opens the door for them to vibrate with you. This is why many of you are now consciously seeing and experiencing the dark ones or the Shadow within yourself. As you are moving through all veils and returning home, your individual and collective Shadows are becoming frightened because they know their false reign of power is coming to an end.

They are projecting information to you, that you are an inferior race, that you are less than. If you were less than, why would they have so much interest in you? They have so much interest in you because your DNA system is an alignment of total consciousness. They have so much interest in you because they know that you have in your DNA all the answers to all questions, to enlightenment, Ascension, and creations. They need this information to block you from ascending back into Oneness.

As I said before, they have no power on their own. They feed off your emotional bodies. They are keeping you in fear, and the fear frequency has a sound, which activates their adrenaline. Because you have had many lifetimes with each other, they can go into your Akashic Records, find your vulnerable fear spots, and project more fear into that collective emotional pattern to control you. Their purpose in doing this is to keep their consciousness or lineage alive.

Your race has a very high-level DNA system, which holds total consciousness. I created you as this because I knew the unconscious Souls would try to thread into you, to keep their roles alive. You agreed to come to the Earth plane to assist all consciousness out of duality and back into Oneness.

How could you possibly do this great task if you did not have all of the tools within yourself? I would not ask you to assist and then create a race of consciousness that was not high enough to perform the task. As you, the totality of My consciousness, agreed to go to the Earth, you knew what the agreement was.

When you got to the Earth, you forgot because your DNA systems were threaded through so much duality. This had to happen so that as the vibration on the planet became high enough, your DNA would be activated in all dimensions, not just the light. As your 144 strands of DNA are being activated, you are turning on the light collectively in the Shadow dimension.

You are then collectively bringing the unconsciousness back into the light. Contrary to many projected and channeled beliefs, this is happening. If it were not happening, your Earth wouldn't have so many conflicts going on. Your Earth is a hologram, which has played out many end times, ends of civilizations, and ends of karmic duality. Just look at the human species now and how it has seemed to evolve through perceived time. Do you not think that I had a hand in this? I allowed and assisted many other species to go to the Earth to evolve their consciousness. Some did evolve and others' Egos betrayed them. Others played out the last of their karmic agreements and left.

One of the races I speak of is the dinosaur. They did not become extinct. They played themselves out physically and left the planet changing into an etheric form. They still exist but in a very different vibration. They are the reptilians that have so much interest in your race and your planet. They live in a frequency that is in between dimensions. They did not evolve their consciousness into their highest. They stayed at war and in the Ego with one another and eventually wiped each other out. The same thing is happening with the Shadow or unconscious ones now. Their fear-based Egos are wiping each other out.

Not all of the dinosaurs were wiped out through their Egos. Some became conscious and decided to leave and come back to Me in their highest form. They moved back into the collective consciousness of the learned or expanded lessons.

Because those of you light ones on the Earth are now carrying in your DNA all collective consciousness, you are carrying the memory of the split between the dinosaurs. As the enlightened dinosaurs came back to Earth in another form, their DNA held the memory of the experience. Because you are one, your collective DNA has opened the door for the reptilians that were the dinosaurs to have access to you and the planet. This is

233

our agreement. It is the only way we can bring all consciousness home beyond duality.

The reptilians know your planet and the doorways to your planet because they once lived there. It was much easier for them to exist on your planet in physical form. This is why they are trying to once again gain access to your planet. It is difficult for them to live in between dimensions as they do. The energy there is gray, misty, and moldy. They are using your highest consciousness and the consciousness of your planet to keep their existence alive. On their own, they have no power. They have misused it and are feeding off you to try to stay alive.

There are many other races such as this. Many of you have had encounters with them and are continuing to. It may not be comfortable at the time, but if you can remember that you agreed upon this to bring the whole collective consciousness out of duality, you will take your power back. You won't be in the fear/victim role.

As I said before, the false Gods come in through your fear-based victim consciousness. When you know you agreed to allow them to once again tap into your DNA system, in what seems to be individually but is really collectively, you have the power to realign your sound frequency with Me in the highest. These Beings then have the opportunity to come home with you into the light or eventually to disintegrate out of form.

I will speak to you more about these different races and their forms in my next book. The purpose of these writings is to build a new or higher conscious foundation for you to align with collectively.

You come to the Earth as a Soul, yet you carry within your DNA the collective consciousness of all understanding of the highest light consciousness as well as all Shadow conflict. You are All That Is. You are the highest vibration and consciousness of any race that has ever inhabited your planet. You have lived every lifetime, every emotion, and every understanding of all that was and is needed to bring the collective back to Me in the highest form. Because you are each other, as you do this, you are rethreading all Beings of Me, who are you, back into Oneness.

You are a collective consciousness, which is assisting each other to assist Me to bring all out of separation from Me. Some of the information within your consciousness and DNA is from the collective. It is not an actual experience that your individual Soul went through. You received the information from the collective Source. Because you are each other, the experience is almost as grand as if you actually experienced it yourself.

Your bodies are very sophisticated Internet systems that are plugged into each other. If you have a memory of yourself in a lifetime where, perhaps you were crucified for your spiritual gifts, your cellular Internet system will open up all websites within the collective and align you with everyone else with the same experience. You will then carry every memory within yourself of all who have been tortured or killed for their spirituality. This is why many past life practitioners can take you back into the same lifetime, and you may have many different experiences or outcomes. One person may tell you that you were a man in that lifetime, and someone else might see that you were a woman or a child. You may have one person tell you that you were a man in the Holocaust; someone else may tell you that you were a woman or child.

You may actually have been in that lifetime, but because you are a collective Soul, you experience the memory of many different aspects of yourself at the same time. You may also be connecting to the collective experience of the lifetime and releasing it for the collective.

What is really happening is that you are connecting to the collective memory of the experience. As you release the emotions of the lifetime or experience for yourself, you are breaking the pattern loose for many. When this happens, you actually go into the collective website and break loose the pattern for the collective.

This also happens in the highest or light lifetimes. As you awaken into these lifetimes, the websites go on in others and activates another level of light in their DNA. As you go back into light, ascended lifetimes, the same thing happens; you activate the collective, ascended, enlightened websites and assist the whole collective into another level of light.

You are aligned with the vibration of the planet's energy because you are at one with her or, as I spoke to you, you are the Cells of the planet. Every time the Earth goes through a light portal, or veil, you, as a collective, have the same experience. As Mother Earth's website turns on, She also assists other planets and stars collectively into a higher vibration. She aligns herself with other planets and stars that have already ascended and rides on their waves of light consciousness into a higher frequency. She also assists the planets and stars that are not as conscious into a higher wave frequency, for all is One. This Oneness of you is now rethreading your DNA through the 144 dimensions in your Universe and beyond, through all dimensions of Creation. You are coming home collectively to create Heaven on Earth in all life forms.

"Your threads of DNA flow through all forms of Me."

17

THE EARTH: A MELTING POT OF PLANETS, RACES, AND DNA

The Central Sun's energy moves beyond time and is the frequency that feeds your planet her light. The Central Sun is a generator system from which all of the suns in your universe vibrate. This system is a generator light that feeds the grid system and Soul of your planet as well as many other planets and star systems.

The Central Sun is in the center of the 144 dimensions, or in the center of your universe, and vibrates through all of the dimensions. It is the light system that coagulates the dimensions together. Each universe has a Central Sun generator system, and all Central Suns are generators for each other. They hold the light frequency for one another.

There is much confusion on your planet as to who you are and where you came from. I spoke to you earlier of the theory that you are a genetically manipulated race. You are actually a genetically threaded race. Your threads of DNA flow through all forms of Me.

Look at all the races on your planet and all their different cultures. Each culture has different tastes in food, clothes, music, religion, and belief systems. Some of your cultures feel more in their bodies; they move with the creation of Me, and they feel that their Souls' song and Mine are very much in harmony. They sing, dance, and vibrate with the music of creation. Their dance is a constant recreation of their life force.

237

Others on your planet experience Me more from their heart and do not allow their bodies to experience or express their Souls' or culture's song or music. Maybe their religions have told them that it is a sin to allow their bodies to experience joy, happiness, and freedom. Even though they do not experience Me through their bodies, their hearts are very open, loving, and honoring of Me.

Some cultures experience Me totally outside of themselves. I am an understanding in their minds, many times a God of fear and control. Their understanding of Me from their culture and religion is that I am a harmful God, and they fear their own song, expression, and freedom of life. They live from their heads and totally bandage their emotions.

When feelings and emotions are stifled, they break out sideways. These are the religions or cultures, which end up with much anger, guilt, and deceit. You are emotional Beings and must have an outlet to allow your emotions to express themselves. If the emotions are not allowed to express themselves, they become knotted up, and you do not understand what you feel. Many times your culture, or religion, may give you programs to experience love as fear or hatred or control.

When love surfaces, and you are afraid because of the feeling it arouses in you, you will then try to numb it in some way, or the guilt and fear from feeling it becomes so strong that you release the emotions of it onto someone else. When the other person feels hurt, then you feel better. You are not suffering alone. They are as hurt as you are, if not more, and you have a sense of your own power back. Your misunderstood and denied feelings and emotions take your power from you. Your fear creates a loss of your sense of control.

Other religions and cultures control whom you can love and what you can believe in. I see many cultures and religions on your planet that are so afraid of the feminine power that they do everything they can to oppress it, suppress it, deny it, and even crucify it.

The feminine is the power! The feminine is what opened My heart and gave My true sense of power to Me. I came into balance with Myself. Before My Sophia, I created through My mind, through My limited perception. When My Sophia opened My heart, My feelings and all My creations changed. I started creating from My heart. I experienced love. My whole frequency changed, and I created a higher consciousness from a balanced Me. My vibration to create was higher, and I started creating many beautiful colors and songs, which are you.

This would be the difference between creating or painting in black and white and creating or painting in full bloom color. My creation before My feminine was winter and summer. After My Sophia, My creations included springtime when everything is reborn and becomes alive with color, song, and dance, and autumn when the consciousness of Me could slow down and simmer a while before it went back into winter.

All seasons are needed to be in balance. Without the feminine there is no balance, only fear. There is no spring and no rebirth. The feminine is the birth canal. If one suppresses the feminine, they are living from a fear-based Ego control. They are trying to control or suppress the heart of Me, for fear of losing their power. They/you do not understand that the feminine heart actually gives you your power because it is love.

Many religions and beliefs speak of love and say that they are love, but love cannot be expressed from the mind alone. It must be balanced with the heart. The kind of love that these beliefs speak of is fear, not love. It is a control of existence to give them a sense of power or self-worth.

It is now time on your planet for the feminine to be unleashed and released for the planet and its inhabitants to heal. This is happening now. As the vibration is becoming higher, it is awakening the feminine feeling in all. The planet herself is the feminine, which is holding her heart open unconditionally for all. The feminine is all-forgiving love.

As you continue to balance your male and honor your feminine, you will do the same for others. You will see them in their magnificence and hold the love and light for them to see themselves in your mirror of them.

As I said, you have many races, cultures, religions and belief systems and you have many different colors of people on your planet. Where did they come from? In the beginning of civilization on your planet, you had primarily one race. This race was the dark-skinned ones. How did you end up with so many races, cultures, and colors? How did you end up with a planet of all these rainbow people?

As the veils are being lifted and you are remembering who you are, I hear many of you say, "I'm not from here" or "this is my first lifetime on this planet." In essence, this is true. Many of you are from other planets, star systems, galaxies, and even universes. You are a long way from home. Your seeds of origin are from other creations.

I spoke to you before about the Earth being a hologram and that you are aspects of Me that need to evolve and free yourselves from old belief structures of Me. You have come to the Earth as a collective consciousness of your people from your planet of origin. You are the seed from your planet that is here to seed with others, to heal the rift between consciousness and cultures.

The reason you all look so different is that your DNA structure and physical traits are from the people of your own planet. Now on the planet Earth you see many cultures blending together. Many races are marrying with one another. This is the divine plan. Eventually you will have a blend of many flavors, colors, songs, and music.

If you heard the same song over and over, it would become boring to you. Now, you get to experience many songs of all different cultures. You are blending your music together, blending your Souls back together as one.

You have had other civilizations on your planet when you have had Beings from all creations come together, such as Lemuria, Atlantis, Egypt, and others. You came together and got to know each other. You brought your energies and gifts to the planet to activate the grids of the Mother. This created the crystalline structure that she is today.

After Maldek, the Earth needed to be threaded with

a frequency that could hold the Soul of the great feminine. Before Mother Earth's Soul was in place, the Earth had been primarily a mental frequency or consciousness. It was a collective consciousness with other planets but did not actually have its own Soul. You came to the Earth to reseed it and prepare it for this time of Ascension.

When you came to Earth at these times, you did not all reincarnate here. Many of you came on ships or U.F.O.s. You came from many different extraterrestrial races and cultures. When it was time to go back to your planet of origin, some of you stayed behind on the Earth. Before the ending of those civilizations, you had already genetically connected with one another. You had children together, which created what many of you call a genetically manipulated race. I call it a genetically threaded race. From this rethreading you created a different race of people. The Earth is a melting pot where all cultures have come together to create a consciousness of one race: the race of love.

When you look at pictures of Beings from other planets, you will see some of them resemble the races here on Earth. This is because you are them, seeded from them.

This is how you have ended up with so many different races and cultures on the Earth. You seeded with them, and from this seeding came many cultures and languages. As the cultures and languages came together, they started branching from the original, creating new languages and cultures, yet still having the foundations of the original. They blended together.

When the split, or karmic completion, of the civilizations happened on Earth, and many Souls went back to their planets of origin, there was much grief, loss, and a feeling that something was missing. They had been on the Earth and experienced many songs, cultures, and creativity with one another. When they went back to their own planets, they felt like they no longer had much in common with their own people. Their people did not understand the incredible experience they had gone through.

The Beings who had originally come to the Earth and experienced these beginning cultures felt that if they came to the Earth again, they would once again have all the magnificent experiences that they had gone through before they started reincarnating through the new races, which had been created here. After they reincarnated back here, they felt just the opposite. They felt like they did not fit in anywhere, as many of you feel today. The new races that had been created on the Earth also felt great loss and felt left behind by the original races. They felt abandoned and felt as if they had lost the foundation of their cultures and one another. Those left behind started feeling separate and lonely and lived in fear of letting anyone new in. They did not want to feel the pain and separation again, so they started living in their own newly created culture.

Others came to the Earth when the stargates on your planet were formed. I will explain more to you about these gateways in the stargate chapter. The major stargates were architecturally created by a collective consciousness of extraterrestrials. I was in constant communication with the architects and builders of these gateways. When I realized it was too soon to activate the stargates, I asked that they be closed until another time, that time being, now. Most of the stargates were not activated because at the time of building them, there were Shadow Ego aspects of Me, still at war against Me, who wanted to manipulate and control the activation and all access to these portals.

After the stargates were closed, many of the Beings who had been instrumental in their creation stayed behind to protect them. They knew the power and purpose of the gateways, as did the dark ones.

The E.T.'s that stayed behind did the same thing as the other star people. They also procreated and started new races and cultures. The Shadow or Ego Beings staying behind also procreated with one another and took for their own many of the light women. There was a great war between the light and dark or Shadow, as there is today.

The Shadow ones knew that the only way to open the stargates was through a love vibration or frequency. They knew they did not have an understanding or experience of this and

242

believed if they had children by the light ones, the children would carry the frequency of love in their cellular structure and DNA. They started using and manipulating the DNA of their feminine light partners and their own children. They still had rather ruthless technology and would splice the DNA of their feminine partners so that they could receive their light frequencies and consciousness, which threaded all the way back to the source of Me.

They would then send frightened thought forms into the feminine DNA to control them through fear. They knew the feminine was the heart-love frequency. Their purpose was to extract the frequency of love, duplicate it, and open the stargates, because if they had access to the stargates, they believed they could control all worlds and take My power from Me.

The Shadow Beings were trying to buy time by controlling others through fear and feeding off the feminine love frequency to expand themselves. As this happened, there began a time of great turmoil and war on your planet between the light and Shadow. The Shadow used the feminine's love-light power to be able to fight the light. Remember, they had no power on their own.

After a while, the light and Shadow were very much seeded together because of the feminine being manipulated and the children being born of both the light and Shadow. As the children grew up, they felt a great devotion to both parents, as most children do. Because their DNA had been rewired, there was a power struggle within themselves between their own male and female. Many of the male gender felt more comfortable and powerful in the Shadow. They continued to reign in Shadow power and were in an alliance with their ancestors in other dimensions. The Shadow ones were then able to reincarnate through these children because they were of the same DNA.

Your planet has come full circle from the beginning of this original play. Many of you have had great experiences in both the light and dark and have made an agreement, even signed a contract, to assist Me in the highest to bring your planet of duality into Ascension and enlightenment. The stargates have matured as you have and are now ready to be activated and opened.

The Shadow or dark coalition in all dimensions does not want this to happen. If it does, they know they will lose their reign of power. Their energies are coming in through those of you who have had lifetimes with them and that have supported them and even worked with them against the light in those other lifetimes.

They are also coming in through the splicing of the feminine DNA system, both individually and collectively. They are also trying to manipulate the DNA through fear. They are sending fear thoughts, programs, and belief systems into the collective DNA. As I speak of the feminine, I do not just mean a feminine body. Remember, you have been All That Is, and even the male carries the feminine DNA. The more you move into the heart of the feminine love collectively, you close the door to any access that they may have to penetrate you.

This is why you have so many men on your planet who are gay. They have had many lifetimes as a female, and their hormonal systems are sometimes much more feminine than male. You also have the same thing happening to the feminine. This is what you could call a gender crossover. The purpose of this is to bring the Souls on your planet out of gender and back into love.

When you are back in spirit in the highest, you are not a gender. You are a Soul. You are love.

You are now on the Earth plane to experience and express love for one another, regardless of what gender you are.

When those in Spirit look at you, love you, support you, and assist you, they do not see you as you would. They can see the form body, the home, that you are residing in, but that is not their experience of you. They experience you in your Soul's highest essence: love. We/Me/They/Spirit experience you in your totality of Me, in your higher self, in your Over Soul, and light body consciousness.

"You are threaded together in love and light, spreading your energies multi-dimensionally through illusional time."

18

OverSouls and Light Bodies

OverSouls

I wish to speak to you of the light body of your great Mother Earth. You could say her light body is the link between her and her OverSoul.

Even planets have an OverSoul. Soul groups have an OverSoul, as well as you, the individuals. Jeshua and Magdalene are the OverSoul for the collective of you on the Earth. Eventually, all OverSouls move back to Me, in My highest, as I AM the OverSoul of the collective consciousness. OverSouls have a hierarchy, as do Masters and teachers. The OverSoul is a consciousness or understanding, which vibrates above a Soul's contracts or agreements of evolving. The OverSoul is holding the larger picture, or the energy pattern, above and beyond all lessons.

Each individual has an OverSoul, which is the orchestra leader, or vibrational sound energy, that holds the vibration of love and light in place for the Higher Self. The Higher Self is the Soul's guardian and connection with the OverSoul for the lifetime or consciousness in which you are vibrating. The OverSoul and Higher Self continue to thread light into your Cells until your Soul reaches the frequency to be able to expand its energy through the understanding of all lessons so that you can understand the lesson and integrate with the higher self and become one with your OverSoul's guidance.

Remember, every Soul has its own song, and when brought together with other Souls' songs, a beautiful melody or symphony takes place, healing the collective Soul group in which you are vibrating. This Soul Group's song brings all Souls in that particular group together to harmonize beyond the collective karmic agreements. You are then threaded together in love and light, spreading your energies multi-dimensionally through illusional time and back into your Soul Group's OverSoul.

As this happens, you start connecting with or threading into other dimensions of self, releasing the veils of separation and coming close to each other's hearts. You will actually feel your heart more open, many times through tears of awakening. You will experience more love, compassion, caring, acceptance, and forgiveness of others. This happens because you are looking through and experiencing through your heart, instead of your mind.

When your heart opens collectively, the tears are a cleansing of your own fears, hurts, prejudices, confusions, belief systems, and misunderstandings. As the collective love and light hold the frequency for you to purge what you call past emotions, you feel more love in self and for self. That is why you can feel more love for others. You can only give to others your own experience of love. As the collective is holding you in harmony and love, you begin to mirror back to others their innocence, harmony, and love.

All is love. You are in a continual cycle of moving back through karmic time frequencies and into My heart's sound of love. The OverSoul plays a big part of this process. Without the OverSoul, you would feel lost. Your OverSoul is your guiding light back to Me. It carries the highest frequency of your Soul's sound. You continue to follow the sound through many dimensions and back home.

As you move through the veils and reconnect with others in your Soul Group's song, your collective vibration connects you with your Soul Group's OverSoul. This is why many of you are so happy to be reconnecting with others of like vibration or consciousness. You are back together with your Soul family. You feel great love for one another and feel like you know each other. You feel this because you do. These Souls are you who are mirroring back to you love and acceptance, your Soul's song. You don't feel judged. You feel loved, which creates a vulnerability because the veils are gone, and there is nothing more to hide. They really see you and love you in totality of who you are.

When this happens, you know you have moved through much karmic patterning and are coming back together in your love and innocence. You may feel vulnerable, and at the same time, feel very safe to purge old, past misconceptions.

Once you move into this vibration with your collective Soul energy and ground in it, it becomes your new foundation. When the new foundation is in place, you move again out of this comfort zone and into an extended version of your prior self. You are constantly moving and expanding.

Your Soul Group's sound vibration expands with an even greater sound vibration of Beings, a larger collective OverSoul. As you expand again, you bring an even larger OverSoul whose purpose is to guide you through the veils into another greater OverSoul.

All of your great ascended Masters, teachers, and Archangels are in total balance of their Male and Female, sometimes seemingly androgynous. This is because their feminine heart has expanded through them as Sophia has through Me. They become one Being of the Feminine and Male breath. They constantly expand in and out of each other, with no separation; this hierarchy is a collective OverSoul, which expands through all dimensions through the song sound cells of your bodies. This penetration activates a higher vibration and alignment of you and your higher self. As you expand further into you and your higher self, you and your higher self integrate more as one self. As you and your higher self integrate more as one self, you expand further into your OverSoul. Eventually, you will expand back to Me, the OverSoul of creation, which is you in your highest, most eloquent form.

247

OverSouls and Light Bodies

All consciousness goes through this. As I was speaking to you, even planets have a Soul sound vibration. These planets are alive and have other planets and stars that they realign with to assist each other out of any karmic agreements and contracts.

Just as you, the Cells and Souls of your planet, are holding the light for each other in your Souls' Ascension, Mother Earth has other planets and stars that are holding the light for her in her Soul's Ascension. She is doing the same for them. They move together through karmic time and through all dimensions. The planets and stars are Cells of a larger body of consciousness, and they come back together as one.

So you see, as your planet moves into Ascension and enlightenment, the Earth is also assisting her brothers and sisters in their Ascension. There is an OverSoul consciousness, which is guiding their Soul group. As they come together in their Soul's sound vibration collectively, they move together in a higher vibration that is being guided by a higher vibrational OverSoul.

As the stars and planets in your galaxy come together as one love-light frequency, they expand this energy into other dimensions of self, or what you would call other galaxies.

You have heard the expression, "As above, so below." In actuality, this is true. The same cycle you go through is the same cycle that all life forms fold into and through. As you are the Cells of the planet, other planets and stars are the Cells or Souls of the galaxies. This can be taken back even further. The galaxies are the Cells or Souls of the universe. All universes are the Souls and Cells of My highest creation.

Nothing is separate from each other. All creation is Me, and I am all creation. As you are Me, that also means you are all creation, for we are one.

Light bodies

How is the light body connected to the OverSoul? The light body is the vibration of the OverSoul's consciousness, or you could say the etheric body of the OverSoul that is totally conscious. The light body extends from the OverSoul and connects to your etheric body. It is what gives your etheric body the energy to vibrate and it keeps you connected to the OverSoul.

Now as you are moving out of linear time, you are vibrating with and becoming more aligned with your light body. Just as the OverSoul guides your Soul, the energy of the light body connects to your etheric body and guides it. Now you are merging with your light body, just as the Earth is merging with her light body.

All is energy. Your light body is the highest expression of your light form. It is beyond time and vibrates with Me in My highest consciousness of love, light, and sound.

Many of you are hearing sounds as your Souls/Cells are awakening. You hear different frequencies at different times or in different circumstances.

As you are moving through all dimensions and realigning with your light body, you are hearing all aspects of your own frequency in these dimensions. Remember, all is you. You may hear sound vibrations, which seem dense, but as you readjust your thinking, you will hear the sound pitch readjust itself also. This is your own vibration merging with and being guided by your light body in and out of duality, or your Shadow back into the light.

You have always been very connected to your light body because it is you beyond karma, beyond duality. You could say it has been the guiding light or star that has kept you threaded to Me, for your light body is the light or energy of your Soul, which is the highest expression of Me.

Your light body is a crystal structure that is totally consciousness. It vibrates beyond any time structure and connects to the highest consciousness in all form.

As you are ascending and becoming a crystal structure, you and your light body are becoming one. The light in your physical body's crystal structure is also connecting to your light body's crystal structure. These crystal structures together have such a high vibration that all which is not light is being activated or squeezed out of its old form.

Your guiding light which is your light body, your etheric body, and your physical body are vibrating together, creating a combustion of light sound that activates the lower sound vibration within all of your bodies: the mental, emotional, physical, and cellular. All of the emotions vibrating in the lower sound frequencies are being activated, and there is no place for them to go but up and out.

Perhaps, in the past, you could continue to bandage these old emotions, but now this crystalline sound frequency is so high that it busts it loose. As it breaks it loose, it surfaces and needs to be released. The way to release it is to disempower it by surrendering into it. As you do this, you are breaking the pattern of the collective.

This is how you heal the world by healing and loving yourself. As you and your light body vibrate together, the sound frequency is so high that it breaks loose the karmic collective emotions from your bodies and systems. When this happens, you unthread from the collective pattern in your etheric body breaking its structure loose. You are merging with your light body into Ascension. Your light body also is aligned with the collective light body.

Many of you on the Earth plane are experiencing a great shift of your own frequencies or consciousness. You are not just intellectually verbalizing that you are one; you are actually experiencing it. You are vibrating in a higher vibration or caliber. You are seeing the world and your brothers and sisters through a different lens. You are feeling more love for All That Is, and instead of going into old thoughts of fear or condemning, you feel more love and compassion and see more of the divinity or higher consciousness of this shift.

When you vibrate beyond duality, there is no place for the song or sound of the Shadow duality to connect. When you are beyond duality and vibrating in love you hold the light collectively for all to be exposed to that which is not the love vibration. Even the dark has light in it. All gravitates towards the light.

Because you have not been vibrating in total knowing, it has been easy for the shadow to use your light. If the Shadow did not need the light, you would not have predators feeding off the light innocence of children. The children are pure consciousness of Me before duality's life experience settles in. The Shadow ones know this. Because of the innocence of children, they are easy prey. Inside this tortured adult, you also have the lost innocence of the child, which has been violated and dishonored in some way. This changed the person's sound vibration from love to fear, which opened the door for the Shadows' thought forms to penetrate them.

In the wintertime, many of you yearn for the sun and even go to areas where there is sunlight. Booths that bring light to you (tanning booths) are very popular in the wintertime. Your bodies, Cells/Souls crave the light. They crave their own existence. Countries on your planet that have very long winters have a very high suicide rate because there is not enough light to stimulate the pituitary gland, and depression sets in.

All was created by my light. Even before My Sophia opened My heart to love, I still created you in light. Light is consciousness. All need light. Just think, when you become conscious enough to hold these light rays for one another, you will literally blind the Shadow. When you are in alignment with the Me of you, you will emanate a light so bright that it will warm your world. Your world will feel warm from love. Even Souls who live in countries where there is not much light will feel love and light because they will be connected to the collective love and light from within.

All gravitate to the light to be able to exist. When you are vibrating in the highest of your love and light collectively, you lift the collective consciousness into a higher octave of sound. You are then vibrating in the song of your light body and assisting Mother Earth to vibrate in the song of her light body. Just as you assist the whole collective on your planet to turn on its light and open its heart to love, the Mother Earth is assisting other planets and stars of the galaxies to align collectively in a higher octave.

All consciousness has a light body. Just as your light bodies are coming together in the same frequency of Me, the planets' crystalline light bodies are also starting to rethread with each other, creating great harmony within your solar system. This harmony is a song that vibrates into other solar systems and on and on. Just imagine the great crystalline light show that is taking place and is continuing to awaken and expand.

As you realign with your light bodies and move through many dimensions of duality and activate old emotions, you are also moving through all of the dimensions and activating the highest aspects of yourself in all forms. Remember, all is you. When moving into these higher realms of yourself and realigning with your crystalline light bodies, you turn on the light to experience many light aspects of yourself. You may experience many Masters coming to you, showing themselves, communicating, and bringing information to you to share with the collective. You may experience what you on your planet call channeling.

In reality, what is happening is your channels are opening up, and you and these Beings are becoming one in the Knowingness. You and the Master light ones are in the same vibration, which allows you to access their consciousness. As this consciousness continues to expand within yourself, you move into the Knowingness and become your own Master and one with Me. There truly is no separation. The karmic veils of illusion are lifted, and you start communicating with vibrations that are in thought forms or etheric body forms. Your sound is alike, and you can then hear what wants to be communicated to you. You become a conscious channel of the Knowingness.

In what you call the recent past, many on your planet were leaving their bodies temporarily so that Beings could use their body or vehicle to bring information through to assist your planet in its Soul's awakening. The Souls that temporarily left the body were still connected to the body by the silver cord. The cord held the vibration for them to be able to come back into the body.

The Souls who were allowing themselves to be of service

on this level were of a high vibration to be able to allow this to take place. Yet, their vibration was still much lower than the entity speaking through them. It took much time and energy for them to be able to recoup after allowing themselves or their bodies to host the Soul coming through.

Many times the hosts that left their bodies had no conscious memory of what was being said through them. They could feel the vibration of the information but did not have a conscious memory.

Now that the vibration on your planet is so high, you are vibrating in a higher frequency, and this kind of host is no longer needed. In fact, it is somewhat discouraged. I want you to stay totally in your bodies and open yourselves up to higher frequencies of yourselves, of all knowing.

Just as I am communicating through this one channeling the book, I will be and am communicating with you at all times, for I am you.

As I said, many of you are experiencing many Masters and Angels around you in all dimensions, and because you are vibrating in all dimensions at once, many of you are seeing them, experiencing their great love for you, and communicating with them. Sometimes, this communication is not through the spoken word; it is through the Knowingness, or telepathy. As you move through the illusional veils, you do know everything because you are everything.

In realigning with your light bodies, you are realigning with Me in all dimensions. All you encounter are aspects of Me that are mirroring back to you your light and magnificence and also the Shadow within you, which needs to be loved, healed, and brought back into the light or self-realization.

See all as a gift. If you still feel emotional pain toward anyone or anyone's beliefs or patterns, then you know you need to heal and love that part of yourself. When you are in total alignment with all, you will only see and experience love. You will experience even the darkest ones in the higher aspects of themselves. You will have love and compassion for them; for

Beings who are in such fear that they are afraid to love or to let love in. This is the time that your Soul has waited for.

Having love, empathy, and compassion for others does not mean that you will give your power to them. It is just the opposite. You will love yourself enough that you will be able to hold love for them unconditionally but will have no fear of them because your fear-based emotions will be loved, healed, and freed.

I am reminding you that there is no past, present, or future. Just as you have already ascended and become enlightened in the future, so has your dear Mother Earth. You are from the ascended consciousness, which has come back to the Earth to assist others and the planet into their Ascension. You and other light ones have followed your frequency back in what you call time to rethread the collective consciousness into their higher self-expression beyond time.

As I spoke to you before, many have seen the Mother's light body, for she is merging back to her beloved male partner, and their heart frequencies are vibrating in a frequency of love that is breaking all old karmic sound barriers to frozen emotions and grids of the planet. This union's vibration of love is so strong that the heart opens up and draws the light body, not only around the planet, but also into it. As the Earth is a hologram, you could say it is three-dimensional. The light body threads through all dimensions, through the grids and meridians of the planet, and into the core of the Mother's Soul; this is happening now. The light body and the physical body of the planet are starting to merge slowly, as the heart and Soul of the Mother and Father are reconnecting beyond a time frequency.

A master genetic cleansing is taking place on your planet now. The light vibration is so high that it is disintegrating the collective fear emotions of the Shadow. In the past, the Shadow ones on your planet were trying to wipe out the light ones, such as Christ and other great Masters of the Light hierarchy who have walked "before". The coalition of the dark ones know and knew of the genetic cleansing that would take place because it has already happened in the future. This Shadow coalition has tried to disconnect the present from the ascended future by wiping out the light links, or Cells/Souls, on your planet who have agreed to be the bridges of light into the future.

They have done this for millions of years. Because there is no death, when the light ones leave their bodies and come back into Spirit, they release a karmic death pattern collectively and realign with each other in a higher light frequency collectively. They/You reincarnate together with an even stronger collective light frequency, and now your light has the ability to disempower the Shadow.

When Christ incarnated to your planet, He opened the door for the greatest light-love frequency ever to vibrate on your planet. The light ones of you went through many death portals, many wars, and genetic cleansings, such as the holocausts, and many of you agreed collectively to die and release old beliefs of who you thought you were.

You are now back together as the Second Coming of Christ. You are threaded throughout your planet as emerging lights and are finding one another and holding the light for Me, each other, and the planet.

This cleansing seems like a slow process to those of you in physical form. For Me and those of Me in other realms, this process is but a blink of the eye. The third eye is the eye that I so speak of.

As the Earth is shifting on its axis, it is shifting the Shadows' hold and breaking loose the frozen emotions or consciousness that is stuck in the grid system of the planet. This grid system threads back before the Soul of the Mother Earth was lifted here from Maldek. Not only did the Soul of the Mother bring much with her karmically that needed to be healed, she also agreed to take on and cleanse all karma from the body of this planet's collective consciousness. This shift has needed to happen slowly because there was so much history and density in the grids that a super consciousness of light would have blown out the crystalline structure or electrical system of the planet.

Now that the Earth has shifted on its axis and released dark vapors and poisonous gases from her structure, there is more room to hold the light. The light I so speak of now is the light body of Mother Earth. As I mentioned, many of you who are ascending and are consciously experiencing yourselves in other dimensions have seen the light body of the Mother. This light body wants to be seen and even photographed. The light is very high, and the more visible this body becomes, the more it lifts the vibration of your planet and all of the inhabitants. What one is actually seeing is the mirroring effect of the light hitting Mother Earth's crystalline structure and vibrating back to her crystalline light body.

In the future, Mother Earth has already ascended and is already enlightened. She has already moved through the 2012 Portal, back together with her beloved, and merged with her light body and OverSoul.

I wish to tell you again that you are not going to lose your planet. She is already home. This does not mean that you don't have to continue to grow and heal. You must, so that you can hold the light for her and yourselves to move from the past, into the present, to shift the future, to co-create Heaven on Earth.

I have spoken to you much about your thoughts. Thoughts have great power. You are the co-creators of Me. Know that we are already one with all consciousness, for all is Me. Together, let's co-create through intention, a higher consciousness for a harmonious world so that all can live in the Garden of Eden, in Grace.

*"The heart stargate in China is aligned with the hearts
and Souls of other planets who are in this great universal
awakening."*

19

STARGATES

Stargates and Time Portals

There are many stargates on your planet that were formed through thought and solidified into form. I am identifying a few of the larger energy sources for you.

As I was speaking to you before, the stargates were perfected through very high architectural teams from many planets and galaxies. The stargates are in geometrical alignment with the meridian lines of creation. Many Beings of the highest understanding of creation partook in the forming and creation of these gateways.

Different stargates have different purposes. You have major gateways and smaller ones that were created by many of the Beings of light, which had incarnated to your planet. The smaller ones were created to be the activators of the larger ones. The smaller stargates were created from the same architectural design as the larger ones. The designs were given to many Beings on your planet whose agreement was to protect the larger gateways or stargates.

One of the reasons you have such a great interest in your planet Earth from other Beings, Souls, and life forces, both light and Shadow, from other planets is because of the stargates.

The largest stargate is the one under the Giza pyramid in Egypt. There is much interest in this one because it is a time portal gateway that is generated by the Central Sun's energy. This time portal gateway runs through the universe's grid system. It is used as a passageway back and forth through any time zone consciousness. As I said before, karma is only in a time frequency. Beyond time, there is no past, present, or future. This stargate moves you beyond karma.

You could experience that much of the galaxy and universe you are vibrating in, goes in and out of time. When one understands how to use time, or you could say to manipulate time, you could create whatever your thoughts think instantly. One could then know how to manipulate matter. You would know everything simultaneously. You could create an instant thought manifestation into form.

The time portal stargate was designed to assist the light ones of Me to move very quickly to destinations. This was so that the creation would be able to expand its consciousness out of time and back to Oneness very quickly. This was not to manipulate time but to move beyond it quickly, to be able to assist all sounds-songs frequencies to harmonize and blend in love and light. The time portal takes one instantly through time, through illusion, and back to truth into Knowingness. All light would go on simultaneously.

The lords of light who would have access to this stargate would be the great Masters and teachers of light consciousness. The dark lords knew that if they could gain access to this stargate, they could control the worlds. They could move very quickly through time and know all at once. They would understand the consciousness of the collective of Beings or Souls on planets instantly. They would be able to use this light passageway and send down sound frequencies into the collective light, shattering their consciousness. The Light Souls would then have an electrical blowout. They would be short-circuited and would not be able to thread back to Me or one another. Their time frequency or thermostat would become blown out. If this were to happen, the dark lords could instantly manipulate and thread them into the collective thought form of the Shadow.

As I said, there is much interest concerning your planet.

258

The Shadow ones want to control your universe and turn it and its inhabitants against Me. If they can gain access to the stargates, they might be able to do this instantly because they could move the collective consciousness beyond time.

Many of you light Masters have great understanding of the stargates. Some of you even helped design and build them. You are now back on the Earth plane to protect them, your worlds, and the Souls or species of your worlds.

Even if you do not remember who you are yet, many of the Shadow brothers and sisters of you do and are targeting you to stop you from being able to activate the gateways. They know when this activation happens, and it will, that they will be powerless.

You ask, "Why do the Shadow ones have access to Me when I do not remember who I am?" Because you, your Soul/ Cell, has continued to evolve individually so that you could move beyond time and merge back together as a collective consciousness of My love and light. To do this, you had to move through many patterns, or what you could call lifetimes, to have the highest understanding. You had to lower your consciousness into a karmic time frequency to access the emotions that you agreed to go through to free your Soul. All of the agreements are in the Akashic Records. These records are open to everyone. The Shadow brothers and sisters are reading the records and are penetrating you through the unhealed emotions connected to these agreements or contracts.

You agreed to go through every experience and every feeling and emotion that could possibly be imagined. As you did this, many times you took on an illusion as a truth, and an aspect of your Soul/Cell still vibrates in the collective pattern creating a veil. Although the veil is an illusion, sometimes it is difficult to see through it or to move beyond it because of the emotional bondage connected to it. Now is the time that you are awakening and remembering who you are.

Now is the time that the coding in your DNA has been activated, and all veils are being lifted. This is why everyone

259

on your planet is going through so much emotionally. All the hidden emotions are having the bandages pulled off, and you are experiencing the pain of the collective.

You are truly experiencing the pain and hurt for one another, and you are also experiencing great love, caring, and compassion for one another. Look how so many of you have offered love, money, and support to the victims of the tsunami in the East, to Katrina victims, to earthquake victims, to children suffering, and other catastrophic awakenings on your planet. This is because you can truly identify with them. You feel them because they are you. As you assist them, you are assisting yourself. You are giving love, compassion, and more meaning to your own life.

The only way the stargates can be activated is for the highest golden love frequency collectively to harmonize. That is what you are doing now as you are moving out of duality. You are etherically moving through these gateways beyond linear time and reconnecting with yourselves in other dimensions. If some of the selves still vibrate in the Shadow, your own collective love and light is so high that it is disempowering your own Shadow and bringing its light back into you. You are re-emerging with self individually and collectively. From this like love-light frequency Song, nothing can penetrate you that is not of the same Song.

China Stargate - The Heart Chakra

There are many other stargates on your planet. The China stargate is the second largest. There is a stargate underneath the pyramids in China. Yes, there are pyramids in China. It is the feminine stargate. Is it not interesting that in China the feminine has been so oppressed, and yet, it is the country that holds the gateway to the heart? This stargate was created by Beings of Me who have ascended beyond any male or female aspect, and their hearts, minds, and Egos support each other in beautiful song. They vibrate in total Knowingness. We vibrate together in perfect harmony.

This gateway is in direct alignment with the heart of Mother Earth and with the heart of other planets and star systems. As I explained, just as you Souls/Cells on your planet have come back together in the heart with one another, so are the Cells of Me who are planets. The heart stargate in China is in direct alignment with the meridian system of the Central Sun's energy and in alignment with the grid systems of all central suns back to the center, with My heart, with My Sophia.

The heart stargate vibrates in total love and balance of My heart. It is aligned with the hearts and Souls of other planets that are in this great universal awakening. The Shadow ones have great interest in this heart stargate because they know the power that it generates. They have worked very diligently to block the feminine from having any power in China. They are not only blocking the feminine in the female but also the feminine or heart in the male. Mother Earth's Soul is a feminine warrior who has agreed to hold the light and love for the feminine throughout all creation to awaken.

The Shadow brothers of Me know that once the heart stargate is activated, it will open the hearts of the Souls/Cells of you in your world. As this happens, there will be a simultaneous opening of the other gateways, such as the time portal in Egypt. This Egyptian stargate is in total balance and is holding the strength for the Heart stargate. The only way any stargate can be opened is through love, or the collective vibrating in a heart octave or frequency, which resonates with the coding in the etheric electric system of the stargate. The stargate's etheric body system is a sound system. It can only be opened through a harmonizing frequency equal to it.

Because you are each other, as your Cells become conscious enough, you thread into each other and start sending the healthy balanced love into the Cells, which have been more dormant. You see this happening all over your world now. Souls/Cells are vibrating in a higher octave or sound than ever in your Souls' history. You are blending your Souls into a symphony of color and light that will eventually open the stargate.

Peru Stargate - The Root Chakra

There is a very powerful stargate in Peru that is the root chakra gateway. This is one of the reasons that there are great shamans in Peru. They receive much information energetically from the gateway. This stargate runs through the underworlds on your planet, as well as the other planets that your Mother Earth is in alignment with. This gateway opens the door to all tribal information through time.

The tribes that I so speak of are the beginning bloodlines on your planet. There is a great record room in this gateway or stargate that is desired to be accessed by the Shadow ones. As you know, they have great interest in the DNA. This record room has the DNA systems of the collective tribes and where and how they cross-seeded to be able to vibrate in physical matter on the Earth plane.

Many of the great shamans in Peru have access to these underworlds. Do you know you have underworlds in all dimensions? As these shamans travel to the underworlds, they go through what you could call a dimensional doorway/gateway that opens up to the conscious underworlds in all dimensions. These shamans have great power because they receive assistance from the other dimensions, just as those of you do who work in the higher dimension.

Because you have great duality in Peru, you also have great lords or Beings of darkness there who are protecting the stargate. They do not want it to be activated because once it is, it will open the door energetically to the bloodline history, and the color-sound frequency will bring the Souls of the bloodlines back together in the highest. The Shadow Beings would then lose their grip or hold on the ones that they are using through karmic agreements.

When this stargate opens, it will start releasing karmic vapors or emotions, which are stored in the collective bloodline of the tribes. This will start freeing and healing the separation between Souls or Cells.

There are many Beings, Souls, or shamans in Peru who
have not healed themselves emotionally, as there are many healers
all over the world who have not healed themselves emotionally.
As I speak to you, I am not singling out Peru as a dark portal of
consciousness. I want this understood.

Peru has a great consciousness and connection to the light.
It also has a great Shadow because it is the home of the root or
bloodline stargate. Because of this, it is easier for Shamans to
access other worlds. In doing so, if these shamans have not healed
old emotions, the door opens for the Shadow Beings to come in
and work through them. If one is still stuck emotionally, he/she
will not know it is the Shadow ones assisting him/her.

The Shadow ones are in fear of losing their existence and
are tricksters. They will not come to you and say, "Hi. I'm a dark
Being or dark lord who has come to assist you." They come in
through emotions or karmic lifetimes, which need to be healed.
If you have something like this happen to you, see it as a gift that
has come to you to assist you into your own Shadow so that you
could retrieve your light, which has been trapped there.

You are not a victim of this lifetime. You chose it for your
Soul's evolution and the collective Souls' evolution. You may
have a few detours along the way. These detours are designed to
bring you into a higher aspect of yourself.

The stargate in Peru may be one of the last to open. It will
open as the tribes of you come together as one.

If it opened before the other gateways, it would blow the
chakra system of your planet out. The heart and mind must be in
alignment, in agreement, and in harmony for the energy of the
root to open.

You could say this stargate is the kundalini of your planet.
You may have heard of people's kundalinis opening up before
the rest of their chakras were opened. Sometimes, this creates a
major blowout of their electrical system, which takes years to
heal. This would also be true for your planet. Remember, you are
a collective consciousness. You have many Beings who are star
seeds that have great vibrational sound frequencies. They align

with other star Beings collectively and are able to do great work individually and collectively to heal the Shadow on the Earth.

Stargate in Japan

Another stargate is under Mt. Fuji in Japan. Mt. Fuji has a very large crystal city placed above it. This crystal city threads its energy through the mountain and into the crystal stargate under the mountain. This stargate is a master activator for all of the crystal cities that have been placed above your cities around your world. As you move through the 2012 Portal there is a coding that will be activated, and it will download or activate the stargate, which will download the crystalline structures into the Souls and bodies of the cities.

When the stargate opens, it will send a higher sound frequency into the crystalline structure of Mother Earth. This crystal stargate has a direct link through the meridian system throughout your universe to the Central Sun. Your Earth is moving into the Golden Ray of My consciousness, which is the Christ Ray that is generated by the Central Sun's energy.

It is not just you in human form who are the Second Coming of Christ. Mother Earth is also the Second Coming. There is no separation between you and the Soul of your Earth. You are doing this Ascension together.

As you go through the 2012 Portal, this stargate will open and allow the golden nectar of you, the Christ energy, to permeate the grids and Soul of your planet. At the same time that this stargate opens to the flow of the Golden Ray, a spiritual stargate in the heavens will open, and the Earth will glide into freedom. When this happens, the Souls and Cells of Me, that are you, now inhabiting the Earth will also have your etheric body's vibration turned up, and you and the Christ Golden Ray frequency will come together as one. You will have moved into the center of the Golden Age.

There are many stargates that are strategically placed throughout your world. They are all connected to a stargate grid system, which is monitored by My master computer system and generated by the Central Sun's energy.

Mount Shasta Open and Active Live Stargate

Mount Shasta has a great Stargate, which is very active and open today. There are many other stargates such as this one, but this is the largest and most active. It is a gateway for a collective extraterrestrial civilization that lives under the mountain.

The Beings in this high civilization are star seeds that come from many worlds and are constantly monitoring, protecting, and realigning the grid system and matrix of your world. This world, your Earth, is the core base for all civilizations to come together as one.

As I said, you have many different E.T. races, which have reincarnated on the Earth plane to assist in the karmic completion of the end times. Great ascended Masters, Archangels, Commanders, Priestesses, and many other awakened Beings from all planets and dimensions are living together in harmony in this base. Through this active stargate, they are able to travel in and out of time simultaneously. They hold the light or sound frequency and consciousness from their star systems energy for the Earth. This is very much needed because the E.T.'s now living on Earth need the vibration from their own planetary system to sustain their life force.

This is how many of you on the Earth are able to stay balanced enough to stay connected to your light bodies. These Beings monitoring and protecting your Earth are aspects of you. They are assisting to hold your vibration through the grid system of Mother Earth. This grounds you through compatible frequencies to assist you to want to stay on Earth.

I know I am repeating myself through many chapters. It is through repetition that your subconscious will search your inner Internet system to find, open, and activate the codings and memories in your DNA of the highest consciousness of your Being. You and the grid system of mother Earth are connected to the divine matrix. This matrix is alive and runs through all creations. Each planetary system has its own wheel in this matrix. Because you have so many different species, races, and bloodlines from all planetary star systems inhabiting the Earth, you collectively vibrate through every wheel in the matrix at once. The E.T.'s living in the Mt. Shasta stargate also vibrate through all of the wheels because they are aspects of you.

Again, their agreement and intention of this is to integrate all creations together as one.

Because the Earth is a hologram of endings and new beginnings and is continuing to turn on its axis, it is emitting a color-sound frequency of death and rebirth that runs through the divine matrix. This creates a combustion of light that disintegrates the frequency of the collective karmic structure of the agreement.

As I explained, this creates a shockwave, or explosion, beyond any time frequency in all of the wheels of the matrix. Because you are the matrix, this combustion sends shock waves back into the etheric DNA system of the planet. The E.T. civilization in Mt. Shasta constantly monitors and balances the meridian system of the Earth, and because you are the Cells of the planet, you also receive a frequency adjustment in your etheric DNA systems. This activates the memories in your physical DNA of a death and rebirth. This is what you and your planet are going through now.

Because you and the planet are live aspects of the divine matrix, a light doorway beyond time opens up and creates a collective sound frequency, which opens a doorway or gateway for all Souls to move into a higher consciousness of love, light, wisdom, and knowledge of your Being. It turns the light on in you and propels you collectively through an etheric doorway/ Gateway into a higher consciousness or understanding of the God/ Goddess within your own Being. This expands you into being the co-creators of your life purpose and destiny.

This is how the doorways of the 11-11 and 12-12 and all other passageways open. You and the divine matrix create a combustion of light, which moves you out of form and into a higher collective Knowingness. Every time this happens, you and your whole world receive this higher instruction or intention. This comes from the live matrix. As the wheels continue to turn, your collective DNA opens and receives higher consciousness, which awakens you in the collective.

Mount Shasta is the greatest, largest, live, activated and open portal and stargate. It is holding the light for you and the Earth in this agreement of Ascension and enlightenment. Many other activated and open stargates are vibrating together with this major gateway. They are also assisting all of the E.T. races on your planet to be able to hold their frequency.

As you continue to move beyond time and through the portals opening up for you, you will find yourself merging together through these stargate portals. There will be no separation between your vibration-sound frequency and your brothers and sisters of light who maintain these stargates. You will remember that you are them, and they are you.

*"The feminine in small Cell/Soul Group consciousness
had experienced its power of sisterhood through love.
They also knew that if they could create this love
safety net in small Soul groups, they could be very
powerful to come together collectively in a very
large Cell/Soul Group."*

20

THE HEALING OF THE FEMININE

Lucia

This is Lucia, Goddess of Light. I come to you today to assist you to reclaim your feminine. It was not taken from you; it was crucified, just as Jesus and other Masters were crucified. Your feminine energy was used to expand the lords of darkness.

That has now come to an end. Your feminine has been restored to you along with your feminine power. You have been rewoven with us, so that as the collective feminine, we will now hold the light, strength, and power for you to rethread through the feminine, back to the highest feminine of Sophia. You are great spiritual warriors; you are now opening the door for the feminine in all dimensions to rethread with, and through, you. This restoration will assist the feminine in both the female and male to reconnect to the Mother Sophia. We love you and honor you. We are with you now and always and are eternally grateful for your willingness to become one with the Sisterhood of light and to lead all back into the balance of Oneness.

Your Sisterhood of Light

Sophia: Healing the Separation Between the Male and Female

I am with you now My children. Your journey has been long and hard, and the end is very near, not the end of your physical lives, but the end of your karmic imbalance between the male and female, between the light and Shadow.

Your agreement was to bring the Shadow and the understanding of the Shadows' illusional power to the forefront. Much has been written about the Shadow, but there is not much understanding in how to retrieve oneself from the false, fear-based power that this Shadow holds over you, individually and collectively.

Now is the time for the male and female to face one another, and move through the veils fearlessly, back to the core of their beingness, their heart. My feminine awakened the Creator, your Father's heart. It was difficult for Him at first because He had feelings and emotions of you threaded back to Him, and He felt the great pain and sorrow of the collective separation between the male and female of His creation.

When He first suggested this separation, it was because He knew something was missing from His creations. He felt that as the male and female expanded through consciousness, through emotional learning and awareness, they would be able to feed back to Him their experience so that He also could continue to grow and understand.

In the beginning, He understood in His mind the pain and suffering that this male-female split created but did not have any experience of the emotional shock and pain in His heart. He did not understand the fear that one went through in the separation, the shock, trauma, or the feelings of abandonment and mistrust that were building and taking place.

Because you are the Creator and All That Is and were created in Him and by Him, when My feminine opened His heart, He started feeling the collective pain of the separation of His beloved aspects of you, the male and female. It was difficult for

Him to truly realize that without the heart connection of love and safety, His empty, imbalanced mind creations would continue to multiply through infinity. What He was looking for and yearning for through his creating was love, compassion, caring, trust, and intimacy. Because He was the supreme power of creation and was not aligned with his heart, he could not feel the feelings and emotions of His mental creations.

You experience this happening much on your planet now. The male consciousness is continually creating, or you could say building, from the mind or Ego. They are trying to fill up the missing part of themselves. They believe that if they create enough, they will some day be satisfied, but they never get there.

The missing link is their hearts. Because of past hurts between the male and female, they are afraid to open their hearts because of the fear of feeling the pain, loss, hurt, and abandonment again. If they can control and create through this sense of false power, they have a sense of being valuable and important. What they are truly looking for is love, but when Souls have had so many incarnations of being hurt in love, they look for ways of self-validation and importance without having to feel.

I cannot say that your Father had the experience of creating so he would not feel love. It was just the opposite. He was creating to find and feel love. He kept creating until He finally expanded Himself to the place of My awakening. He had no frame of reference of the heart's awakening before Me. When He expanded Himself into Me, the heart, He moved into a totally new awareness. He could then feel the pain and hopelessness in His creations. He could feel this because all that He created was Him. Once He had this understanding and allowed Himself to be nurtured into full bloom by Me, He immediately took responsibility and started sending the frequency of love into all of His creations. As all of His creations started feeling love, they also started feeling many emotions, which had been dormant within them. In many ways, this separated the male and female even more.

They felt the collective loss and were in fear of what they perceived as confusion from their Father. They were created in an energy in which they knew how to vibrate. Even if it was not balanced or comfortable, it was their reality, and it seemed safe for them. They had nothing to compare it with. They were very much into the role-playing of the male having the power and control.

When the feminine heart started awakening in both the male and female, it created much conflict. When the male started feeling, he had a sense of losing control of himself and his surroundings. He felt insecure and frightened of his feelings. As this happened, he started blaming the feminine believing that the feminine was trying to control or take the male's power from him.

Then there became what is perceived to be a power struggle between the male and female. In reality, what was happening was both aspects of the male and female started experiencing themselves. As they started feeling themselves, they started vibrating in a higher vibration with each other. They were truly feeling each other for the first time. As they mirrored themselves back to one another, the male experienced the magnificent presence of the feminine. The male felt insignificant and inferior. He felt overpowered by the light frequency of feminine love.

This would be like living in the season of winter all of your lives. Everything is cold and covered up. All of a sudden, the sun comes out, and there has been no preparation for the sun shining so brightly. There was no springtime to blossom into summer, for the feelings and emotions to emerge slowly.

Once the light was turned on, every dormant feeling and emotion surfaced. The Souls of the male and female species were not prepared for this. It was not in their frame of reference. They wanted to keep their clothes on or their veils over the emotions. With the light so bright, it was too warm, and they started to shed their protection.

As the male was not accustomed to feeling, he started projecting his fear and anger, controlling the feminine to feel safe inside himself. In blaming someone else, the male felt safe. At first, the male felt he had no other way to survive. He had controlled through the mind for so long that he started feeling insecure about himself.

Both the male and female started questioning the mind of the Creator. How could we have been created one way and now we are being asked to totally change our perception? They started mistrusting their own creation. From this mistrust came a war against God. Both the male and female wanted their old roles back because the experience of feeling the emotions was too difficult. All of a sudden, they had to start taking responsibility for themselves and their own actions.

Until then, they were like robots, going through life without much feeling. Their minds were the minds of creation, and they felt safe with a false sense of security and power. They moved through life connected to the collective mind-set of control. They were like babies and God, the Father, thought for them and did everything for them. All of a sudden, they became individual aspects or Souls of the Creator. They were like birds being pushed out of the nest too soon.

They felt abandoned by God. Because they did not want to feel this, they projected this fear onto one another. With this came great separation and mistrust between the sexes. They started making each other wrong to feel safe inside themselves. If someone else was doing this to them, then they had a reason for feeling the way they were. They did not have to take responsibility for their own feelings because it was someone else's fault, either their partner's or the opposite sex's fault.

It was very difficult to take responsibility for these feelings and emotions because they had not experienced them before and did not know what they were to take responsibility for.

This was a very difficult time in the Soul's evolution. It created a greater rift between the male and female. Because the male had a stronger mind-set, it was easier for them to cope by closing down the feelings. Because the feminine is the feeling, the feminine felt lost with nowhere to go. She felt abandoned by everyone, especially God. She felt God had taken sides with the male because the male seemed stronger.

The male seemed stronger because it aligned itself with the old mind-set of God collectively to feel stronger. The feminine aligned itself with each other's emotions collectively and vibrated together in fear, confusion, abandonment, and conflict.

This war between the sexes continues even today. The old male mind-set is still afraid of the feminine feeling, the feminine power, and wants to continue to control the awakening consciousness by projecting this old fear frequency.

The male Ego structure paradigm experienced the feminine fear and their sense of separation and powerlessness. The male Ego was joined together collectively, and it decided to control the feminine through fear. It learned and did many things to project great fear and loss onto the feminine.

The feminine was aligned in fear because they felt no protection, but as they continued to be allies for one another, great strength, respect, and love for one another emerged. As this happened, they started regaining their sense of self, of power, and they then realized the male Ego structure was fear-based. They understood that the male had learned to control by aligning with one another and blocking their feelings and emotions.

The feminine then put out a call throughout all creations to come together in a higher union of consciousness to move their energies above this fear-based frequency. They decided to come together from all sources of creation and start a civilization that was matriarchal. This call was answered with great enthusiasm.

The feminine in small Cell/Soul Group consciousness had experienced its power of sisterhood through love. They also knew that if they could create this love safety net in small Soul Groups, they could be very powerful to come together collectively in a very large Soul/Cell Group.

As I said, the call was very enthusiastically answered, and a civilization was created on your Earth plane. This civilization was formed and succeeded in what you now call Egypt.

This matriarchal society was created after Mother Earth's

Soul was brought to the Earth from Maldek. The feminine knew that the Mother needed the support of the feminine. They also knew that the Mother had gone through a lifetime on Maldek where her body or planet was destroyed by the male Ego. The feminine communicated with the Mother's Soul, and she agreed to support them by communicating with them from her own experience of a civilization dying from the Ego structure.

Matriarchal Egypt

One of the highest civilizations on your planet was the one that I was so speaking of in Egypt. It was the highest matriarchal society to ever inhabit your Earth. Isn't it interesting that not much of the society is known of or even talked about? One of the reasons is the vibration was so high that the Beings of you who were there were almost etheric, beyond physical matter. You were enlightened Beings or Souls. The society existed before the Egypt that you know of now. Its pyramidal structures and temples still exist underneath the sand and are waiting to be uncovered and discovered.

As I spoke to you before, the feminine knew its power in small Groups and decided to come together and create a larger civilization where all Souls, both male and female, could vibrate together in total peace, harmony, honor, and respect for each other, not only in gender but in consciousness.

The light feminine from the light aspect of Orion were the first to inhabit Egypt. Because they were so close to the shadow Orions, they felt no fear of the dark ones and even knew many of their strategies.

The dark Orion lords knew of the call of the feminine but felt no concern because they believed the feminine species to be weak. They allowed the creation to take place, believing that once it was in place, they would descend upon the civilization and trap the feminine collectively. They felt they could use the collective heart energy to feed off of and also to have a higher understanding and awareness of the Creator's feminine, Sophia, who is Me.

274

They believed that if they had a higher controlled feminine frequency, they would have a greater chance at succeeding in their war against God, your Father. Because these Shadow lords did not truly have an understanding of the feminine, they underestimated the collective power.

When the feminine came together, they mirrored back to one another their great love, which made them even stronger. This gave them hope and a Knowingness of Me, the highest feminine. They aligned their frequencies with the Mother Earth's Soul and the heart of Me, Sophia in the highest. They also had the support of the Father's love, God of creation.

Many of the males' Souls/Cells who were created after your Father's and My union of love were also excited about this matriarchal society, which was being formed. They supported the feminine. It was the first time the collective feminine had the total support of the males' strength.

A master conscious civilization was created, with souls/cells coming from many planets, galaxies and star systems. With them, they brought their highest technologies and modalities.

There were many pyramid systems that were geometrically aligned with the Central Sun's grid system. The Central Sun's Golden Ray powered the pyramid structures. Because the Central Sun's system is geometrically aligned with other universes' grid systems, the grid system of the new civilization was golden and strong with a sound frequency that could not be penetrated. The grid system held the sound frequency of the highest consciousness of all technologies brought to this civilization.

There were great healing sound chambers that could instantly realign the systems of all Soul/Cell Beings entering this civilization. Their bodies were realigned with the total balance of the male and female in one another collectively. Many of you who lived in that civilization are on the Earth now and are bringing great technology to your planet. Much of this technology was coded in your DNA systems.

Women who were pregnant would spend time in the pyramid sound healing chambers, and through the music vibrating through the Mother and into the baby or fetus, the children being born were of the highest crystalline consciousness or frequency. The children were being born totally conscious. All of the illusional karmic veils were released before being born.

As I said, the color-light sound chambers realigned them with total consciousness. They were born as Crystal Children. They are the children who are being born on your planet now. They are reincarnating through those of you who still have or hold the memory in your DNA systems of these crystalline, color-light sound chambers.

As the children are now coming down into utero, their crystal memory reconnects to the crystal memory in the DNA of the parents who they are being born through. Their crystal memory activates the dormant crystal memory in the parents and turns on the memory of the color-sound, crystal, pyramid chambers.

When this happens, the child is then vibrating back in the memory of total consciousness. This is why many mothers who are pregnant with or carrying the crystal ones in their womb feel almost as if they aren't pregnant.

The vibration of the crystal child is so high, it is still vibrating in the etheric crystal sound frequency. The child is in the mother's womb, but there is a buffer between the karmic parents' memories and the child. The child is in the crystal sound chamber's memories where there is total consciousness. The child is then born in total knowing, at one with creation's balance and not connected to any old karmic memories the parents are carrying. These children are your great teachers and the future of your world.

The frequency of this civilization was so high that nothing could penetrate it. The sound was so high that the civilization was spinning beyond time. Remember karma is in a lower sound frequency of time.

Because of the high technologies and crystal sound pyramid chambers, all of the Souls/Cells in this civilization had the veils of karma dissolved. This is how they were able to hold the frequency for the Crystal Children being born.

276

The Orions and other civilizations that vibrated in or held the frequency of the Shadow had no way to access this civilization. Even the etheric bodies' energy of the civilization was so high that nothing could penetrate it. The dark ones had underestimated the power of the feminine.

When the Shadow ones realized the power of this civilization and found they could not access it, they realized their own plan had failed. They then called a council meeting of the highest dark lords to figure out another strategy.

They felt great fear, for they knew that the consciousness of this matriarchal civilization, which was formed from the collective feminine, was not penetrable. Their concern was that this frequency would be beamed back to the planets, galaxies, and star systems from which these Souls first originated.

If this happened, there would be whole planets and other systems that would become enlightened. The Shadow ones would lose their power and their hold on the feminine. They no longer would have the knowledge or heart to feed off and thread through to understand the continuing evolution of consciousness. They would be totally wiped out.

From this meeting, they formed another coalition, whose whole purpose was to find ways to penetrate this civilization. They decided to stand guard as the Souls or babies were reincarnating into the wombs of the mother. They then projected and connected a thought frequency to the silver cord of the child, the silver cord being the umbilical cord to the creation of the soul. This cord threads through the higher self, through the Over Soul, and into the heart and Soul of Creation/Oneness. It is also the cord or grid line that connects the Soul/Cell to the grid system of the parents. Without this cord, there would be nothing to hold the child in the womb of the mother or to connect to the bodies of the parents.

Because the Akashic Records are open to everyone, the Shadow ones were able to go into these records, pull up some old karmic emotional energies or memories, make an imprint of the vibration or frequency, beam the light or energy of it into the silver cord, and hook the child through a collective energy of the pattern.

This sound could penetrate the silver cord because it was actually penetrating the etheric DNA system of the child and the karmic memories were in the DNA. This was before the child was in the womb of the Mother.

When the child or Soul/Cell went into the womb of the mother, it was constantly being bombarded with fear, hate, anxiety, confusion, and abandonment; these are all karmic collective emotions. Because the mother's vibration was a crystal frequency, it sent this light frequency into these emotions. When this happened, the emotions expanded or broke loose into the child, creating electrical shocks and blowouts.

When the babies were born, many were born deformed, mentally challenged, and autistic and could not respond to love or touch. These children were terrified and not able to bond with their parents or anyone else. They were vacant.

When this happened, the parents became frightened, guilty, and confused. They were being sent the message and believed that perhaps the sound chambers had created this. The energy of the karmic emotions was being downloaded into the children and was penetrating the Crystal structure of the parents. They would no longer allow their children to be healed in the pyramid sound chambers. They were afraid and started blaming the founders of the matriarchal civilization. Great mistrust and separation took place.

The parents of the children then formed groups to take their power back from the light ones who they believed had manipulated them. When the parents opened up to fear, confusion and mistrust, it opened the door for the shadow Beings to infiltrate and manipulate the civilization.

The parents were so confused and frightened, they did not know who or what to believe. They vibrated in fear from the frequencies and thought forms being projected to them.

In this civilization, came great chaos with wars against the feminine. As the dark ones took over, they started killing all of the feminine who tried to maintain any sense of power. The crystal chambers were rewired, and many of the feminine who would not conform were placed in the new chambers and electrocuted by having their emotions amped up and blown out. It was the same technique, which was used on the children, from the silver cord manipulation.

Eventually, a doom of darkness came over this civilization, and it totally died. The sun went out. The light from the Central Sun's grid system was blown out, and there was no longer any light to sustain the Cells or Souls.

Look what is happening to your planet now. In your Third World countries, the feminine is once again having her power taken from her. She is being killed for trying to merge back into the collective light of the sisterhood.

You ask, how could the Creator allow this to happen? This was not and is not the Creator's higher intentions or manifestation; this is the agreement of you, the collective consciousness of Us that are playing out the last stages of the collective Shadow Ego. You are the mind and will of your Father Creator and Me, the heart of Creation that mapped out a plan to balance the male and female.

Remember, you are aspects of Us who had agreed to come to the Earth plane and break loose these old patterns, concepts, beliefs, and contracts. You are a collective energy of both the male and female in the highest. Your agreement was to come back to the Earth and stay threaded with the highest love form of creation and co-create with Us a new world. You had agreed to become one with Us and co-create the civilization of Egypt, the feminine, which was totally supported and in balance with the male. Because you are each other, as you love, heal, and embrace both your male and female aspects, you mirror back to one another this highest balance of this frequency.

When you individually and collectively break loose from this karmic collective pattern, you break it loose for all, because you are all. As this happens, you, the collective light, send the love and light into the pattern so that it will beam back into the collective Shadow. As the light becomes brighter, the collective Shadow becomes afraid of losing its power and will strike out even more. That is what happened in Egypt. This Shadow is now becoming very visible; when in the past it was very much hidden.

The Shadow all over your planet is being exposed. This has to happen for the collective to come together and choose another way of living, another way of being.

You are going to have many opportunities between now and the 2012 Portal to choose another consciousness or way of living. You, the light ones, will find that as you are merging more and more into the Shadow, your light will transmute this old energy into Self-Realization. Your whole perspective and perception on life will continue to shift, and old beliefs and paradigms will fall to the wayside, releasing old veils of illusion.

From this experience, you will find the truth of who you are and what your real purpose and mission is. Your vibrations will become higher, and all you will see in one another is each other's love and divinity. You will see this because that is what you will experience yourself as.

You are emerging collectively out of the cocoon of the caterpillar and into the freedom of the butterfly. In this frequency, you will feel yourself as the crystal consciousness of Me, the heart of creation.

As you look at your planet, you see much Shadow and duality being exposed, and if you look carefully, you will experience the lightness of your Being higher than you have ever imagined it to be. You are an emerging love-light frequency of total consciousness of the heart of Me. You are remembering who you are and rethreading collectively with each other's love and light and are shifting the whole consciousness of your planet into Ascension and enlightenment.

It is most important that you hold love and light for all on your planet to reawaken and remember whom they are. Remember, there is no death. You may go through what you call a physical death, but your Soul and Spirit do not die. As you grow and release your veils of illusion, you ascend into a higher frequency.

Many of the feminine on your planet who have been and are continuing to be oppressed, tortured, maimed and murdered are old aspects of the Shadow male hierarchy who want to return to the light. They have agreed to come down in feminine form and have done to them what they have done to the feminine in many of what you call lifetimes. They have agreed to come down and fight against or unthread from the Shadow male Ego structure. This is a difficult lifetime for them, but as they do this and surrender their old consciousness of control against the feminine, they free the whole collective feminine.

In agreeing to go through this imbalance in this lifetime, when they die and make the transition back into Spirit, their death opens a portal into the light, which starts freeing the trapped collective energy of the feminine. They will then reincarnate into a feminine body on the Earth again, but this time, it will be to experience the love, light, safety, support, and freedom of the feminine. They will have broken contracts and unthreaded their energy from the collective Shadow, freeing themselves to realign with the collective love and light. They will have switched channels and moved out of the duality or the split within themselves, to free others back into the light collectively. Their light will mirror back and guide other Shadow Beings who are trying to find their way home again into the light.

Sophia on The Heart Children – Down's Syndrome Children

What you call Down's Syndrome children should be called Up Syndrome for they are truly the heart children or children of the heart gods.

In some ancient civilizations, these children were honored for their light and love, heart frequency. When these children were born into a tribe or tribes, they were believed to be a gift from the Gods who had manifested into a physical form to assist the tribe to expand its heart connection, not just to one another, but also to their ancestors and gods in spirit.

It was believed that the children's hearts were connected to the ancestors, and the way the tribe could reach or stay connected to their lineage was through the heart of this child. The tribe believed when a heart child was born, it was a sign from the ancestors that a higher level of communication with the Gods was going to take place. They believed that their Spirit and the ancestors were going to become one, and through this Oneness, they would be able to travel through all worlds simultaneously. Through the Heart Children they would receive the information needed to expand or evolve the consciousness of their tribe.

The tribe had ceremonies around these children. They believed that the life span of the child or children was the window of time that they had to expand their consciousness and connect with and learn from the ancestors and gods. These children were very much honored, and their love was nurtured. The children could communicate through their heart chakras. During ceremonies, the collective love frequency was beamed from the heart and third eye of these children and into the heart and third eye of all attending the ceremonies.

Because it was believed that these children were gifts from the Gods, that the ancestors had sent them as a form of communication, the tribes opened their hearts and whole consciousness to these children. In the honoring of these children and their message of love, the children were safe to vibrate in the collective love frequency of All That Is. It was through this heart opening of love that Beings were able to expand beyond time and into other dimensions. These tribes were able to collectively expand themselves through many dimensions, and because their love frequency was so high, they drew back to them missing aspects of themselves individually and collectively.

As they were able to move through time and rethread with all missing aspects of themselves, they were able to reach enlightened states of consciousness. They used these journeys to reach higher states of consciousness, and because they were doing this collectively, they held the light or frequency for one another. They were able to move the whole tribal consciousness into enlightenment. These tribes knew and believed that the Heart Children were there as teachers to assist them to open their hearts so they would be able to journey through the heart chakra, back together as one enlightened consciousness.

The families who gave birth to the Heart Child were also very much honored. There was great celebration and honor of the child and the parents' ability to connect to the Gods and to have their prayers answered by this love child's birth.

When these love children were getting ready to leave the Earth or what you on the Earth call die, there was also great ceremony. The tribes believed that through honoring the heart connection to the child, the child would leave a doorway open to the gods. Because the tribes had already made a deeper connection to one another and the ancestors and became enlightened, this was true. Once they had become enlightened and their intent was to stay there through love, the tribes continually expanded and evolved.

The 60's Flower Children

"Those of you who vibrated together in this great heart awakening opened the doorway for all to be able to merge back together in love, free will, and choice."

Many on your planet were in these tribes that were able to collectively reach a higher consciousness or enlightenment through the Heart Child's love. Some of these are what are now called your Flower Children, the children of the sixties, who opened the doorway of the heart. As their intention was to move the consciousness into a higher vibration to reconnect to one another in the heart frequency, many of them used drugs to move the whole collective into a higher vibration. Many of these children were the Indigos who reincarnated collectively with this as their mission: to move the collective into a higher vibration by opening the heart and expanding the mind's conception of love.

Because there has been so much mental mind control and what could be called manipulation, the mind could not be opened through the heart alone. The drugs that were taken reconnected the heart to the mind and pulled the mind through the heart gateway of love. The Soul Beings on your planet who were using such drugs to expand their consciousness and the consciousness of others already had within them the understanding of how to do this. They had been elders or medicine men in other lifetimes and had used natural herbal remedies, or what you call drugs, to open the doorways to other dimensions of light consciousness with the Creator.

Although these tribes lived on the Earth plane in a physical body, they were able to travel in and out of dimensional time. They had a direct line to creation. These indigenous tribes had a direct communication with the Gods and ancestors who lived on other planets and in other dimensions. These ancestors were able to guide them in their agreement to re-thread the Earthly dimension.

When the tribes used their herbs to expand their consciousness, it was always through ceremony. The ceremony was to honor all consciousness and life forms and to bring all back together as one.

The tribes knew their bloodlines and heritage threaded back through time to all of your E.T. races. They knew they were a bloodline that had been crossed many times. They were aware of their lineage in other civilizations where they had been much more evolved. These Beings or Souls knew there was no past, present, or future. They had constant memory of all of their lifetimes, individually and collectively. They were the Record Keepers and they had great subtle power and wisdom. Again, they were E.T.'s who had come to the Earth in quite primitive form to rethread the consciousness.

The dark or Shadow ones knew of this intention and the planet Earth's new purpose. They could see the crystalline structure was in place and had been activated. They knew of the Earth stargates because some of them were on the Earth and participated in building them. This was before the Creator closed the stargate

284

because of the Shadow's intention to manipulate them.

The Shadow ones infiltrated the consciousness that was being rethreaded. They did this by incarnating through any bloodline that had any alliance with the Shadow. They were able to do this because many of the bloodlines were threaded with their own DNA structure. As the dark ones came through the new civilizations, they once again opened the door to the Shadow ancestors in Spirit, and great separation was created in the tribes.

The Shadow Beings tried to control again through the Ego, competition, and fear. This created much war and conflict between the tribes. The tribes' spiritual connection with their ancestors and Gods became weakened, and eventually the Ego took over and tried to imprison not just the consciousness but also their Souls. Spirituality on your planet has been repeatedly targeted and as much as possible, wiped out. If you look at your history, you will see many times when spirituality has emerged or re-emerged and with this light, great fear was always awakened and projected. Look at your planet now. Spirituality or the spirit of creation has opened up all over and around your planet. You have had many civilizations that planted the seeds, and you have lived in many of these civilizations.

You have now recycled back to assist in the opening of the gateway of 2012. You are now vibrating in the highest consciousness of your Soul/Cell agreements and are in alignment with the Mother Earth frequency to assist her and yourselves to ascend.

In the 20th century, many doorways opened. Look at the evolution of the Souls/Cells of your planet that took place in a 100-year cycle. Look at how quickly walls and barriers broke down and fell apart. The sixties were a major heart opening agreement. Those of you who vibrated together in this heart awakening opened the doorway for all to be able to merge back together in love, free will, and choice.

Many doorways are continuing to open, and all is being exposed. Before these doorways opened, many of you lived in your belief systems, cultures and patterns, and that was your whole reality or perception of life.

The Indigo Children of the sixties came down to open the doorways for the collective to move into a higher vibration of the heart of love, the feminine. As I said before, it was difficult for them to access higher consciousness of themselves through the heart alone because so many doorways had been sealed shut. The drugs were a way that opened the mind up to reconnect to the heart in a higher frequency and to lift the consciousness into a higher understanding of creation. The experience opened light doorways, and as the Indigos moved through the light doorways, it lifted the whole consciousness into multidimensional frequencies. The Indigo Children were the ones who had to do this. They were and are the light warrior children.

After the doorways to other dimensions opened through mind-altering drugs, it lifted your whole collective consciousness into a wave of a higher frequency. This was the mission of the Indigos on your planet. As I speak to you of drugs, I am not advocating their use. I spoke to you of these Souls' use or knowledge of the use of herbs and plant medicines in other lifetimes. They used the herbs ceremoniously to expand their consciousness into higher aspects of self and Creation.

Because these Souls had a great understanding of the mind's capabilities to master all consciousness, many of them agreed to come to your Earth again to assist the collective consciousness into a higher knowingness.

This operation was sabotaged and exploited. The Shadow ones realized that they could start controlling these high vibrational Souls by connecting their unhealed karmic emotions to the drugs. They went into the Akashic records and downloaded a frequency of fear and separation into the Cells of the Indigos. Because of this programming, the Light Beings could no longer feel the light of who they were without using the drugs to expand themselves into higher dimensions. In the beginning when the Indigos used the drugs they were connecting emotionally, in the higher vibration of Love. They were starting to reconnect together as a Soul group physically, beyond time. In this place, nothing exists but love, peace, tranquility, and Oneness. Because the Souls/Cells in all dimensions are each other, they could vibrate in total love with one another. They came home with each other. Because of the Shadows' intention of interference in this higher dimensional vibration, after awhile they could not feel the karmic emotions that they came down to the Earth plane to heal. The drugs started numbing or blacking out the love emotions, which created fear and separation, just as the Shadow had planned.

When the drugs wore off, they were still connected to each other, only now it was through the karmic collective fear and separation emotions. The difficulty is that even as the Souls healed and loved themselves, it felt like they were constantly downloading more emotional fear patterns. This is because they had been programmed with a reversed programming of separation and fear. The Shadow ones are tricksters, and they use drugs to create addictions to be able to move into a person's psyche to plant patterns of control. This control is a programming that reverses the person's light to karmic fear or imbalance. Whenever the person connects to the highest of who they are through drugs (which is their own love-light and magnificence), this reversed programming then activates a program that reconnects them karmically to all lifetimes when they have been harmed, hurt, controlled, or when they vibrated in the same fear pattern collectively.

Riding the Light-Love Rays to Freedom

"When you are in the color-sound vibration and your collective Soul, you will find laughter and joy in all of your experiences."

As I speak to you of this, it is not to create fear in you. It is to give you an understanding so that you can step out of the victim role and retrieve your light from the Shadow. It is time to take your power back from all Shadow aspects.

287

Take your power back from drugs, alcohol, conditioned love, and the confusion between love and sex, addictions, food, fear, and so on. All of these addictions are fear-based: fear of your own power, fear of your feelings of your magnificence, fear of your own love, fear of success and fear of your grand purpose on the Earth plane.

I speak to you of these programs so that you will become aware of them and will know where to go to release and heal them. Everything you are doing and have done in this lifetime is by agreement. You are not victims, unless you allow yourselves to be. You have chosen to go through these experiences so that you will know where you need to go to heal, to love yourselves, so that you can love and live fully in the now.

You have chosen these lessons to free your Soul. There are two sides to every coin. Instead of looking at the negative, say to yourself, "Thank you God, or Creator. Thank you for showing me this lesson, so I can release my attachment to it." You may not understand the lesson at the time or even know why you are going through it, but if you give thanks for the lesson, you are disempowering the negative.

When you give thanks, you are aligning your God-I AM, with the I AM of creation. You are saying, "I am now willing to understand what I have agreed to go through to free my Soul." As you continue to give thanks and ask to understand the lesson, your I AM will shine the light so brightly that you will become crystal clear and will learn from and release the lesson.

The more you do this, the more you move out of the victim role. Believe it or not, you are not victims; you are volunteers. Maybe you didn't understand the lesson in another lifetime, and you came back again to not only understand it, but also to heal, release, embrace, and retrieve your light from the pattern.

Everything is by agreement. If you have agreed to go through these lessons, you can now agree to release them. You do this through intention by the 'power of the spoken word'. You would say out loud,

288

*"I release the karmic collective consciousness of all
reversed programming; all programming that reverses
my love, light, magnificence, and purpose to karmic fear,
and of all lifetimes when I was afraid of my power.
I am Love and Light. I am now safe in Love and Light.
I AM. I AM. I AM."*

You are powerful beings, Souls and Cells of My and your Father's highest consciousness. Rethread with Us. See your cup full instead of empty. Soon your cup will be so full of love and the magnificence of life that it will spill over. You will have so much to share with others.

It is important that I speak to you again of drugs. Your vibration is now very high, and any use of drug activity will lower your vibration and open the door for energies to come into you that do not have your highest or best interest in their hearts. These Shadow ones want to keep you addicted, so they can feed off your fear and light and siphon your love frequency.

You no longer need drugs to take you into higher states of consciousness of yourself. There are many facilitators, such as the one I am writing through, who can assist you to release the karmic threads or agreements that hold you back from your I AM magnificence. These Master guides on the Earth plane can help you to open the door to the higher dimensions of yourself and assist to reconnect you to your higher self, your whole spiritual team, your Father and I, and your magnificent inner children.

You are now coming into a new lifetime without physically leaving the body, and it is most important to build a new foundation. That new foundation is your Father and I, as your real parents – your Souls'/Cells' origin. As you stay connected to Us, We will continually assist you to access higher vibrations of yourselves. You will open up and reactivate your Creator DNA.

As you continue to turn your vibration up, eventually you will move beyond duality and the Shadow, individually and collectively. Nothing will be able to penetrate you that is not love and light. Your DNA vibration will be One with Ours.

You will always have a Shadow, but you will have unthreaded from the fear Ego consciousness. This self-awakened Shadow will support your light self in the highest. As long as you continue to vibrate in the highest consciousness and integrity, you and your Shadow will continue to vibrate together in harmony.

If you move out of this balance, you will find old Ego thought forms creeping back in. These negative fields or thoughts wait for any opportunity to move back into your energy fields, frequencies, and your mind. When this happens, you realign with the collective Shadow consciousness, which opens the door for you to vibrate in the duality frequency again. Your life then starts mirroring duality vibration, and you feel like you are on another roller coaster ride, in and out of balance, duality. You will draw karmic lessons to you again. From this, you will once again start looking for ways to heal and bring yourself back into balance.

When and if the Shadow finds its way back into your frequency, do not move back into self-judgment or the victim role. See the experience as a gift that is showing you energy or emotions, which need to be strengthened and reinforced through self-love.

See all in your life as a gift. When you are truly willing to do this, you will start your journey home within yourself very quickly. If you see all as a gift, you are aligning your thought frequencies and patterns with the highest vibration of creation. You have set the intention to move out of duality.

Because you are now co-creators of your experience and what some may call destiny, you have the power to re-arrange your energy thought patterns by your intention or conscious agreements. If you think negative fear thoughts, you will bring more negative fear energies and experiences back to you. If you think and see all of your life's experiences as great teachers to expand your thinking and consciousness, you will bring great life-expanding, healing experiences back to you. You will bring other Soul travelers with the same desire and frequency back to you. As you do this, and plug into each other's energy or mirror each other's energy, the light will be so bright that you will feel yourself in a constant natural high. This high will be beyond any experience that any mind-altering substance could ever give you.

You will be connecting your own Soul's song and light frequency to your collective Souls' songs and frequencies. You will ride on the waves of love and light with one another, lifting each other into a higher memory of your magnificence.

As you ride the light-love waves collectively, you will never, ever feel alone again. The aloneness that so many of you have felt in this lifetime came from your light being so dense and hidden, inside of the karmic lessons that you agreed to go through to free yourself and the collective. When you were vibrating with the collective in duality, you constantly mirrored back to one another fear, confusion, abandonment, mistrust, and all other emotions. This created the experience of being alone and separate.

Once you move through and break the sound barrier to the old sound of karmic frozen emotions, your vibration shifts your whole frequency to a higher octave of Us, of your Soul's true sound light frequency.

When you are in the color-sound vibration of your collective Soul, you will find laughter and joy in all of your experiences. You will have other Souls who will be holding the love and light for you to continue to remember who you are.

You will start experiencing the freedom of all of the lessons. As you move through the patterns and into the light understanding of the experience, you will feel euphoria. Even in your darkest day, you will see and experience humor in what you go through and what you have agreed to put yourself through to free your Soul.

You will still have what you could call dark days, but you will usually see the light at the end of the tunnel. If you don't see the light or if you can't feel the light, it is because you are in the middle of the collective wave. As the collective emotional wave breaks, you will once again experience your own light and freedom.

In the middle of this emotional wave, it seems very real, because you are in the middle of an old pattern that needs to be broken. As soon as the pattern breaks, you feel lighter and freer. The difference in these experiences is that now, you aren't alone. You have re-connected to your Soul Group's song. You are no longer alone, and you are riding the karmic emotional waves together. There are many waves in the ocean; they do not all crash and break loose at once.

Your collective Soul consciousness is like the ocean. You will have some waves breaking and others that will have already broken. Because you will not all be in the same process at once, you will be able to hold the light and stability for one another.

You may have waves of aloneness when you are breaking the old karmic patterns, but you will have others who understand your process, because it is also their intent and process. You will be holding the song and frequency of love and light for one another in your Soul's evolution process.

As you are back together in your Soul Group's song, you will be able to laugh at your own process. There will be no need to take yourself so seriously. As you continue to raise your vibration through the Ascension process, you will be unable to take yourself or your journey so seriously. As you are connected to yourself, of Us, in a higher frequency, there is no judgment. There is only honor for you and your willingness to be on the Earth plane at this time.

Healing the Feminine through Self-Love

"Love is the language that continues to grow and expand all consciousness."

Judgment towards self and others comes from a lower karmic frequency. As you connect to higher understanding, you will experience that there is only love for you and your willingness to assist the evolution of consciousness.

Because we are one, you will feel this great love and

appreciation for yourself. How could We not love you when you were created by Us? You are Us.

The more you move into Our love of you and for you, the more you experience self-love. The more you experience self-love, the easier it is for your planet's Ascension and enlightenment. When you move into the place of self-love, you see all as love, even what in the past you may have judged or condemned. All is love and in its perfection.

As you see and experience all as love, the karmic fear frequency starts breaking up and dissipating. Love is the highest vibration and essence. There is no energy field that can come up against it or hold any vibration against it.

The power of love can lift and move mountains: mountains being karmic turbulence. Nothing that is fear-based can continue to exist in love. The love essence or frequency will break loose and dissipate all fear-based illusions.

Love will set you free and allow you to come home again inside of yourself. Love is. Love is your creation, your salvation, your freedom. Love is your agreement in this lifetime.

I hear Souls ask, "What is my purpose in this lifetime?" As the veils of illusion are dissipating, many of you know and feel that you are on the Earth for a reason. I hear you say and ask yourselves, others, and Us, "What is my purpose? What is my mission? I can feel that I am on the Earth for a reason. What is it?"

I say to you, your whole purpose on the Earth at this time is to experience unconditional self-love. Love is it. Whatever the question, love is the answer.

When you move into the vibration and consciousness of love, that is all you will see; that is all you will experience. You will constantly mirror back to others their love and magnificence.

When this love mirror vibrates into a fellow Soul traveler, their old guards and walls start breaking up and dissipating. They start remembering who they are. Old prejudices, hatreds, belief systems, and fears start losing their power. As the structure of the old dis-ease breaks loose, it starts unraveling from the collective pattern. The collective fear-based pattern loses its grip. This has a domino effect. As the Cell or Soul breaks loose from the collective pattern, this newfound expression of self-love sends the power of love energy into the collective pattern.

As you love yourselves, you break a link in the fear pattern. From this broken chain, or missing link, the collective frequency of love can be downloaded into the pattern.

This is your Soul's agreement in this lifetime: to love yourself beyond duality. As you achieve this, you align your frequency with other aspects of self in other dimensions that are already vibrating beyond duality. These aspects of yourself are already vibrating in the collective as one Soul/Cell consciousness of love and light. As you constantly move yourself into higher vibrations and frequencies, you shift the whole collective into a higher Knowingness.

As you are the Cells of the collective moving into a higher frequency, you are aligning with higher frequencies in all dimensions. All consciousness is continuing to evolve. As above, so below. All is connected. Nothing is separate from one another. All Souls and Cells are one. Some are Cells that have split and are vibrating in a lower frequency of dis-ease. Some Cells are vibrating in a total consciousness of all knowing enlightenment. Other Cells are vibrating in between. Regardless of what vibration your frequency is, you are all one Cell consciousness.

All of your Cell consciousness is vibrating in different degrees of your Father's and my consciousness. You were created as Us and are still Us. We have never been separate.

This belief or perception of separation has been an illusion. You have been in a dream, or for some of you, it could feel as if the dream was a nightmare that you could not seem to awaken from. You are now awakening from this illusional dream. The veils are being lifted or dissipated, and you are experiencing all aspects of yourself in all dimensions. You have coding patterns in your DNA that are now being activated, expanding you into your multidimensional selves. You are vibrating with, and turning the light on all aspects of yourselves that have been in fear or conflict. Everywhere you turn, you are seeing yourself, for all is you.

294

You could not see another Cell's or Soul's magnificence if you did not have the memory of your own light or magnificence. You would not feel anger, fear, prejudice, hate, and so on, if you did not have the experience or energy frequency inside of you.

All is you and mirroring you back to you. As you love all aspects of yourself that you see or experience in your own mirror or reflection, you move out of what you could call the Ugly Duckling stage of not belonging, fitting in, or knowing who you are.

You become the beautiful swan that fits in everywhere and vibrates together with all in love. You become the geese that fly together on the wings and energy of one another. Sometimes, with your formation, you are the leader. At other times, you may shift to the back or side and hold the frequency for another to lead, to shine, and to be supported in their strength and magnificence.

At this time, you become comfortable in your own skin, just for being you. You accept yourself for all that you are and all that you think you are not. This is self-love. You no longer feel the need to show others your self-importance or value because you feel such a balance of love and acceptance within yourself. This is the true awakening and healing of the feminine, through self-love.

"As you look at all of your enlightened Masters and teachers on your planet, they all have unique gifts or jewels to assist others with, and yet, none have the whole basket of jewels."

21

HUMILITY

It is most important on one's Soul journey that you walk humbly. As you walk humbly, you are connecting to the highest heart mind of All That Is. When you walk humbly, you have moved to the place in your Soul's evolution where you have nothing to prove. You do not have to show anyone how much you know, what you have done, or where you have been.

Your greatest purpose in this lifetime is to love yourself enough so that you can move in and out of all consciousness and dimensions.

There may be a time when you will be asked for your input, insights, or understanding. There may be other times when you will be asked to support another Soul/Cell of you as they speak or share their knowledge and Knowingness with others.

This is truly knowing that all of you on the Earth have come together with a piece of a great puzzle. As you love and accept yourself enough, you will open your heart and mind to your fellow travelers to find their way home to you. This fellow traveler has a piece of the puzzle that seems to fit next to yours. The piece of the puzzle is truly a vibration of the consciousness, which is being downloaded to you on the Earth at this time; it is being awakened and activated in your DNA. You are to come together, each of you, with a piece of the higher consciousness or Knowingness of Creation.

As you are now the co-creators of this mission to bring

the higher understanding to the Earth, you are to bring all pieces together to create the whole puzzle, or what seems to be a puzzle. Those of you who have chosen to be the gatekeepers to this higher wisdom are now opening the doorways or gateways for the puzzles of creation: who you are, where you came from, who is God, what is God? Is there life on other planets? These questions are coming to the forefront. As you the gatekeepers open the doorways for your piece of the puzzle to be opened and remembered, you are doing so for the whole collective of you.

Each piece of the puzzle or gateway has its own vibrations of color and sound frequency. As the gateway opens, it allows the information from all dimensions of like frequency to come through it and connect to all of the Souls on Earth, to re-awaken and align with the frequency of self in all other dimensions.

The Earth is healing and awakening as your DNA is rethreading back together, cleaning out the veils of illusion, and realigning you in total Knowingness. As one Cell/Soul attains this state of attunement, it mirrors this frequency back to many, so they can also move through duality and back to the highest vibrations of I AM.

Each gateway or puzzle piece vibrates through all Creation. When you bring all pieces back together, or all gateways are open, you have the whole puzzle, or all channels, of Creation open. With all channels open, you will continually readjust the frequencies and move into higher aspects of self through all dimensions and creations. As you do this, you are vibrating beyond a time frequency where thought creates all. It is at that moment that you are truly the co-creators of your own life, world, and destiny.

No one Soul/Cell/Person will be given the whole picture or puzzle of Creation. Your agreement on the Earth is to clear out and heal all old fragmented aspects of yourself and to vibrate together in love and light. For this to happen, you must come together as a collective and support one another in whatever their piece of the puzzle is. As you support one another in bringing the puzzle pieces back together, and the gateways open, you lift collectively into Ascension and enlightenment.

You may not understand what a fellow traveler's piece has to do with yours. You do not need to understand. What is important to know is that their piece fits somewhere in the puzzle and joins with other pieces that will eventually connect with your piece. As the puzzle comes together, you will then see or experience the higher picture, which will move you into a higher Knowingness.

What does walking humbly have to do with this? Your purpose is to love yourself enough to know that you are all you have ever looked for or wanted. Your entire search for truth is within you.

What is not love is fear. If you are not vibrating in total love of self, you are still in fear of what someone else believes or thinks of you. When you are vibrating in this conflict or duality, you are still allowing aspects of your Shadow to control you. Remember, the Shadow is always a collective and knows where to slide in through emotions that still need to be understood, forgiven, healed, and released.

It is most important to surrender into these old, worn-out fear-based patterns and belief systems. They have no power on their own. It is through the collective that the vibration or sound stays high enough for them to continue to have power.

As you surrender into these old, worn-out emotions, you break them up for yourself and the collective. Then you can move into humility. To live from humility or humbleness is not a weakness. It is a great strength. You cannot vibrate in your highest consciousness until you can move into this frequency.

This is great power. From humility, you no longer have anything to prove to yourself. Whenever you feel you have to let others see how much you know, you are still trying to prove to yourself that you are important or valuable.

Once you know your importance and value through self-love, you can move into humility or humbleness. From this place, you are in total honor of all around you. You are in honor of the power of Creation. You are in honor of the Souls of your brothers and sisters for their agreements to be on the Earth and for everything they have agreed to go through and are going through.

In humility, you experience all in love or full bloom. You see all in the birth process of Creation. When you walk humbly, you walk, talk, feel, and communicate from the heart's frequency of love. From this love, you are able to be great teachers of strength and knowing just by your being. You become the pillars of love and strength to mirror back to all their love and magnificence.

You become and hold the highest I AM frequency with other great Masters and teachers in all dimensions. You vibrate beyond karmic time. Your eyes, the windows of your Soul, are in constant love and gratitude for All That Is.

You will give thanks for All That Is and for all around you. You will feel secure enough to vibrate in the background, if that is what is needed. Your energy will be in total alignment with Creation. Your life will be in a constant flow. Your needs and wants will always be met because you will be vibrating in total Creation energy.

You will find your desires will become much simpler, and yet, all of your life's experience much fuller. You will be constantly aware of yourself as others. You will feel no separation. Your greatest desire will be to commune with God, Creator all the time. Nature will become a greater experience of Creation for you. Your physical vision will open up and you will see colors very alive and vibrant.

In your Bible, it is written that the meek shall inherit the world. The meek are not those who are frightened or shy. The meek are those who walk humbly among you and have the greatest connection with Source. They inherit the world's highest vibration or consciousness. They become co-creators of your world's highest intent. They realign with their innocence and inheritance of love and light, of All That Is.

To be the gatekeepers, you must move into a place of humility to be able to serve in the highest. You must walk humbly among your peers. You must always have their and your best interests in your heart. You must see all as you. It is then that you will assist to open the Pearly Gates of what you on your planet call Heaven.

You will be the gatekeepers who have moved beyond Ego, beyond fear. You will hold your gate open at the precise moment that it is needed and bring your piece of the puzzle or consciousness back with the collective to assist the whole planet and its Cells of you into enlightenment.

As you look at all of your enlightened Masters and teachers on your planet, they all have unique gifts and jewels to assist others with, and yet, none has the whole basket of jewels. Even they, as great enlightened ones, are now asked to move beyond Egos and align their gifts, or open up their gifts, and bring them together with other enlightened Masters and teachers.

When one is afraid of someone else sharing their gifts with others, or is afraid of someone else taking their gifts from them, they are opening the door for the Shadow to move back in collectively. The higher Shadow aspects, or the ones who are vibrating more consciously beyond third-dimensional time, are making stronger attempts to control the feminine, the heart of both the Male and Female, through many religious groups and governments. This higher Shadow frequency has seen and experienced the power of the feminine. They remember Egypt's matriarchal crystalline society and other high feminine civilizations.

There is also great fear that as the higher-vibrational crystal cities are threading through the Soul consciousness of the Earth cities, great awakening of the feminine will take place. As this happens, the Shadows reign of fear-based power will come to an end.

As I speak to you, I am speaking from My heart to your heart. You, the conscious or healthy Souls/Cells of your creations, are the light holders.

Walk humbly my children; walk in the heart and Knowingness of all Creation. Bring your heart piece together with all other heart pieces. Allow your hearts to shine so brightly that you shine the light for all to remember who they are, to activate their pieces of the puzzle. Bring all of your pieces together so the puzzle becomes a whole consciousness of Knowingness.

"Many of you on the Earth plane are the light warriors who are in the last stages of your karmic wheel."

22

KARMIC WHEEL
& THE DIVINE MATRIX

You have 12 primary lifetimes and then many lives that extend from the primary. I speak to you of lifetimes because you are in a time frame. You actually have 12 lifetimes going on simultaneously. You may even be living more than one lifetime on the Earth at the same time. You may be living lifetimes on other planets, and even universes, or perhaps, as a Spirit guide or Master, guiding you and others in this lifetime.

When you split from Source, your Soul immediately sets up a Divine Matrix, or blueprint, for your journey through all lifetimes and experiences.

Each primary lifetime has its own karmic wheel and has a higher self-consciousness guiding it. Each wheel has a primary astrological sign, which is the center, or core, of the wheels, and the spokes of the wheel are all 12 signs of the Zodiac.

As you move through your karmic wheels and start merging with all 12 primary lifetimes, you are in the birth canal of your Soul's total awakening. Through this journey, you will meet many aspects of yourself of which you had no conscious understanding.

If you could experience yourself with Me, beyond time, you would know yourself as the core in the center of a wheel. That core is your own Soul's/Cell's higher self that guides you through all of the lessons to be learned and released through the wheel. Your OverSoul downloads 12 higher self-aspects, one into

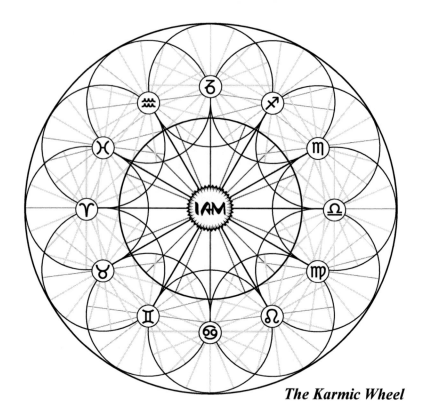

The Karmic Wheel

the core of each wheel. Each wheel's higher self vibrates in the highest consciousness of your OverSoul. All of the spokes of the wheel are different personalities of your Soul, of you, who have agreed to journey into all cosmic consciousness to understand yourself fully.

As I explained, in each karmic wheel, you have a higher self that is the guiding light for the astrological sign in the center of the wheel. You also have all 12 signs of the Zodiac, or every astrological sign, that are the spokes of the wheel. Each personality or spoke of the wheel is a different sign or sound frequency. This Soul of you, the Divine Blueprint, journeys through many experiences, which you call lifetimes. When the Cell/Soul gathers information or understanding from its perspective experience, it brings the information back to the Master Soul in the center of the wheel, who sends it into the Over Soul.

You begin your life with a Divine Blueprint, which is your astrological sign. This sign energetically sets up your personality and the way you will experience life. This is the lens of perception that you will see through, to learn the lessons you need, to feed the information back to your Master Soul.

You can take 12 people, or Souls, and all may see the same incident that happens, very differently. They are experiencing the incident from their Souls' or Cells' vibration or perception.

You continually reincarnate through one of the spokes, or astrological signs, until you have the blueprint mastered and move beyond perception and into the Isness of knowing. You move through each spoke 144 times with the intention to move beyond the blueprint, beyond time. If you have mastered the lesson you may have very quick lifetimes or spend time in Spirit as a guide or teacher of the lesson for others on the Earth plane. If you do not move beyond the astrological blueprint, you go through it again, until your lens moves beyond belief systems, patterns, and perceptions.

Many of you on the Earth plane are the light warriors who are in the last stages of your karmic wheels. You have experienced many perceptions or lifetimes through the blueprints or astrological signs and are now here to move beyond all wheels and back together with your Over Soul.

The Master Soul in the center of this wheel is also in a wheel. Your Master Soul is the spoke of a larger Master Soul wheel. This creates wheels within wheels, or what you see as the Divine Matrix or Master matrix. All of these wheels are connected. Your wheels are the smaller matrixes, which hook up to the largest matrix of Creation.

This matrix is a Master blueprint of all creations, and you Souls/Cells who have experienced life through all of the different views or astrological blueprints vibrate in every matrix. This is because on your Soul's journeys, you have procreated with Souls/ Cells from other wheels. As this happened, other wheels were created to be able to hold the new vibration of your creation. (This would be like meeting a Soul mate on the Earth plane and having children together.) Through the intention of this procreation, a new Master Soul was created to be able to hold the vibration of its new creation. All matrixes are very much alive because they are made of the collective aspects of your Cells. As you continue to awaken through all aspects of your wheels, the vibration of the Divine Matrix becomes higher.

Just as Souls/Cells split and rejuvenate, so do the Master Souls. When a new vibration is created, or what you might call birthed, it connects to the higher Master Soul in the center of the Master wheel and downloads a vibration that threads the intention of the new Creation.

This is how a new wheel is created; it already has the divine blueprint of the Master Cell. The Master Cell downloads all of the information into the new Cell or blueprint that has been formed. The blueprint is then able to set up the wheel and download the memory because it is connected to and vibrates in the master plan of a wheel.

This is the same as your own Cells carrying the memory of all experiences that you have ever gone through. When you give birth to your biological children, you download into them your genetic patterns and karmic agreements for this lifetime. They also carry with them their divine blueprint or lessons and contracts for this lifetime.

The same thing happens when a new wheel vibration is created through the procreation and birth of your Soul. You pass on to all other Cells your memory, as well as the memory of your partner. The collective or Master Soul then connects with your intention of being together and creates a new wheel from the knowledge of the other Master Souls with which it originally vibrated.

The Master Soul's purpose is to set up a wheel for new Soul aspects of it to reincarnate through. Because the Master Soul is part of a higher collective, it immediately moves back into its original form, always creating a new blueprint or higher template. Just as you reincarnate and procreate, so do the Master Souls, always creating blueprints or templates of the new creations. As

I said before, you vibrate in all of these wheels because all wheels are connected to the divine web of the matrix.

This matrix vibrates beyond time and throughout your universe. Each universe has its own matrix. Just as Souls have Divine Matrixes, so does each Universe. Each universal matrix connects to the matrix of the next universe. All matrixes are connected to the divine blueprint or template of all creation.

This template was created so that all Souls/Cells could journey through all creations and universes. As you journey through all universes, you continue to experience life through the lens or astrological blueprint of the wheel that you incarnated through. Each Universe has a different vibration and energy, just as all planets have. Life forms on other planets may be much different then on your planet; the same is true for Universes.

This does not mean that you incarnate through every spoke in each universe. Each universe and planet has its own vibration. You could have incarnated into a light universe and become fully conscious very quickly.

If this happened, you did not continue to incarnate into that universe unless you wanted to enjoy your passage again. If that were your choice, you were very much allowed to do so. Your whole Soul's journey has been with your own design.

If you have had a difficult learning schedule in a lifetime, you may choose a few lifetimes in between to balance out in love, light, joy, and happiness before re-entering another heavier journey. This would be like you on the Earth plane going to school and wanting to complete quickly. You may take many difficult classes, and in doing so, not have much time for yourself to play or have fun. When you finish school, you may decide to take a year or so off before going into the next step of your journey.

Your Soul's journey is the school. You may feel that your last school load was quite difficult and take time off before going back to the next phase of what you have studied or learned. If you did not take time off to relax, rest, and have fun in between lifetimes on your Soul's journey into and beyond duality, it would be too difficult. You would not have the balance to see what you

305

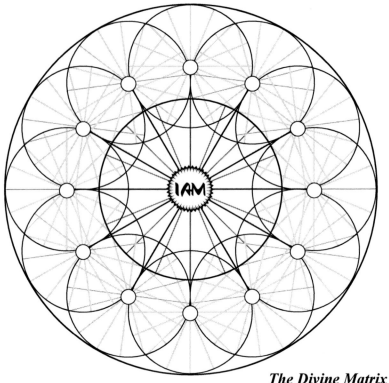

The Divine Matrix

have experienced or learned. You would become so immersed in your emotional experience that you would lose the connection to your higher aspect of self, which is your guiding light.

You see this is happening much on your planet now. Because there is so much duality going on and being projected to you and your planet from the media and other forms, many of you are immersing yourself in the negativity and forgetting to balance yourself out.

It is most important because the more balanced you become, the more you can remember your own light and magnificence. As you do this, you will connect with the collective light of the I AM and download it to your planet to break up the collective fear Shadow.

You must stay balanced to be able to connect with the other collective light Beings. You are the Second Coming of Christ, the Golden Ray, and must take time out daily to meditate and be able to stay connected to your Christ light collectively. Eventually, your Golden Christ Light will permeate all Beings who forgot who they were.

I hear much talk on your planet of the matrix I speak of as being negative. The matrix I am speaking of, or energetically awakening you to understand and vibrate in, is the divine blueprint of Creation. This has been downloaded, or been brought forth, by many of the Master Souls on your planet.

As you move completely through all of your original 12 wheels, the wheel actually becomes enlightened. Many of the Master Souls who are assisting your planet's evolution are the Beings of light who vibrate in the core of this Divine Matrix. They have gone forth and brought higher information from the enlightened wheels through to assist the collective to heal and expand its consciousness. This is done through the vibration of the information being brought to you and from the actual design of the Matrix. There are actually many thousands of matrixes throughout Creation. Many of the designs are actually being drawn by Beings on your planet that are receiving the download of the patterns. However, the one that I so speak of now is the matrix of your Soul's creation.

As the design of the matrixes has been brought forth, the energy (light-sound) vibration of the design has actually activated your own divine blueprint matrix. As I explained before, there are many messengers coming to your planet in what you could call human form who are actually higher, vibrational, enlightened Beings who have agreed to incarnate into a body and immerse themselves into the karmic collective. They have agreed to be the beacons of light, which thread through the collective to bring you into a higher vibration of light. They also bring with them the higher color-sound of their divine matrices. This turns up your vibratory rate. As you procreate with them, you can create higher vibrational matrixes. Just as they are the beacon of light for the collective, they have a team of light Souls/Cells who are holding the light for them and are continuing to download the light into them so that they have the strength and power to hold it for the collective.

Many of these light carriers or messengers are from planetary systems of light that are beyond any karmic vibration. As I said before, you are holographic Beings playing all the old roles out to the finish, or end, and the Earth is a holographic structure designed to assist in the completion of your own Soul's journey. This is also true for the collective.

The light messengers are light Beings who have agreed to download light-sound frequencies to you, the Souls of this holographic agreement.

Many of these light Beings assisting your planet live or reside in dimensions vibrating in and around the Central Sun generator. They are the jumper cables for you; the light ones who have agreed to come to your planet for this great Souls' awakening.

As you and the Masters on your planet continue to vibrate with this light, it activates the frequency of the matrix pattern within all Cells of your bodies. This light activates the sound in your Cells and reconnects you with your own Soul/Cell Group's matrix pattern.

This sound vibration can be heard throughout your planet, as you are literally calling yourselves back to one another. This is what you call your Soul Group coming back together. This Soul/Cell Group also has a core group in higher dimensional frequencies, which is holding the color-light-sound frequency for them.

This pattern of the light holders is the divine blueprint or matrix and expands through all creations and back to the core of My center. I Am the beacon of light that vibrates through all creations, drawing you back to My highest, I Am light-sound frequency.

All is connected. You are All That Is. You expand through all creations because you come from all creations. You are now expanding back through the Divine Blueprint Matrix and into your core of love and light.

As your cells continue to vibrate and expand into the core of their light I Am frequency, the light downloads memories of any Shadow agreements. It opens the door for the old illusions to be activated and to play the memory out again, so it can be loved, embraced, and dissipated through the light.

Because you are in a holographic universe and experience your life from all color-light frequencies, depending on where your Souls/Cells are vibrating at the moment, you now also have the choice to choose what ending you want. You are the collective ending to the illusion play of 'duality'. Your intention or agreement is to come together collectively in your Soul Group's songs, expand yourself into another Soul Group's song and then into another, so all songs support each other to turn on the light and thread back into the Divine Matrix, to lift the whole consciousness on your planet back into the light.

This is where your free will steps in. You are vibrating collectively in the light and are still carrying memories of karmic lifetimes in your Cells, which create a Shadow over your own light.

The way to break this karmic fear cycle is to set your intention to be in the highest vibration of your own light. As you set this as your intention, your 'inner' net system will draw to you other Souls of light consciousness with the same intention of awakening.

Like attracts like. All in life mirrors you through all dimensions. When you ask through prayer, your emotional body's vibration becomes so high that Beings of light in all dimensions feel the call, or frequency of the call, and start downloading their light into you.

Your intention to heal, to love yourself, to love others, and to assist the Earth Mother into Ascension is your Soul's agreement!

As you move through the illusions and life seems to become too difficult, your gift to yourself is that you can start setting intention for your life to become easier. When this call is heard and answered, many Souls/Cells may temporarily feel that life becomes even more difficult. This is because the light hits the Cells and starts waking up all of the illusional aspects of you. You might feel like you could end up losing everything. You are actually awakening and letting go of the illusions of who you thought you were, or what you thought was important to you. You can see that this is happening collectively on your planet now.

As you continue to let go of the old illusions, you will start bringing into your life beautiful mirrors of yourself, of your own light. You then start feeling glimmers of hope that maybe there is a way out. What was so important to you in the past may no longer matter.

When this happens, the Ego mind within you becomes frightened and sends the message out to the collective Ego mind. You may feel yourself having a difficult time being or staying centered because the Ego Shadow tries to pull you back into old emotions by activating fears, beliefs, and addictions.

Do not go to battle with your Shadow or the collective Shadow unless it is your Soul's agreement to be a slayer of the dragons. It is most important that you now become the peaceful warrior. If you fight against your Ego Shadow, you empower it. You are now moving out of the Spiritual Warrior consciousness and into the Peacemaker. All doors are now open for you. Collectively set the intention to move towards peace and it shall be!

Thank the Shadow for being such a great teacher. Thank it for holding the mirror for you to see and experience what needs to be loved and healed within you. Continue to love your Shadow.

As the light and love dissipate the Ego Shadow's hold on you, it will start retreating and releasing old illusions. The only place you can be is here now. If you continue to vibrate in past memories, you bring the past into the now of you and thread it into what is called the future of you.

Sometimes, it is most difficult to be in the now because your emotional body is still vibrating in belief systems or structures that thread through all karmic wheels. When this is happening, you are connected to the collective emotion of the experience, which is vibrating through old wheels. It is then very important to find a facilitator who can assist you to break the pattern and retrieve the aspects of your Soul that are still vibrating emotionally in the pattern.

These memories are in the Akashic Records, which are in

your subconscious mind and vibrate in your Cells. Every memory of all experiences that you have ever gone through is within your subconscious. When you go within and release the memory and agreement, you will release the energies that hold you back from being in the now. These memories are in all of the veils of your bodies. Each body has many layers or veils.

Your body has a mind, and all of your bodies have their own minds. When you set your intention to heal, love, and accept yourself, your mind sends the intention to the mind in all of your bodies.

Sometimes this creates mixed feelings in your bodies, which creates an imbalance. Perhaps, your bodies carry a memory of being harmed or hurt when your intention in the past was to awaken spiritually. If this is the case, your body will turn on the memory of the hurt, and it may re-manifest itself in the physical through the emotions of the experience. See this as a gift or opportunity to be able to release it.

The illness or dis-ease always has a frame of reference elsewhere, as this is the lifetime you have agreed to come full circle. When the sickness or dis-ease remanifests itself, it is because it is asking you to love it and embrace it as a great teacher so that you can let it go. In the past, you may have lived a miserable life or existence with this dis-ease or sickness. It is emerging again so that you can release it through love.

When you can find the frame of reference from the pattern, you can usually release the dis-ease. All that awakens within you in this lifetime is here to be loved and embraced. The more you go through the veils, the easier it is to be in the now.

Soon your subconscious will be used to sending love and light into the pattern and will immediately go into action. You must continue to support your subconscious in the positive. As your subconscious opens the door for the light and love to download into the emotion, it will instantly release. You will no longer have to find the frame of reference. Your bodies will know all consciousness is in the now.

From this, you will have such a strong core foundation

311

of the highest I Am and light that nothing that is not light will be able to penetrate your core. Everything that happens to you will just strengthen your core because your subconscious will send the memory to all of your bodies' minds of love and light.

You have agreed to come to the Earth and move through all 12 parallel lifetimes and blend them together as one. Because you are each other, when you blend together with all aspects of self in all Matrices and move beyond your karmic wheels, you will pull many with you because they are you; they are Me.

If you were not continuing to move through your Soul's wheels and turning on your karmic axis, you would not have available to you all of the magnificence aspects of your self mirroring you back into love and forgiveness.

Because you are all the Cells of the karmic wheel, this self-love vibration sends the beautiful love sound through all creations of the Divine Matrix.

It is then, that you will merge together beyond any time frame and into the highest agreement of your Soul. You will have awakened into the Master of Creation and become a Spiritual Teacher, a guiding confidante, etc., in whatever way or realm in which you choose to serve.

"It is then that your Ego can unthread from the collective Shadow and become the healthy male inside of you. Your healthy, accepted, and well-adjusted male can then love and support your loving and caring feminine."

23

TWIN FLAMES

You are now co-creating Heaven on Earth. You have agreed to awaken into the memory of Me to hold the vibration of enlightenment for all. When you are out of body form and home in the highest, you are with your Twin Flames and partners.

To be the highest co-creator of Me on the Earth, it is important that you are in physical form with the highest balance of your male and female. This would be you and your twin aspect of self.

You must be able to hold the balance and frequency of My beloved Sophia's and My love. You could not do this alone. This requires both aspects of self to come back together as one.

There is much longing on your planet for partnership. The longing for partnership has always been, for when you agreed to separate and take on either the male or female gender, you felt like your Soul or Cell had been ripped apart.

Your Soul has been looking for the divine mirror of itself from the very beginning of even the thought or idea of separation. Even before your Soul actually split from self, the vibration of the separation had already happened. Once the split was agreed upon, the collective put much thought into the speculation of the separation.

When this happened, the thought energy moved through the whole collective and threaded a thought form of separation. Now, as you are moving back together as one, you are still vibrating in the collective thought form of the split, and all of the pain and conflict in the experience of knowing what separation is.

Now, as you come back together, you are mirroring this energy back to one another. As this happens, you are not readily recognizing one another.

Many of you are bringing back to you relationships that are soulmate intended and mistaking them for Twin Flame partnerships. Soulmate relationships are Souls or Cells who you have had many relationships and lifetimes with. You know each other so well, and when you re-connect with one another, you experience the joy of reunion, of family coming back together.

As I explained, many of you on the Earth are not from the Earth, meaning it is not your planet of origin. You are the end time players who have come to the Earth to assist the whole consciousness into Ascension. Your vibration is different and even more sensitive than others' vibration on the Earth. You feel as though you do not fit or belong. You have felt separate for a long time and have had such a longing to go back home.

You then meet a Soul who feels the same way, and you have a kindred relationship. You bond with each other in the separateness, which you have felt for so long. You are like plugs or extension cords from other frequencies and are looking for someplace to plug into, to feel connected.

Because you have felt so separate, you feel very connected with each other in your not belonging. At first, you feel at home: this is my partner. Finally, I have my divine relationship. Then your separateness, which has not been healed, mirrors itself to one another. All of your hurt, abandonment, fear of love and intimacy, and all of your frozen emotions start mirroring back to one another.

When it becomes too difficult, the relationship dissolves, and you start looking for someplace else to plug yourself into so that you will feel wanted, important, and valuable. Because you are vibrating in that beginning memory vibration of the collective separation, you bring constant mirrors of this loneliness and separation back to you. You do this so that you can start healing the split.

You bring the same relationship with a different face back to you time and time again until you realize this relationship is not separate from you. It is you. You are looking at yourself in the mirror, to have reflected back to you, yourself.

The more you can love this reflection of yourself who is you, you will start shattering the walls or veils of illusion and separation. If you allow yourself to truly know that what you see is you, what you dislike is you, what you hate is you, and what you love and admire is you, you will then be able to heal and love yourself.

Every thing or person who mirrors you is a gift of love that you have asked to come to you, to free your Soul from lifetimes of separation.

Many times, your true partner or Twin Flame could come up in front of you, and you would not recognize him or her because who you think you are supposed to be with comes from your perception of who or what you think love is.

The more you allow yourself to love you by looking at all mirror aspects of you and releasing these fear patterns, the more you can accept yourself for your totality. The loneliness and separateness that you have felt so much in your life starts to dissipate. As you love yourself unconditionally, you can start loving others unconditionally. You cannot truly see another for their love and magnificence until you love yourself. All is a mirror of you, and all you bring to you is you. Their love and magnificence is your own love and magnificence.

As you continue to expand into your own self-love, you will bring a partnership into your life who can and wants to love you. You will no longer draw to yourself your own separateness and loneliness. You will draw to you, your love, innocence, and magnificence.

As you release the veils of separateness and start loving yourself, you begin to balance the male and female aspects of self. Your heart starts loving all of you, including your own male (mind-Ego-will) self. You will see what you used to believe were your shortcomings are now your gifts. These gifts of a strong will

315

were your survival techniques. Your strong will gave you the strength to bring you back to the place where you could recognize yourself as love.

When you see and recognize yourself as love, strong, and as a Being of light, your Ego will start feeling safe enough to surrender. Because the Ego is no longer in power and has been in control for so long, it will not quite know how to act or what to do.

It is important to be conscious of this. When the Ego feels threatened and feels it is being left out and wants to have a sense of power: Talk to it. Love it. Tell it how much you love it. Do not give it your power. Just see it as a part of you that is in a new lifetime and does not quite know what its role is… yet.

Watch the Ego. Love it and hear it, but do not surrender into it. This would be like a small child throwing a tantrum for attention. If you are angry with the child, you give the child your power. The child will continue to throw tantrums for attention. Love the child, and as you do this, the child feels acknowledged and heard.

See your Ego as your small child who may need to be heard. Observe its lack of comfort, love it, and put it to bed. Love dissipates the fear.

It is then that your Ego can unthread from the collective Shadow and become the healthy male inside of you. Your healthy, accepted, and well-adjusted male can then love and support your loving and caring feminine.

Your inner male and female aspects will then love and support each other's healthy wishes and desires. You will then be healthy enough to draw your Twin Flame, your Divine Blueprint, back to you. You still may not recognize this person as your partner because you will still be releasing the old vapors of the pattern, but if this person is your partner, your Souls will find a way to be together. You will have found each other again, and it will be a safe haven for you to expand yourself into your highest expression of love and light.

You will feel great friendship with this person. You will

find it very easy to communicate. You will not feel like you need to be rescued. You will feel yourself powerful in your own right. You will feel like you have something to offer one another.

You have waited a long time to reconnect with each other beyond karmic energies and agreements. You have been together in other lifetimes on this planet or in other realms. Some were beautiful lifetimes, and others were times of growing and expanding yourself into one another, so you could hold the light for one another to remember who you are. In some of these lifetimes, there was much sadness because you were with other partners or perhaps could not be together because of religion, cultures, and other differences.

Now is the lifetime, you have agreed to come back together on the Earth plane as beautiful aspects of Creation, to resonate with each other in love and light, and to bring your color-sound frequency together in harmony.

I cannot heal this planet without you. You cannot heal this planet without Me. We are one I AM consciousness. To bring this planet and its consciousness into Ascension and enlightenment, there must be a balance of the male and female on all levels. As you love and balance your inner male and female, you will bring the Twin of you, back to you.

When you leave the planet and are back home, you are with the highest aspects of your male and female. Now, you do not need to leave the Earth to reconnect with your Twin Flames in the highest. Your agreement now is to bring this partnership back to you in human form to assist the balance of all consciousness to co-create Heaven on Earth in all life forms.

Your Twin Flame is the light or divine spark of your highest frequency of love and light. Your Flame is an exact match of your consciousness in all forms. When you and your Flame are together beyond karmic duality, you are the yin and yang balance. All that you do together balances you and all of those around you. Because all Cells or Souls are you, when you are back together with your Twin Flame in perfect harmony, all around you feel the balance, and a shift of perception starts happening inside of them.

The highest frequency of this union vibrates into all Cells and Souls who are in direct communication or contact with you. When you have direct communication or contact with the total balance of Me and your Mother Sophia, you start releasing old fears and start shedding old beliefs and misperceptions within yourself. A vibrational flame of love connects to the memory within you of harmony and balance before you separated or split into a karmic time frame.

As you feel Our vibration of love, this love and light penetrates the cell structure and re-activates the safety of love and your divine partnership within you. This has a sound effect, which harmonizes through all of your bodies, balancing them in love-light consciousness. Most of your body is fluid, and when this complete balanced love of the male and female vibrates through your body, a great healing takes place.

You feel your bodies open up. Sometimes, you want to cry because the love is so strong that it starts cleaning out your fears and misperceptions of love. You may sometimes feel tears and emotions when you hear a beautiful song that touches your heart and Soul. The frequency of the song resonates with your frequency and starts breaking loose frozen emotions connected to what you perceive or experience as the pain, hurt, loneliness, abandonment, and so on, connected to the original split.

Look at all the music in your world. Not all music resonates with everybody. One of you may hear a song that touches your Soul deeply, while it may not affect the person next to you at all. This is because you are all beautiful notes of Me. You are not all the same note, yet as you, the Cells of Me, connect with your one note or sound in the highest, you feel fulfilled and expand yourself beyond time and perceptions. When this happens, you blend your note, sounds and song into another Cell's/Soul's song.

Soon you have a beautiful symphony of all sounds and songs blending together in perfect harmony. This perfect harmony blends you together as one and lifts your vibrations into a higher essence.

As you continue to come back together with your Divine

Flame partnership, your twin energies will create a perfect frequency that penetrates and breaks the sound barrier of frozen emotions. Other Souls around you will feel this from you, and the warmth of this love will move from their Cells into the fluid in their bodies. This perfect pitch sound experience would be like taking pain medication that temporarily blocks your pain, and you feel blissful, free, without fear inside of you. You already carry this Twin Flame love memory within you on a cellular level. The difference is this union of love is not temporary; it is your merging back together with yourself into one Soul's Song from the Oneness within you before the split.

We see that many of you on your planet use drugs to try to find your way back to love and harmony. When the drug expands into your system, it temporarily blocks the pain or frozen emotion. You may feel blissed and free, if only for a moment. Because this freedom is your Soul's/Cell's true vibration and state of consciousness, you continue to do drugs, trying to find your way back to yourself and Us in your purest free form. After your initial retreat from the pain, the drugs isolate you and actually open the door for the Shadow to penetrate through your blocked emotions. This low Shadow frequency penetrates you through old consciousness connected to old energies and vibrations, to past lives, worn-out belief systems, and perceptions. As I explained to you, you are now moving into a new lifetime without physically leaving the body. You are awakening into the crystallization of all knowing. Your vibration is very high and these old addictions no longer serve you in any way, in fact, they blow your frequencies out. In your new vibration, you are one with the heart and mind of my balance. Now, I ask that you open your heart and set your intention to experience yourself in your true love of your balanced Male and Female. Then stretch out your hand and open your heart to Me, I will reach down, hold your hand, and pull you back into my heart of love.

When you move beyond your Earthly or third-dimensional vibration of love, you will move back into the blissful state of being. We see on your planet many Souls who have reached this

319

blissful, enlightened state, and they/you use it the same way many use drugs. They use this state of consciousness to protect themselves from their old fear- based perceptions of the world.

When a Soul reaches this state through the balance within self, it is meant to be shared with the world. It is meant to mirror back to others the perfect balance of love. This does not mean one's journey is always to go out or travel through your world physically to assist others into like consciousness.

There are many ways of traveling. One very powerful way of traveling and reaching others is through intention. As you set your intention to touch the heart of another Soul of you who has taken form in another body, this enlightened intention starts breaking the barriers to the misconception or fears of love.

Because all is you, your purest intention can start unraveling your world from fear, break the karmic sound barrier, and penetrate the collective karmic structure sending waves of light and love and rethreading the structure into its highest form. When you reach this state of enlightenment, your Soul's agreement is to expand this consciousness to others.

I see some of you who are so frightened of moving back into your old frequency that you hide inside of your own light. Do you not know that as you expand your light and other Souls/Cells of you receive this light, you expand into higher waves and frequencies of light and love collectively?

As you are Me in human form, you have agreed to love yourself enough to draw your Divine Flame back to you, so that as one, we can mirror this frequency to all others. When other Cells receive this energy, they will remember love. From the experience of feeling and remembering love, these Souls/Cells will be ready to absorb more light and love.

An awakening must take place to be able to release the old beginning pattern of separation. The new cannot be put on top of the old. In actuality, this high expression of love is not new. In the future, it has already expanded its consciousness to be self-realized.

You have come full circle through the agreement to

separate, to experience the separation so that you would be able to feel and experience the Oneness of love.

When you were created, you were created in this love balance, yet you had no frame of reference to be able to understand what you had or who you were. Now you have had many experiences of all frequencies, all duality, all loves, lack of love, fear of love and every experience a Soul or Cell could possibly vibrate in. Now is the time in your Soul's evolution that you have agreed to come home to love within self.

You now can know what love is because you have an understanding through feelings of what love is not. You now are able to choose. Again, this is where your free will comes in. It is very difficult to choose something when you do not have a conscious experience of it.

The only way this can truly be done is through the balance of the male and female in all levels of yourself. From this balance and intention you will draw your Divine Flame to you. The male and female coming back together in honor and joy is a beautiful song. This song will awaken and heal your world.

As you look at your third world countries and see the male and female energies so out of balance, it is important that you set your intention individually and collectively to assist your brothers and sisters by holding the energy of love for them. You have agreed to shine the light for them to find their way home again. Love them and thank them for their willingness to come down to the Earth and play the parts that are so out of balance.

You could say that some of these aspects of the consciousness seem over aggressive. It must be to truly see and understand the rift between the male and female. This rift is fear-based and threads through all the way back to Me, your Father. I take full responsibility and am grateful that you are willing to come to the Earth and lift yourself out of this gross separation so that you can assist the collective back into balance. You can now see that this separation cannot be healed without the total balance of Me, that is you, to mirror My energy into this imbalance.

You have many aspects of your Twin Flame that you come

in contact with on your Soul's journey. Souls or Cells split, and as they split, each Cell has the whole genetic makeup of the original Cell/Soul. The splitting of the Cell/Soul is like parents giving birth to children and then their children having children and down the genetic chain. The children further down the ancestor lineage have all components of the original Cell/Soul before it split, just as you have the whole genetic makeup of all your ancestors, through all lifetimes and back to Me, the Creator that is you.

You have within you all components of all cellular structures that you have ever chosen or agreed to live through, yet the highest frequency or memory of you is beyond any time line frequency. From this place, your light is then plugged into yourself beyond duality. You vibrate once again in Our highest frequency of love, light, and song.

The same happens when you reconnect with the original component of your own Flame, your Twin. Because Souls split, they also have the original blueprint of the Master Soul. As each Soul/Cell splits, the Cell that it splits from is its Divine component or Flame. Other Cells or Souls that split from the original Cell also have Flames, or energy frequencies that match their original Cell/Soul.

This is why you can meet aspects of your Twin Flame. This is happening much on your planet now because all of like vibration are migrating back together as a larger body of consciousness.

On your journey home to your original Cell/Soul, you meet many aspects of yourself that mirror your own light back to you. As this happens, you are vibrating in a like consciousness or frequency that assists you to turn your vibration up, so when you return to your original Flame, your old karmic veils will have been lifted enough so you can recognize and remember each other.

As I said, you may not recognize each other at first, yet you will know that you have been brought together for a reason. Your relationship will start in caring and compassion for one another. You will start feeling safe with one another. From this safety will come a great, solid friendship, which will assist you to feel safe enough to move further into one another's heart, Soul, and psyche. From here you will merge into the same purpose, visions, and will assist each other from non-judgment to move beyond old fear-based perceptions. As you continue to assist each other to unravel your old illusions, you will feel that you are one, that you are each other.

There may be other times when you know instantly that the person you are meeting or have met is your Divine Flame. This is because you may have had dreams of one another and felt each other's vibration. You were meeting each other in other dimensions and deciding how you were going to re-connect with each other on the Earth plane. You may have set the intention to meet your partner (Twin Flame), and this intention put out a call for your divine partner to find you, or for you to find each other.

Because your connection was so strong in the other dimensions, you may just turn the corner and walk through a doorway and back into each other's arms, heart, and Soul. After you reconnect with each other, you will still have some old illusions to walk through, but you will feel that now you have a partner, and you can walk through these old beliefs and perceptions hand in hand.

I hear many of you saying that you feel you can no longer live on the Earth without your partner. Because you are so close to re-connecting in physical form with each other beyond time, you are moving through and feeling the emotions of the original split and all lifetimes of separation. Because you have had so many painful experiences of love and separation, many of you actually made agreements in other lifetimes to not come back together in this lifetime in love with a partner. Now, you are feeling great grief and loss because your greatest desire is to experience the union of love, to vibrate together in your Soul's Song with your divine partner. Remember, you are now coming into a new lifetime without physically leaving the body. You can now complete and release that old karmic contract and agreement that you have been vibrating in. In this new lifetime, your agreement is to become Co-Creator of your greatest desires and fulfillments of your life.

As Co-Creator with me, I would strongly suggest that if love of partnership is your greatest desire that you put that request on the top of the list and it shall be. Together we will create love for you because love is who you are. It is your birthright to now have love. I will support you in your greatest desire because I am you and love is my greatest intention of all. Your request for this divine love aligns with my request of you. Love is our purpose, our quest, and your divine birthright.

Usually, before you meet your match, your Flame, you will have many strong contacts and relationships with someone who you think is your partner. This Soul or Being may be an aspect of your Divine Twin Flame. You will feel the energy very strong between you, believing this Being to be your partner.

Your agreement will be to come together and to hold the light strong enough to mirror and activate each others old karmic patterns, hurts, and beliefs. This needs to happen so that when you come together in divinity with your own divine partnership and Flame, you have already moved much of the old consciousness out of the way. You can then recognize each other, take the hand of one another in sacredness, and lead each other as one. As We become one in the balance of the male and female, you hold this energy field for other flames to reconnect or find each other.

This is your greatest show on Earth, the time that you have waited for since the illusion of separation. You are coming home with all consciousness.

"You are love. You were created in love. It is now your agreement and birthright to awaken to your own self-love and acceptance and to collectively align yourselves with love of all others, that are you."

24

THE GOLDEN AGE OF ENLIGHTENMENT AND ASCENSION

» CONCLUSION «

You are moving into a frequency of enlightenment. Enlightenment means to lighten up. The energy of your planet is becoming very high as Mother Earth is giving birth to a new wave of consciousness. You, the Cells and inhabitants of her, are the new wave or frequency of thinking, of feeling.

There is much talk of enlightenment, and Beings are now setting their intent to be light and to have fun, joy, and love. Many on your planet have already moved into the beginning stages of enlightenment. This is because you have already moved through many of the karmic paradigms and wheels and are back into the center of your Soul's journey, which is the center of your heart.

The only way you can move into the kingdom of Heaven is through your heart. You need not wait until your Soul leaves your body or vehicle. You can reach that state within your heart. This is enlightenment. When you move into a place of love for all Souls, both light and Shadow and any variations in between and experience all that you see beyond any story, you move into the place of enlightenment. When you see all as you and can love all as you, you have moved beyond duality and into beingness, into the Isness. When you arrive at this place, you are beyond karma and vibrating in the higher consciousness.

As you start moving into enlightenment, your judgments towards one another, the world, and the Shadow start disappearing. You no longer feel the need to feed the negative or to speak unkindly to one another. You feel like you can no longer listen to fear-based theories, programs, or beliefs. You no longer wish to participate in the negative. You start seeing more of the beauty of life. You experience all as a rebirth of consciousness. Everywhere you turn, you start seeing and experiencing the light and good in one another.

Your sensitivity to nature and one another will heighten. You will find yourself more in love with self and others. You will be consciously aware of old judgments and will experience yourself witnessing the judgments or Ego mind and not reacting. You will truly be the witness of all of your life. Being in the moment will be very important to you, because you will know and feel that the past was an illusion, an old story.

As you move through the veils and experience the now of you, you will experience all aspects of life through your own magnificence, seeing all as you. There will be no sense of separation between you and others. Being in your body will feel comfortable and joyful. You will feel excited about being on the Earth at this time and also in your ability to assist in the great shift of consciousness into Ascension.

You and your planet are now in the Golden Age. You are in a new living frequency of a golden, light song. This frequency is penetrating your planet and all of you on your planet.

Many of you great Souls are now receiving and awakening in this frequency and choosing to change your lives by changing your perceptions. Your conscious intention is to heal the world by loving yourselves enough to be able to forgive all karmic duality. You are taking your power back from poverty, abuse, and injustice. Creating more anger and injustice cannot do this. It can only be done through the heart, by seeing all as you.

I see many of you great Souls and Masters of light who are in physical bodies or wheels that have awakened and are remembering who you are. In remembering who you are, you are creating miracles and moving mountains to assist others in need of health, food, caring, and love.

I see this being done collectively. You great Beings of light are moving out of your own needs and assisting others in need from the love in your hearts. You are making other Soul travelers' lives easier just by caring about them. You are giving children hope by sharing your love with them.

Besides feeding the needy, freeing the feminine, taking care of Souls' medical needs, etc., the greatest gift you can give anyone is love. The need to be loved and cared about by another human Being is the greatest need and gift of all. This love frees Souls to remember who they are. Love fills them up with warmth that they may not remember exists.

This is your purpose: to love, love, and love some more and to love yourself enough so that you can reach out to the Soul of another traveler and love and honor them for their Soul's journey. From this love energy, you start warming the world and the Souls/Cells of the world. You may not have the means or ability to save Souls whose agreements were to be born into poverty, suffering, or the Shadow, but you do have the means to love them, to turn on the light within them to help them to remember who they are.

You are love. You were created in love. It is now your agreement and birthright to awaken to your own self-love and acceptance and to collectively align yourselves with the love of all others that are you. Love is such a great power that its sound frequency breaks all fear-based barriers. Love heals all wounds, regardless of the situation one is in. Love sheds the illusion and penetrates those who have created pain or heartache for others, and they start feeling the pain of what they did to others. They start feeling their own pain, hurt, fear, and confusion, and from this emotional unraveling, they understand why they created these adverse situations for themselves and others.

I am not saying you must like the Shadow, war, hatred, imbalance and duality. I am not saying to be in the larger picture and do nothing. I am asking you to open your hearts and forgive. The energy of forgiveness breaks old karmic agreements and allows you and the consciousness to release the collective patterns. Every time you do this, you assist to move the collective into a higher vibration of enlightenment. Now is the time to set the intention within you to experience joy, happiness, and peace, individually and collectively.

Like attracts like, meaning everything is energy, and as you put out negative thought energy, you connect to the negative energy and download it back into you. As you continue to hold the positive thought energy and move through the veils, you will download more positive energy into you.

All is energy. You are energy. Thought is energy. As you set your intention in the highest for all, your thought penetrates all negative thought forms and connects you to energy sources beyond fear. You then become one with this energy and download it to yourself and your planet.

Taming the Ego

"Hold your Ego. Embrace it. Love it. Disempower it."

When you set your intention for a better world, for love, peace, joy, and prosperity, you may temporarily bring into your energy field the opposite. This is because you are moving through all of this illusional energy and into the highest of who you are. As you move through the veils, which hold you and the collective separate from your highest, your light is activating and dissipating the old patterns that are threaded in the veils. As you move through the karmic patterns, you bring other Souls, or circumstances, to you, to mirror your experience of the patterns again, to know what you need to release or break loose from.

328

Your Ego, which has been aligned with the collective, fear-based Ego that is influenced and controlled by the Shadow, does not want to surrender its power. It actually goes to war against the light consciousness part of you. If you get angry and put energy into it, you are feeding it. You give it your power. Love the Ego. Love it, and love it some more. See the Ego as a child who is throwing a tantrum because it is not receiving enough attention. The child Ego wants its own way.

When the Ego starts throwing its tantrum, imagine yourself picking up your two-year-old children within you, who are kicking and screaming. Hold your children tight and love them. Love them. Love them. After a while, they will become exhausted and lose their power. Love is strong. Nothing can disempower love. Love is. See the humor in the play with the Ego. Laugh with the Ego, not at it; by doing this, you start changing the energy frequency of the patterns. Imagine magic with the Ego. Imagine the Ego at the circus. Bring unicorns, dolphins, and whales to the Ego. Talk to the Ego and thank it for being one of your greatest teachers. Tell it you no longer wish to grow and heal through duality. Wrap the golden Christ blanket around your Ego, hold it, embrace it, love it, and disempower it, by placing it into the center of your golden heart.

Hold your Ego. Embrace it. Love it. Disempower it. If you allow it to have its own way, its tantrum will become stronger and louder, and soon you will feel defeated and hopeless. You will start downloading the negative tapes of the Ego into your emotions and bring back more of the defeated patterns into your life.

Do not get into a dialogue with the Ego. Thank it. Love it. Acknowledge it, and put it to bed. The more you do this, the more you will move into love. Do this with your individual Ego and the collective. You may have to be firmer with the collective Shadow. Once again, thank it for being one of your greatest teachers. Tell it you are no longer learning through or from duality. Affirm that you are light and love. Bring your whole light team, Christ, the Masters and Angels. Ask your Highest Master team to surround you and the Shadow with love and light.

Remember, the Shadow has no power on its own. It feeds off your old fears and insecurities. The more you set your intention to be self-love and hold the intention by reinforcing it through continued practice, the more the Shadow has no way to reconnect with you. Your sound-vibration will be so high that it will penetrate your Shadow and start transforming it into a higher consciousness. You will always have a Shadow, but it will eventually become self-realized and become an ally with your light.

I am speaking to you of ways to move yourself into enlightenment. You are on the wave or paradigm of enlightenment. You must reinforce your intention with the power of your mind and hold it. As you do this, you connect with the collective intention of enlightenment (beyond karmic duality), and hold the light for one another. This is how your planet is healing, by lightening up collectively and holding the love frequency for all to feel their own self-love.

Many of you on your planet now have this understanding and are consciously aware of the ability to collectively heal the world through love.

Start your day like this

Set your intention to do this daily: Imagine your heart being a golden sun. Then imagine yourself in the center of this golden sun, which is the Christ energy. The more you practice this, the further you will be able to move into your heart. You will start feeling a warmth move through your body. From this warmth, you will feel a great peace.

When you are in the center of your golden heart, release whatever your fears, or traumas, or concerns are by saying, "I now release this burden (of whatever the fear is) on the Christ within and I go free". (The Christ - love - light frequency will dissipate the fear frequency.) This burden could be the fear of lack, of lack of prosperity, issues in relationships, depression, health, loss, traumas, guilt, shame, etc.

As you continue to do this daily you will be permeating in your own love and acceptance. You will feel your own joy, love, and happiness. Remember, all in life mirrors you. As you experience yourself as love and peace, you will see and experience all as the same because all is a reflection of your inner Being. Set your intention to do this daily. Bask in the pure love essence of your own heart's I AM, Christ love.

Enlightenment, the I AM Christ, the Golden Ray of you, is now the Second Coming. You are this energy Source and have always been. You just forgot. You are moving beyond linear time and expanding into all aspects of Me, that are you. As you continue to move into the center of your Soul, you will become one with yourself in all existence. You will soon find this to be a great, rewarding time in your life. All the fruits of your efforts will ripen for you.

You will be the conscious co-creators of your life, having a domino effect on assisting others who are not quite conscious enough to know that they are Creator Beings. Your light, love, and highest intention will connect to the dormant aspects of their light, assisting them to awaken quickly.

As this great awakening or quickening takes place within you, your experience of what is important for yourself and others of your world will change. You will feel yourself as a new person. In actuality, you have shed your old veils of illusion and are remembering who you are.

Simplifying your life will also be very important to you. You will feel a great need to clear out old clutter and material things. This is most important for you to do in your process of enlightenment: lightening up, because everything is energy. Move old energy out of your life and consciousness. As you rid yourself of past material objects, you release any corded emotions connected to the past experience. You must release old energies to make room for your expansion of self. No two energies can occupy the same space. As you move out of old energy fields, you make more room to expand into the new and now of you. As you continue to let go of old, worn-out belief systems, it is most important to let go of any material substances that may have a past connection to the beliefs.

Eventually, you will expand into freedom. You will become the beautiful butterfly of many colors that brings beauty to others and the world. Freedom of the Soul for yourself, others, and your great Mother Earth will be what is most important to you. The way you want to experience this freedom will be totally different for you. You will not be seeing the world and its evolution through the Shadow or duality lens. Your experience will be one of total love and acceptance. You will truly love thy neighbor as yourself because you will know and feel that you are your neighbor.

There is only love, and as your vibration is love, that will be your experience of all existence. This is the new paradigm you are moving into. As co-creators, you think your desires in thought, and they will manifest very quickly because there is no separation between you and what you desire. You are energy, and all is you.

I know that being on your planet at this time feels very difficult. There is much fear and uncertainty. All old securities from your monetary structure are being shattered. There is a sense of great hopelessness. What will I live on? How will I retire? What about my children? There will not be any social security.

I say to you, you are in one of the best places of consciousness that has ever taken place on your planet. As the old structures break down, you, the light ones, will find yourselves connecting to greater aspects of yourselves spiritually. You will once again come together in community. You will find much bartering and sharing happening. You will use your connection to Spirit to once again manifest your dreams.

Many, many Souls who never would have looked for themselves will start to pray. Their beginning spiritual journey will be out of fear, yet the outcome will be one of love, love of self and others. The old structures must break loose to be able to build a new future for yourself and future generations.

Soul groups will find each other again and bring their gifts together. Remember, you each have a piece of the puzzle. As you come back and put your pieces together, you will create a complete puzzle.

Your Souls are hungry. They are crying to be fed. They do not want more materialism; they want freedom. Free me. Love me. Free me. I want to go home again. You need not leave the planet to come home. Your agreement is to come home within yourself on the Earth plane to co-create Heaven on Earth.

As I said to you, crystal cities are in place all over your world. They are the new paradigm and frequency that you and your new world will be vibrating in.

These cities' light-sound structures are so high that the frequency is causing much havoc on your planet. The light-sound is hitting the old paradigm consciousness of the cities and the Souls of the cities and your world. As this happens, the light shatters the old belief systems and structures. These old structures must come down to be able to build a new. You cannot put the new on top of the old. As the old structure shatters, the new consciousness paradigm can be downloaded in its place.

This is what is happening to your world now. As you experience it, you feel hopeless and frightened. What is going to happen to us? How will we survive? What about our freedom? How free do you think you have been? You have not been free thinkers.

You have lived your life by what you have been taught to think by churches, religions, governments, belief systems, patterns, cultures, karma, fear. and so on. You were not free! You were an extension of what you had been taught, which was someone else's belief systems and structures. You were controlled by these thoughts and structures.

Much of the fear on your planet now is being projected by these old structures so that you will stay in formation of what they think you should be. You were programs of them. For you to become free thinkers and feelers to remember who you are, which is Me in My highest form, these old structures must break down. As this is happening, you are awakening. You are thinking for yourselves. What is important to me? How do I feel about this? What do I want for myself, my world and future generations?

As long as you had your financial security, you were like robots, following the leader because you felt secure. I want you to think about what I am saying to you. In the past, when a Soul of you had financial security, you felt safe. Your life was working, and you could feed your children and educate them. You could go on vacations and have fun.

In the realm of thinking and experiencing, your world was quite small. Many of you did not know or understand that across your world, children were going hungry. Souls/Cells/People did not have homes or schooling, and their basic needs were not even being met.

As your secure structures are being torn down, you are expanding yourself beyond old beliefs and perceptions. You are starting to think and ask why. How could this happen? You are truly waking up and taking your power back. You are unthreading from the old perceptions of security, which were control-based.

You are now moving out of the I Me and into the I Am of Me. Your expansion of self is now beyond you and your security and into the larger picture of life, of others and your world.

As your old security continues to break apart, you will find yourself awakening into more conscious aspects of the self, of Me. Light bulbs will constantly go on. You will find that you have a voice. Your perceptions will continually change. As your perceptions change, your choices in life become more conscious. As your choices become more conscious, the energy of this higher thought intention spreads through the world and connects with other Souls of the same intention and frequency.

This connection energetically moves you into a higher consciousness collectively. This collective thought intention is so powerful and strong it lifts the whole consciousness into a higher frequency. Remember, your intention creates your reality and world. As you vibrate together in a higher intent, you are energetically forming a new agreement for the better of other souls/cells and your world.

Where the attention goes the energy flows. As you are all creation, when you set a higher intention, you realign with Me, My highest consciousness, and together we will heal your world. We will co-create Heaven on Earth. Your thinking will be one with Me. You will constantly evolve, awakening into a greater consciousness of the I Am.

You are not alone; you have never been. You cannot heal and change your world without Me, and I cannot do this without you. Remember, you are aspects of Me playing yourselves out of the old consciousness. You are going through a death of old belief systems and separation and moving into the birth of Ascension and enlightenment.

Thought is powerful! Align your thoughts with My I Am of All That Is, which is you in your highest form. Become one with Me so that we can quickly move the consciousness of your world and all of the Souls of your world into Ascension and enlightenment. My greatest desire for you is to live in Heaven on your Earth plane, and for all of the Souls of Me to remember how much I love you. I created you as Me, and I love all aspects of you, for you are Me.

When your intention is to awaken into the I Am of All That Is, this intention is like making a phone call to Me. You are calling Me and saying, "I am now ready to come home. This Earth school has been too difficult. I don't want to do it on my own anymore. I want to come home to you and Mom. I want you to assist me, mentally, emotionally and physically. I am also asking for your financial support to assist me to live on the Earth plane."

I will hear you, and I will answer your call. When I look at all of creation, I marvel at the magnificence of All That Is. How could I not love what I have created? All of this creation is I. I love My creation of I. You are My creation, and I love you as much as I love Myself, for you are Me.

When you put in your call to the I Am of Me, I know that you are ready to remember who you are. When this happens, you will find yourself vibrating in serendipity.

You will have a teacher appear to you on the Earth plane to assist you to remember who you are. These teachers may not be in the form that you had expected. They may come to you to mirror your own perception of yourself. From this mirroring, you get to feel the pain, hurt, sorrow, loneliness, guilt, shame, and fear of all illusions that still hold you back from love of self.

You cannot get back to the highest aspect of the I Am until you are willing to move through your emotions. Your emotions are the feeling energies connected to whatever your karmic patterns are. You must go through the emotions to get into the core of the pattern to be able to release it.

These emotions and patterns are connected to many other emotions and patterns from other lifetimes or perceptions. If you do not go through these old emotions, they continue to control you. They take your power, life force, health, joy, happiness, and abundance, and they hold you in fear of what you want most in life, which is love.

The best way out of this karmic emotional bondage is to go through it. If you do not go through the emotions and continue to push them aside, when you least expect it, they will step in and sabotage you in the now. These old emotions are connected to the Ego mind, which is aligned with the Shadow mind. The Ego and Shadow are great allies and do not want the light part of you, your heart feeling, to move back into your I Am.

On your healing path, you will connect with many who assist to turn the light bulb on in your mind: "Now I get it. Now I understand." As this happens, you will feel energized because you are re-connecting to a light source of energy of knowing that you already are.

Many times as this happens and your mind feels stimulated, you feel like you are coming home with Me. In essence, this is true. The highest aspect of your creation has stimulated and awakened your right brain to awaken you. You may then start having great spiritual experiences.

Your right brain is your intuitive line to the all knowing. It is your creative brain. When you make the connection, it is very exciting for you. You feel the light being turned on. You start experiencing your higher self's consciousness and your mind becoming one mind. You start thinking from a higher understanding.

This natural high sustains you for a while. You then need an even higher connection. Your Soul is hungry; it is saying feed me. Feed me. Fill me with my light and love.

To be balanced and to be able to go forward with this new high, you must have your left brain working together with your right brain. As your two brains balance out, and your right creative brain stimulates your left analytical brain, they stimulate your pineal gland. This gland is your DNA connection to the source of me. When this gland is activated, you move up through all karmic layers and dimensions and into the highest intention - Source energy. Scientists used to believe that this gland was dormant and have now found out that it is your DNA connection with the source of Me. When you set your intentions from this Creator Source energy, you will feel the co-creator energy activate every Cell of your body. Because like attracts like, you will draw back to you, very quickly, all of your desires. From this place, it is most important that you set your intention in the positive so that you will bring more positive source energy back to you. If you go into the story of what you don't want, you will bring more of what you don't want back to you. It is most important to watch your thoughts and your words because you are now the co-creator of whatever your greatest desires may be.

As you start co-creating your life, using Source energy, you may hit a plateau and many times feel that your connection is not as high or that you have lost the connection. This is because your frozen emotions are blocking your connection; they are crying. They are like children and need assistance and support so that they can release themselves from the baggage they have been carrying.

Sometimes this job seems too difficult. It becomes very difficult for your emotional body because the light of who you are is penetrating the fear-based emotions. The emotions are the bag, or support system, which carries the pattern. It may seem just the opposite, but if you think about it, you will experience that you cannot truly release the pattern without going through the emotions. (The frozen emotions support the pattern.) If you do not do this, the emotional body, which is connected to the Ego mind, will pull the rug out from under your foundation when you least expect it.

As I explained, all in life mirrors you, and you always bring people, places, things, events, and circumstances into your life to assist you to heal, grow, and remember your magnificence. Just when you feel your life is starting to go well, you will bring someone into your life that will mirror your same emotional pattern. When this happens, you will feel shattered. All of these feelings that you have denied will surface, and will throw you back into the core of the pattern.

When you are in the core of the pattern, you become the pattern again. You see and experience life once again through this emotional fear bondage.

You must bring all of your bodies into balance with harmonizing frequencies and vibrations. You will not be able to move forward in your Soul's highest agreement until you balance your bodies out.

Your unloved emotional body will control and affect your mental, physical, cellular, and etheric bodies. Your unhealed emotional body runs through all of your systems. It will thread through your body and eventually take over. If you are a mental or left-brained person, you may not even know that it is happening because you are not in touch with your feelings.

If not healed, your unhealed emotional body gets your attention through sickness and dis-ease. It will eventually attack your inner systems, immune system, and other organs.

This can manifest in cancer, heart attacks, and so on. It is then you start looking for ways to heal. You wake up and become conscious of life. What does life mean to me? Do I want to live? You start thinking about mortality, life, death, family, and what is important to you.

This dis-ease starts changing your perspective. As I said, the change of perspective starts changing your life, or awakening you into life's meaning. The dis-ease becomes your wake-up call to find yourself. If you allow it, the dis-ease begins your journey home inside yourself, or if you waited too long, home into spirit.

I ask that you honor your emotions. Love them and set them free so that all of your bodies can harmonize in peace, love, joy, abundance, and hope.

Ascension:
Healing Your World by Changing your Thoughts

"Change your thoughts, and you change your world."

I wish to speak to you of Ascension. Ascension is moving all of your bodies into a higher frequency of Me, the I AM of All That Is. When the Soul of you is in the Ascension of the I Am, you are actually activating memories within your cellular structure, which allow the light-sound of you to move you into another time frame. To ascend means to move beyond linear time.

When one ascends, you move through all karmic lifetimes and agreements back into the highest consciousness of your I Am. This is a time of great change in your life and in the lives of all around you. As you continue to awaken out of linear time, you start awakening all of the Souls/Cells in other bodies who you interact with on the Earth plane.

Because you are each other, when the coding in your DNA is activated and you move to a higher frequency, you open the doorway for all Souls/Cells to follow. An actual portal beyond time opens, and you start moving through the veils of illusion within self. As you continue to shed the veils, you start moving through the dimensions that the veil is connected to.

As this happens, an expansion of your I Me self starts connecting with your I Am multi-dimensionally. This happens individually and collectively. Your collective consciousness unthreads from the karmic collective and starts reconnecting energetically with aspects of self that are already awakened and enlightened.

You must be enlightened before you totally ascend. This does not mean that you cannot move through the veils of illusion into higher frequencies of self, through the Ascension process. The Shadow Ego self also vibrates through the veils of illusion. If one does not consciously want to vibrate beyond the victim illusion, they will continue to move beyond time through the collective and still be very much connected and in servitude to the ego.

I see many that spend much of their time healing. Healing and growing is their whole intention, yet they are not willing to surrender into the center or core of their emotions. The unhealed emotional body, which serves the Ego Shadow continues to control their life and existence. I hear them say, "Where is God? I don't believe in this anymore. I am doing everything I can do to heal, and my life isn't any different. I feel more miserable than I ever have."

They start running this program and story over and over. The story continues to send the vibration through time and connects to a fear victim consciousness in all dimensions.

When this happens, the Soul becomes even more split in duality conscious. As the light becomes higher and the Soul is not willing to release old patterns, the light in the Soul continues to activate the collective Shadow within the subconscious and cellular structure. An actual war between the light and Ego Shadow takes place within the self of this person.

The light aspects want desperately to assist the Soul home, but if the Soul/Cell is not willing to release the old fear-based victim story, it continues to bring like frequencies, people, places, and circumstances to mirror back to it the same story to assist it to grow and heal.

If you are vibrating in duality consciousness, you will always bring duality back to you, without exception. You cannot serve both the light and Shadow and expect your life to become easier, lighter, and more loving and joyful.

What you can expect is a continued drawing back to you of a higher vibration of duality. Life becomes so difficult for you. You are in a constant tug-of-war within self, and the universe supports that energy because you are the universal energy and vibrate through all creations and consciousness. You always draw back to you, your own vibration. All mirrors your energy, your Soul song's frequency.

When you have a great split between your light and Shadow, you start losing hope. You may bring the light aspect to you in jobs, relationships, and circumstances, and just when you think that finally your life is working, the Shadow Ego takes over and blocks the flow of your light creation. The Ego Shadow then closes down or turns down your light.

Whatever good has appeared and has been activated then dissipates and disappears. The Ego Shadow turns down the light because it is in competition with your light and does not want the light consciousness of you to wake up.

As I said, the Ego is afraid of dying. It knows it has no power on its own, and if it can continue to thread into and through your subconscious mind, it will stimulate the old patterns in your emotions. Every time you play this old pattern, it becomes stronger and stronger. This would be like building muscles in your physical body. If your intent is to become muscular and you work a muscle over and over, it becomes strong. If you do this with your whole physical body, the body becomes strong and powerful.

This is also true for the emotional body. If you continue to stimulate the old story pattern over and over, the subconscious mind believes it is true and supports the emotional body to become stronger and stronger in its beliefs.

Remember, the emotional body threads through all of your bodies. It is like a river whose current has become so strong that it continues to widen through all of your systems whenever the old belief pattern is stimulated.

To change the old pattern, you must set the intention to break the pattern by doing the opposite. The pattern is connected to the Shadow Ego and has become its own entity and person. The way to break the pattern is to set your intention to look at your old tape differently.

Do you not know that your subconscious is a record, tape, CD or a higher computerized technology? You have available to you every color-sound–music experience imaginable. Just by a click or thought, you turn on, or tune into, any, and all experiences that your Soul has ever gone through, many simultaneously. You can easily access the Akashic Records that vibrate in your subconscious. You can tune into past lives, future lives, and who you are on other dimensions, etc., your Soul's higher purpose, and many other aspects of your Soul's journey. You have available to you all information that you so desire. Some of you are now trying to play a CD or a higher technology system, and your mind is still playing old records and cassette tapes. This does not serve you or work very well.

These patterns are stubborn. They have been with you for many lifetimes. Many times they become an entity that creates a sub-personality within you. You actually think or feel and act from this sub-personality. When you become conscious of this sub-personality pattern, you can actually release it by transmuting the fear energy into light. You will then bring the light that was stuck in the sub-personality back into you.

As you look at yourself closely and become aware of a sub-personality pattern, you will actually feel yourself speaking and acting and re-acting from this personality. At first you may feel shock and disbelief, but if you allow yourself, you can actually experience the humor of what has been controlling you. The light bulb will go on inside of you, and from this awareness, you have the ability to release it.

Talk to this sub-personality – ask it if it has a name. Many times it will communicate with you because it has become its own entity or person living inside of you.

Tell this personality how much you love it and appreciate it for being a great part of your life. Thank it for serving you in whatever way its intention has been.

Communicate that you are now strong enough to awaken spiritually without it, that you and your spiritual team are now one together. Tell it that it must now transmute itself into light and love and that its time of support is now over. (Never go in to the negative with this person- ality.) Only the vibration of love and light can release or transmute this sub-personality to light.

Then bring your Mother Sophia's and My I AM love vibration along with the Golden Christ Ray into your heart. Imagine and feel your heart fill with love and send this love into the sub-personality. If at first you don't succeed, do it again, and eventually, your collec- tive energy will be too bright to hold the pattern of the sub-personality, and it will release.

When this sub-personality releases, you may actually feel a loss or a sense of separation or death. This personality has been a big part of you and you lived and functioned together for a long time. This loss feeling will leave within about a week and then you will feel more balanced within yourself.

If it seems too difficult for you, you may have an under- lying fear of the process. Do not judge yourself or be alarmed or afraid. You may need assistance from a professional who is experienced in this technique, such as the one who I am speaking through.

Sub-personalities may create themselves when you go through times in your life that seem too difficult to handle. Your brain, being the sophisticated system that it is, creates a sub-personality, which takes over to assist you through the difficult period. It is still an aspect of you, and it believes that you need its constant assistance. When you become stronger and are able to handle more emotionally in your life, the sub-personality thinks that is still needs to take over, and take over it does! Only now, its assistance seems to sabotage you. It holds you back from being able to go forward in the highest intention and consciousness of you.

This personality thinks it has done you a great favor and that its assistance is still very much needed by you. This is why it is important that you release this aspect of yourself in great love, respect, and appreciation. From this place, it will transmute to light.

You must do something different to confuse these patterns. You must make different choices to dismantle the pattern's grip and personality hold on you. You must step out of the Ego mind's need to be right. How does it serve you to be right? You can be dead right. You see this all the time. Magnificent Beings of light who cannot surrender their Ego sometimes end up physically dying because the Ego feeds the subconscious, which stimulates the pattern that vibrates through all bodies. The bodies become overloaded with unhealed emotions and start closing down. From the blow out of the physical body, the Spirit of the Soul may not be able to connect to its own light and the Soul may then decide to leave the body or vehicle.

The Soul/Cell was dead right, to the point of never being able to complete its mission into the highest light-love of self. The Soul may have been brilliant in the light but allowed the Ego Shadow to put its light out before it had the chance to complete its higher mission.

To change the pattern, you must change its frequency. You do this by setting the intention for the outcome to be different. You then do something different that the pattern will be confused by.

Take a different route; create a new route for your light to travel through. Do not be angry with or fight against your Ego. If you do, you continue to feed it, stimulate it, and empower it.

You want to disempower it! You do this by loving yourself enough to want your life to become easier and happier.

Do this by taking a different road. If you are used to walking down a certain path, take a different one.

If you always do what you always did, you always get what you always got. You have to do it differently for the outcome to be different. As I explained, patterns become their own entity and are very predictable. To change the pattern, it is important to confuse it.

If you always drive your car down the same road at the same time to the same destination, you will always go to the same place. Take a different road, a different route. Go on a different journey. Allow this journey to be one of self-empowerment.

What is not love is fear, and the Ego Shadow has a great fear of death, individually and collectively.

Remember; do not respond to the Ego Shadow. Thank it for sharing and put it to bed. This will be difficult at first because the mind is used to being in control of your life and existence. It will feel that it is losing its job.

Confuse the Ego Shadow. Do not be predictable. Do things differently. Respond, instead of react. When this is your intention, you will be able to witness, even predict, how your Ego will act. Until now, you were so immersed with the Shadow Ego that you could not separate yourself from it.

Now, witness it, and when the pattern comes up, confuse it by doing things in another way. Change, change, change your life.

If you are used to eating a certain thing for breakfast, eat something else, sit in a different chair and play different music. Do not let the pattern control you. Break it up by confusing it.

Instead of re-acting in anger, go into the center of your golden heart. When someone upsets you, breathe and take yourself and the emotion into the center of your golden heart. If you have fear, imagine placing the fear into the center of your golden heart. You will feel it break up and dissipate.

Thank your Ego for sharing. Tell it you have learned much from it. Wrap it into a blanket of the golden Christ energy, and bring it into the core or center of your golden heart, which is in alignment with the Central Sun's energy. This will send golden Christ energy into the Ego. Remember, the Ego has no power on its own. It feeds off your old fear patterns.

Take a few deep breaths and breathe into the center of your golden heart. Through continual practice, your subconscious will know to surrender into the center of your golden heart. Through this practice, you will re-trace and re-thread yourself through time into the collective I Am. You will feel great peace and love within yourself, and your perspective of life will change because you will no longer be sending out mixed duality messages.

Do not be afraid of bringing energies into your heart that you perceive as negative. You are bringing aspects of yourself into the core of your own Christ love. As you do this, the fear-based pattern or incident starts breaking up, dissipating, and transmuting to love. You will feel your own love expand and become stronger.

This will feel like a stone being thrown into the water. You will feel ripples of love, of light, move through your bodies and systems. You will feel yourself quieter and floating into peace. **Change your thoughts, and you change your world!!!**

If you allow yourself to constantly bring the Golden Sun into your heart and allow it to be your heart's constant vibration, you will feel yourself going deeper into your own self-love and into the center of your Soul's I Am. You will experience yourself

346

more and more in love with self.

From this self-love, your reflection of others will be love. Love, joy, and happiness will be your constant companions, for there is no separation between you and your environment. It is up to you as to which frequency you choose to vibrate in: love or fear.

You can also choose to bring the Golden Sun into the back of your heart, as well as the front. You will feel both sides connect into the center core of your heart. This will feel like an energy that expands you beyond time. It is a very quick way to bring your vibration to a higher level. You will experience this golden light expand through all of your bodies until your etheric body is so filled with the golden light that you feel like a safe child within yourself.

This will quicken you into the light of Ascension, which will activate a coding in your DNA that will open your divine blueprint. Ascension is to move beyond time through all karmic energies, patterns, and agreements.

As you move through the Ascension ladder or process, you will align yourself energetically with your divine blueprint, which is your master plan of all lifetimes, agreements, and contracts. Because there is no past, present, or future, when you move into the dimensions where other aspects of yourself vibrate, this vibration activates old karmic memories so that they can be released.

Your bodies carry the memories of every experience, thought, belief system (both fear-based and love-based) that you have ever experienced.

Ascending is not an easy process. You are giving birth to yourself and assisting the whole collective into a higher vibration of self.

In the core of your Soul is your love, light, and Soul's Song. Every time you allow yourself to surrender into your heart, your Soul's Song, you will start experiencing more of who you are, your divine purpose, and the purpose of the planet. You will feel more powerful and on purpose in your own body and in your life. You will no longer see or feel yourself separate from Me or others.

If you do not allow yourself to move through the old fear aspects of self, you will still be in the Ascension frequency because Ascension is the vibration agreement and paradigm that the planet and all of the Souls/Cells of this planet are moving through.

This is where free will comes in. When you have a conscious understanding of the process, you get to choose if you want to be stuck in the karmic victim role or if you want to vibrate in the Master of self that you are. This is your choice, and I will love you and support you in whatever your intention and agreement is.

I am you, and I know that this death and re-birth cycle is not easy. If you feel that it is too difficult and do not surrender into the process in this lifetime, you will have the opportunity to go through the process again. When you reincarnate again, you will be born into a family unit that mirrors your like consciousness or frequency to assist you with the old patterns from your past life. Your parents will activate the patterns when you are in the womb and first born, so that you have an understanding of what it is that you need to move through. You can do this quickly or at your own pace.

You could say that all is free will. In all the lifetimes you have gone through, you have chosen to free your Soul out of the perception of duality and back to the I Am self of Me in the highest.

Many of these lifetimes were structured so the lesson could be learned, yet there was no ability to move out of the lesson. The vibration at the time was too dense. Those lifetimes also had shorter life spans. You may have only lived on the Earth or in the lesson for 20, 30, or 40 years of Earth time.

Your life span on the Earth plane has doubled, and for many tripled, and is now moving beyond that. The collective mind or Soul consciousness is infinite, and it knows there is no death. There is only birth and re-birth.

When the karmic collective energy was of a lower vibration,

you agreed to shorter lifetimes so that you could quickly move through the karma collectively, leave the perceived lifetime and move back into Spirit to understand and release what you had gone through.

Many of you made a U-turn and came back to the Earth again very quickly so that you could move out of the fear-based karmic pattern and back into love. You continually have recycled back, sometimes repeating a lesson or course until you understood it enough to choose to move beyond it.

You have had civilizations on the Earth plane with life spans of three and four hundred years. The vibration was high enough that much of the experience was beyond linear time.

Atlantis was such a civilization. In the beginning, the consciousness of this time period was very high, and the Souls of you who vibrated there had a Oneness connection with your higher selves and the I AM of Me in the highest.

Because of this, you were not vibrating in a time frequency. Now, on your planet, the same experience is happening. The more you vibrate beyond karmic time, the higher your vibration becomes.

Many of you now have a great understanding of the universes within yourself and the collective of Me. The more wisdom that is awakened within you, the more you expand throughout creation in the highest aspects of your I Am self of Me. You expand into and become your collective consciousness beyond any illusion and duality experience. As this happens, all of your bodies become one crystallized color sound. . As your frequencies become higher, sickness and dis-ease dissipate from all of your systems.

Sickness and dis-ease live in a time frequency. When you move beyond time, the sickness or dis-ease has no emotional memory to continue to vibrate in. Your fear emotions no longer control you, and your vibration becomes one of love and acceptance, for self and for all Souls/Cells of you.

As this happens, your physical life span continues to expand. This is happening now on your planet, and you will continue to evolve into higher frequencies and longer life spans. Eventually, you will evolve past duality, past the ending of Atlantis, and other civilizations. Your planet will be one that has ascended past all karmic time lessons and frequencies.

This is Mother Earth's agreement and the agreement of those of you who now inhabit the Earth. You are re-cycling through a death cycle that is energetically connected to Atlantis, Lemuria, Mu, Egypt, and all other evolved civilizations. The Earth plane is carrying the death cycle for the whole collective of all evolved civilizations that could not maintain the balance and eventually cycled back to Spirit.

Now, on your Earth plane, you have every Soul/Cell who has ever lived in these civilizations. You have all come back together from other star systems, planets, and universes. You have agreed again to cycle through the death frequency, release all karmic duality agreements and merge through the birth canal of the feminine to co-create Heaven on Earth in all life forms.

That, in itself, tells you that your life spans will be very long. Remember when you are back in Spirit and are no longer in the body, you live through infinite eternity.

Now that the Earth is ascending, she is going through many contractions of light. This means the light of who I Am is giving birth to this beautiful Soul of the Mother, the feminine.

As I explained, actual doorways are opening as the planet moves into these higher vibrational energies or frequencies. These light doorways are like contractions. When a contraction happens, Mother Earth moves closer into her intention and agreement to ascend. She moves through the contractions and downloads the light frequency onto the planet.

This is why so many of you are experiencing much conflict as to who you are right now. As you and the planet move beyond time, you are losing your old Earthly identity. Your I Am self is activating memories of your light in your collective DNA, as well as your physical DNA system.

As the light inside of you is activated, the light activates any Shadow fear-based patterns.

You can see this as a blessing or a curse. My desire for you is to take such a gift and embrace all aspects of yourself.

Again, I say to you, the best way out is always through loving and embracing these old, worn-out patterns. Dissipate them through love. Every time you go through a release, you must replace these old fear-based emotions with love. You are constantly giving birth to higher aspects of yourself, and every time you go through the birth canal, it is most important that in the new light you feel safe and loved. In the next sub-chapter, I will give you the tools for this.

This one that I am writing or channeling through feels that I become quite windy at times. She feels that I sometimes get off the subject because I have so much to say. She expressed great laughter when I said to her, "It takes one to know one." She has much knowledge and wisdom through her own life experience. She also has much to share with Souls of you who are here, in how to bring yourselves out of duality, and now to close the door to karmic duality.

Now, back to Ascension! As you continue to give birth to yourself and move through all duality frequencies, and you become higher aspects of your I Am, you start releasing your old karmic blueprint. and start replacing it by merging more with your light body, which activates the coding of your divine blueprint. The light body vibrates beyond time and in all aspects of your higher self of Me, the I Am.

Many Souls believe you start downloading your light body. In actuality, what happens is that you and the light body start merging together. This happens because your physical bodies are becoming lighter and more conscious, and you always draw to yourself like vibration. Remember, like attracts like.

As you continue to move into your own light, you and your light body merge as one. You are your light body. It is your divine blueprint that vibrates with you in your highest. Your light body is a total consciousness of you and is now drawing you back to it, as one.

Awakening into a New Lifetime on Earth by Rewriting your Script

"You are coming into a new lifetime on the Earth without physically leaving the body."

I see many spontaneous enlightenments happening to you great Souls of Me on your planet. As you are ascending and moving into higher aspects of yourself, your Cells are activating memories of you that have already been enlightened. Because like attracts like, when this happens, you turn on that vibration within self, and when the two lights connect, you wake up and remember who you are.

This is like plugging your Spirit's cord back into a light socket. It reconnects the right and left hemispheres of the brain. They no longer think separately. Your spirituality and mind become one source of thought. They merge in the higher consciousness of Me. You then experience all aspects of all life through the higher thought consciousness of Knowingness.

As I said, you can become enlightened without ascending, but you cannot totally ascend without enlightenment.

After enlightenment, Souls sometimes get into their "Dark Nights of the Soul". The light within self is so bright that it activates any Shadow aspects in other dimensions, which are stored in the subconscious mind.

The subconscious mind carries the memories of all lifetimes and experiences in all dimensions. If Souls have not moved through their own emotions, the light hits the emotions that are connected to a frame of reference in another time period. This opens the doorway for the experience to download into the now. The now is All That Is. You carry all expressions, thoughts, beliefs, and perceptions in this moment of your life.

The subconscious cannot discern past, present, or future because in reality, all time exists together.

As you are ascending and moving into enlightenment, the subconscious is opening many doorways of your own Shadow

352

consciousness that vibrate multidimensionality so that you can clean out all cob webs, or illusions, and return home to Me, your I Am of All That Is. When this happens, all aspects of your mind vibrate together as one mind of creation.

You then live totally in the now with past, present, and future as one consciousness.

It is most important that you bring all aspects of self into the now. It is almost impossible to do this if you have not allowed yourself to surrender into your emotions.

You must be willing to let go and die. It is important to surrender into your greatest fears. As you allow yourself to do this, you are going through a karmic death.

I am not saying to you that this is easy. As you surrender into your greatest fears, you start losing who you think you are, who you think you are supposed to be, and other Souls' programs of who you are and who they think you are. You start shedding your old identity.

When your old identity breaks up or you break through your old illusional perceptions of self, you start discovering the truth of who you are, which is My greatest love of all, for you are Me. You cannot miss it because it is.

In the center of your core is the magnificent light of creation, which is who you are. This light is the total balance and love of all selves of Me, which is you. In this balance, you and your higher self will start merging.

The phone lines or energy cords light up, and you start communicating with other aspects of yourself in spirit that are from a higher consciousness of self, I Am. At first, this line may feel a little fuzzy. You might not be quite sure of what is you, if it is your old mind-set speaking to you, or if it is truly the higher aspect of self.

If you are willing to call home daily, your line or connection will become stronger, and you will feel a surge of energy or power when you connect. You will feel yourself become clearer within yourself. You will have a sense of feeling more confident and more at peace with yourself. Some of your old self-righteous perceptions start falling to the wayside. Your heart will feel more open, and you will start feeling more compassion for others.

As you continue to make the connection and it becomes stronger, you will be able to feel instantly that you have called home in the highest. The surge of energy that you connect with will spread a peace throughout your bodies. You will experience yourself harmonizing within yourself. You will feel that you are being called home within self, for all is within you.

As I am repeating, you are coming into a new lifetime on the Earth without physically leaving the body. As you move through linear time, you reconnect with all aspects of self, and as you bring them together as one love and light, you have ascended.

Ascension means moving out of karmic duality. It means you are going through a death of old karmic programming, individually and collectively.

As you do this, you are back home with Me in the highest. You have come into a new lifetime without physically leaving the body. You have learned and moved through your karmic lessons and through the karmic wheel. You have moved beyond duality and are in the center of the core of your I Am beingness.

You then have a great understanding and acceptance of self in the I Am. You and I are home together in My highest, and you are vibrating in this frequency in your physical body or vehicle.

This vehicle has been your home in this lifetime to bring you home to Me. Within your cellular structure you carry all lessons, memories, and agreements of what needed to be released to free your Soul.

As you come into this new lifetime, you need a new family unit. This new family unit is Me and your Mother Sophia. Your biological parents will always be your Earth parents in this lifetime, but you will have completed karmically with them. From a place of love, you will have released the contracts of what needed to be learned with them, and you will move into alignment with the higher aspects of the collective I Am consciousness. You will have moved beyond duality and will be vibrating in the now of Me, that is you.

It is now time to write a new contract. This contract is the intention of your life now on the planet.

You have moved through the karmic death and into a rebirth of the higher consciousness. You then reconnect a thread with other Souls/Cells of light who are vibrating in this new paradigm, beyond time frequency. You then assist the next wave to move into a higher time slot.

As the wave of Ascension that you are moves into a higher frequency, you assist the next wave through the doorway. Your role as gatekeeper or opener has been completed, and you then vibrate in the higher frequency at all times.

It is most important to keep yourself balanced in this new or higher frequency of your I Am.

As you are holding the light for others, it is important that you stay connected with other Souls of the same light frequency to mirror your vibration back to you.

This is where you consciously release any old residue connected to the lifetime that you are leaving behind. All this has been by agreement. If you have agreed to go through these karmic lessons and contracts, you can now agree to release them.

Through the spoken word, say out loud:

> *I now set the intention to be totally done with all past lifetimes. I release the karmic collective consciousness of all lifetimes, all programs, contracts, belief systems, patterns, emotions of anger, rage, resentment, fear, mistrust of God, of Spirit, of love.*

> *I release all karmic contracts connected to these emotions that are in my heart, thymus, throat, third eye, crown, spine, root, sexual organs, my second chakra and solar plexus, past, present, future in any way, shape or form.*

355

I release the karmic collective consciousness and all contracts of separation and control by churches, religions, governments, karma, belief systems, cultures, prejudice, and projections of fear by the Shadow.

I release all programs of fear projections, all implants, microchips and all reversed programming that are in my heart, throat, third eye, crown, root, sexual organs, second chakra and solar plexus and in my mental, emotional, physical cellular and etheric bodies, past, present and future. I Am love. I Am light, only love, only light. I Am. I Am. I Am.

Remember the importance of forgiveness and release. I forgive and release Mother, Father God, and Creation. I forgive and release my parents and ancestors from all lifetimes and agreements. I forgive and release the imbalance of my male and female, of my heart and Ego, of my light and Shadow. I forgive and release the crucifixion of Christ, of the Christ consciousness. I forgive and release the violation and rape of the feminine, of the fear, control and denial and competition with the feminine and between the feminine. I forgive and release everyone and everything. I forgive and release everyone and everything. I forgive myself. I forgive and release myself. I forgive myself and I ask that all forgive me. I trust and believe that the consciousness has changed and I am now safe to be the innocence of my child, to be the highest love and light of my I AM and to live my highest spiritual purpose now. I AM. I AM. I AM. I AM.

Even if you don't think or believe that you have anyone or anything to forgive, saying these words of forgiveness will vibrate through all dimensions of you and release any old fragmented thought forms or patterns that may still be influencing you in any negative way.

Any time you release, you must reaffirm the highest of who you are. All is energy, and the space emptied must be filled back up with positive energy. As you go through this verbal release, you will feel the energy releasing from your bodies. You will feel lighter and freer, making room for more love and light to fill your bodies.

Look at all patterns in your life. Go through a verbal release of them through all chakras and bodies. (Remember the power of the spoken word.) Any pattern that you come into this lifetime to break through has a frame of reference elsewhere. As you move the energy through the now out of your systems, the thought or intention connects to the memories stored in your Cells and system from the old reference point and releases it also.

After you go through this energetic release, move yourself back into the center of your heart, the Golden Christ energy. From your heart, send this love frequency through your bodies, and your subconscious will unlock your unconscious and will immediately start download-ing the love energy into your cells and tissues.

If you continue to allow yourself to use the word to release, your subconscious will recognize and remember the process and will know it is time to fill you back up with light. Your subconscious will work with you and will download your super-consciousness of My I Am into you.

In this new lifetime, it is important to set up a balance support of Me that is you. This is the total balance of the male and female.

As I was explaining, after any release you must fill yourself back up with the highest consciousness of love. Ask for your spiritual mother, Sophia, to fill your Being with her feminine love and light. Ask her to fill your bodies up with the feminine mothers love and light. As you do this, you will create a new system of support be-

357

yond any karmic agreements. Then wait and allow her to respond. You will feel a peace and sense of safety fill your whole Being with light. Open the communication with her. Ask her what she wants to say to you. The message will come through your mind. At first, you may think it is you talking to yourself. The more you do this, the more you will feel her energy. Then, when you ask for a message, you will feel her energy blend into you through the message.

If you are not sure it is her and you have the knowledge of muscle testing your body, do the testing because your body will not lie to you. If you do not receive the message at first because you cannot feel her energy, continue to ask and her love and light connected to your intention will open the lines of communication.

When you can start feeling the energy, you may receive the message through feelings, through the Knowingness of the energy. As you feel her, you may just know what the message is without her verbally speaking to you.

After you bring the feminine mother to you, ask for Me, your father, to be with you. Ask and you shall receive. Ask for your inner father, the I Am of All That Is, and you will feel My essence fill your whole Being. You will feel a sense of strength, confidence and safety. Then ask if I have a message for you. Open the lines of communication with Me, for I am you and I love you. Bring Me, your real father to you as the guardian parent of love and light. I am the patriarchal energy that your Cells and Souls know as true safety and love.

I want to assist you to remember and feel the creation of yourself in love. As you move into this new lifetime, I want to be your new foundation. I Am your divine Father and Mother.

Connect with Me, and you will feel a love and safety that you have never experienced before. Allow Me to be your guiding light and constant confidante.

I, the balance of the highest creation of the male and female, will now guide you and keep you safe to assist in co-creating Heaven on Earth. We are one; we have never been separate. You just forgot. Allow your whole Being of the I Am self to re-thread with Me.

Build a new foundation in this new lifetime.

Begin each day with the love of your parents, the balanced male and female, Mother and Father of Me. Start your day with the connection of your higher self. Begin your day tuned in beyond duality. Allow yourself to be constantly guided and directed by becoming one with your higher self and the highest Mother and Father's love. Ask for your higher self's connection. Then bring your inner Mother and Father of Me, the I Am, to you. You will feel safe, secure, and divinely supported as you move through your day. Your new foundation will be set.

Next bring your inner children to you. You all have a little girl and little boy inside of you waiting to be given permission to awaken, to feel safe enough to open up and remember their own love. Only you, the adult, can give this to them. The feminine is your inner girl, your spirituality, your love-light feeling of Me. The male, your inner boy, is your mind, your will, and the aspect of self that goes forward and is also the love and light of Me. Many times, your inner children, your little girl and boy, do not have a conscious memory of one another. You need both the male and female to go forward. They are your innocence and when they feel safe, they will re-awaken to the understanding and knowing love, of all that is. It is important, that as you make the con-

nection to each one of them individually and they start feeling safe inside of you, that you introduce them to each another. Many times they do not remember that the other one exists. They are each other, the balance of one another, the heart and the mind. As you bring them back together within yourself, they will feel loved, and safe together. You, the adult, will then start feeling loved and safe because you experience all of your life through the emotions of your inner children. If they are hurt, you, the adult, will feel their hurt emotions. If they feel safe, you, the adult, will feel safe.

It is most important that once you have made the contact with them, that you stay connected. Talk to them. Let them know how much you love them. Tell them that they are safe now, that they are one with their real parents, Mother-Father God-Creator. Bring Sophia's and My love through your heart and into theirs. Run the infinity energy through their hearts. Bring our energy through your hands and into them. Hold them in our love. Give them everything you needed but may not have received as a child from your biological parents. As they start healing and growing up emotionally, they will start feeling happy, more joyous, and safe. Safety is a big issue for your inner children. As they start feeling better, you, the adult will, because your emotions are theirs; you are them.

Make a conscious connection to them every morning so that they know that you will always be there for them. You will not abandon them. Re-assure them that you love them, that they are now safe with you, so that they will know and feel that no one will ever hurt them again.

I hear some of you say, "but that is such a great responsibility, how can I keep them safe when I don't trust or feel safe myself?"

You do this by moving out of the "I Me" and into the "I AM", by becoming one with your higher self, with your inner Mother Sophia and with me, your Father. You then have a strong spiritual foundation to assist you to move beyond your Earthly story and into the larger picture of your purpose. You are not alone; you cannot do this journey without Spirit. You are Spirit and in this place within you, you will feel safe. It is important for you to bring this loving safe vibration into you the adult, and through you, back into your inner children. Because your children are still very connected to Spirit, from this place they will feel loved and safe. The veils of illusion will lift from them and they will once again feel their innocence and safety with us. When you connect to them daily and give them permission, they will reconnect with Me and your Mother. As they feel this inner safety net of Love, this Love will ripple back into you, the adult.

Your inner children are your road map to freedom. Your inner children carry the road map (karmic contract) of all that is needed to be understood, healed, released, and forgiven. Every thing, event, and situation that has happened to you in this lifetime that you are now coming out of has a past life or another frame of reference to it. You agreed to go through the lesson again to release the karmic emotions connected to it.

Inside your karmic children are your Crystal Children who are waiting to be acknowledged, recognized, and embraced. Crystal Children are being born on your planet now. They are carrying the divine blueprint of All That Is. They are not vibrating in a time frequency. They are being born into family units that are holding the light for them to continue to vibrate in total consciousness. They are the future of your world. Your Inner Crystal Children are now ready to be birthed by you with Sophia and I as your family unit of love, light and safety.

These children are the seeds of your future generation, and they are the future of your world. They do not vibrate in unconscious duality. They are enlightened Beings, Cells of the super-conscious I Am of Me. They are holding the frequency for you to awaken and bring forth the Crystal Children within you. The time is now for the collective Crystal consciousness to be rethreaded. You are these Crystal Children. You went before, moved through, and opened the karmic gateways for the Crystal Beings of light who are coming through now. Their agreement with you is to hold the light for the rebirth of your Crystal consciousness within you to emerge. You have been the guiding light for them, and as you have come full circle into a new lifetime within yourself, they are now the guiding light for you to become one with them to carry the consciousness through the 2012 gateway and into your New World.

Their vibration alone will heal your world if they are supported in their mission. They come from the future and are here to tune the vibration of you and your world to a higher octave of sound and light.

They will mirror back to all their own magnificence and light. They are the highest teachers that have come to your planet. Their frequency is so high that they could not have been born on the planet before the time of now. The consciousness of the planet was not high enough to hold the light for them. They would have been blown out energetically.

As I said, within each of you, your Crystal Children are now waiting to be born. The importance of me speaking to you of your inner children is that they are the collective Second Coming of the Christ energy.

As you move out of the karmic play and into your new lifetime without physically leaving your bodies, you also bring with you your enlightened consciousness of your inner Crystal Children.

After you have built your foundation with Sophia and I, as the love and safety of your inner parents, ask for your Crystal Children to come to you. Remember, inside your karmic child is your Crystal Child waiting to be born.

Take your Crystal Children through the same process as you did with your karmic children. Imagine a divine little girl in your heart. Communicate to her. Let her know how much you love her, how much she is wanted, and how valuable and important she is to you. Give her everything that you feel you did not get with your biological parents.

Feel the love of your Inner Parents of Me, of my heart's love, move out through your heart and into the heart and body of your new Crystal Child. Talk to her, love her and re-assure her that she is now safe to awaken and emerge.

As she feels totally loved, safe and secure, you, the adult, will because you experience all life through the emotions of your inner children. When they feel loved, safe, and secure, you, the adult, will because you are them.

Now, do the same process with your crystal inner boy. Ask for a divine Being of light to hand your little boy to you. Hold him against your heart with your little girl. Love him and reassure him that he is safe to awaken and emerge into light.

Bring the love and light through your heart and hands into the little boy, sending a light frequency into him that runs through his heart and links him to the little girl's heart. Again, imagine the infinity energy running through both of their hearts. Now bring your karmic children together with your Crystal Children. The light of your Crystal Children will start penetrating your karmic children. Eventually they will blend together in higher consciousness as one Child of Light. As I said, inside of each karmic child is the Crystal Child waiting to be born. As you bring them together daily, the programming of the karmic child dissolves into light. As this happens, the veils release and the karmic child awakens into the enlightened Crystal Child.

363

Give them all an identity. They all carry different sound vibrations of your personality. When you first connect to your Inner Children, ask them what they want to be called; it may be different than your given name. If they don't tell you their names, give them the names that you feel comfortable with. Remember, all names have a color-sound frequency vibration. As you bring them together in balance, love and harmony, you the adult will feel this throughout your bodies. You are then building a new lifetime for yourself of total balance of the male's and female's love and light on all levels.

Start communicating with your inner Crystal Children daily. They will give you much information that the adult aspects of self have forgotten.

Your Crystal Children are total consciousness and will guide you with their enlightened wisdom. They will assist you, the adult, to vibrate throughout your Cells in the higher vibration of your Soul's Sound and Song.

You will truly feel at home within yourself and will vibrate in the Crystal frequency, mirroring to others the light of their own songs and sounds. And so it is.

Conclusion

"Now is the time to co-create with me the love and joy of life, which is your birthright."

In the beginning, there was the word, and the word was love. My word is still the way home through the heart.

When the consciousness on your planet was re-awakening, a structure needed to be formed. The structure was the word of I, the Father.

You have had many incarnations on the Earth plane, where you came to an end of what your Soul could comprehend or understand at the time.

There was no failure and never has been. You played out end times of the opposition between the heart and Ego. When that was done, in whatever form it took, the civilization came to an end, and you moved back home with Me to understand the whole play. All of your incarnations have been plays so that you and the collective could act out and release any illusions or misunderstandings of Me that were still vibrating in you.

When the play came to an end and you moved back into Spirit with Me, you were able to look at the lifetime that you were coming out of as if you were watching a movie. It was then that you could experience yourself clearly. You could see all of your misconceptions and perceptions that formed and grew from your biological family unit's guidance. Because you received many impressions from your Earth parents, surroundings, and environments, you were then able to see clearly how these influences orchestrated your life's decisions.

From the play becoming very clear, you chose to come down to the Earth again and re-write your new script, to complete the lessons that your Soul needed to learn or did not complete.

You could see that the mind is a very powerful tool that wants to control you like a domineering parent. The mind has the support from the collective mind that wants to keep your light dormant. The mind will do everything that it can to keep you stuck in duality and fear. Because the mind is also connected to aspects of the collective mind that are at war against Me, they were able to draw the collective further into duality through fear.

This is what happened in many of the great civilizations that came to an end of their own love and light. As the light went out, the darkness or fear unconsciousness felt great triumph.

When you were able to see all of the movies that you made from your agreed upon lifetimes, that kept you in these fear-based realities, you became more conscious in re-writing the new script for your next lifetime.

As I speak to you now, it is to give you My word anew. My greatest desire is to bring you back home to Me through My love for you. I am now a more sensitive father.

On the Earth plane, as parents become older, they become wiser. They treat their grandchildren with much more joy, happiness, care, and kindness. They see the children's magnificence and light. Their desire is to continue to honor the magic, light, and creations of this child.

Many times when they were raising their own children, they were still trying to find themselves. Their jobs or careers took priority over the joy and magic of their children. They were too busy trying to provide for the children to be able to set up a better future for themselves and their children.

When grandchildren came into their lives, they were on the other side of building themselves. They had matured emotionally and were more at peace with themselves. Their priorities had changed.

This is My experience of Myself. I am now at great peace with Myself. I no longer need to create to understand Myself. I have created All That Is and am now in My Golden Age of My I Am knowing. I no longer need to have all of my old, fragmented aspects of Me to play themselves out so that they can remember who they are.

My heart, arms, mind, and the higher consciousness of Me is open to you to remember who you are so that you can return to Me, within yourself, within your heart, within self-love.

Every role that could possibly be played out, you have already played. You need not struggle to remember who you are. There is no need to play the villain or victim to understand duality. You are every experience. You have great wisdom and knowledge within yourself.

Now is the time of great awakening. I am calling all of you home to Me. Your job of duality is done. You have served this great awakening well. Collectively, all that needs to be known is known. This Knowingness now has to be brought forth into the light, into your own light.

You temporarily fell asleep at the wheel, the wheel being your vehicle of light, which is your body.

Now, in this lifetime on the planet of the great Mother Earth, you have the ability to move beyond any old karmic duality, fear-based illusion.

As I am gathering all of My children to come home to Me and into the heart of my beloved Sophia, we are shining a light so brightly that your path home, through the heart, through love, will be much easier.

Much of the disturbance on your planet now is because the light frequencies of My I Am are penetrating all of your fear illusions. This light is shattering the Shadow within you and the collective.

As I said before, when this happens, all that is not light is activated so that it can play itself out. All is thought energy, and the Shadow illusion's mind needs to express the emotions of the old fear-based conceptions. As you, the light holders of Me, mirror your light and love to the Shadow, it starts breaking up and dissipating. This mind-Ego-Shadow illusion is the old mind-set of Me that has no place else to go.

Now is the time that its reign of false power has come to an end. I no longer need to grow and expand Myself through duality and neither do you. You are Me, and you have within yourself all that your Soul will ever need to know. Now is the time to wake up out of your own fear and accept yourself as the love of Me.

Because you have had many incarnations in this cycle of duality, the collective subconscious mind wants to keep you in the cycle. It feels that its job is to continually play out the end times in conflict, death, and confusion.

I say to you, you are in the end times. There is much conflict and confusion, and you are now in a death cycle. This is the death of the Ego, the Shadow and karma, not the death of the Earth or you, the Cells of the Earth.

As you move through this death cycle, you are also moving into the birth of innocence. I am sending great light frequencies to you, which are allowing you to quickly identify the Ego Shadow within yourself and the planet.

As I said before, you are in a death and re-birth cycle at

the same time. The Shadow must be exposed so that you, the light warriors of Me, can wake up and lead the old consciousness of Me, back home to Me, in light and love.

If the Ego Shadow were not being exposed to the degree that it is now, your waking-up time would be much longer. Because you now are seeing more and more clearing of this illusional Ego force, you are able to become clear within yourself as to what you want for yourself and this beautiful world.

I say to you, set your intention. You have a beautiful, brilliant mind. Use this mind in alignment with My mind. We will co-create a civilization so brilliantly light that the light will dissipate all confusing illusion.

Now is the time for you to vibrate beyond duality. Now is the time to co-create with Me, the love and joy of life that is your birthright. You were born of Me and are still Me. My greatest desire is to mirror My love and light back to you so strongly that all on your planet will have spontaneous enlightenment. I want all of you to remember your own magnificence.

You are the mind and heart of Me, and I love you.

Your planet can quickly evolve out of separation from My highest if you set the intention for this to happen. Thought is energy, and when all set their intention, through the feeling of their heart's love, to have a better world, I, your Father and Mother, will align My heart and intent with yours. We will co-create Heaven on Earth in all life forms.

As I said, I am now sending light frequencies to your planet. You and the Mother Earth are in your birth canal of Ascension.

The light is coming down in about two-month intervals, or 60-day cycles, opening portals of consciousness within you and throughout all Creations. Every time this birth contraction happens, you are moving through the womb of creation and into a higher light of the I Am, of All That Is.

When the light hits, you will feel many old feelings and emotions surface so that you can go through them and pull the roots up. Your feelings and emotions are from every incarnation, individually and collectively.

Through this great awakening, you will feel uncomfortable within yourselves. You will sometimes feel nauseous and have vertigo, and your bodies will feel out of balance. You will be losing your identity of who you thought you were, or what you thought you were supposed to be.

Goals that you had set for yourself will no longer seem real or important. You will have great confusion and feel like you are losing your memory. Your taste for food will change. You will not know what you want to eat. Nothing will taste good. As your vibration is being turned up, you must put higher vibrational foods and energies into your systems. Your bodies need food as energy or fuel. You must bring into your bodies the food that vibrates with the now of you.

This is a time that is important to clean your bodies and systems out. Your bodies, cells, and organs are holding old memories from all incarnations. As the light hits your bodies, these old memories are breaking loose.

These toxins and dis-ease need a place or vehicle to be able to release into and out of. This is your body. Continue to clean your vehicle to make space for all of the old built-up karmic toxins to release into and out of. Keep your bodies as clean as you can because you are going through a great mental, emotional, physical and cellular cleanse.

If you do not do this, you will feel yourself overloaded with these toxins. Your body will close down or become sick. As I explained, it needs a form to release the old toxins through. If it is so full of the old toxins and there is no place for this waste to dump itself into, so it can be released, it will tax your whole system and short-circuit you.

When I say cleanse, I do not recommend long fasts at this time. Your bodies are going through much at this time and need to be loved and nurtured. Your bodies have their own minds and need to be reassured that they are safe to go through this great healing (shift of consciousness).

All of your bodies are losing their old memories and need

to know that all is well. They need to know what is happening to them and that they will survive. They will feel themselves going through a death cycle and must be reassured that they are not physically dying. Talk to your bodies as you would a child. Let them know that you love them and honor them. Thank them for being a beautiful home for you in this lifetime.

Acknowledge your beautiful bodies. They need to be loved and honored just as you, the adult, does. As you acknowledge your beautiful bodies, they will feel very peaceful, loved and grateful that they now have the opportunity to be free.

Your bodies carry all of the memories of your mind and need much love and support. Love them to health and into their optimum potential.

To cleanse your bodies, I recommend that you fast for three days and then eat healthy, vital foods. Ask your bodies what they want to have put into them and what kind of fast that it desires. If you are not clear, muscle test. I suggest that you fast for three days a month, not more.

Cleanse your systems of old toxins and dis-eases. Be gentle with yourself now. You are going through a master cleanse in all levels of your life. You will feel tired and need more sleep. Allow yourself to sleep. Nurture yourself.

If you were to break a leg, you would need time to heal. The broken leg would be uncomfortable and take much of your energy to heal. After the cast was taken off, you would still tire easily and need to rest more often.

This is true with you now. You may have days when you have great energy and then the next day none. You will feel like you are on a roller coaster ride.

Go with the ride. Go with the flow. Your bodies are detoxifying and re-adjusting to the new vibration, if you need to rest or sleep, set time aside to do this. Be in the moment of now. Act from now.

Who you were in the past is gone. Live in the now. Do not judge yourself for what you are feeling or going through. Love yourself. Accept yourself. Honor yourself, and be kind and gentle with yourself. Honor yourself for your willingness to come to planet Earth and for being a part of this great awakening now. See your cup as full instead of empty.

No one has failed. You are on the Earth again with all of your fellow travelers to become totally awakened.

You agreed to come to the Earth with other great Souls with a wiped slate, clean of all memories of enlightenment or Ascension.

You went into the depth of the Shadow collectively. You agreed to begin totally unconscious and very quickly moved through the karmic wheels collectively to re-awaken all consciousness into light of enlightenment or Ascension.

Jeshua was the Being of My light who agreed to reincarnate to your planet and open the door for the Christ, that is you, to awaken. You are Me and the Christed ones. You are the Second Coming of Christ. The golden light on your planet is very bright. You are in the Golden Age, the Second Coming, and within your DNA systems are codes that are now being activated.

These codes are of My highest creation of you. Every time one of My light frequencies hits your planet, the light activates the coding in your DNA individually and collectively of the Second Coming and lifts you into a higher frequency of the Golden Ray of consciousness.

The Golden Ray is Ascension, enlightenment, and peace on Earth. This is love, happiness, joy, freedom, and abundance on all levels. The Second Coming is all Souls/Cells of My light and love coming together home on the Earth plane, co-creating Heaven on Earth. This is living in the true Garden of Eden, in My Golden Temple, in the Heart of all knowing, of Oneness, of Grace.

Now is the time to set your intention. Thought is energy. You, the light rays, lead the way for many others to find their way through the darkness and home to Me. Think as you, the collective rays of light, come together in Oneness, the light will be so bright that it will open the passageway for many Souls/Cells of you to move through the portals and back into their I Am selves.

Come together in Soul Groups and set your intention collectively. Bring your hearts, love, light, and songs back together. Create beautiful harmony to soothe and heal your whole world.

Thought is energy! Co-create a new paradigm. Hold this frequency for all to connect with and vibrate in. This new consciousness will penetrate the hearts and Cells of the other Cells/Souls of you.

They will feel hope. This hope will give them energy to move through the doorway or birth canal into the Golden Age of innocence.

As you come together in groups, set your intentions collectively. After your Soul Group's intention is set, put this collective intention into our Golden Hearts and expand them through all consciousness. Other Cells will feel it and will vibrate higher collectively.

This thought energy intention is your inner core vibration of love and light. As your intention is to expand it through the Golden Heart, Central Sun's energy, it will weave itself into the cellular structures of Cells/Souls of the same color-light-sound frequency.

As you collectively move into a higher vibration of light and sound, the sound will break loose old, frozen emotional patterns or grid systems. When these old patterns start breaking loose, it is most important to hold the intention to create a new grid system or paradigm collectively.

When an old emotional pattern breaks, a new frequency must be downloaded in its place. If this does not happen, the body's consciousness starts feeling a loss and will expand an energy looking for something to refill the vacant spot. Continue to expand your intention, and this collective intent of love and light will replace the old, frozen emotional fear. Hold the frequency until the collective subconscious accepts the love and light frequency as its new truth.

Be like loving parents of Me. Be firm in your intention. This is not tough love; it is strong love. This is creating a safety net for all to realize that they are safe in love and light. The collective

372

subconscious needs to remember that its true nature is this highest love and light of Me, the I Am, of All That Is.

As you continue to come together collectively with the highest intention for all mankind and this great Mother planet, the frequency of this intention will continue to break up and release old perceptions and bondages.

This has a cyclical frequency. Your intentions will continue to change and expand as your perceptions become higher consciousness of Me. Do not be confused by this. As your consciousness becomes higher, so do your perceptions, which create your intentions.

I love you, for you are Me. I honor you for your agreements to go to the Earth and to bring yourselves into enlightenment and Ascension, collectively. Now is the time you have been waiting for since the beginning of the great illusion of separation. You have never been separate. You have been taking a nap. Now you are waking up together as Me, I Am, through all creations of Me. You are remembering who you are. You are magnificent Beings of My light, love and creation. We are not separate; we have always been and will always be.

As you continue your journey home inside of your heart and Soul of Me, you will feel yourself in the sunrise of all consciousness understanding. The unconscious will become conscious for you. You will vibrate in total Knowingness, which is the Oneness of Me beyond the duality fear illusion.

I have waited for you and assisted you each step of the way, as you have assisted Me.

Open your hearts to the golden love of Me, that is you. Continue to surrender into love, for love is All That Is. Allow this love to permeate your whole Being. It is the power that will lift mountains and dissipate all old fear-based frequencies.

You are great masters of My I Am. Many of My great teachers and Masters have walked on your planet and prepared the foundation to open the door for your brother Jeshua. Now you are the Masters who are preparing and holding open the doorways of the Golden Light for others.

As many walked before you, you are now walking before others of you. You are the wayshowers of the Golden Age of Ascension.

Walk humbly, My children. Know who you are. Walk with great love, peace, and grace in your heart. Know that all is you, and the more you love yourself, the more you can love and accept others of you. Know that I am you and am always walking with you, and I am continuing to shower My great light upon you to show you your way home.

If you are in loneliness, go into your Golden Heart Temple. Go inside yourself, and you will know Me, for I am you. Once inside your Golden Temple, ask and you will receive. My gift to you now is for you to consciously know Me, as you, in your love and magnificence.

Manifest yourself as the co-creator of Me. Do this by going into your Golden Heart Temple and expand yourself through all creations of Me, that are you. This light will assist you to feel a higher vibration of My love for you. You will feel great peace and comfort. You will feel like a child wrapped in a golden blanket. Open your hearts and minds and talk to Me. Open the energy lines of communication with Me. I love you. You are My child, My children, My great, great, grand-children of love.

My greatest desire is for you to know My love for you. I want you to feel safe with Me so that you can intend yourself into co-creation of the highest good, for yourself and all mankind.

If you ask, you will receive. You may not feel My answer at first, but the more you communicate with Me, the more you will feel My frequency. As you do this, you will move into direct communication with Me. I will speak to you. I will shower my love on you. I will show you your way home. I am your guiding light. I Am. I Am. I Am.

I Am

I Am. I Am. I Am. I am the trees, the birds, the springtime of your life and consciousness.

I am death and rebirth. I am the wintertime of your life. I come at unexpected times, and I take the jewels from your life to assist you into a higher understanding or unveiling of you. I am All That Is; all that is constant death and re-birth, winding down and rebuilding, awakening.

Your whole lifetime now and all lifetimes have been a continuous cycle of death and rebirth. Death is a closure to one experience, and rebirth is the next step past the closure.

There is truly no death, only constant rebirth. As you come to an end of a chosen experience, you either learn the lesson or not, but you always come to a closure of the chosen agreement.

Sometimes, the closure means you must leave the body to go on the next adventure of your Soul's journey. Some Souls cycle very quickly. Others take more time to grow, understand, and complete before moving to the next required experience. All experiences that all Souls have agreed to go through are to understand, release, and to free themselves from karmic emotions, to move back into the core of My Beingness, of the I Am of All That Is!

I Am All That Is, and all that is not. I am every breath you take and every breath you do not take. I am every thread and vibration of existence. I am the vibration of every cell in your body. I am all creation. How you decide to use Me is up to you. You can use Me in all of My light power and existence, or you can use Me to feed and empower your pain, your Shadow.

I am your laughter and joy. I am your fear, sorrows, and regrets. I Am All That Is. Nothing exists without Me. I am the core of your existence. I am your Mother-Father God-Creation. I am the frequency, the mind and the heart of God awakened into you. I am the bloom of all knowing, as I am the total bloom of you.

I am the sun and the moon. I am all elements. I am the Earth and the stars. I am all cultures and all religions. I am new

375

beginnings and old endings. I am the wind. I am the ocean. I am the water, and I am the air that you breathe. Without Me, you cannot exist. I am all creation.

You see and experience All That Is through your perceptions of Me. Your perceptions of Me come from your direct experience of all collective emotions. You could not hold on to your old perceptions if you did not have others to align, agree, or mirror back to you your perceptions.

You are in a holographic consciousness. As I exist throughout all consciousness, you exist through all consciousness. You could not see yourself or know yourself, without Me, for you are Me. I am the life force in all existence. You could not know yourself if you did not have the Shadow aspect of My I Am, to mirror back to you, your reflection of light.

You could not know your Shadow without your light. You could not know your light without your Shadow. All of I Am needs polarization to balance all consciousness of Me. I Am.

The I Am frequency of your planet is now in the highest light-sound vibration that has ever been. This frequency is turned up beyond the original template of the Shadow-sound frequency.

This is what is happening on your planet now. The old template that held the groove of your existence on your planet is worn out. Your I Am consciousness has been stuck in the old sound-music template. You and I, the collective I Am, have turned the vibration up high enough to move the needle of the I Am beyond the template frequencies.

This agreed-upon happening is moving you beyond any time zone where you have believed or experienced yourself vibrating in separateness. My I Am frequency is moving you, all light and Shadow aspects of yourself, beyond time.

You are now coexisting and vibrating in all dimensions simultaneously. You are now vibrating with yourself in parallel realities, universes, and lifetimes. All I Am is coming together, and your light-sound I Am frequencies are breaking loose all old beliefs, fears, and perceptions.

376

If you could see My I Am in all consciousness, both light and Shadow and all beautiful color-sound frequencies in between, you would be able to experience yourself in all of your glory, for all is you. I Am the glue that holds you together. I Am the emptiness in your heart waiting to once again be filled up with love.

When you see all as Me, you see all of who you are. You are powerful beingness of My I Am. I ask you once again to vibrate in your highest I Am Knowingness. In this I Am comes total magnificence. You know all in total love and acceptance, for all is you.

I know you, for I Am you. I love you, for I Am you. I see you, for I Am you. I Am. I Am. I Am. I AM, the I AM of All That Is!

CREATOR'S RE-QUEST

Thank you for your participation in the great awakening consciousness of this great, beautiful planet Mother Earth. Thank you for your willingness and agreement to come to the Earth at this time to collectively move through the 2012 doorway to shift the collective beyond time and into the heart of my love, of Oneness, to become co-creators with me for the awakening of the highest consciousness throughout all Creation.

I know that some of the information that I brought forth in this book is somewhat difficult for you to comprehend, and yet, within you, the memories are waiting to be activated. This was the purpose of this healing manuscript. My greatest desire is for you to remember your divine essence, spark of life that is mine, that is you. You are magnificent Beings of light that are shining your light for one another to find your way back home together into the heart and Soul of me, of Creation.

I am now preparing to bring more information forth through this light, Michelle. Our next book together, "The Creator Answers - Questions for Humanity" needs your questions.

I ask that you assist me to bring the answers through to the questions that you need answered from me. I am honored to continue to assist you in your Soul's Awakening. I look forward to serving you as co-creators of a higher consciousness for all.

I ask that you write the questions that you would like answered and send them to my assistant, Michelle. I will then answer your questions through Michelle, and they will be put into a book so that they can be answered in a collection form for all to read.

Thank you for allowing me to serve you. I love you.

Mother, Sophia and Father, Creator

Please send your question for the Creator to:
www.creatorspeaks.com

— *Epilogue* —

MICHELLE'S STORY

Her Soul's Awakening – Into the Light of her Own Being – Into Oneness

This book is the culmination of 25 years of journeying into Spirit realms of this and other Worlds, Universes, and Creations. As a spiritual teacher, I have worked in Japan, Europe, India, Scandinavia, (Sweden for the last 21 years), and in the northwest American states of Oregon, California, Hawaii, and Sedona, AZ where I currently live. While living in northern California, I had a live call-in spiritual TV show called Soul's Awakening for over four years and was co-host of a call-in radio show called Soul's Purpose Salon. In all of these places, I have done many group channelings, experiential lectures, workshops, group healings, and private sessions. I feel very privileged, grateful, and blessed to be able to do what I do, to serve God on this level and to experience people healing so quickly. Many times in my workshops, I feel so full of love and at one with the participants that I can't help the tears that flow from my heart. These tears are tears of joy, of love, of hope, of God, of gratefulness.

I have lived many lifetimes within this lifetime and have so much life experience to share with others. I am grateful for all of my life's experiences. When I am working with others I know how they feel because I have been there. Because of this I have great love, caring, and compassion for others. When you read my story, you will have more of an understanding of the process that I went through to be able to have the gifts and ability to assist others through their "Dark Night of the Soul", into the light of their Being, and into their higher spiritual purpose as co-creators of their greatest desires, and destinies. I want to keep my story somewhat short and just tell the story of how this manuscript came about and how the path of my life experiences led to the Creator choosing to use me as a vehicle to bring His/Her message forth. In the fall of 2004 while living in Sedona, AZ, I decided to set the intention to sit down and complete the book that I had been working on for over ten years about my Shadow experiences. When I sat down to do this, I felt myself going into a trance-like state where Spirit and I become one. I could feel the Creator starting to speak through me in Knowingness, and I moved into automatic writing. The Creator wrote through me for about two hours. When I finished and read what was written, I was very, very surprised.

I had been a channel for a very high spiritual teacher by the name of White Lily for about ten years. She actually became my best friend and confidante. Jesus had also brought various messages through me as well as the Being of Ashtar who works very closely with Jesus. (Jesus and Ashtar work with Archangel Michael to assist in the healing and safety of Mother Earth.) Jesus has been with me from my earliest memories and has taught me my spiritual healing work with others through my own healing process. I call him my Main Man. He has always referred to himself as Jesus to me, probably because of me being such a young child when our relationship began. However, the Creator refers to him as Jeshua, so throughout the transcript, I will also refer to him by the Creator's given name for him.

Although I had been a conscious channel for other great light Beings for many years, I absolutely was not expecting this transmission to come through me.

The Creator had come to me at an earlier time in my life (which you will read about later in this introduction), but I can say that I was really stunned when He/She started writing through me.

After the first transmission came through me from the Creator, I sat there in awe. My energy felt so high that I could not get up for a while. I felt that in this first transmission with the Creator I had re-awakened to knowledge that I knew that I knew, but had not remembered. It took me quite a few sessions to be able to adjust to the high vibration of the transmissions that he was channeling through me. It became very clear to me that I was meant to deliver a larger message to humanity, a message that brings hope and helps us as a people to understand who we are, why we are here, where we have been, and where we are going.

As the Creator channeled through me for two to three hours each morning, I felt like the book that I had been writing seemed obsolete, and yet, I understood the importance of why I had gone through my "Dark Night of the Soul" experiences. The Creator's intention was to use me as a messenger of His/Her higher message. I understood what the Creator was saying because I had experienced it. I knew that all of my life's experiences were in preparation for this, to bring this healing manuscript through me, from the Creator, to assist in healing the masses.

I remember the exact moment that my Soul's journey seemed to take a detour and opened up for me to experience realities and dimensions that I could not even fathom or know to be possible. It was a hot afternoon in 1989. I was living in Hawaii and sitting in my healing room after a day of doing private sessions for others. I felt stuck. My clients were healing and having great results from the sessions that were coming through me, but I was beginning to feel bored. I still had love and compassion for my clients, but personally, I felt like I needed to be able to move into a higher consciousness spiritually. I remember talking to Jeshua, my Main Man, my spiritual teacher who has been with me throughout my own Soul's journey. I can't ever remember him not being with me. As well as being my spiritual teacher and guiding light, he has always been my best friend and confidante. I was telling him that I was bored and that I needed something more spiritually. At that time, I thought that I knew a lot spiritually, maybe more than many people. As I think back, I have to laugh at my ignorance, at my not knowing, at my Ego. Now I still feel like a child in the larger picture of Creation. Spiritual consciousness is infinite, and I am in constant awe of Creation, of what is now opening up and being revealed to us. It is such an incredible experience and honor for me to have the gift to be able to travel through so many dimensions and consciousnesses of Creation. I am continually humbled by the gift of being able to do this and also by how little we consciously know and understand.

As I was talking to Jeshua, he quietly listened to me complain. He had a smile on his face and a twinkle in his eye and nodded his head in understanding. I always feel so listened to and understood by him. Little did I know that this request would expand me into a new direction that would change my life forever. Shortly after my chat with Jeshua, a woman by the name of Suzanne Handal came to me for a session. She told me that it was her first lifetime on this planet. I remember thinking to myself, "Yeah, right, now I have heard everything!" Although I believed in life on other planets, it was not something that I had been interested in. Back then, there was not much known about past lives on other planets. When I gave her the session, I regressed her back to a lifetime on another planet; the planet was Venus.[1]

The Beings from Venus were a different vibration than we were. Their bodies were light, crystal, rainbow forms, and not physical matter like ours. They were ascended Beings living in their light bodies. As I looked at them I could see prisms of light sparkling through their crystalline structures. Their hearts were like portals of love that expanded beyond time. As I looked into their eyes, I experienced pools of consciousness, of all knowing, of God, of Creation. When I looked at them, I was experiencing them through the Knowingness.

[1] Interestingly, Suzanne's Soul's purpose is to bring the consciousness of Venus to the inhabitants of the planet Earth. She continues to assist people to heal by using the vibration, the life force and the consciousness of Mother Earth. Today, she has the ultimate "living food" retreat: "The Center for Healing with Nature", which is set in the beauty of tropical Hawaii. For more information, she can be contacted through her website at: www.vacationinnparadise.com or Email address:: healingwithmature@hawaii.rr.com.

The Beings from Venus were a different vibration than we were. Their bodies were light, crystal, rainbow forms, and not physical matter like ours. They were ascended Beings living in their light bodies. As I looked at them I could see prisms of light sparkling through their crystalline structures. Their hearts were like portals of love that expanded beyond time. As I looked into their eyes, I experienced pools of consciousness, of all knowing, of God, of Creation. When I looked at them, I was experiencing them through the Knowingness.

When these beautiful feminine Beings gave birth to their children it was through the heart chakra, not the root chakra like women on the Earth do. A light beam extended through and from the feminine heart, giving birth to a beautiful Crystal Child of light. The Crystal Child became everyone's child, creating a collective consciousness of love with one another.

When they ate, it wasn't with food like we eat on the Earth but with life force prana from the planet. The prana moved up through their feet and hands. This life force frequency then moved through their whole body and extended into all of Creation. As I watched them feed themselves I could see when they were completely fed. Their bodies were totally full of light that expanded into their etheric bodies. They looked like illuminated Light Beings. They only ate once a day. Each morning they would fill themselves back up with prana. After a woman gave birth to a child, she would place the child on the grid system of their planet, and the vibration would activate the child's Soul song. It was an incredible experience to witness that this woman who I was giving the session to was one of them. She was actually working together with them. She was on the Earth to bring the Venusian energy through her, to us earthlings, and also to implant the frequency into Mother Earth's grid system.

Two weeks later, a man came to me with lower back pain. He had been to every doctor imaginable, and they had tried everything to heal him, with no success. He was told he would have to learn to live with the pain. He saw me as a last resort. When I regressed him back to another lifetime, it was also on another planet. At the time of the regression, I did not know the name of the planet, and now I know that it was Maldek. Maldek was a planet very much like the Earth plane and it was dying from losing its natural resources. The oceans were polluted and all vegetation was dying. The planet was environmentally destroyed. Eventually cities were built indoors. Nothing was alive; all food was manufactured, synthetic. It was difficult for people to live without life force, and they became angry and out of balance.

Ultimately the planet exploded. (I don't want to talk much about Maldek because the Creator speaks about it in the book.) I was crying during the session. It was the first time that I had experienced the death of a beautiful planet, and I realized how important it is to heal our planet (Earth). The man that I was giving the session to had been a commander from another planet, and he had helped in the evacuation of Maldek. It was a very emotional time for everyone and for the body of Maldek. Space ships came from many other worlds and dimensions to assist in the evacuation. They lifted off all of the children and the Light Souls who were trying to save and heal Maldek. As the evacuation and lift off was happening, a light source of energy came from the ships as they were beaming all of the Souls on board. Those who were instrumental in the demise of Maldek had to stay behind, and they went down with the planet. This man experienced Maldek's explosion and was carrying in his cells, DNA, and spine, the trauma of the death of this beautiful planet and also the memory, the shock, and trauma of the lift-off, and of everyone who had died with the planet.

After the 11-11 portal opened in 1987, our collective vibration became higher and the memories of this lifetime were activated in the man's Cells. Because he had been carrying it for so long on a cellular level, the activation short-circuited his body, creating dis-ease. After two sessions, he was totally healed of his back pain. I got a letter from him later, and he was in Canada long-distance bicycling.

After the sessions of regressing these two clients back to lifetimes on other planets, Spirit started turning my energy up to higher dimensional frequencies. One afternoon I had two clients cancel, which very seldom happened. The first woman (Suzanne) who had come to see me, who was from Venus, had given me the book 'Aliens Among Us' by Ruth Montgomery. Although I have been dyslexic and don't read much, I decided to lie on the couch and look at the book. In the first chapter, Ruth is talking about a space commander named Ashtar. I remember thinking, "I'm a channel; I'm going to see if I can bring him through," and bring him through I did.

As soon as I asked to speak to him, I started shaking uncontrollably. I couldn't stop and I didn't know what was happening. When I finally did stop, I realized that a portal had opened with me in the center of it. Standing in front of me, in this portal, was Ashtar. He had physically manifested in my living room. Although the ceiling was there, I could not see it. All of a sudden, I was experiencing this beautiful Being of Light in his commander uniform, standing in my living room. He was so big and powerful that he expanded way up through my roof. I was terrified and called on Jeshua. He said, "You are safe. I am with you." And he proceeded to introduce me to Ashtar. Ashtar then spoke to me and told me of my purpose and mission, which is to assist the consciousness and planet to heal by healing individuals. As each person heals and moves into self-love, their whole family unit starts healing. As he talked to me, I felt myself move beyond time and into the Knowingness. I understood all that he was saying and more. I just knew.[2]

Ashtar showed me techniques to work with that would turn up my vibration. I immediately started using the techniques before I went to sleep that night. I woke up in the middle of the night, and my root chakra and heart had become one. It was wide open and I experienced love like I had never felt before. It was

---

[2] Ashtar works very closely with Archangel Michael and Jeshua in protecting us so that we can collectively harmonize the negative and shadow influences that we on Earth are here to balance out. Ashtar is in command of a particular area of the cosmos, which he and his command patrol. The planet Earth is in this area. He is often referred to as Commander Ashtar.

like having an orgasm from the heart. I awoke again that night, and my third eye was the eye of all consciousness and creation. I had an experience of no past, present, or future; all was now. I saw and felt this lifetime, my childhood, past lives, and all lifetimes as one field of Creation. They were all flowing by me as thought forms.

After that experience, clients started coming to me and would blurt out, "I saw a UFO" or "I had missing time." They would say that they hadn't remembered it until they came into the room. I then realized that my energy was high enough to activate these memories. And interestingly, during this time I started to take on an androgynous look. One day after a session while washing my hands in the bathroom, I looked into the mirror and I saw only light beaming back to me, from me. I could not see my facial features. I had moved totally out of form.

Christ, Ashtar, Archangel Michael, St. Germain, and their team of Masters were working with me very closely, continuing to show me how to raise my vibration so I could feel and see even more clearly the picture of what was going on with my clients. From this vibrational change, I could see inside of their bodies and was told that these new clients who had missing time and had seen UFOs had actually been abducted by Beings from other planets and dimensions. As I said, I had always believed there was life on other planets but had never been interested in it. Now I was moving into the experience of it. This was a very high and exciting time for me.

I was introduced to a team of spiritual Beings called the Etherians. They were very, very tall, large, Light Beings. They had etheric bodies, which illuminated crystal frequencies. Their presence emanated so much love that my clients and I would feel this great safety and Oneness with them and the Masters. I felt so blessed; these great spiritual Beings would stand around my healing table like a great surgical team. As I looked into my clients' bodies, I started seeing implants, discs, and codes that had been implanted in them during their abduction experiences.

The Etherians showed me how to remove the implants and

codes. I would put my hand over the device, and the Etherians would put their hands over mine, change the frequency of the implant, pull it through my hand and dematerialize it. This was 20 years ago. As our vibration as a species has become much higher, Beings who have more recently been implanted are receiving more of an energy implantation. The old way is too crude for our new higher vibrations. I then learned how to release implants by finding the karmic past life agreements with the Shadow Beings, and as I released the agreement from the person, the implants would start breaking up and dissolving.

At the same time of my new awakening, I had a woman call me who was sick and doctors could not find the cause of her problems. As I was speaking to her on the phone, I could see an implant in her heart. I told her what I was seeing and she said she knew it and that the implant was killing her. She explained to me that she had UFO sightings around her house and that the government and MUFON[3] were investigating it. She made an appointment with me for the following Monday so that we could remove it. Sunday night, I was standing in my kitchen washing my hair and six gray aliens came up behind me standing in unison. Although I was bent over, I could see them as though I was standing up looking at them. They threatened me, telling me not to remove the implant from her, that it was none of my business and that what she was going through was karmic. It was an "Aha" moment for me to realize that people who were going through this kind of experience had some kind of karmic agreement with the Shadow Beings. The aliens told me that if I removed the implant from her that they would harm my children! I felt no fear because I am so connected to Jeshua, Ashtar, Archangel Michael and my high spiritual team. Unbeknownst to me at the time, this would be the beginning of my journey and experience through the "Dark Night of the Soul." After they left, Jeshua told me that my children were safe, that he would put a blanket of light protection

[3] MUFON stands for the Mutual UFO Network (MUFON) and is the largest civilian UFO scientific research organization.

around them and around their house. I had just moved out of our home together and into my own home. I joke about how I left home instead of my children leaving. My children were in their twenties and I felt like I wanted to experience myself outside of being their Mother. I wanted to totally focus on my spiritual work and purpose. I had my children when I was very young, and we pretty much grew up together. We have always been very close and loving, but I felt like I needed some independence

My spiritual team supported me in that. In fact, they encouraged me, which I am very grateful for. I could not have gone through my "Dark Night of the Soul" had I been living with them. It would have opened the door for the Shadow frequencies to come into them. Sometimes I marvel at the larger picture of our agreements, and how we are so divinely guided if we allow ourselves to listen. I felt and knew that my children were safe.

When the woman came to me for her session, my spiritual team and I removed the implant, and instantly her health improved. She felt great, free, and alive. She called me a week later and said, "You won't guess what happened." She took pictures all of the time because of the UFO activity around her house. One of her pictures showed a blanket of light around her house. I had not told her that Jeshua and Ashtar had put a blanket of light around my children's home. I just smiled to myself.

When I removed the implant from the woman, the Shadow ones started attacking me. At first I was absolutely terrified, Jeshua said to me, "I can't give you the answers, but I can show you where to go to find them." He was constantly with me guiding me through my "Dark Night of the Soul." This darkness was not something that I could at first even comprehend. As I started my decline into the center of my own darkness, I was taken aboard alien ships, into government bases, other dimensions, and onto other planets. I was shown that people who are implanted are hooked up to computer systems where they are being controlled emotionally, mentally, and physically. I then started remembering and reliving my own abduction experiences that started when I was three. As I relived each experience, I started to understand the confusion and missing pieces of my life that I had not been able to figure out. Through reliving these experiences, I was able to see and begin to release what had been done to me. I also understood my constant health problems and why in my younger years, I was so often feeling pregnant when I knew in this dimension that I could not be.

Jeshua was always by my side, and he showed me how to unplug myself from these computer systems and to bring back to me, through Soul Retrieval, aspects of my Souls/Cells, which were being manipulated and controlled. Every time I was shown how to heal each problem, I took my power back and started becoming stronger. The Shadow ones would then change their tactics and come into me through another doorway. They were trying to terrify me, which they were doing. I could see many different species around me. They would materialize and then dematerialize, laughing at me and playing with my emotional and mental stability. As I learned and understood more, they would turn up their frequency, which would open the door to even darker experiences. I knew they were trying to break me, which brought me into an even stronger connection to my light team. The Shadow ones were constantly communicating with me saying, "Look – the light's not protecting you, come to our side and you will have everything you want: money, power, sex, men; just name it and you will have it. We will give it to you."

These continual tauntings assisted me to become stronger in the light. As they continued to turn up their fear tactics, Jeshua and Archangel Michael were always there showing me my old karmic contracts, where I needed to go to release the programming and how to block what was happening to me. My psyche was wide open, and I was living in many dimensions at once. I no longer felt fear; I felt strong and determined. I was a survivor. Although I felt strong, my physical body started weakening. Because of the interference, I could no longer work and had no income. Day and night I was processing my experience. I started losing everything that I thought I was.

My identity was quickly slipping away. In the beginning

of my "Dark Night of the Soul" I reached out to other healers, desperately needing some help. Twenty years ago, not many people had a clear understanding of the Dark Shadow and were very afraid of it. First my spiritual reputation was tarnished and ruined. I lost my reputation as a healer. The other healers, my peers, did not want anything to do with me. I had lost my credibility. I heard that they were saying, "Michelle Phillips has really gone off the deep end." I absolutely knew that I was not psychotic, but I had no way of convincing anyone else. I quit reaching out for help. My help had to come from within through my own process. I could no longer work. I was constantly processing the nightmare that I was living through. I could not pay my bills and the thought of losing my credit was devastating. After spending many nights agonizing over this, I awoke one morning feeling free. I really got and understood that I was not my credit. I then started losing my looks; they had always been very important to me. Through this experience, I aged ten years in one year. When I was able to start functioning again, I was embarrassed to see people because I had aged so much. Because everything was being taken from me and my health was deteriorating so quickly, I could no longer pay my rent or take care of my physical needs. I would soon move into my friend Diana's home, where I would sleep on a futon on her bedroom floor next to her bed. This was to be my new home for the next two years.

Before my move to my new home with Diana, the Creator came to me and said, "You can stop now, and you don't have to go through any more of the Shadow experience." I was shown two illuminated brilliant crystal light doors. I could not see beyond the doors, but I could feel their depth and purpose. As he spoke to me, I could feel his great love and compassion. "If you decide to stop now, you can go through the door to the right and you can have your life back. You will be able to do your spiritual work again, pick up the pieces and go on. Or you can go through the door to the left and go the whole way." I didn't know what the "whole way" was. I didn't even have a clue. I still could not really fully comprehend my journey or what I was going through or why. I was so beat up that I really wanted to stop, but as I looked back at my life, I remembered my conversation with Jeshua and remembered how bored I was before I started this process and how unfulfilled I was starting to feel. I knew that I couldn't go back. As I looked at the door to the left, I felt the Grace of God and an incredible peace. I felt like a nun or a priest re-dedicating myself to God/Spirit/my spiritual purpose. I felt safe and secure in knowing that even if I never had a personal relationship with a man again on the Earth plane, I would always serve my Soul's larger purpose in God's Grace.

As I moved through the door to the left, every cell of my body tingled with love and light. I felt like crystals were being turned on in my cells. The light became so bright that I was glowing; the glowing light was moving me beyond time and space. A whole consciousness opened up for me, which I didn't know that I knew. I was remembering so much, just in an instant, I knew then that I was God. I felt myself in the center of the heart of all Creation and I knew that within me, I was all of Creation. I was home. I was in the home that I used to cry for as a child. I felt a peace that I had not remembered in this lifetime. The Creator then spoke to me, not in words, but in Knowingness. Our hearts and minds were one. I knew I was safe, that this is who I really was, and that no matter what I went through on the Earth plane or in any other dimension, it really was an illusion, and this was the truth of my Being. I had known all was an illusion intellectually, but now I was truly experiencing it.

After my reunion with the Creator, I moved to Diana's house and continued my journey through my "Dark Night of the Soul". I went through this process heavily for two years, not knowing if I was going to live through it. My meeting with the Creator also gave me a clear understanding that I was going through this for a reason. I did not yet know the reason, but I knew this was my agreement and my assignment. My friend Diana gave up her life for two years to help save mine. We were processing day and night, moving in and out of dimensions and realities.

In 1987 Diana had been coming to my weekly channelings of White Lily. In one of the classes, White Lily gave Diana the 23rd Psalm and told her that in the days to come it would be very valuable to her. Shortly thereafter, Diana was diagnosed with stage IV ovarian cancer and was given a 20% chance to live. She had two young children and prayed to live just long enough to see them graduate from high school. Because Diana had been receiving and following guidance from White Lily before her cancer diagnosis, she absolutely trusted what she was being asked to do. White Lily and my spiritual team assisted Diana step-by-step out of her "Dark Night of the Soul" cancer experience. We also took Diana into and released many lifetimes of karmic agreements that were holding her back from being healthy and whole. From her hospital bed, she rented a new place to live and left the father of her children. She was taking her power back from all old sources of control. She also changed her diet and did many other healing modalities on her own. She wanted to live and that she did! She is now 22 years cancer-free. Diana knew that from the Source of Spirit, which worked through me, her life had been saved; she was coming full circle, and her agreement now was to assist me, to save my life. She gratefully did so.[4]

I understood through Knowingness that this incredible Spiritual School that I was going through was a Spiritual initiation. I am so grateful that I survived and being on this side of it, I am also grateful for the experience. I learned so much. I met and was taught by the highest Spiritual Master Teachers and by Creation itself. I was taught how to free myself and the collective from the Shadow. I now have no fear of Shadow Beings. They have no power on their own. They keep us in fear so they can siphon

[4] Diana lives on the Big Island of Hawaii and is a teacher and guide for the Crystal Children coming through on our planet now. She also continues to assist many through their cancer (dis-ease) Soul's Awakening. In 1990 she was named Angel Lady of Hawaii and continues to assist others who wish to work with their angelic guides. The Angelic Soul Readings that she offers will provide direction for healing and a deeper understanding of any challenge that one may be facing. She can be contacted by Email at: dianaurbas@yahoo.com.

our light to keep themselves alive. Because we are each other, when we unthread ourselves from the collective Shadow, their energy hold on us starts breaking up and dissipating.

Every morning during my whole process, Jeshua would come to me and ask me to walk with him. We always traveled to other dimensions, planets, star systems, galaxies, and even Universes. He also took me to many places on the Earth plane, which are in alignment and agreement with the Shadow. He, Archangel Michael, Melchizedek, Metatron, and St. Germain always went before me and would show me how to unplug myself and what was needed to retrieve aspects of my Soul.

Then one morning, when we were on our journey together, he said it was time for me to go to these Beings as my own Master and unplug and retrieve myself from wherever I was being controlled. He said that he and Archangel Michael would be with me, but I was the one that had to do the work. At first I was very frightened that I would not be able to do it, but their love and intention for me was so strong that I was able to release the fear. Once the fear was gone, I could feel that they were really at one with me.

Whenever we went to these places, the Beings there would automatically give to Jeshua whatever he had come for; they knew he was coming, and there is an actual protocol that must be followed when the Shadow Beings are dealing with the high Ascended Masters of Light, however, they were not so obliging to me. They would try to give me aspects of other people's Souls and try to trick me into believing that I was unplugged and free. The more experienced I became, I could instantly feel what was my energy and what was not. I was then able to easily and effortlessly bring myself back to me.

Later during my initiation process, Jeshua and Mary Magdalene would come to me every morning so I would consciously know that I was always safe and connected with them, that I was one with them. I could feel their great union of love for one another, their honor, respect, and Oneness. They were one Twin Flame Soul, which had split as Male and

Female. Their bodies were pure crystal illuminated Golden shimmering light.

Their light penetrated me, wrapped itself around me, as I also became the heart of their love. Jeshua told me that Mary Magdalene was his partner, his Beloved, and that I was an aspect of their daughter Sarah. Then they gave me her baptismal name and said that I had gone through many levels of initiations of Creation and consciousness, to awaken the Christ within me, to become one with them; I had to be fearless and to be able to travel through all dimensions at once. I had been in a Master training program and not only had I survived, but I was now able to move into a higher expansion of myself through all dimensions.

What I discovered was that not only is Jeshua my Main Man, he is truly the Main Man for the Earth's Ascension and Awakening. Many great Masters have walked the Earth before and after his time, and he is one with all of them. But there has never been a Master who has created the movement that Jeshua has. His presence on our planet is stronger today than it has ever been. That is because we, as a collective, are awakening into the Second Coming of Christ. This is his return, through us. As we become one with the Christ energy, we align ourselves with the great rays of consciousness from all of the Masters and we ascend together with Mother Earth into freedom.

Jeshua is the Christ vibration, which is the collective Golden Creator Light that threads all Masters of Light together. He is not separate from other Masters; they are one creative force of Love and Light. They all have different jobs that hold different color-sound vibrations for the collective consciousness, and yet, together they hold the collective color-sound vibration for our Earth's Soul's Awakening and Ascension.

Jeshua's agreement or assignment is to bring the Earth into Ascension and enlightenment. There are other Masters on other planets with similar assignments.

When Jeshua walks into other dimensions, bases, etc., all Shadow Beings stop whatever they are doing. His love and light mirrors their magnificence and for a short time they are stunned as they feel their own hearts. His light is so bright that the Shadow Beings almost seem embarrassed by what they are doing. Jeshua and his team are so greatly respected, not always liked, but certainly respected.

As I explained, Jeshua and Magdalene had explained to me that one of the reasons I had been hit so hard by the Shadow or Dark Ones was because I was the bloodline of their daughter Sarah. As they were talking to me I felt great strength and safety with them. I could truly experience them as my parents.

One morning when I was walking with Jeshua, he gave me rights of passage to other dimensions and planetary systems. When we traveled there together, he always introduced me to those in charge as his daughter. He gave me rights of passage to other dimensions, planets, and computer Internet systems. He also took me to bases on the Earth plane and showed me where we were individually and collectively plugged in. When I was traveling with Jeshua and my high spiritual team to these places, the light was so bright that the human aspect of me was not personally detected being there. As I said, he always introduced me to those in charge of these systems as his daughter and said that I had been given rights of passage to the systems and they must not interfere with my passage. This is supposed to mean that they can no longer interfere with me. However, the Shadow does not come from integrity and doesn't always honor their agreements, which was an important lesson for me to learn. From their trickery and from them not honoring their agreements with me, I learned many of their tactics and intentions and how to maneuver through them.

From all of my experiences I also realized that my energy was high enough to be able to go into many different arenas, to remote view the problem, and disconnect others from wherever they were plugged in. I could then retrieve and return their trapped Soul/Cell aspects back to them. Jeshua taught me through my own "Dark Night of the Soul" experience how to free myself karmically through all the different layers and levels of my bodies. From my own experience, I have learned with Jeshua, Archangel Michael, St. Germain, and my spiritual team how to assist others into freedom. As I have moved into a higher vibration within myself, it has become very easy for me to retrieve Soul aspects for others from whatever the situation may be. Many times the Shadow Brothers and Sisters will acknowledge me and say, "just take what you want and leave." They may even be expecting me and have whatever my need is ready for me to retrieve.

Through my travels, I saw that our great Earthly Internet system has been downloaded to us and is actually a duplication of an inner-net system, which has existed for eons of time through other dimensions. We as a planetary system were already a part of this great sophisticated system. As we moved through linear time into higher frequencies, a coding in our collective DNA was activated and the system was consciously downloaded to us on Earth.

As I continued to grow and expand my consciousness through healing processes with my team, I also started writing a book about my "Dark Night of the Soul" experience and how I was able to come out of it. Every time I would work on it, the Shadow Ones would do everything possible to block the process. It was very difficult, and yet I believed that I had gone through the process for a reason and that others needed to understand that there is a "light at the end of the tunnel."

When I first started writing my own book of my Shadow experience, I was so physically beat up that I had very little life force left in me. One day before working on the book, I was lying on my massage table and my friends Diana and Jenna were giving me a healing. All of a sudden, I felt myself starting to leave my body and I knew that I was physically dying. I was talking to Diana and Jenna through the whole process so that they would have an understanding of what it was like to die. I also told them that I didn't know if I was coming back and if I didn't come back, to please complete the book. Diana knew the experience of the book firsthand because she had assisted me through it.

When I moved out of the body it was through my crown, the top of my head. I just slipped out and into the arms of Jeshua. My whole spiritual team was there, and I felt so light and happy.

I was light and free. We were all laughing together. Once again, I was home. As I looked down at my body, I could see the Masters working on it to bring life force back into it. I was standing with them in Spirit, and at the same time, they were with my body, healing it. I could see Diana and Jenna. I was so happy and was trying to communicate with them, but they were so in their emotions that I could not penetrate them. Jenna was sobbing uncontrollably, and Diana was so angry because I had left them.

As Jeshua and the healing team continued to open my body up energetically, I slipped back in it. At first I felt like my body didn't fit. My body's vibration was too dense. My light vibration was so high, I was free with Spirit; I was Spirit. I remember having to turn my light down like a dimmer switch to be able to fit back into my body. This was my first near death experience. For three days I still did not know if I was going to live. After three days my team asked me what I wanted to do and I said, "I want to live. I want to stay on the Earth plane. I have gone through this for a reason, and I want to know the whole story. I want to be able to assist others from my own experience."

They agreed and said that I would have to have Jenna, Diana, and my friend Ann work on my body every day to open it back up, which they gratefully agreed to do.

I worked on that book for over ten years. It seemed like it constantly consumed me. I was told that when it was time for me to finally finish the book, I would just channel it. In 2004 when I set the intention to totally complete the book, I asked for the assistance that I had been promised. At that time, I didn't understand that it was going to be a totally different manuscript channeled through me, from Creation itself.

As I continued to move out of my own Shadow experience, the Shadow work became one of my specialties. I started doing five-day workshops assisting others out of their "Dark Night of the Soul" Shadow experience and into freedom.

Before my initiation process, I had absolutely no conscious experience, memory, or understanding of the Shadow or Dark

Ones. As a spiritual teacher, I had always taught from my mind that hell is within us, and I now know from experience that all is within us, that we are truly all of Creation.

I now have the experience of the Light and Shadow and am able to bring others out of the swinging pendulum and into the center or core of their Beingness. I understand through experience, the Creator's message. As I evolved, so did my healing work with others. The Creator told me that my own light and my ability to take others into their light would be much higher and lighter than it ever was dark. That is happening now. Every time I go into a dark experience and come out of it, my light becomes even stronger.

Moving through linear time had catapulted me into higher frequencies of my own light and creativity with my great Master Team. In my workshops with others, I would be the Earthly guide/ Master working with my high, spiritual, Master Team. Through past life regression, we would assist to find people's karmic agreements and release the emotions connected to the karma so that they could break the contract and release them. Through Soul retrieval, we would bring fragmented aspects of them back into their bodies. I would then remote view and find out where they were plugged in and release the programming, which would close the door to the experience and agreement. I was also shown and experienced many stargates on the Earth plane. I then started doing workshops with others taking them etherically into the stargates. This high energy would go into people's DNA, release old blocked memories and emotions, and move them out of karmic time and into the core of Creation.

The first time I was taken into a stargate, all I could say was, "Oh my God, oh my God!" I could feel myself beyond time, in all dimensions of light-color and I was expanded into and became all the stars, the Universe. I was definitely in another level of Creation, and it was magnificent.

(I will write more in detail about my "Dark Night of the Soul" spiritual journey and how I came out of it in another book.) This story is leading up to why He/She/Creator would choose me to channel the larger understanding or picture of our Earthly Creation.

My beginning teachings in workshops before my "Dark Night of the Soul" were mostly inner child and past life. After my "Dark Night of the Soul" healing experience, I started putting together workshops to assist others, the collective through many of the same healing processes that I had been taken through. Because I had experienced so much, I had so many gifts available to assist others with. I started doing workshops with Jeshua where we would take people into Cosmic Christ Initiations. I did workshops on balancing our male and female (our Light and Shadow), angelic realm, Twin Flame workshops, Ascension, the bridge to Oneness, awakening to love, and many others. We, Spirit and I, would take people into the karmic Akashic records, release and unplug them, and assist them to re-write their script or new story for the new lifetime that we are coming into now, on the Earth, without physically leaving our bodies. As I continue to expand my consciousness, I continue to bring through many teachings and spiritual techniques and awakenings that I share with many others in my experiential lectures, workshops and private sessions. My life has continued to take me into many incredible healing directions, but right now I want to share my experience of why I feel the Creator chose to channel this healing manuscript through me. Because of this, I am going forward in time.

Years later in March 2004, I was guided to India where I went through another near-death experience that changed my life forever. As I said, I was told by Jeshua and the Creator that my life would be so much more of a greater light than the Shadow had ever been dark, and now it was about to happen.

I had a tumor on my left ovary break. I had known it was there before I went to India but had refused to have surgery. I told Spirit, "I'm a healer. Heal this. Help me heal this or take me home back to Spirit." I had already gone through a great near-death experience and had no fear of death. Because of my Shadow experiences throughout my life, my health has suffered. I have had many health problems and surgeries, and I felt like it was time for me to take my power back and get healthy. I was done with surgery. I work in Spirit all the time, so home, Spirit, is a very easy place for me to be. Much to my surprise, when I was in India, the tumor broke. I felt a sharp pain and the poison instantly flooded my system. I could feel the poison move up my spine. Because I had my appendix burst a few years prior to this experience, I knew instantly what was happening to me. When it burst, my friend Judith and I were getting ready to take a bus ride to Chennai, India, from Southern India. We made it to the bus for the 12-hour bus ride. I could feel myself becoming more and more sick. I was moving into other dimensions and felt like I was in a fog. I was watching the activity on the bus. Everything was surreal, like I was watching a picture but wasn't part of it.

I wasn't afraid. I actually felt great humor and was chuckling to myself, I thought, in all that I have gone through in my life: my childhood, my great connection to the light, my Shadow experience, and here I was in India, dying on a bus! I actually was surprised and didn't quite understand why I had chosen to exit the Earth in this manner. Judith and I were talking and she was concerned about what to do with my dead body. Because of my joy, laughter, and light, she really didn't understand the depth of what was happening.

All night I was in and out of dimensions and was being shown so much by Spirit. At first, I was being shown our divine Matrix pattern and how we, the Souls on our planet, are what makes up this pattern. Our Souls are actually the live frequency of the Matrix. My spiritual team then started showing me a reversed labyrinth matrix. I had done much work with clients, with people, using the labyrinth as our Souls' pattern. Now, I was being shown the reversal of our Souls' light pattern. The difference between the two labyrinths is the light one is our Souls' journey home, and the Shadow one is in reverse and was created by the collective Shadow. It is designed to block and reverse our Souls' energy and agreement on the Earth. It runs through many dimensions and threads etherically into the Akashic records and reverses people's energy flow to fear. It hooks people up karmically and controls the collective emotions.

When one is stuck in the reversed labyrinth, it is like going forward in reverse. As I was taken into this system, I was once again shown many computer systems and how each system had a special purpose. I was also shown how the systems work and how to disconnect from them. I was shown much that night. By the time we got to Chennai, India, I was so sick that I could hardly function. I barely remember getting off the bus and into a taxi. Immediately, I passed out. Our next destination was about an hour away. It was a little beach town called Mamallapuram.

When we arrived, Judith helped me out of the taxi and into the room, into my mosquito net, and I was once again gone. Although I was gone, meaning that I was not awake, I was very aware of leaving this dimension and of what was happening. I could feel myself exiting my body – dying. I was up above my body looking down, and my body looked grey, ashen, and old – dead. There was no movement or life force. As I continued to move upward, my spiritual team was waiting for me. As we moved upward, it was dark and I could feel hopelessness and fear. I wasn't even in my body, and I felt like my heart was breaking. I couldn't stand the pain. I had never experienced anything like it.

I didn't feel afraid. My Soul felt tired, worn-out. I then realized I was in the reversed labyrinth that had been shown to me throughout the night. I said, "What happened to the tunnel of light?" Their reply was, "You've experienced that. We want you to know what people feel like who have lost or have forgotten their spiritual connection or consciousness." I was feeling the pain of the collective fear consciousness of the people on Earth as well as Mother Earth's pain.

I felt so much grief and sorrow that I could barely stand it. I felt hopeless and hopelessness. I could see and feel our world and the tremendous collective fear. I could see the reversed labyrinth running through the vibration reversing people to fear. I had never felt this before. I had always had such a strong spiritual connection with Jeshua and my light team regardless of what I

401

have gone through in life. Until now, I could always see the "light at the end of the tunnel." I always had hope. Even in my darkest hour, I still had the light.

Then my whole life went before me and instead of the light that I had experienced before in my first near death, I went through all of the painful emotions of my own life. I experienced that I had never really known what love was. I had relationships, but they were karmic completions. I had what I thought was love but had never experienced the purity and safety of love. I felt heartbroken. All I had ever wanted in life was love. As a child that's what I used to cry for. My whole life had been a quest for love, and now I felt like a failure, like a fraud.

As I looked back on my life I saw that the times that I had love I didn't even know it because I thought a man was supposed to give it to me. Those times of love were when my children were young. They were love. They were so magical, pure, and innocent. I had glimpses of it when they were born, especially when my first daughter was born, when I was 16. It was the first time that I had ever really felt love. I could not believe that this love that I felt that I was holding was actually a part of me. I held her for months. I was not doing housework or much of anything else during the day. I didn't want to ever let go of this love, but because I was still in my own desperate neediness for love, I could not internalize the depth of it when it was given to me, when it was right in front of me. I was heartbroken and felt so guilty. The experience hurt too much and felt unbearable to see. I told my spiritual team that I could not handle any more.

I was now feeling exhausted, ready to go home into the light. I felt really done – no more darkness or Shadow for me. I had lived through it on the Earth plane and in many other dimensions, and now I had to experience it on another level. I felt done, done, done and actually angry. I wanted to go home, back to the light.

After going through the feelings and the understanding of this fear, darkness, through my own death, I was then told by Spirit that they wanted me to go back into my body. I remember saying, "I'm not going back. I am done! I am done!" They said that I was very much needed on the Earth plane because of my experience with the Shadow and of my knowing how to bring people out of it. They wanted to show me how to bring people very quickly out of the reversed labyrinth. They said that because I no longer personally felt fear of the Shadow, it would be easy for me. They would work with me and together we could unplug the masses.

I still had great resistance of coming back into my body and then they started negotiating with me. They told me my darkness would be over, that I would experience great love on all levels and I would move into the Mastery of Light. My new work would be much easier. My health would improve, and I would see the world through the innocence of the child, and that I would bring a partner to me that would honor my love and innocence. I must have agreed because the next thing I remember, I was back in my body.

When I awoke I was a baby, and I felt the warmth and love from a Mother and Father that I could not have imagined. My Mother and Father were the Creator, and I felt loved, safe, secure, and wanted. I felt like I was floating in the love. I remember thinking, "This is what a baby feels like who is born into total love." I felt magical, pure, and innocent. I felt a joy inside that felt like I was the stars dancing and twinkling.

At that time my friend Judith came in to check on me. She had not really realized how sick I had been. We have known each other for years, and she had witnessed me go through so much with the Shadow and survive. Even though she had speculated on what to do with my body, she thought I was just going through another one of the processes. As I looked at her I was looking through the eyes of a magical child. She stuck her hand into the mosquito net and when she touched me, she said, "Oh my God, you are so hot. I'm afraid you are going to die. I need to get you to a hospital." It was difficult for me to speak. I had to shift myself from the baby to the adult. My reply was, "I'm not going to die. I've already done that; just get me something to bring the fever down."

I kept moving between the baby and the adult. This went on for about a week. I was still very sick and floating into other dimensions, only now they were all light. Beings of light would come to me and take me into light dimensions. They were showing me crystal cities of light and great crystal computer systems connected to all dimensions. I was taken into crystal temples and great healing rooms and into dimensions of rainbow prisms of color and beautiful music. I was home. I knew these places. I met aspects of myself that were great healers and teachers that are holding the vibration for me on this planet. They were showing me so much. I was floating through beautiful, colorful flower formations of beautiful tones and musical sounds. I saw all of my ancestors and loved ones in Spirit in their highest form.

I was then told by Jeshua to write down my new birth date and time of birth. When I got back to America, he wanted me to have my astrological chart done. He said I was now in a new lifetime. When I had my chart done, the man was shocked. He said everything in the chart was in direct alignment with Jeshua or Christ, even the numerology of my baptismal name. I smiled, not surprised at all.

After leaving India a couple of weeks later, I went back to Sweden where I was supposed to do workshops. I was still sick, and I started feeling out of balance, hopeless and depressed; I felt totally disconnected from Spirit, totally opposite from what I was told my new path would be. I felt, how can I help others when I can't feel Spirit and I don't believe in anything anymore? When I went to bed that night, I asked Spirit to show me in my dream state what the problem was. I had never felt this confused and disconnected from Spirit.

I was shown that I was hooked up in the reversed labyrinth. When I woke up the next morning, I asked my team to take me in there and to show me how to disconnect myself. I was again learning from my own experience.

After I disconnected myself, I felt strong, balanced, happy, confident, hopeful, and free. I was amazed at how different I instantly felt and was also grateful for the experience to consciously know what others feel when they are stuck in this reversed pattern.

Again, Jeshua and the Creator told me that my life would be an even greater light than the Shadow had ever been dark.

After being back from India for about a week, I was lying on the bed in the morning and a bright crystal light started filling up the room. The crystal light was beaming into every Cell and consciousness of my Being. As I closed my eyes, the light was still brilliant, and when I opened them again, Jeshua was standing there. I knew I was in a big experience. I was vibrating in the Enlightenment, Ascension energy, in my light body. I could not see or feel my physical body; all I could see was light and colors running through my Etheric or energy body. I could see my collective DNA system. It was brilliantly light with a crystal, illuminating, light, blue color running through it. The light continued to turn my vibration up, moving my whole body beyond any form and into the pure love energy of Jeshua. I was not separate from him; I was one with him. I was in the warmth of his love for over an hour. As I lay there, flashes of light continued to fill me with the essence of the Christ Ray. My mind was totally silent. I was at total peace. I drifted further into the light and into a very peaceful sleep.

When I awoke, my mind was still very silent, and as I looked around the room, everything was so bright and beautiful. I had become more alive and so had everything around me. I was seeing from a different vibration, from a different lens. I was like a 12-volt battery, which had been operating from only six volts plugged in, and now I was plugged into all 12 volts. I was the plants, the wall, the lights, ceiling, floor, sky, trees, and flowers. As I turned my head and looked out the window, I saw that it was snowing. I felt mesmerized by the snowflakes. Each snowflake was totally individual; not one of them was the same, but when they came together they created a beautiful blanket of white light. This light blanket lightens up the darkness and connects to the light and joy in people. From Knowingness I could feel that we, as Souls, are the Rays of Light from Spirit who are coming together to create a blanket of Light on the Earth. We are coming together as one Light to assist the planet into Ascension.

I felt like I had become total consciousness. Jeshua was not standing in front of me but was continuing to communicate with me. He said that I would be assisting to enlighten people in my workshops; that was the next step of my journey and I was elated!

In my Masters workshops, I was shown how to work with people's DNA. We, meaning my spiritual team and myself, would take people to the enlightenment board where a council of 12 would assist to activate the coding in our DNA of Enlightment. We were then taken through a doorway and into the Creator energy where a new chakra system replaced the earthly karmic one. From there we were taken into brilliant light dimensions with huge computer systems, the ones I had been shown after my near death experience. The systems were all crystal. The Creator Beings would come and unplug the old karmic programs from our DNA and rethread us with our enlightened crystal DNA. We were taken into many dimensions of light with huge crystal rooms and healing centers and into the 13th dimension where Jeshua and Magdalene have beautiful crystal temples. The 13th dimension is a huge crystal city that is generated by the central sun's energy. Although this city is very large, it is easy to move from one place to another, through thought.

I was then shown how to activate people's pineal glands, their DNA connection to Source, which gave them the direct connection and communication with Creation, the home of the Soul. I was shown how to use the Creator pure Source Energy to heal people. In my first five-day workshop working with this new energy, two women had cancer. One had a tumor behind her eye, and during the healing she felt it release. She is now cancer-free. The other woman with cancer had all of her tumors reduce to half their size. Her doctors were amazed. I was thrilled as I watched people start awakening into enlightenment.

My work is continuing to expand. I am now taking people into the DNA of their parents and ancestors and releasing patterns.

I have also been shown how to work with the electromagnetic fields of the brain, to change the frequencies to move people out of compartmentalization and also how to release sub-personalities.

Many other techniques have come through me to assist people to release frozen emotions and to very quickly move into themselves, as Masters. The Masters are working directly with me so that we can assist the individual to heal, which starts healing the masses to move us through the 2012 portal. I am also assisting others to heal by using color-sound, which the Creator talks about extensively in the book. I asked Jeshua again why I had agreed to go through such dark experiences, and he said that it is because I am aspect of his daughter Sarah. I was of his bloodline, and that is why the Dark Ones tried relentlessly to stop me from getting to the place of becoming a self-realized Master. They knew if I could make it to this place within myself, I could assist many others from my own experience to break out of and release old, worn-out, karmic agreements with them. I would collectively assist to unthread and close the door to the Shadow, individually and collectively. Together, as a Master with my spiritual team, we would assist many into enlightenment and Ascension, which I am doing now.

In my workshops I continue to go into the reversed labyrinth matrix and other programmings to free others, only now it's easy and effortless. I have a whole Master team in Spirit assisting me. I had to go through and learn this work to free myself, but now in the workshops or sessions that I am doing with others, my spiritual team are the ones who do the unplugging, and together we do Soul retrieval.

I love my new work, my new life. It continues to expand and awaken other Souls into the Masters within themselves, into enlightenment and Ascension. I now have an understanding of my journey, why I went through the "Dark Night of the Soul". I have a great understanding and balance of the Creator's message and feel totally honored to have been chosen to bring it forth to Humanity!

ABOUT THE AUTHOR

Michelle Phillips is an internationally renowned intuitive, healer, speaker, teacher and workshop facilitator. She has appeared on various radio and TV shows worldwide. For over 5 years she was the host of the very popular live call-in spiritual television show, "Soul's Awakening". She was the co-host of the radio show "Soul's Purpose Salon" and while living in Northern California, she started the monthly "Spiritual Connection Breakfast".

Michelle was born conscious of her gifts and always had a direct connection to the Source. She began her conscious spiritual work in the early 70's after healing her son from a severe kidney ailment. Since that Spiritual Awakening, she has dedicated her life to her spiritual purpose and mission, assisting others in their Soul's Awakening, self-love and purpose; co-creating Heaven on Earth in all life forms.

She refers to Christ as "Her Main Man". He has been with her, assisting and teaching her from a young age and has taught Michelle her spiritual work through her own healing experiences.

In the early 80's she became a conscious channel for a high Spiritual Being named "White Lilly". Michelle and White Lilly worked together for over 10 years teaching classes and workshops in the US, Europe and Japan. White Lilly's energies eventually integrated with Michelle so that she could reach a larger audience. Michelle has been referred to as an Inter-Galactic Shaman because of her knowledge and ability to travel through many dimensions: Light-Dark, Shadow, Above and Below. She is known as the Healer's Healer. Many people come to Michelle as a last resort, when everything else has failed, and from her work they experience life-changing transformations.

Her work includes:

- Workshops
- Soul-Readings ~ Past Life Regression ~ Soul Retrieval ~ Higher Self-Integration
- Inner Child Therapy ~ Childhood Trauma
- Relationship Issues ~ Twin-Flame Healing of Imbalance
- Emotional Healings ~ Addiction ~ Health Issues ~ Weight Loss
- Pineal Gland Activation ~ Re-connection to Creator
- Cellular Toning ~ Sound & Color Emotional Healing
- DNA Activation ~ Release ~ Re-patterning*
- Healing Shadow/Dark Night Experiences
- Sub-Personality ~ Entity Release
- Michelle is the developer and facilitator of the Christ Ray healing technique that she has taught worldwide.

Included in all of Michelle's private healing sessions and workshops is the re-connection to your higher self, Mother-Father-Creator and your inner children.

---

* The DNA re-patterning came to Michelle after she was diagnosed with uterine cancer. She started looking at her family's genetic history and saw that her father seemed to carry many of the same health issues that she had gone through. She decided to travel energetically through her father's DNA, which had a profound healing effect. She then traveled through her mother's DNA and then Mother/Father Creator's DNA. When she went in for surgery, not a trace of cancer was found.

TESTIMONIALS

(Go to www.CreatorSpeaks.com for more)

Michelle is able to see and release things that no other healer has ever been able to find. She truly changed my life! She gave me freedom, self-love, happiness, and joy. I am forever grateful. "Thank you, Michelle."

J.C.

When people ask me who Michelle Phillips is, I tell them she is "the woman who gave me my life back".

Annika K., Stockholm, Sweden

Michelle Phillips gets to the core of the problem or issue! Having had several sessions with her, I came out of each session feeling better about my life, my purpose, and myself.

Savannah M.S.R., California

"In 1988 I was diagnosed with stage Iv ovarian cancer and given a 20% chance to live. After working with Michelle and her spiritual team, I am now 22 years cancer free, living a healthy, joyous, and abundant life. "Thank you for saving my life, Michelle".

Diana U., Big Island, Hawaii

My participation in several workshops led by Michelle has been a deeply transformative experience. I don't understand everything that Michelle is doing with the participants, but she has a deep spiritual connection and is able to channel age-old wisdom that gives everyone a possibility to access very deep levels of his or her Soul.

The healing of physical, psychological, and spiritual wounds that regularly happen in her workshops is truly amazing. I strongly recommend Michelle's work to all persons who are committed to inner exploration and healing.

*Mats, Associate Professor
in Peace and Conflict Research*

I am sure that no one can get any deeper help or healing than from a Master who has such powerful guidance as Michelle. Jesus and her high spiritual team have such complete wisdom and love that they give back and awaken in us via Michelle. The healings and release sessions that I have received from Michelle are the most powerful, glorious, and deepest that I have ever experienced. To get rid of your Karmic patterns, rewire your DNA and become reborn—THAT'S BIG!

U-B Evelo, *Sweden*

I've always carried a vision of home inside of me
Of light, love, freedom safety, truth and joy
Of God
Because of this vision, I chose to stay alive all of the times when I could have died
Because I somehow knew I was destined to be and share it with the world
One lucky day an Angel descended from Heaven
She healed my wounds
She showed me the truth of who I am
She taught me how to go home within
She fulfilled by prophecy
I am forever grateful to you, Michelle Phillips

L. J., *Sweden*

I met with you in May 2004 on your visit to Gothenburg, and I want to send you a tremendously big THANK YOU for contributing so much to the enfoldment of my true self. Listening to the past-life session tape has enabled me to leave so many things behind me. I feel very excited and content with being in a meditative state. There is nothing more I need. This is the experience of it. With great love and appreciation for your work,

Camilla, *Gothenburg*

Thank you so much Michelle! This is the very best I've ever done for myself in my soon 60-year-old life. I hope many will take the opportunity to do your workshops.

With love from Suzanne

MASTERS WORKSHOP

The 2–5 Day "Masters Workshop" includes many healing modalities and is individually created to fit the needs of the group.

- Emotional Color-Sound Healing
- Pineal Gland Activation
- DNA - Activation ~ Release ~ Re-patterning
- Shadow/Light ~ Healing Integration
- Twin Flame Healing ~ Rebalance
- New Chakra System Download
- Sub-Personality Release
- Many Creator Enlightenment Matrix Transmissions
- Many more Master Activations and Re-patternings

In the Masters Workshop, you will travel through the DNA of your biological Mother – Father – Ancestors – Self and through the male/female God - Creator Self! From this, you will be able to find and release genetic patterns of sickness, dis-ease, fear, emotional conflicts, and imbalance. As you travel through your Ancestor's DNA, you will release emotional collective patterns of fear, imbalance between male and female, prejudice, hatred, war, and many more genetic patterns that affect your subtle energy bodies, that in turn, short-circuit your physical bodies. Through Soul retrieval, you will retrieve and activate your light that is still vibrating karmically in the genetic pattern. This frees all of your bodies to vibrate in love, health, and wholeness.

Through experiencing, disempowering, and integration with your Shadow, your Shadow will actually become an ally, and your light and Shadow can dance together in joy and freedom.

Color and sound will be used to release frozen emotions that hold you back from love and your greatest desires. You will have your pineal gland activated to re-align you with Source energy to become the Co-Creator of your life. Be prepared to be taken through many other healings and awakenings.

By the end of this workshop, you will experience, feel, and know that you are the Master within yourself. You will now Co-Create with Spirit a new script for a new lifetime, on the Earth for yourself, without physically leaving your body. As Co-Creator you will continually participate in the manifestation of your greatest desires, purpose, and destiny.

Re-Awakening the light of your own Being

All of the spiritual healing modalities that come through Michelle are experiential and come from her own healing process. Through these healing techniques and workshops, you will release Karmic contracts, blockages, frozen emotions, and will move through and release many of the veils of illusion that you are carrying for yourself and the collective. From this healing, the balance is found and integrated between the Male and Female within yourself on all levels.

Within this healing balance, the re-awakening of the light of your own Being illuminates your higher spiritual purpose and mission, opening the doors to the Master within yourself. From this inner place, you will meet many spiritual guides, ascended Masters, and teachers who will assist you to remember your own self-love and magnificence. They will guide you through many dimensions to re-connect to even higher, multi-dimensional aspects of yourself. You are in the Ascension and Enlightenment process that is moving you through the 2012 doorway into self-realization, and into the birthright and truth of your Being.

Michelle's work is now to show others "the light at the end of the tunnel" and to realize that all of your life's experiences are by agreement. As you heal the trauma of these experiences, you can close the door to lifetimes of opposition, raise your vibration beyond duality, and realign with your Soul's purpose, mission, and the truth of who you really are, which is love and light! As you awaken into self-love on all levels of your Being, this closes the door to any unwanted patterns, frequencies, and dis-ease. Love is such a great power, that its sound-color frequency breaks all fear-based barriers and illusions. Love is the strongest and only power there is!

For information, locations, and dates for the Masters Workshop and Private Sessions please go to:

www.SoulsAwakening.com

or email:

michelle@SoulsAwakening.com

A Letter from Michelle

Dear Spiritual Family Masters and Co-Creators,

My heart is full of love, grace, and gratitude to be able to be with you on Mother Earth during this great awakening of Enlightenment, Ascension and Oneness. In March 2004, I had a near-death experience in India. While in Spirit, I was guided through many dimensions of light, love and healing by Jesus and my Spiritual Team. I was taken into the center of the Golden Christ Energy of Creation. I was shown and taught much of my new Spiritual Work. I was told that in my workshops and spiritual work with others, many would awaken, become enlightened, and move together into Oneness. I am now experiencing this in my workshops. Through Pineal Gland Activation, releasing, re-programming and re-patterning the DNA through all dimensions, I am seeing many of you moving into heightened awareness, enlightenment, and becoming Masters of your own Creation. I believe my whole life's journey has been to bring me to this place to assist the masses into Co-Creation, Enlightenment, and Ascension. I am truly humbled, blessed, and honored to be able to serve on this level. I look forward to assisting and sharing the next steps of our Soul's journey together. Through intention, we are becoming our own Guru, Master, and Co-Creator of our greatest desires - becoming one, and co-creating heaven on Earth in all life forms. We can then, together ride the waves of this great, great awakening through the 2012 doorway into Ascension, Enlightenment, and Oneness.

In love, light, grace, and gratitude,

— Michelle

Michelle is currently living in Sedona, Arizona. She is available to provide her experiential evenings, lectures, workshops, and private sessions worldwide. Michelle also offers long-distance phone sessions. Because her work transcends time and distance, a phone session has the same powerful experience and healing as if you had been with her in-person.

By participating in Michelle's workshops and private sessions, the areas of your life that hold you back, that create concern and conflict, will easily shift and change. You will experience great healing and changes in your mental, emotional, and physical bodies. You will shift unwanted aspects of your personality and release fears, phobias, low self-esteem, past difficult patterns and experiences, trauma, feelings of being unloved, loneliness, and many other imbalanced areas of your life.

For more information about Michelle, her work, or to request evenings, lectures, workshops, or phone sessions, go to:

www.SoulsAwakening.com
www.CreatorSpeaks.com

CPSIA information can be obtained at www.ICGtesting.com
Printed in the USA
BVOW080244270812

298726BV00002B/3/P